WILLIAMS-SONOMA

A TASTE OF THE WORLD

FEATURING THE BEST RECIPES
FROM AROUND THE GLOBE

GOLD ST.
PRESS

Contents

About This Book

Food is our common ground, a universal experience.
—James Beard

Food is a living tradition, one that connects us directly to our families, our communities, and our histories. But food is also how cultures connect and combine. From the earliest explorers to modern-day globetrotters, travel has always meant the introduction and adoption of new foods and techniques.

It's difficult to imagine Italy before marinara sauce, France without its master *chocolatiers*, Thailand's curries lacking handfuls of spicy chiles, or Mexico's tacos empty of tender, spit-roasted pork or charred bits of beef. Yet, all these ingredients were unknown before travelers transported plants and animals over the Silk Road and across the oceans. Fortunately for us, cooks have long welcomed new foods into their kitchens, endowing the world with a legacy of experimentation and continually expanding the globe's menu.

This book, as its title promises, offers a small taste, a sampling of cuisines from around the world. No book, even one as hefty as the volume you now hold, could capture all the flavors nor encompass the vibrancy of foods enjoyed in countries near and far. But neither can most of us travel so extensively. With the chapters that follow, we open a tiny window onto a vast, flavor-filled landscape. The recipes range from traditional foods that have been enjoyed for centuries to more recent creations and interpretations. Organized by ingredient and identified by their countries of origin, they allow you to see how people in Mexico, India, and the Middle East cook their chickpeas, or to compare China's savory fried "doughnut sticks" to New Orleans' sugar-dusted beignets. Peppered throughout the chapters, you'll also find short features that delve into regional specialties (Champagne or tapas), key ingredients (Asian produce or Italian salumi), and helpful techniques (flambéeing bananas or pleating dim sum).

Venture through the book at a leisurely pace. Then head into your own kitchen to take part in this great, global exploration of cuisines.

—Thy Tran

BREAD AND PASTRY

Crust and Crumb

BREAD AND PASTRY AROUND THE WORLD

Bread is eaten in some form in every region around the globe. It appears at the table throughout the day—dipped in yogurt for breakfast, rolled around savory fillings at lunch, spread with jam for afternoon tea, or laid alongside a rich stew at dinner. From the most basic unleavened flatbreads to elaborately decorated loaves, bread provides both sustenance and celebration.

At its most basic, bread springs from a simple mixture of flour, water, and salt. Placing great importance on their daily loaf, ancient cultures worshipped beneficent goddesses of grain, measured wheat fields with precise math, and devised sophisticated tax codes for different classes of bread. For millennia, bread remained flat, patted by hand and cooked on a hot stone. Then, over time, creative bakers on every continent refined bread into the striking diversity of today's loaves, buns, and rounds. Early on, thin, crackerlike breads, such as the crispbread eaten by the Vikings, were crucial for survival under difficult conditions. Light and compact, these dry breads could be stored without molding and carried on long journeys by warriors and explorers, to be

eaten dried or reconstituted with water. But it was the ancient Egyptians' discovery of leavening that ultimately transformed the shape and flavor of bread. Inoculated with yeast, bread dough ferments into sourdough. The yeast spores grow and multiply, causing the dough to rise and giving the bread a lighter texture. This discovery led to the array of leavened breads eaten today, from France's chewy baguettes and Italy's olive-oil-enriched focaccia to eastern Europe's bagels and America's fluffy sandwich loaves. But the world of contemporary bread also encompasses eastern and western steamed breads, sweet and savory fried breads, decorative, celebratory enriched breads, and breads that are made to be partnered with fillings and toppings of all kinds.

FLATBREADS

Descended from ancient versions, some crisp flatbreads, such as Norwegian *lefse* and Indian *papadums,* are regional specialties. Jewish matzo is perhaps the most widely known variety. Softer flatbreads, such as India's *chapati,* the Middle East's *lavash,* Mexico's tortillas, and Greece's pita, remain staples around the world, since they can be made quickly and easily each day to meet a household's needs.

In countries like Afghanistan and India, where food is eaten with the hands, diners tear off small pieces of flatbread and use it to bring food to their mouths, wrapping bits of meat or soaking up rich sauces. Much more than an optional accompaniment, these breads are integral to the act of eating. Some cultures have developed methods of folding and layering dough to lighten their unleavened breads and give them a flakier texture. Examples include China's scallion pancakes and Malaysia's *roti canai.*

LEAVENED BREAD

European bakers perfected leavened breads with a firm structure and crisp crust. The bread of medieval Europe is strikingly similar to whole-wheat (wholemeal) bread baked today. Abundant forests provided fuel for baking large loaves in brick ovens, and wheat crops thrived in Europe's cool climate. Cultures based on rice, corn, millet, and other warm-weather crops created breads that are much softer or flatter. Ethiopian *injera,* for example, has leavening, but its teff flour creates distinctively thin, tender bread.

After the invention of convenient chemical leavening, such as baking powder and baking soda (bicarbonate of soda), came denser, more durable leavened breads, such as classic Irish soda bread. Quick breads became the standard on the prairies of the United States, where biscuits, hoecakes, hush puppies, corn bread, fry bread, pancakes, and johnnycakes were cooked in cast-iron pans over open fires. The leavening powders were light and portable, thus establishing traditional breads for each region of the country.

STEAMED BREAD

In the cool climate of northern China, steamed breads were the staple long before rice became accessible to the populace. Filled buns are common for breakfast and snacks, but for centuries plain steamed wheat bread called *mantou* was eaten daily. The light, delicate bread served with Peking duck is a modern example of China's old staple.

New England's colonists combined abundant rye and corn with their precious stores of wheat, then steamed bread in covered pots in their fireplaces. Steaming—a longer, gentler process than baking—allowed farming families to leave the kitchen for long periods of time. Some families still steam their Boston brown bread in empty coffee tins.

FRIED BREAD

Deep-frying, best suited for small amounts of dough, results in crispy, intensely flavored breads and pastries. Deep-fried foods were once enjoyed during feast days, as oil and butter were rare and precious, and today some of our favorite treats, from doughnuts and funnel cakes to sweet and savory beignets, emerge from hot oil. Centuries ago, Catholic households across Europe fried numerous treats, including sweet and filled breads, on Fat Tuesday, the day before the Lenten fast begins. Polish *paczki* and Italian *chiacchiere di Carnevale* are both descendents of these pastries.

FILLED AND TOPPED BREAD

Bread is the perfect base for savory ingredients such as spiced meats, seasonal vegetables, and creamy cheeses. Pizza is most closely associated with Italy, but across Europe and the Mediterranean, variations abound. From Spain comes the extra-thin *coca*. The *pissaladière* of Provence boasts a topping of caramelized onions and anchovies. In Turkey, individual rounds support lamb and pine nuts.

Enclosing ingredients in a crisp crust produces portable foods. Sandwiches and street foods such as Malaysian curry puffs, Indian samosas, Chinese roast pork buns, Argentinian empanadas, Italian calzones, and eastern European knishes have all become popular beyond their native lands. Doughs that envelop meaty fillings tend to be richer than plain bread, as the extra butter, lard, or oil helps create a moisture-proof barrier. Cornish pasties were once made with sturdy bread dough to survive the workday but now use more delicate pastry.

ENRICHED BREAD

Enriched and sweetened breads, many in special shapes, help define important holidays. Celebratory breads include fruit-studded stollen given for Christmas in Germany, hot cross buns enjoyed on Good Friday in England, and Greek Easter bread decorated with dyed red eggs. For the Jewish Sabbath, braids of challah grace the table, and *pan de muerto* fills Mexican bakeries on the Day of the Dead. No longer limited to holidays, these treats can be enjoyed year-round.

Pizza with Onion and Arugula

Most neighborhoods in cities such as Naples, Rome, and Florence have at least one pizzeria, and the best have wood-burning ovens twice as hot as the average home oven. They also have talented *pizzaioli* (pizza makers) who pull and twirl the balls of dough to the size of a plate and a thinness that ensures a crisp crust.

For the dough

1¼ teaspoons active dry yeast

2 tablespoons lukewarm water (105°F/40°C), plus 1¼ cups (10 fl oz/310 ml)

2 cups (10 oz/315 g) all-purpose (plain) flour

2 cups (10 oz/315 g) semolina flour, plus extra for dusting

½ teaspoon salt

2 tablespoons extra-virgin olive oil

For the topping

1¾ cup (6 fl oz/180 ml) canned plum (Roma) tomato purée

1 lb (500 g) fresh mozzarella cheese, shredded or sliced

1 large yellow onion, sliced paper-thin

4 cups (4 oz/120 g) tender arugula (rocket) leaves

MAKES 4 PIZZAS

1 In a small bowl, dissolve the yeast in the 2 tablespoons lukewarm water. Let stand until creamy, about 3 minutes.

2 To make the dough, on a large work surface, sift together the flours and salt into a mound and make a well in the center. Pour the yeast mixture, the olive oil, and ¼ cup (2 fl oz/60 ml) of the lukewarm water into the well. Swirl the liquid into the flour, slowly adding the remaining 1 cup (8 fl oz/250 ml) lukewarm water at the same time, until a rough dough forms. Knead vigorously, stretching and pressing against the work surface, until the dough is soft and smooth, about 10 minutes.

3 Cover the dough with a damp towel and let rest for 5 minutes. Divide the dough into 4 balls, cover again, and let rise until doubled in bulk, about 2 hours.

4 Place a pizza stone or unglazed tiles on the bottom rack of the oven and preheat to 500°F (260°C). Place one dough ball on a lightly floured work surface (leaving the others under the towel). Punch it down, flatten into a disk, and dust with flour. Roll out or stretch the dough into a 12-inch (30-cm) round, turning and dusting it regularly with flour.

5 Sprinkle a baker's peel or rimless baking sheet with semolina flour and lay the dough on top. Cover with one-fourth of the tomato purée. Scatter with one-fourth of the mozzarella and one-fourth of the onion slices, then transfer to the stone. Bake until the cheese is melted and the crust is browned, 5–8 minutes. Roll out and prepare the remaining pizzas as the previous one bakes.

6 As each pizza is removed from the oven, scatter with 1 cup (1 oz/30 g) arugula leaves. Serve, then place the next pizza into the oven.

Pizza Bianca

POPULAR FILLINGS

Pizza bianca is often eaten plain, preferably just out of the oven, but almost every snack bar in Rome offers it split horizontally and filled as a sandwich. Most Romans like it stuffed with ripe fresh figs and prosciutto. But the fig season is short. *Mortadella* or prosciutto and fresh mozzarella is a classic, while *bresaola* (air-dried beef) and *rughetta* (arugula/rocket), with or without shaved Parmigiano-Reggiano, is decidedly modern. Tuna and marinated artichoke hearts are another time-tested combination.

WHERE TO FIND PIZZA BIANCA

Just about every *panificio* (bakery) in town bakes *pizza bianca* and every corner store sells it and will fill it with something easy. Shops that serve *pizza al taglio* (by the slice) often also sell *pizza bianca* filled with sautéed greens or other ingredients. Two good ones to try are Pizzeria Leonina, on the street of the same name near Via Cavour, and Pizzeria Florida, on Largo Argentina. But true aficionados go to the shops that specialize in *pizza bianca* cut and filled to order.

At Frontoni, on Viale Trastevere, no one will bat an eyelash at unusual requests. *Puntarelle* paired with salami? Eggplant (aubergine) and smoked mozzarella? No problem. Roscioli, on Via dei Chiavari, fills its superb pizza with simpler fare, such as *bresaola*. Finally, the famed Antico Forno in Piazza Campo de' Fiori opened a separate shop to sell its ready-stuffed gourmet *pizza bianca* with fillings such as zucchini (courgette) flowers and mozzarella.

High on the list of things that make Romans proud is *pizza bianca*, the sublime flatbread that is white and soft inside and golden brown and crisp on top. When the pizza is filled with ripe figs and prosciutto, a local favorite, it is called *pizza e fichi,* a term that has come to mean "as good as it gets."

MAKING PIZZA BIANCA

MIXING For each batch of *pizza bianca*, flour, water, salt, and cake yeast are put into a giant mixer, which first combines the ingredients and then kneads them to yield a smooth, elastic dough. The dough is left to rise for up to 6 hours.

SHAPING AND KNEADING The risen dough is cut into portions each weighing about 4 pounds (2 kg). Each piece is shaped by hand into a 24-inch (60-cm) loaf, sprinkled with flour, and left to rest for about 15 minutes. The loaves are then kneaded and stretched. After the dough is worked for about 5 minutes, it emerges as a slim shape approximately 6 feet (2 m) long. The pizza's characteristic dimpled surface is made by the baker's fingertips, which work over the surface as if he were playing a piano.

BAKING The pizzas are brushed with olive oil and transferred on a long, narrow *pala* (peel) to the oven, where they bake at 500°F (260°C) until crisp and golden. They are then slipped onto a shelf and left to cool.

Lamb Flatbread

Small open-faced meat pies like these are popular café food in Syria, Lebanon, and Israel, as well as in Turkey. The dough is a cross between that used for an Italian pizza and Turkish *pide* bread. Add the chiles if you prefer a little heat.

For the sponge

2½ teaspoons (1 package) active dry yeast

1 teaspoon sugar

½ cup (4 fl oz/125 ml) lukewarm water (105°F/40°C)

½ cup (2½ oz/75 g) unbleached bread flour

For the dough

4½ cups (22½ oz/700 g) unbleached bread flour

2 teaspoons salt

2 tablespoons olive oil

1½ cups (12 fl oz/375 ml) lukewarm water (105°F/40°C)

For the filling

2 tablespoons olive oil, plus extra for brushing

1 large yellow onion, finely chopped

4 cloves garlic, minced

1 lb (500 g) ground (minced) lamb

1½ cups (9 oz/280 g) peeled, seeded, and chopped tomatoes

½ cup (2 oz/60 g) minced fresh mild green chiles (optional)

½ teaspoon ground allspice

1 teaspoon ground cinnamon

½ cup (¾ oz/20 g) chopped fresh flat-leaf (Italian) parsley

Salt and freshly ground pepper

¼ cup (1 oz/30 g) pine nuts

¼ cup (⅓ oz/10 g) chopped fresh mint

MAKES 12 FLATBREADS

1 To make the sponge, in a small bowl, dissolve the yeast and sugar in the lukewarm water. Stir in the flour and let stand in a warm place until bubbly, about 5 minutes.

2 To make the dough, place the flour in a large bowl and add the sponge, salt, olive oil and lukewarm water. Stir until a soft dough forms. Turn the dough out onto a lightly floured work surface and knead until smooth and elastic, 10–12 minutes. Shape the dough into a ball, place in an oiled bowl, and turn to coat evenly. Cover the bowl with plastic wrap and let rise in a warm place until doubled in bulk, 45–60 minutes.

3 Meanwhile, to make the lamb filling, in a large frying pan over medium heat, warm the 2 tablespoons olive oil. Add the onion and sauté until tender, about 10 minutes. Add the garlic and lamb, raise the heat to high, and sauté until the meat begins to brown, 5–8 minutes. Add the tomatoes, chiles (if using), allspice, and cinnamon and cook uncovered, stirring occasionally, until very thick, about 30 minutes. Stir in half of the parsley and season with salt and pepper. Let cool.

4 Turn the dough out onto a lightly floured work surface and knead briefly. Divide into 12 equal portions and form each portion into a ball. Cover with a kitchen towel and let rest for 30 minutes.

5 Preheat the oven to 350°F (180°C). Spread the pine nuts in a small frying pan and toast until fragrant, 6–8 minutes. Let cool.

6 Raise the oven temperature to 500°F (260°C). Roll out each ball of dough into a 6-inch (15-cm) round. Space the rounds well apart on baking sheets, brush lightly with olive oil, and divide the filling evenly among them. Sprinkle with the pine nuts. Bake until the crusts are golden, about 6 minutes. Sprinkle with the remaining parsley and the mint and serve at once.

Pita Bread

Now ubiquitous beyond the region, pita bread is a staple in the Middle Eastern diet. The simple, puffy flatbread might be slit crosswise and stuffed with a variety of fillings or cut into wedges and used to scoop up delectable dips and spreads.

1 tablespoon active dry yeast

Pinch of sugar

1½ cups (12 fl oz/375 ml) warm water (105°–115°F/40°–46°C)

2 tablespoons olive oil, plus extra for greasing

1½ teaspoons salt

3½–4 cups (17½–20 oz/ 545–625 g) unbleached all-purpose (plain) flour, plus extra as needed

MAKES 10 PITAS

1 In a bowl, dissolve the yeast and sugar in ½ cup (4 fl oz/ 125 ml) of the water and let stand at room temperature until foamy, about 10 minutes.

2 In the bowl of a heavy-duty mixer fitted with the paddle attachment, combine the remaining 1 cup (8 fl oz/250 ml) water, the oil, salt, and 1 cup (5 oz/155 g) of the flour. Beat on medium speed until creamy, about 1 minute. Add the yeast mixture. Beat in the remaining flour, ½ cup (2½ oz/ 75 g) at a time, until the dough pulls away from the sides of the bowl. Switch to the dough hook. Knead on low speed, adding flour 1 tablespoon at a time if the dough sticks, until stiff and sticky, about 3 minutes. Transfer to an oiled bowl and turn once to coat with the oil. Cover loosely with plastic wrap and let rise at room temperature until doubled in bulk, 1–1½ hours.

3 Place a baking stone on the lowest oven rack and preheat to 450°F (230°C). Turn the dough out onto a lightly floured surface, divide into 10 pieces, and form each into a ball. Roll out the balls into rounds about 6 inches (15 cm) in diameter and ¼ inch (6 mm) thick. (If the dough does not roll out easily, let it rest, covered, for 10 minutes.) Arrange the rounds on a floured kitchen towel, cover with another towel, and let rest until puffy, about 15 minutes.

4 Preheat a baking sheet for 6 minutes, then brush it with oil. Transfer 3 or 4 dough rounds to the hot baking sheet and place it on the baking stone. Do not open the oven door for at least 3 minutes. Bake until puffed and light brown, 6–7 minutes. Stack the pitas on a plate and cover with a kitchen towel. Bake the remaining pitas, then serve warm.

INDIA
Chapati

In northern India, *chapati,* also known as *roti,* is baked by *rotiwalas,* who belong to a special subcaste. The men are the bakers, while the responsibility for making the dough and cooking the stuffing may fall to female family members. The *rotiwalas* often work for small eateries called *dhabas,* where *chapatis* accompany all dishes.

1½ cups (7½ oz/235 g) *chapati* flour or whole-wheat (wholemeal) flour

½ teaspoon salt

4 tablespoons (2 fl oz/60 ml) *usli ghee* or unsalted butter, at room temperature

1 tablespoon whole milk

½ cup (4 fl oz/125 ml) water, or as needed

MAKES 12 CHAPATIS

1 Place the flour and salt in a large bowl. In a cup, combine 1 tablespoon of the *usli ghee* with the milk. Work the liquid into the flour mixture, using your hands, then add the water, gathering and pressing until combined. If the dough looks too dry, add 1–2 tablespoons more water. (Overly wet dough will be too sticky to roll.) Turn the dough out onto a lightly floured work surface and knead for 3 minutes. Cover with plastic wrap and let stand for 15 minutes.

2 Divide the dough into 12 equal portions and form each into a ball. Roll out each ball into a round about 6 inches (15 cm) in diameter, dusting often with flour.

3 Heat a griddle or frying pan over high heat until very hot, then reduce the heat to medium-high. Cook each round until brown spots appear on the underside, about 30 seconds. Turn and cook until the second side is spotted. Using a clean kitchen towel, press one edge of the bread, causing the trapped steam to puff the bread. (It is not essential that the breads puff.) Transfer it to a work surface, brush lightly with some of the remaining *usli ghee,* and place in a covered container lined with paper towels to absorb condensation. Serve at room temperature.

Green Onion Pancakes

These savory pancakes, made of unleavened dough, are layered with green onions and pan-fried until flaky. To prevent the onions from breaking through as the pancakes are formed, and to ensure that they cook properly, chop them finely.

2 cups (10 oz/315 g) all-purpose (plain) flour

1 cup (8 fl oz/250 ml) boiling water

3 tablespoons sesame oil

Coarse or flaked salt for sprinkling

1¼ cups (3¾ oz/110 g) chopped green (spring) onion tops

Vegetable oil for frying

MAKES 6 PANCAKES

1 Sift the flour into a bowl and make a well in the center. Pour the boiling water into the well. Using a wooden spoon, quickly work the water into the flour to make a fairly stiff, but not dry, dough. Knead lightly in the bowl until the dough forms a ball. Remove the dough from the bowl and brush lightly with some of the sesame oil. Invert the bowl over the dough and leave to cool, about 6 minutes.

2 Knead the dough very lightly until smooth and elastic, brush with more sesame oil, and place in a plastic bag. Set aside for 30–60 minutes.

3 Using your palms, rock the dough back and forth to form a log about 10 inches (25 cm) long. Cut the log into 6 equal pieces and form each piece into a ball. Roll out each ball into a very thin round about 7 inches (18 cm) in diameter, brush generously with sesame oil, sprinkle with salt, then cover evenly with one-sixth of the green onion tops. Roll up the round into a cigar shape, twist into a tight coil, and brush the top with sesame oil. On a lightly oiled work surface, flatten the coil with a rolling pin to make a round about 5 inches (13 cm) in diameter. Try to avoid having the onions break through the dough.

4 Pour oil to a depth of 1 inch (2.5 cm) into a large, wide, shallow pan, and place over medium-high heat. When the oil is hot, cook 2 or 3 pancakes, turning once, until golden brown, about 3 minutes per side. Arrange on a platter, sprinkle with salt, cut into quarters, and serve at once.

Crisp Cheese Crackers

2 cups (8 oz/250 g) shredded
Comté or Gruyère cheese

½ cup (2 oz/60 g) grated
Parmesan cheese

6 tablespoons (3 oz/90 g)
unsalted butter

1 cup (5 oz/155 g) all-purpose
(plain) flour

Pinch of cayenne pepper

2–3 tablespoons chopped fresh
chives

Coarse sea salt

MAKES 24–28 CRACKERS

1 In a food processor, combine the cheeses, butter, flour, and cayenne. Process until well combined and crumbly, 40–60 seconds.

2 Transfer the mixture to a piece of plastic wrap and shape it into a log about 2 inches (5 cm) in diameter and 6–7 inches (15–18 cm) long. Roll up the log in the plastic wrap, patting it to form a smooth, even shape. Refrigerate for at least 1 hour or up to overnight.

3 Preheat the oven to 350°F (180°C). Unwrap the dough and slice into rounds about ¼ inch (6 mm) thick. Arrange on 2 ungreased baking sheets, preferably nonstick, spacing the rounds about 2 inches (5 cm) apart. Sprinkle each with chives and a pinch of salt.

4 Bake the crackers, 1 sheet at a time, until light golden brown, 10–15 minutes, rotating the pan halfway through the baking time. For crispier crackers, bake for up to 3 minutes longer. (If the edges brown too much, the crackers will taste bitter.) Serve at once.

Chickpea Pancakes

½ cup (2½ oz/75 g) millet flour

½ cup (2½ oz/75 g) chickpea
(garbanzo bean) flour

1 teaspoon minced garlic

¼ teaspoon cumin seeds,
crushed

2 fresh hot green chiles, seeded
and thinly sliced

¼ cup (⅓ oz/10 g) chopped
fresh fenugreek or fresh cilantro
(fresh coriander)

1 teaspoon salt, or to taste

2 tablespoons vegetable oil,
plus extra for frying

½–¾ cup (4–6 fl oz/125–180 ml)
water

MAKES 8 PANCAKES

1 In a bowl, combine the flours, garlic, cumin, chiles, fenugreek, salt, 2 tablespoons oil, and water. To make thick pancakes, add ½ cup (4 fl oz/125 ml) water; to make thinner pancakes, use up to ¾ cup (6 fl oz/180 ml) water. Whisk until thoroughly blended.

2 Heat a nonstick frying pan over medium-high heat until very hot. Brush the surface with a little oil. Pour about ¼ cup (2 fl oz/60 ml) of batter into the pan. Quickly tilt the pan to coat it evenly with the batter. Cook until the underside of the pancake is browned, about 2 minutes, adding a little oil around the pancake during cooking to ensure that it browns nicely. Flip the pancake and cook on the second side until browned, 30–45 seconds longer. Transfer to a plate in a warm oven and cook the remaining pancakes. Serve at once.

Caramelized Coca

Popular in Catalonia, *coca de vidre* is a thin sheet of dough flavored with anise and pine nuts and caramelized with sugar until it is hard and crunchy. Hence the name, which translates as "glass coca." The long, thin board of crisp pastry crumbles into shards as you bite into it, causing a shower of sugary crumbs.

For the dough

3¼ cups (1 lb/500 g) all-purpose (plain) flour

1 teaspoon baking powder

1½ cups (12 fl oz/375 ml) whole milk

1 teaspoon salt

1 tablespoon sugar

2 tablespoons extra-virgin olive oil

1 teaspoon anise liqueur such as *anis seco*, Pernod, or pastis

2 tablespoons extra-virgin olive oil

¾ cup (4 oz/125 g) pine nuts

½ cup (4 oz/125 g) sugar

½ cup (4 fl oz/125 ml) anise liqueur such as *anis seco*, Pernod, or pastis

MAKES 4 COQUES

1 To make the dough, sift the flour into a large bowl, add the baking powder, and whisk to combine. Add the milk, salt, sugar, olive oil, and anise liqueur. Mix with your hands into a smooth, elastic dough. Form into a ball, cover with a kitchen towel, and let rest for 20 minutes.

2 Preheat the oven to 425°F (220°C). Oil 2 large baking sheets.

3 Cut the dough into 4 equal pieces. Pull each piece into a thick sausage shape. On a lightly floured surface, roll out each piece of dough until it is as thin as possible (about ⅛ inch/3 mm thick), yet still easy to handle. It should be roughly three times as long as it is wide and have rounded ends. Carefully transfer to a baking sheet.

4 Prick the surface of each dough piece all over with a fork. Brush with the 2 tablespoons olive oil. Sprinkle with the pine nuts and sugar. Bake until golden brown, about 15 minutes. Immediately drizzle the pastries with the anise liqueur. Serve warm or at room temperature.

The *coca* is Catalonia's most famous pastry. It takes many forms, both sweet and savory: from the roasted-vegetable topped *coca de recapte* to the sugary *coca de vidre* (page 29). *Les coques* are always popular but are particularly abundant during the processions and parties held during carnival.

Les Coques

TYPES OF COQUES

The word *coca* signals a pastry base. From the popular *coca de recapte*, topped with anything from peppers to salted herrings to sausages, to the typical Balearic Islands' *coca*, topped with spinach, pine nuts, and raisins, what characterizes *coques* is variety. They can be sweet or savory, crowned with cinnamon and lemon, glacéed fruits, nuts, cheese, mushrooms, ham, anchovies, or tuna and tomatoes. Others are filled with such delectables as shredded pumpkin or custard.

ESCRIBÀ

Tourists walking down the Ramblas market street in the heart of Barcelona often stop in amazement at the jewel-like Pastisseria Escribà. The beautiful gold-and-green art nouveau storefront acts as a magnet for anyone interested in early-twentieth-century design.

Once you enter the shop, however, academic concerns take second place to appetite. Escribà is a treasure trove of fine sweets both local and foreign, with a bounty of almond cookies, sugary *coques* studded with pine nuts, and specialties like *brazo de gitano* (gypsy's arm), a cream-and-sponge-cake roulade, or *rambla,* a biscuit-and-chocolate truffle cake. The members of the Escribà family are the aristocrats of Barcelona *pastissers*. The business was founded in 1906, and Antoni Escribà, the patriarch of the firm, is as famous in Catalonia as chef Ferran Adrià. He even has his own entry in the Catalan national encyclopedia: "A man of great culture and sensibility."

MAKING COCA DE LLARDONS

MAKING THE PASTRY *Coca de llardons* is the quintessential Catalan *coca*, simple and delicious when freshly made with the best materials. The basic ingredients are flour, butter or lard, minced pork fat or *panceta* (the *llardons*), sugar, and pine nuts. First, the dough—flour, butter or lard, salt, and water—is mixed, then kneaded by hand.

ROLLING AND DIVIDING Next, the dough is rolled out into a thin sheet, the *llardons* are sprinkled on top, and the dough is folded over and rolled out again. It is then divided into pieces, and each piece is rolled out one last time into an elongated strip with rounded ends—the shape of the classic Catalan *coca*.

FINISHING AND BAKING The shaped pastries are finally brushed with melted lard or butter and generously sprinkled with sugar and pine nuts. They are then baked at a high temperature until the sugary topping is browned and crispy, which takes about 20 minutes. The *coca de llardons* is best eaten warm, with a steaming cup of hot chocolate or coffee, or a glass of sparkling *cava*. *Salut!*

Iron-Skillet Corn Bread

This is old-fashioned corn bread, dense and grainy, with no sugar and a slight tang from buttermilk. An iron skillet is not essential (any ovenproof pan will work), although it is traditional in the South. Many cooks still use rendered bacon fat in place of the oil and then crumble bacon into the batter. The hot-pepper jelly is also a regional specialty. Use jalapeños for a milder jelly, serranos if you prefer it hotter.

For the jelly

1 red, 1 green, and 1 yellow bell pepper (capsicum), seeded and coarsely chopped

4–6 jalapeño or serrano chiles, seeded and coarsely chopped

6½ cups (3¼ lb/1.6 kg) sugar

1½ cups (12 fl oz/375 ml) cane vinegar or cider vinegar

1 bottle (6–7 fl oz/180–220 ml) liquid pectin

For the bread

⅓ cup (3 fl oz/80 ml) corn oil

1⅔ cups (8½ oz/265 g) yellow cornmeal

⅓ cup (2 oz/60 g) all-purpose (plain) flour

1 teaspoon sea salt

1 teaspoon baking powder

½ teaspoon baking soda (bicarbonate of soda)

3 eggs

2 cups (16 fl oz/500 ml) buttermilk

MAKES 8–12 SERVINGS

1   To prepare the jelly, first sterilize the canning jars: Place 6 half-pint (8-fl oz/250-ml) jars in a large kettle, cover with water, bring to a boil, and boil for 10 minutes. Remove from the heat and let the jars stand in the water until ready to fill. Put self-sealing flat lids in a small saucepan, cover with water, bring to a boil, and boil for 5 minutes. Remove from the heat and let the lids stand in the water until needed.

2   In a nonreactive saucepan, combine the peppers, chiles, sugar, and vinegar. Bring to a boil, stirring to dissolve the sugar. Boil, stirring frequently, for 3 minutes. Let cool for 2 minutes. Add the pectin and stir for 2 minutes.

3   One at a time, remove a jar from the hot water, drain well, and fill to within ¼ inch (6 mm) of the rim. Wipe the rim clean, put the flat cap in place, and screw on the ring band. Let stand until cool, then check the seal; the lid should be concave. Let stand for 24 hours before using. If the seal has not worked, store in the refrigerator for up to 3 weeks. If it has worked, store in a cool, dark place for up to 1 year.

4   To make the corn bread, pour the oil into a 9- or 10-inch (23- or 25-cm) cast-iron frying pan and place in a cold oven. Preheat the oven and pan to 450°F (230°C).

5   Meanwhile, in a large bowl, whisk together the cornmeal, flour, salt, baking powder, and baking soda. Make a well in the center. In another bowl, whisk together the eggs and the buttermilk. When the oven reaches 450°F (230°C), add the egg mixture to the dry ingredients and stir gently just until blended. Remove the hot pan from the oven and swirl the oil to coat the bottom and sides, then add the oil to the batter, whisking quickly to blend. Pour the batter into the hot pan.

6   Bake until the edges are crusty and brown and the surface is golden, about 15 minutes. Let cool in the pan for 5 minutes before slicing. Serve hot with the pepper jelly.

Pissaladière

This is the pizza of Provence, rich with onions that have been cooked down with herbs, butter, and olive oil to make a thick, golden, caramelized confit. Black olives and anchovies round out the flavorful toppings.

For the confit

4 tablespoons (2 oz/60 g) unsalted butter

3½ lb (1.75 kg) yellow onions, cut into slices ¼ inch (6 mm) thick

1 bay leaf

4 large fresh thyme sprigs

4 fresh winter savory sprigs

1 teaspoon freshly ground pepper

½ teaspoon salt

4 tablespoons (2 fl oz/60 ml) extra-virgin olive oil

For the dough

5 teaspoons (2 packages) active dry yeast

1 cup (8 fl oz/250 ml) lukewarm water (105°F/40°C)

1 teaspoon sugar

1 teaspoon salt

2 tablespoons extra-virgin olive oil

About 3½ cups (17½ oz/545 g) all-purpose (plain) flour

20 anchovy fillets

20 oil-cured black olives

2 teaspoons extra-virgin olive oil

2 tablespoons minced fresh marjoram

MAKES 10 SERVINGS

1 To make the confit, preheat the oven to 300°F (150°C). Cut the butter into pieces and put them in a shallow baking dish. Place in the oven to melt, about 5 minutes.

2 Remove the dish and place half the sliced onions in it. Tear the bay leaf into pieces and scatter half over the onions. Add 2 each of the thyme and winter savory sprigs, ½ teaspoon of the pepper, and ¼ teaspoon of the salt. Drizzle with 2 tablespoons of olive oil. Repeat with the remaining onions, seasonings, and olive oil to create a heap. Bake, turning the onions every 10–15 minutes, until they are light golden brown and reduced by half, 1–1½ hours. Remove from the oven; discard the bay leaf pieces and herb stems.

3 Meanwhile, to make the dough, in a small bowl, dissolve the yeast in the warm water. Add the sugar and let stand until foamy, about 5 minutes.

4 In a bowl or food processor, combine the yeast mixture, the salt, 1 tablespoon of the olive oil, and 3 cups (15 oz/ 470 g) of the flour. Stir or process until a silky but firm ball forms. If the dough is too wet, add the remaining flour a little at a time. If the dough is too dry, dribble in warm water. Turn the dough out onto a well-floured work surface and knead until smooth and elastic. Oil a large bowl with the remaining 1 tablespoon olive oil. Place the dough in the bowl and turn to coat with the oil. Cover the bowl with a damp kitchen towel and let stand in a warm place until doubled in bulk, 1–1½ hours.

5 Punch down the dough, re-cover with the towel, and let rest another 30 minutes.

6 Position a rack in the upper third of the oven and preheat to 500°F (260°C). Punch down the dough and turn out onto a floured surface. Roll it into a rectangle about 13 by 19 inches (33 by 48 cm). Sprinkle a little flour onto a 12-by-18-inch (30-by-45-cm) rimmed baking sheet. Lay the dough on it, pressing it up the sides. Spread the dough with the onion confit, then arrange the anchovies and olives on top. Bake until crisp and lightly browned, 12–15 minutes.

7 Immediately drizzle the *pissaladière* with the 2 teaspoons olive oil, then sprinkle with the marjoram. Cut into rectangles and serve warm or at room temperature.

Onion Focaccia

For variations on this focaccia, try sprinkling the dough with finely chopped fresh herbs, a mix of sun-dried tomatoes and black olives, or cheeses such as crumbled Gorgonzola or grated Asiago (in which case, omit the salt).

1 tablespoon active dry yeast

1 tablespoon sugar

1½ cups (12 fl oz/375 ml) warm water (105°–115°F/40°–46°C)

½ cup (4 fl oz/125 ml) olive oil, plus extra for brushing

1½ teaspoons table salt

4–4¼ cups (20–21½ oz/625–670 g) bread flour, plus extra as needed

½ cup (2 oz/60 g) chopped yellow onion

Coarse sea salt for sprinkling

MAKES 1 SHEET

1 In the bowl of a heavy-duty mixer fitted with the paddle attachment, dissolve the yeast and a pinch of the sugar in ½ cup (4 fl oz/125 ml) of the water. Let stand at room temperature until foamy, about 10 minutes. Add the remaining water and sugar, ¼ cup (2 fl oz/60 ml) of the olive oil, the table salt, and 1 cup (5 oz/155 g) of the flour. Beat on medium speed until creamy, about 1 minute. Add 1 cup (5 oz/155 g) of the flour and beat on medium-low speed for 2 minutes. Stir in the onion. Switch to the dough hook. On low speed, beat in the remaining flour, ½ cup (2½ oz/75 g) at a time, until a soft dough forms and starts to pull away from the bowl. Knead on low, adding flour 1 tablespoon at a time if the dough sticks, until it is moist, soft, and slightly sticky, about 6 minutes. Cover the bowl loosely with plastic wrap and let stand for 20 minutes.

2 Line a heavy rimmed baking sheet with parchment (baking) paper and brush the paper lightly with oil. Turn the dough out onto the prepared sheet. With oiled fingers, press and flatten the dough into an oval about 1 inch (2.5 cm) thick. Cover loosely with oiled plastic wrap and let rise at room temperature until doubled in bulk, about 1 hour.

3 With your fingertips, make deep indentations, about 1 inch (2.5 cm) apart, all over the surface of the dough. Drizzle with the remaining olive oil. Cover loosely with plastic wrap and let rise at room temperature for 30 minutes.

4 Place a baking stone on the lowest oven rack and preheat the oven to 425°F (220°C). Sprinkle the bread lightly with coarse salt. Place the pan on the stone and bake until the bottom of the bread is lightly browned, 20–25 minutes. Serve warm or at room temperature.

Hot Cross Buns

Every Good Friday in the nineteenth century, cries of "one-a-penny, two-a-penny, hot cross buns" reverberated around the streets of London as vendors sold sweet buns marked with a cross. The spicy fruited buns originated in Tudor times, and by the reign of Elizabeth I they were so popular that their sale was restricted to the serious observances of burials, Christmas, and Good Friday. Today, hot cross buns are eaten throughout much of the year, for breakfast or tea, or as a snack.

For the buns

½ cup (4 fl oz/125 ml) whole milk

2 cups (10 oz/315 g) bread flour, or as needed

2 tablespoons superfine (caster) sugar

½ teaspoon *each* fine sea salt and ground cinnamon

¼ teaspoon *each* ground mace and freshly grated nutmeg

⅛ teaspoon *each* ground cloves and ground allspice (optional)

1½ tablespoons cold unsalted butter, diced

1 teaspoon rapid-rise yeast

⅓ cup (2 oz/60 g) *each* dried currants, golden raisins (sultanas), and mixed candied citrus peel

1 large egg, beaten

For the pastry crosses

⅓ cup (2 oz/60 g) all-purpose (plain) flour

1 tablespoon unsalted butter, diced

1 teaspoon superfine (caster) sugar

For the glaze

2 tablespoons whole milk

1½ tablespoons granulated sugar

MAKES 6 BUNS

1   In a small saucepan, warm the milk to 105°F (40°C), then set aside.

2   Sift the 2 cups bread flour into a large bowl. Stir in the superfine sugar, sea salt, cinnamon, mace, nutmeg, and ground cloves and allspice (if using). Rub the butter into the mixture until it forms fine crumbs. Mix in the yeast, then the currants, raisins, and candied peel. Make a well in the center and stir in the egg and enough warm milk to form a soft dough. If it is sticky, add a little more flour.

3   Turn the dough out onto a lightly floured work surface and knead until smooth and elastic, about 10 minutes. Return the dough to the bowl, cover with plastic wrap, and let stand in a warm place until risen by a third, 3–5 hours.

4   Lightly oil a baking sheet. Turn the dough out onto a lightly floured surface and knead for 1 minute. Divide into 6 equal pieces. Shape each piece into a ball and place on the prepared sheet, flattening it slightly. Cover lightly with plastic wrap and let stand until very puffy, about 45 minutes.

5   Preheat the oven to 400°F (200°C). To make the pastry crosses, sift the flour into a small bowl. Rub in the butter until the mixture forms fine crumbs. Mix in the superfine sugar. Stir in 1 tablespoon cold water to make a firm dough. Turn the dough out onto a lightly floured surface and roll into a rectangle about 8 inches (20 cm) by 2 inches (5 cm) and ⅛ inch (3 mm) thick. Cut the pastry into 12 strips, each about 4 inches (10 cm) long and ¼ inch (6 mm) wide. Brush with water and arrange 2 strips in a cross on top of each ball, brushed side down. Bake until golden brown, about 15 minutes.

6   Meanwhile, to make the glaze, in a small saucepan over low heat, combine the milk and granulated sugar and cook, stirring occasionally, until the sugar is dissolved, about 5 minutes. Raise the heat to high and boil vigorously until the mixture is syrupy, about 30 seconds.

7   Transfer the buns to a wire rack and immediately brush with the hot glaze. Serve warm or at room temperature.

Almond Stollen

¾ cup (3 oz/90 g) slivered blanched almonds

2½ cups (12½ oz/390 g) all-purpose (plain) flour

⅔ cup (5 oz/155 g) granulated sugar

2 teaspoons baking powder

½ teaspoon baking soda (bicarbonate of soda)

½ teaspoon *each* ground mace and grated nutmeg

½ teaspoon salt

½ cup (4 oz/125 g) unsalted butter, at room temperature, plus 2 tablespoons, melted

½ lb (250 g) cream cheese, at room temperature

1 large egg

2 tablespoons amaretto

½ teaspoon *each* vanilla and almond extracts

½ cup (3 oz/90 g) *each* golden raisins (sultanas) and finely chopped dried apricots

½ cup (2 oz/60 g) dried tart cherries

Confectioners' (icing) sugar for dusting

MAKES 1 LOAF

1 Preheat the oven to 350°F (180°C). Line a baking sheet with parchment (baking) paper.

2 In a food processor, combine the almonds and 1 cup (5 oz/155 g) of the flour. Process to make a fine meal. In a bowl, combine the almond mixture with the remaining flour, granulated sugar, baking powder, baking soda, mace, nutmeg, and salt.

3 In the bowl of a heavy-duty mixer fitted with the paddle attachment, cream together the butter and cream cheese on medium speed until fluffy, about 2 minutes. Add the egg, amaretto, and vanilla and almond extracts. Beat until smooth. Reduce the speed to low and beat in the raisins, apricots, and cherries. Beat in the dry ingredients, ½ cup (2½ oz/75 g) at a time, until a stiff batter forms, about 2 minutes.

4 Turn the batter out onto a floured board and gently knead a few times to make a cohesive dough. Transfer the dough to the prepared sheet. Pat into a thick oval about 10 inches (25 cm) long and 8 inches (20 cm) wide. Make a crease down the center of the oval with a chopstick or the blunt edge of a knife and, without stretching, gently fold the long side over to within ¾ inch (2 cm) of the opposite edge, forming a long, narrow loaf with tapered ends. Press the top edge lightly to seal.

5 Bake until the stollen is lightly browned and a toothpick inserted into the center comes out clean, 40–45 minutes. Remove from the oven and brush lightly with the melted butter. Dust with confectioners' sugar. Let cool completely on the baking sheet. Dust once more before serving.

Pain au Levain

In sourdough language, a *levain* is a firm starter, a chef, a mother, or just old dough. Some bakers claim to use a *levain* that has been in their family for hundreds of years. Whether you start it fresh or get a beloved starter from a friend, remember to pinch off a piece of the dough before you shape the bread so you can then pass it along. You can also experiment with using different quantities of the starter when you make the dough to change the personality of the loaf.

For the first stage starter

1 cup (4½ oz/125 g) unbleached all-purpose (plain) flour

⅓ cup (2½ fl oz/80 ml) cool water (78°F/26°C)

For the second stage starter

1¾ cups (7½ oz/217 g) unbleached all-purpose (plain) flour

½ cup (4 fl oz/125 ml) cool water (78°F/26°C)

For the dough

1 cup (8 oz/250 g) starter

3½ cups (28 fl oz/875 ml) cool water (78°F/26°C)

1 tablespoon sea salt

¾ cup (4 oz/125 g) whole-wheat (wholemeal) flour

7–8 cups (2–2¼ lb/875 g–1 kg) unbleached all-purpose (plain) flour

MAKES 1 LOAF

1 To make the first stage starter, combine the flour and the water in a ceramic or glass bowl. Stir with your fingers or a wooden spoon until well blended—the starter will be soft and sticky. Cover the bowl with plastic wrap and let stand for 72 hours. The starter should rise slightly and take on a fresh, acidic aroma.

2 To make the second stage starter, uncover the starter and scrape it into a bowl. Stir in the flour and the water, mixing well. The starter should be firm but not too stiff. Cover with plastic wrap and let stand for 24–48 hours. (A longer wait will produce a more acidic loaf.) When the starter rises and bubbles, it is active and you are ready to bake.

3 To make the dough, combine the 1 cup starter, water, and salt in a very large bowl, stirring with your fingers or a sturdy whisk. Add the whole-wheat flour and 5 cups (25 oz/775 g) of the all-purpose flour, 1 cup (5 oz/155 g) at a time, mixing well after each addition. Continue mixing until it is thick and spongy. Add the remaining 2–3 cups (10–25 oz/315–630 g) all-purpose flour while working the dough by hand, folding it over itself to incorporate air and using only enough flour to form a soft, slightly tacky dough. Cover with plastic wrap and let rise until doubled in bulk, 8–12 hours.

4 Line an 11-inch (28-cm) basket or bowl with a kitchen towel rubbed with flour.

5 Turn the dough out onto a work surface heavily dusted with flour. The dough should be quite slack. Cut off about 1 cup (8 oz/250 g) of the dough and set it aside to use as the starter for future loaves (see note, at right). Shape the remaining dough into a large, round ball. Gently place it, seam side up, in the towel-lined basket. Pinch the seam together with your fingertips. Cover with a damp kitchen towel. Let the dough rise until doubled in bulk, 4–6 hours. (If it becomes extremely loose and jiggly, it has overproofed; skip the slashing process in step 6.)

6 Position a rack in the lower third of the oven, and preheat to 450°F (230°C). Fill a spray bottle with water for misting the dough. Sprinkle the top of the loaf with ¼ cup

(1¼ oz/40 g) all-purpose flour and spread it evenly over the dough. Place a heavy baking sheet on top of the loaf and, holding the basket and pan together, invert them. Remove the basket and towel. Using a sharp, serrated knife, slash a crisscross into the top of the loaf.

7 Mist the loaf with water, and immediately put it into the oven. Bake for 30 minutes. Reduce the heat to 400°F (200°C) and continue baking until the crust is dark and the bread sounds hollow when tapped on the top, 25–30 minutes. Transfer to a wire rack and let cool completely before slicing.

Note: Store the 1 cup (8 oz/250 g) reserved levain dough in a covered container. If you are not going to use it within 2 days, store it in the refrigerator and feed it every 5–7 days. Gray or green mold is the result of good bacteria growing; simply scrape it off. If it turns pinkish and smells bad, throw it away. To feed it, stir in ½ cup (2½ oz/75 g) all-purpose (plain) flour and 2 tablespoons cool water—it should form a rough, soft ball—and let it stand at room temperature for a few hours or overnight before returning it to the refrigerator. Before using it to start a new batch of levain, let it stand at room temperature and ferment for 6–8 hours. The less frequently levain is used, the more sour it will be and the slower the dough will rise. If you use your levain infrequently, feed it every day for 3 days before using.

FRANCE
Le Boulangerie

The famous French baguette is demonstrably egalitarian, perfectly at home in the shopping *sac* of an elegant mademoiselle or the tool satchel of a carpenter. Some say it was invented by Napoléon, who insisted on the long, slender shape so soldiers could stuff it into a trouser leg and keep their hands free for battle. But it was actually created just before World War I in response to consumer demand: people wanted less *mie* (interior) and more crust. The long loaf of the day, which measured some 30 inches (76 cm) and weighed about 5 pounds (2.5 kg), kept its length but shed all but one-half pound (250 g) of its weight, resulting in the now-familiar slim baguette.

In the decades following World War II, the quality of bread in Paris—and throughout France—was in free fall, as bakery chains, with an eye toward the bottom line, leapfrogged across the landscape. A national "good bread campaign" was launched early in the 1990s to fight this trend, and many Parisian bakers joined the movement.

Among those who helped Parisian bread regain its good reputation was the late Lionel Poilâne, who took over his father's bakery on the Rue du Cherche-Midi in the early 1970s. Throughout his tenure, he campaigned to educate people about the joys of traditional bread, and his daughter Apollonia continues the crusade today. No bread lover should visit Paris without making a trip to Poilâne, home of the *miche Poilâne,* a huge, round country loaf that sets the standard in Paris and around the world.

The slender baguette, prized for its crisp and tender crumb, is a relatively recent invention. It first appeared in Paris in the early twentieth century, replacing the more traditional rustic round loaf known as a *boule,* from which the word *boulangerie* comes.

WOOD-FIRED OVENS

Most bread in France today is baked in electric industrial ovens, but at Poilâne the bread goes into a wood-fired oven, modeled after the ovens of ancient Rome. Made of brick, stone, and cast iron, it burns wood in a hearth below the stone "floor." A hole cut in the oven floor is plugged with an iron funnel called a *gueulard,* which can be positioned to direct the flow of heat. The oven's ceiling is low, trapping the heat more effectively.

Poilâne's signature *miche* is a dense, chewy, moist loaf with a crusty exterior. Much of the texture is due to the long fermentation and rising process—the loaves take six hours to make from start to finish. But the way the loaf is baked also contributes to its heft. The intense heat of the wood-burning oven extracts extra water and air from the dough. A loaf starts out at about 4.85 pounds (2.2 kilograms), but weighs just about 4.25 pounds (1.9 kilograms) after baking. Finally, the wood imparts a slightly smoky flavor to the bread—a rustic touch that an electric or gas oven could never duplicate.

MAKING PAIN POILÂNE

MAKING THE DOUGH Behind every *miche Poilâne* is the *levain,* a natural sourdough starter that leavens the bread and gives it its characteristic mildly acidic taste. The baker combines the starter with flour, water, and salt. The mixture is kneaded in a metal vat for fifteen minutes, then left to rise for two hours. Finally, the dough is put into a large wooden box to rest for another hour.

FORMING THE BOULES Bakers at Poilâne divide the dough into loaf-sized portions, then they weigh each one to make sure it is exactly 2.2 kilograms. The portions are molded by hand into rounds, and the loaves are set into individual wicker baskets lined with linen, which absorbs humidity and encourages further fermentation. The dough rests in the baskets for two hours.

BAKING THE BREAD The baker turns the risen loaves onto wooden planks, marks the signature P in the crust with a knife, and slides the loaves into the oven, where they bake at 450°F (230°C) for an hour. Logs burn below the loaves, imparting a slightly woody flavor to the finished bread.

Ham and Cheese Quesadillas

Authentic quesadillas—a popular street food throughout Mexico—are traditionally made with *masa* and cooked on a *comal*. They are filled with countless combinations of meats, cheeses, vegetables, and chiles. The simple quesadillas here are stuffed with tangy cow's milk cheese and thin slices of salty ham.

For the corn tortillas

1 lb (500 g) freshly prepared *tortilla masa* **or 1¾ cups (9 oz/ 280 g)** *masa harina* **for tortillas**

1 teaspoon sea salt, or to taste

1 cup (8 fl oz/250 ml) plus 2 tablespoons warm water, if using *masa harina*

For the filling

1 tablespoon safflower or canola oil (optional)

5 thin slices Port Salut, white Cheddar, or other full-flavored cheese

5 thin slices good-quality ham

5 teaspoons salsa

Guacamole, homemade or purchased

MAKES 5 QUESADILLAS

1 To make the tortillas, if using fresh *masa*, put it in a bowl and knead together with the salt, adding a little warm water, if needed, to make a soft dough. If using *masa harina*, put it in a bowl, add the warm water, and mix with your hands; allow the dough to rest 5 minutes, then add the salt and knead for 1 minute. Shape into 10 golf ball-sized balls, then cover with a damp kitchen towel.

2 Heat a large griddle, cast-iron frying pan, or *comal* over medium heat. Put 2 sheets of heavy plastic inside a tortilla press. Place a *masa* ball between them and gently press with the top plate. Remove the tortilla from the press.

3 Slide the tortilla onto the hot griddle and cook until the underside is freckled, about 30 seconds. Flip it over and cook for another 20–30 seconds, then flip back to the first side for just a second. Transfer to a tortilla warmer or stack on a plate and cover with a towel.

4 To make the quesadillas, add the oil (if using) to the frying pan or *comal*. Top half of the tortillas with a slice of cheese and a slice of ham, and spread the ham with 1 teaspoon of salsa. Cover with the remaining tortillas. Place in the hot pan 1 at a time. Toast until the cheese begins to melt. Flip over and toast the other side. Serve warm, with guacamole on the side.

Pea and Potato Samosas

Samosas are typically served as an appetizer, accompanied with a mildly spiced mint, cilantro, or tamarind relish or a fruit chutney, such as mango. They are easy to make at home and can be served piping hot as a snack, along with traditional Indian sweets. Amchoor powder, made from ground dried green mangoes, has a fruity, sour taste—it can be found at well-stocked Indian markets.

For the filling

½ lb (250 g) new potatoes

2 tablespoons coarsely chopped fresh cilantro (fresh coriander)

1½ tablespoons sunflower oil

½ small yellow onion, finely diced

1 small fresh green chile such as serrano, or to taste, finely chopped

½ teaspoon peeled and finely chopped fresh ginger

½ teaspoon cumin seeds

½ cup (2½ oz/75 g) fresh or frozen English peas

2 teaspoons amchoor powder or fresh lemon juice

½ teaspoon garam masala

Fine sea salt

For the pastry

1 cup (5 oz/155 g) all-purpose (plain) flour

¼ teaspoon fine sea salt

1 tablespoon unsalted butter, melted

¼ cup (2 oz/60 g) plain yogurt, plus 1 tablespoon

Sunflower oil for deep-frying

MAKES 12 SAMOSAS

1 To make the filling, place the unpeeled potatoes in a saucepan with water to cover generously. Bring to a boil and cook until tender, 25 minutes. Drain and let cool. Peel the potatoes and cut them into ¼-inch (6-mm) cubes. In a bowl, combine the potatoes and cilantro.

2 Meanwhile, in a small nonreactive saucepan over medium-low heat, warm the sunflower oil. Add the onion, chile, ginger, and cumin seeds and cook, stirring occasionally, until the onion is soft and golden, about 15 minutes. Stir in the peas and 3 tablespoons water. Raise the heat to medium, cover the saucepan, and simmer, stirring occasionally, until the peas are tender, about 8 minutes. Uncover and continue to cook until any excess moisture has evaporated. Stir in the amchoor powder and garam masala. Add this mixture to the potatoes and stir gently to combine. Season with salt and set aside.

3 To make the pastry, sift the flour and salt into a bowl. In a small bowl, stir together the melted butter and 2 tablespoons warm water, then immediately add to the flour and stir to combine. Stir in the ¼ cup (2 oz/60 g) yogurt. Turn the pastry out onto a lightly floured work surface and knead until it forms a stiff but pliable dough, about 5 minutes. Divide into 6 equal pieces.

4 Form each piece into a ball and dust with flour. Using a rolling pin, roll the pastry into a thin disk about 6 inches (15 cm) in diameter. Cut the disk in half. Place a spoonful of filling on one half of each semicircle and brush the edges with some of the remaining 1 tablespoon yogurt. Fold the pastry over the filling to form a triangle. Pinch the edges to seal.

5 Pour sunflower oil to a depth of 4 inches (10 cm) into a large, heavy frying pan, and heat over medium-high heat to 375°F (190°C) on a deep-frying thermometer. Working in batches to avoid crowding, carefully add a single layer of samosas and fry until golden brown, about 4 minutes. Transfer to paper towels to drain. When the oil returns to 375°F, fry the remaining samosas. Serve warm.

Roast Pork Buns

Bread is as much a part of a Chinese meal in the north as rice is in the south. Vast grain fields in the northern provinces provide the wheat needed for the noodles and the many varieties of baked, fried, and steamed breads. As Chinese kitchens traditionally were not equipped with ovens, steaming and dry cooking on a griddle were the economical and effective ways to cook breads.

For the starter

1 cup (5 oz/155 g) all-purpose (plain) flour

¼ cup (2 oz/60 g) superfine (caster) sugar

1½ teaspoons active dry yeast

¾ cup (6 fl oz/180 ml) lukewarm water (105°F/40°C)

For the filling

10 oz (315 g) Red Roast Pork (page 283), diced

1½ tablespoons hoisin sauce

1 tablespoon cornstarch (cornflour) dissolved in 3 tablespoons water

For the dough

1¼ cups (7½ oz/230 g) all-purpose (plain) flour

2 teaspoons baking powder

1½ tablespoons melted lard or vegetable oil (optional)

⅓ cup (3 fl oz/80 ml) lukewarm water (105°F/40°C)

MAKES 20 BUNS

1 To make the starter, in a small bowl, stir together the flour, sugar, and yeast. Make a well in the center. Pour the lukewarm water into the well and stir with a fork to mix thoroughly. Cover with plastic wrap and set aside in a warm place until bubbly and doubled in bulk, about 3 hours.

2 To make the filling, in a small saucepan over medium-low heat, combine the pork, hoisin sauce, and cornstarch mixture and heat gently, stirring, until the meat is glazed with the sauce, about 1 minute. Set aside.

3 To make the dough, in a large bowl, sift together the flour and baking powder. Make a well in the center. Add the lard (if using), dough starter, and lukewarm water to the well and, using your fingers, work the mixture into a smooth dough.

4 Form the dough into a ball and transfer to a lightly floured work surface. Using your palms, rock the dough back and forth to form a log 20 inches (50 cm) long. Cut into twenty 1-inch (2.5-cm) pieces. Gently roll each piece into a ball, then, using your fingers or a rolling pin, flatten it into a 3-inch (7.5-cm) round that is thinner on the edges than in the center. Place about 2½ teaspoons of the filling in the center and pull the dough up and around it, twisting and pinching the edges together at the top.

5 Cut out 20 pieces of waxed paper or parchment (baking) paper, each 1½ inches (4 cm) square. Place the buns in 2 steamer baskets or on 2 racks of a metal steamer with a square of paper beneath each, spacing them ¾ inch (2 cm) apart. (If you have only 1 basket, cook them in 2 batches.) Let rise for 10 minutes.

6 Bring water to a simmer in the steamer base. Place the steamer baskets or racks over the simmering water, cover, and steam until the buns are well expanded and dry on the surface, about 8 minutes. Serve at once.

Originating in the teahouses of China's Guangdong province, the first dim sum were midday treats for the leisured classes. Today, dim sum is served to masses of diners in multistory canteens, the preparation of dim sum is considered a high art, and every dim sum parlor has its own repertoire.

Dim Sum

By late morning on Saturdays and Sundays, dim sum restaurants from Hong Kong to San Francisco are packed with eager diners. They have gathered to share a meal of flaky pastries, steamed dumplings, and stuffed buns, all served on small plates and intended to "delight the heart"—a loose translation of *dim sum*.

Modest dim sum establishments may have an à la carte menu or a few servers circulating with trays laden with small plates. But at larger establishments, food emerges from the kitchen on a steady stream of carts, which the servers maneuver through the crowded dining rooms. As they pass, they sing out the names of their dishes—*ha gau* (steamed shrimp dumplings), *siu mai* (open-faced pork and shrimp dumplings), *cha siu bao* (barbecued pork buns)—and diners select the ones they want. You can always beckon a waiter over to get a closer look, and he or she will lift the lids of the steamer baskets.

At the biggest dim sum houses, the weekend repertoire may include seventy-five to one hundred choices, from the familiar steamed dumplings and wonton soup to stuffed vegetables, fried squid, barbecued meats, steamed chicken feet, green (spring) onion pancakes, and sweet bean pastries. It is tempting to fill your table with the first tantalizing delights you see, but dim sum enthusiasts know that it pays to be patient. Each time you make a selection, the waiter will mark your bill—most dishes are moderately priced, but some specialties, such as roast suckling pig, are more costly.

In Cantonese, the dim sum meal is known as *yumcha,* literally "drink tea." Traditionally, it is the only Chinese repast accompanied with tea (*cha* is generally served after the food), and many dim sum houses offer a selection of teas, from the light and fragrant chrysanthemum to the robust *pu-erh,* which is said to counteract dim sum's richness.

MAKING BARBECUED PORK BUNS

ROLLING DOUGH Cantonese *cha siu bao* (barbecued pork buns), served at every dim sum house, begin with sweetened, yeasted wheat-flour dough swiftly flattened into small circles with a rolling pin.

STUFFING AND FORMING The filling includes finely chopped barbecued pork stir-fried with garlic, soy sauce, oyster sauce, and sugar. After the filling cools, chefs use chopsticks to place a small portion on each round. Using their fingers, they seal the buns with rapid-fire pinching and pleating.

STEAMING The buns, with their surface swirls, are set aside to rise before steaming. In a hot kitchen, that doesn't take long. Before steaming, each bun is placed on a square of thin paper so it won't stick. Diners peel the paper off the bun.

SERVING Snow-white *cha siu bao* go from the steamers to the rolling dim sum carts, still in their lidded bamboo baskets. The servers will keep the lids on to keep the buns warm, announcing the contents as they stroll past each table.

Beignets

Beignets, French for "fritters," take many forms. In France, they are most often stuffed—with everything from fruit to seafood. In the United States, the word is closely associated with the New Orleans version, a deep-fried, sugar-dusted rectangle of pastry that is one of the city's most famous offerings.

2½ teaspoons (1 package) active dry yeast

¼ cup (2 fl oz/60 ml) warm water (105°–115°F/40°–46°C)

4½ cups (22½ oz/700 g) all-purpose (plain) flour

3 tablespoons granulated sugar

¾ teaspoon fine sea salt

1 cup (8 fl oz/250 ml) whole milk

4 tablespoons (2 oz/60 g) unsalted butter

1 large egg

Peanut or canola oil for deep-frying

Confectioners' (icing) sugar for dusting

MAKES 12 BEIGNETS

1 In a small bowl, sprinkle the yeast over the warm water and let stand until creamy, about 5 minutes. In a food processor, combine 3 cups (15 oz/470 g) of the flour, the granulated sugar, and the salt. Process briefly.

2 In a small saucepan over medium-low heat, combine the milk and butter and heat gently until melted. Remove from the heat. With the processor running, pour the milk mixture through the feed tube and process until blended. Add the egg, yeast mixture, and the remaining 1½ cups (7½ oz/235 g) flour and process just until a soft dough forms.

3 Preheat the oven to 200°F (95°C). Line an ovenproof platter with paper towels. Pour oil to a depth of 3 inches (7.5 cm) into a deep, heavy saucepan or a deep fryer and heat to 360°F (182°C) on a deep-frying thermometer.

4 While the oil is heating, divide the dough into 2 equal pieces. On a well-floured work surface, knead 1 piece briefly until soft but not sticky. Roll into a rectangle about ¼ inch (6 mm) thick. Cut into 6 equal rectangles. When the oil is ready, place 2 or 3 rectangles in the oil and fry, turning once, until puffed and brown, about 2 minutes per side. Transfer to the paper towels and keep warm in the oven. When the oil returns to 360°F (182°C), cook the remaining rectangles, and then repeat with the remaining dough. Using a fine-mesh sieve, dust the beignets generously with confectioners' sugar and serve at once.

Fried Doughnut Sticks

Though the Chinese finger food known as a "doughnut stick" is deep-fried, it is not sweet like a western doughnut. Still, the tendency of Chinese cooks to fry dough rather than baking it—ovens being rare in China—may explain the existence of Chinese food and doughnut shops common to large cities in the west. In China, these doughnut sticks typically accompany *congee,* or rice porridge.

1¼ cups (6½ oz/200 g) self-rising flour

2 teaspoons baking powder

1½ teaspoons salt

½ teaspoon baking soda (bicarbonate of soda)

⅓ cup (3 fl oz/80 ml) plus 1–2 tablespoons lukewarm water (105°F/40°C)

Vegetable or peanut oil for deep-frying

MAKES 10 DOUGHNUT STICKS

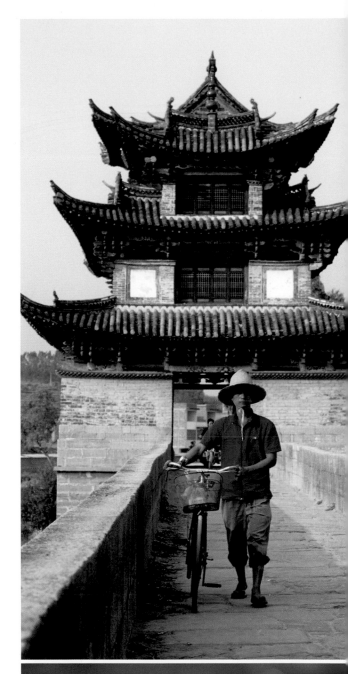

1 In a bowl, sift together the flour, baking powder, salt, and baking soda. Make a well in the center and pour in the ⅓ cup (3 fl oz/80 ml) lukewarm water. Stir to mix well, adding the 1–2 tablespoons water if needed. Knead lightly in the bowl for about 30 seconds to form a very soft dough. Cover with a kitchen towel and let stand for 15 minutes.

2 Turn the dough out onto a lightly floured work surface and knead again very lightly until smooth, about 30 seconds. Roll out the dough into a strip about 4 inches (10 cm) wide and 16 inches (40 cm) long. Using a sharp knifc, cut crosswise into 20 strips each 1 inch (2 cm) by 4 inches (10 cm). Press the strips together into pairs, sealing the seam with the back of a knife along the length of each pair. Working from the center of each, use your fingers to stretch the dough gently to about 10 inches (25 cm) long.

3 Pour oil to a depth of 2½ inches (6 cm) into a wok and heat to 360°F (182°C) on a deep-frying thermometer, or until a piece of dough added to the oil begins to bubble and turn golden within 30 seconds. Place 3 or 4 doughnut sticks in the oil and fry, turning frequently, until golden brown, about 1½ minutes. Transfer to paper towels to drain. When the oil returns to 360°F, fry the remaining doughnut sticks. Serve at room temperature.

GRAINS

From the Field

GRAINS AROUND THE WORLD

Myths around the world relate how rice, corn, quinoa, rye, wheat, and barley were each the gift of generous gods. As the basis of daily meals, these grains are indeed the foundation of life. All are the seeds of grasses—or cereals, named for Ceres, the Roman goddess of agriculture—but their individual variations help define the unique characteristics of cuisines from Chile to China.

Much of the global diet depends on grains. At their most basic, grains serve as a neutral yet nutritious base for a small amount of vegetables and meat, but in fuller times, cooks transform them into complex and festive dishes. Indian *biryani*, Spanish paella, and Moroccan couscous mark the heights that humble grains can achieve. Although amaranth, millet, sorghum, oats, and a multitude of other grains are eaten as staples in many regions, the three most common grains globally are rice, corn, and wheat. Spreading far beyond its native regions in Asia and West Africa, rice has adapted to diverse climates, resulting in thousands of varieties that provide a range of colors, flavors, and textures. From black to red to gold, from sweet and sticky to flowery and

dry, rice offers more variety than any other grain. Corn was cultivated thousands of years ago by the Incas of Peru, the Mayans and Aztecs of Mexico, and the Anasazi in the American Southwest. It has since served as the basis for a variety of foods, from simple popped kernels to elaborately filled, wrapped, and steamed tamales. Though most often ground into flour, wheat is also eaten in whole- and cracked-grain forms. Traditional pairings in world cuisines—such as corn and beans in Latin America, rice and tofu in Asia, wheat and chickpeas (garbanzo beans) in the Middle East—have long been valuable for providing complete proteins. But even now, when we eat grains for enjoyment as much as sustenance, these recognizable combinations shape cultural and culinary identities.

RICE

In areas with colder and shorter growing seasons, short, plump, and starchy rice grains evolved. Japanese sushi rice and Italian Arborio are examples. Warmer areas such as the Middle East, India, and Southeast Asia developed fragrant, long-grain varieties. These include *sadri*, basmati, and jasmine, which cook to a dry, fluffy texture.

The pilaf method of cooking rice echoes in much-loved dishes such as *pulao* in India, *polo* in Iran, and *plov* in Russia. Long-grain rice, sautéed first in butter or oil along with a variety of aromatics, simmers gently in broth over a low flame. Other ingredients often find their way into the pot, from a pinch of saffron to an incredible array of fresh seafood. European cooks might stir in tomatoes, fresh peas, wild mushrooms, a splash of wine, or squid ink, while cooks in tropical countries might enrich their rice with coconut milk or palm oil. A sprinkling of fresh cilantro (fresh coriander), mint, lemon zest, or fried onions will finish the rice before it arrives at the table. The *biryani* of Pakistan and India is the epitome of such dishes. Served at weddings and other festive occasions, it involves layering basmati rice carefully with marinated meats and complex spices, and then cooking the aromatic mixture in an earthenware pot sealed tight with dough.

Leftover rice boasts a pantheon of dishes. Around the world, a variety of soups, salads, and fillings highlight already cooked rice. In China, fried rice is a featured course at formal banquets. In Italy, leftover risotto is bound with cheese and deep-fried as *arancini*, a popular treat.

In the United States, South Carolina cooks perfected rice dishes. The marshes and tidal rivers of the Low Country proved ideal for growing rice, and soon a new crop was established in the colonies. Bringing with them the cuisines of West Africa and the West Indies, plantation slaves made dishes such as gumbo, jambalaya, red beans and rice, and Gullah rice an integral part of the American South.

Starchy, short-grain varieties lend creaminess to desserts. The grains are pounded into Japanese *mochi* or simmered slowly in milk to make creamy rice pudding, a dish that has become a favorite in some form on nearly every continent.

CORN

To this day, corn is the most important food crop in the Americas. When explorers brought it home to Europe in the 1500s, it became especially popular in Italy. A small amount of corn was boiled in a

large amount of water to make polenta. This could be eaten warm and soft like a thick porridge, or after it had been spread and cooled on a wooden board until firm. Cut into thick slices with a string, cooled polenta was served much like bread during lean times.

Removing the hull and seed transforms corn kernels into hominy. Native Americans add whole hominy grains to endless soups, stews, and side dishes. Grits, a dish special to the American South, features ground hominy simmered in water or milk much like Italy's polenta.

WHEAT

Farro is a variety of wheat that grew wild in the Fertile Crescent. This ancestor of modern wheat famously fed the Roman legions, who carried it throughout Italy. The central regions of Tuscany, Lazio, Marche, and Umbria continued to enjoy its chewy texture and nutty flavor even as more easily cultivated wheat varieties were developed. More nutritious than other grains, farro has regained popularity and appears now in soups and salads far beyond Italy's borders.

Semolina refers to milled durum wheat, a hard and large-grained variety that gives Italian pasta its firm bite. In addition to golden-hued breads and desserts in southern Europe, semolina flour appears in couscous, an important staple in Morocco and Algeria. Although actually a fine pasta, couscous is prepared and served much like a grain. Traditionally, North African women made couscous by rolling together both coarse and finely ground durum wheat with salted water. Pressed through a sieve to form tiny granules and then dried in the desert sun, it could be stored indefinitely. Cooked over simmering stews or broths to absorb their flavorful steam, couscous becomes the base for a wide variety of dishes.

In India, many know semolina as *sooj* or *rava*. Stirred with mustard seeds and curry leaves for a savory *uppuma*, a fluffy pilaflike dish enjoyed at breakfast, or simmered into a rich pudding with cardamom and cashews, the wheat granules adapt well to the diverse regional cuisines of the subcontinent.

Bulgur, similar to couscous, consists of whole-wheat (wholemeal) grains that have been cracked, steamed, and then dried. Tossed with lemon juice and an abundance of parsley, it becomes the refreshing tabbouleh salad in Lebanon and other Middle Eastern countries. In Syria, bulgur is shaped into balls with spiced, ground lamb to form kibbe. Turkish cooks prepare it like a pilaf, lacing the wheat with nuts, dried fruit, or savory bits of meat.

Baked Rice with Meatballs

Here is a baroque version of *arroz al horno*, or baked rice. Meatballs, chicken, pork, and chickpeas are buried in the rice in this specialty of Elche, a small town in Alicante province surrounded by date-palm groves. This is an ideal dish for home entertaining, as it can be assembled up to four hours in advance and then finished in the oven just before serving.

For the meatballs

½ lb (250 g) ground (minced) lean pork or veal, or a mixture

½ cup (1 oz/30 g) fresh bread crumbs, soaked in milk or water to cover and then squeezed dry

¼ cup (1½ oz/45 g) almonds, ground

3 tablespoons chopped fresh flat-leaf (Italian) parsley

1 egg

Grated zest of 1 lemon

Salt and freshly ground pepper

1 red bell pepper (capsicum), halved lengthwise and seeded

6 tablespoons (3 fl oz/90 ml) olive oil

3 cloves garlic

4 cups (32 fl oz/1 l) chicken stock

1 whole chicken breast, boned with skin intact and cut into 1-inch (2.5-cm) pieces

½ lb (250 g) pork, cut into 1-inch (2.5-cm) cubes

Salt and freshly ground pepper

¼ lb (125 g) thick-cut bacon, cut into ¼-inch (6-mm) cubes, or sweet pork sausage, sliced

2 cups (14 oz/440 g) Spanish short-grain rice such as Bomba or Calasparra

1 cup (7 oz/220 g) drained cooked or canned chickpeas (garbanzo beans)

7 eggs

¼ cup (2 fl oz/60 ml) milk

MAKES 6 SERVINGS

1 To make the meatballs, in a bowl, combine the meat, bread crumbs, almonds, parsley, egg, and lemon zest. Season with salt and pepper. Mix well and form into balls about 1 inch (2.5 cm) in diameter. Set aside.

2 Preheat a broiler (grill). Place the bell pepper halves, cut sides down, on a baking sheet. Broil (grill) until the skin blackens and blisters. Let cool, covered loosely with aluminum foil, then peel away the skin.

3 Preheat the oven to 350°F (180°C). In a large ovenproof frying pan over low heat, warm the oil. Add the whole garlic cloves and sauté until tender, 2–3 minutes. Turn off the heat. Using a slotted spoon, transfer the cloves to a blender. Add the roasted red pepper and ½ cup (4 fl oz/125 ml) of the chicken stock, and purée. Set aside.

4 Season the chicken and pork with salt and pepper. Heat the oil remaining in the pan over high heat. Add the chicken and brown well on all sides, 5–8 minutes. Transfer to a plate. One at a time, brown the pork, meatballs, and bacon. Set aside with the chicken.

5 In a saucepan over high heat, bring the remaining 3½ cups (28 fl oz/875 ml) stock to a boil, then reduce the heat to maintain a bare simmer. Add the rice to the oil remaining in the frying pan over medium heat. Stir well, then add the pepper purée and cook for a few minutes until well blended. Add the simmering stock, chickpeas, and reserved meats. Bring to a boil, reduce the heat to low, and cook uncovered, stirring often, about 7 minutes. Transfer the pan to the oven and bake, uncovered, until most of the liquid is absorbed, about 10 minutes. (If making the dish ahead, cover and refrigerate. Reheat in a 325°F/165°C oven until warmed through, then continue as directed.)

6 In a bowl, whisk together the eggs and milk. Pour the mixture over the rice. Raise the oven temperature to 500°F (260°C) and continue to bake until the top is browned, 5–8 minutes. (If the top fails to brown after 8 minutes and the pan is flameproof, slip it under the broiler for a few minutes until browned.) Remove from the oven and let stand for 10 minutes before serving, then serve directly from the pan.

Paella

Though originally from Valencia, paella has spread all around the Mediterranean coast, with every region boasting its own version. This one originates in Barcelona.

4 cups (32 fl oz/1 l) chicken stock

Juice of ½ lemon

4 large artichokes

Coarse sea salt

1 teaspoon saffron threads

3 cloves garlic, thinly sliced

6 boneless chicken thighs

⅓ lb (155 g) pork loin

½ lb (250 g) pork sausages

7 oz (220 g) cleaned squid

1 cup (8 fl oz/250 ml) olive oil

1 yellow onion, thinly sliced

1 red bell pepper (capsicum), seeded and cut into 1-inch (2.5-cm) pieces

1 lb (500 g) ripe tomatoes, peeled, seeded, and finely chopped

2½ cups (1 lb/500 g) short-grain rice such as Bomba or Calasparra

1 cup (5 oz/155 g) fresh or frozen English peas

6 oz (185 g) monkfish or hake fillet

24 large mussels

12 medium shrimp (prawns), peeled and deveined

Fresh flat-leaf (Italian) parsley

MAKES 8 SERVINGS

1 In a saucepan, bring the stock to a gentle simmer, then maintain it over low heat.

2 Fill a bowl with water and stir in the lemon juice. Remove the tough outer leaves from each artichoke and slice off the top 2 inches (5 cm) of the remaining leaves. Cut the stem off at the base and discard. Quarter the artichoke lengthwise, then scrape out and discard the fuzzy choke. Place the quarters in the lemon water.

3 Using a mortar and pestle, grind the saffron with 1 teaspoon salt, then grind in the garlic. Set aside. Cut the chicken, pork loin, and sausages into 1-inch (2.5-cm) pieces. Slice the squid into rings, leaving the tentacles whole.

4 Place a 16-inch (40-cm) paella pan or a wide, heavy frying pan over high heat and add the olive oil. When the oil is hot, add the chicken, pork, sausage, and squid, and sauté until golden, about 10 minutes. Using a slotted spoon, transfer the meat and seafood to a plate. Set aside.

5 Drain the artichokes and add to the oil remaining in the pan. Add the onion and bell pepper and sauté over medium heat until the onion is translucent, about 3 minutes. Return the meat and squid to the pan and stir in the tomatoes. Add 2 ladlefuls of the hot stock and simmer 1–2 minutes.

6 Stir a little stock into the mortar with the saffron mixture, then add it to the pan. Add the rice to the pan, followed by the peas and all but ½ cup (4 fl oz/125 ml) of the remaining stock. Stir thoroughly.

7 Cut the fish into 1-inch (2.5-cm) pieces. Scrub the mussels with a stiff brush and scrape off their beards, or remove the mussels from their shells if desired. Arrange the fish, mussels, and shrimp on top of the rice mixture, discarding any mussels that do not close to the touch. Return the paella to a simmer and cook until the meat and seafood is cooked through and the rice is tender but not too soft, about 20 minutes. If mussels are in their shells, discard any that failed to open. If all the liquid is absorbed before the paella is done, add a little of the reserved stock.

8 Turn off the heat and cover the pan with a clean kitchen towel. Let stand for about 10 minutes to allow the flavors to mingle and the rice to absorb any remaining juices. Garnish with parsley and serve warm, not hot.

Spanish Charcuterie

FUET

Long, thin, and dry cured, this salami-like sausage is made with white wine, pepper, and spices. It often develops a layer of natural white bloom on the surface. *Fuet* is a favorite for snacking. It is served, skinned and thinly sliced, with the popular tomato-rubbed bread or put into the lunches of children. The sausages are almost certain to be found in the picnic basket of any Barcelonan heading out of town for the weekend.

BOTIFARRA BLANCA

This firm, white sausage has been produced for at least four hundred years. Mildly spiced, juicy, and aromatic, it is made with a mixture of lean meat and gelatinous cuts. Some *charcuters* like to add egg to the mixture, in which case it becomes a *botifarra d'ou*—a specialty of carnival celebrations, especially in Barcelona. *Botifarra blanca* is usually seared, grilled, or fried and is a popular accompaniment for *mongetes* (stewed white beans).

BOTIFARRA NEGRA

Botifarra negra is the Catalan version of blood sausage, or *morcilla*—those types made with fatty meat and blood. It often contains minced onion and various spices, including cloves, black pepper, and allspice. Since it has been preboiled, it can be thinly sliced and eaten without further cooking. More commonly, however, it is sliced, fried briefly, and served as part of a lunch platter, perhaps alongside eggs and potatoes.

JAMÓN SERRANO

This exceptional cured ham, although not in the same league as the best Spanish *pernil ibéric*, is produced in the Pyrenean town of Olot. Though the qualities of a good serrano ham are not widely known outside of Spain, they are widely appreciated. The rich, sweet-salty punch of flavor makes it a natural partner for a dry sherry. Other excellent cured hams come from Jabugo, Dehesa de Extremadura, and Guijuelo, Spain's three great areas of production for *ibéric* ham.

FUET

CATALANA

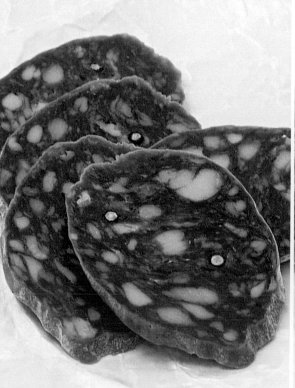

SALCHICHÓN DE VIC

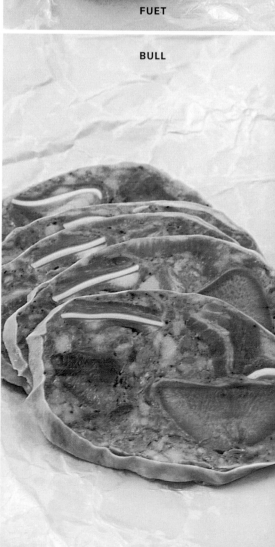

BULL

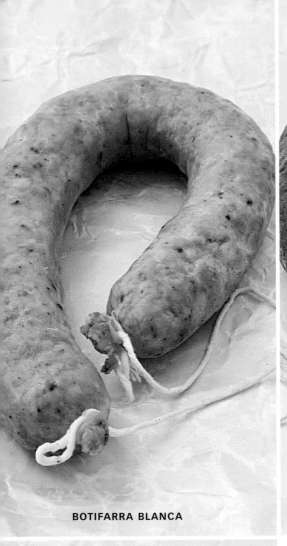

BOTIFARRA BLANCA

BOTIFARRA NEGRA

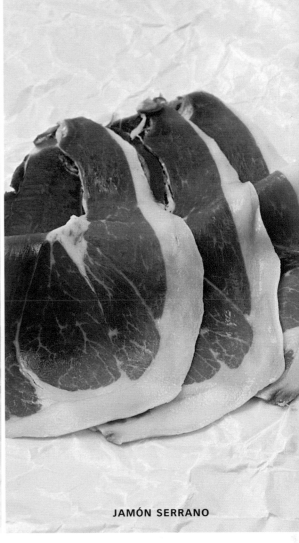

JAMÓN SERRANO

SOBRASSADA

CATALANA

Many Spanish *embotits* have Catalan equivalents. *Catalana*, however, is unique to Catalonia. Some food historians believe it to be the oldest of all Catalan sausages. Primarily made of lean meats, it has a firm texture and is generally large in size to make slicing easier. It is often flavored with white wine or black pepper, or in luxurious versions, pieces of black truffle. *Catalana*, like *bull,* makes a superb sandwich filling.

SALCHICHÓN DE VIC

Undoubtedly the best-known Catalan *embotit*, as well as the most prestigious and expensive, this specialty sausage (also called *llonganissa*) is one of the world's great pork products, equaled only by the finest artisan salami from Italy. It is best eaten in thin slices, and is typically served with crusty bread or toast drizzled with olive oil. The recipe, as followed by artisan producers in the town of Vic, is surprisingly simple; the only spices used are salt and pepper.

BULL

The name of this classic sausage is derived from the verb *bullir*, which means "to boil." The raw materials include variety meats from the pig, such as ears, feet, and the parts around the head and jaws, which help create the dense, sliceable texture. The thickly chopped meats are mixed with spices and pimentón, stuffed into skins, then boiled, cooled, and sliced thinly for eating in sandwiches, on toast, or as part of a mixed salad.

SOBRASSADA

Dry-curing meat is impossible in the hot, humid climate of the Mediterranean islands, so the people of Majorca, Ibiza, and Minorca have developed another technique: they add large amounts of pimentón to preserve the sausage meat for *sobrassada*, turning it bright orange in the process. *Sobrassada* is found in various forms—thick links in Majorca, thin links in Ibiza, or packed into small tubs. This delicious sausage is perfect with tomato-rubbed bread.

Shrimp and Basil Fried Rice

2 tablespoons vegetable oil

Salt

2 cloves garlic, minced

2 small red Fresno or serrano chiles, seeded and chopped

¼ lb (125 g) shrimp (prawns)

4 cups (1¼ lb/625 g) cold cooked long-grain white rice

1 tablespoon light soy sauce

1 tablespoon fish sauce

¼ teaspoon sugar

2 green (spring) onions, including 1 inch (2.5 cm) of the tender green tops, chopped

½ cup (¾ oz/20 g) firmly packed fresh Thai basil leaves

¼ cup (⅓ oz/10 g) coarsely chopped fresh cilantro (fresh coriander)

MAKES 4 SERVINGS

1 Peel and devein the shrimp, leaving the tails intact.

2 Heat a wok or deep frying pan over medium-high heat. When the pan is hot, add the oil, salt, and garlic and stir-fry until the garlic is light golden brown, about 30 seconds. Add the chiles and shrimp and stir-fry until the shrimp begin to turn bright orange-pink, about 30 seconds.

3 Add the cooked rice, crushing gently to break up any clumps, and stir-fry until heated through, about 2 minutes. Add the soy sauce, fish sauce, and sugar and stir-fry to combine thoroughly. Add the green onions and basil leaves and stir-fry just until the leaves begin to wilt, about 30 seconds.

4 Transfer the rice to a serving plate and garnish with the cilantro. Serve at once.

Yangzhou Fried Rice

1½ cups (10½ oz/330 g) long-grain white rice

3 tablespoons dried shrimp (prawns), soaked in ½ cup (4 fl oz/125 ml) boiling water for 10 minutes

½ cup (2½ oz/75 g) shelled English peas

½ cup (3 oz/90 g) corn kernels

3 tablespoons vegetable oil

2 eggs, beaten

½ cup (3 oz/90 g) diced bacon or ham

½ cup (2 oz/60 g) diced yellow onion

1 small, hot red chile, seeded and chopped

1 tablespoon light soy sauce

Salt

MAKES 4 SERVINGS

1 Rinse the rice in a sieve, then drain well. Pour the shrimp and its soaking water through a sieve held over a heavy saucepan. Set the shrimp aside. Add the rice and 1¾ cups (14 fl oz/430 ml) water, cover, and bring to a boil. Reduce the heat to low and cook until tender, 16–18 minutes.

2 Meanwhile, in a wok over high heat, bring 1 cup (8 fl oz/ 250 ml) water to a boil. Add the peas and corn and boil until tender, about 2½ minutes. Drain; set aside on a plate.

3 Wipe out the wok, add 2 tablespoons of the oil, and place over high heat. When the oil is hot, pour in the eggs and cook, without stirring, until lightly set, about 30 seconds. Break up the eggs, then transfer to the plate. Return the wok to high heat, add the bacon, onion, and chile. Stir-fry until the onion is golden, about 1½ minutes. Add to the plate.

4 When the rice is ready, add the remaining oil to the wok over high heat. When it is hot, add the shrimp, the cooked ingredients, the soy sauce, and 1 teaspoon salt. Add the rice and stir-fry until thoroughly mixed. Serve at once.

Red Rice with Achiote

This garlicky orange-red rice looks like the familiar Mexican red rice, but achiote paste—made from the brick-red seeds of the annatto tree—lends a flowery flavor.

2 medium-large ripe tomatoes, chopped, or 1 can (14½ oz/ 455 g) chopped tomatoes, drained

½ cup (2½ oz/75 g) chopped white onion

2 cloves garlic, chopped

1 tablespoon achiote paste

⅓ cup (3 fl oz/80 ml) safflower or canola oil

2 cups (14 oz/440 g) medium- or long-grain white rice

3 cups (24 fl oz/750 ml) chicken stock

1 green bell pepper (capsicum), roasted and seeded, then cut into short, narrow strips

5 fresh flat-leaf (Italian) parsley sprigs, chopped, plus extra for garnish

Sea salt

MAKES 8–10 SERVINGS

1 In a blender, purée the tomatoes, onion, and garlic. Add the achiote paste and blend until well mixed. Pass the mixture through a sieve.

2 In a heavy saucepan over medium heat, warm the oil. Add the rice and cook, stirring, until it starts to turn lightly golden, about 5 minutes. Stir in the tomato purée and fry, scraping the bottom of the pan occasionally, until the purée is absorbed, about 3 minutes. Stir in the stock and add the bell pepper, the 5 parsley sprigs, and 1 teaspoon salt. Reduce the heat to medium-low, cover, and simmer the rice until almost cooked through, about 25 minutes. Remove the pan from the heat and leave covered for 10 minutes.

3 Toss the rice with a fork, then spoon into a warmed bowl, garnish with parsley sprigs, and serve.

THAILAND
Pork, Rice, and Coriander Soup

For the garlic oil

¼ cup (2 fl oz/60 ml) vegetable oil

6 cloves garlic

6 cups (48 fl oz/1.5 l) chicken stock

1 tablespoon preserved radish

2 tablespoons fish sauce

⅛ teaspoon ground white pepper

¼ lb (125 g) ground (minced) pork butt or shoulder

1½ cups (7½ oz/235 g) cooked long-grain white rice, preferably jasmine

3 tablespoons coarsely chopped fresh cilantro (fresh coriander)

3 tablespoons chopped green (spring) onion, including tender green tops

MAKES 6 SERVINGS

1 To make the garlic oil, heat a small frying pan over medium heat. Add the oil and heat to 325°F (165°C) on a deep-frying thermometer. Meanwhile, chop the garlic and drop a bit into the oil. If it sizzles without burning, add the rest and fry, stirring to break up any clumps. When the garlic begins to turn golden, after about 3 minutes, remove the pan from the heat and let the garlic continue frying until golden brown, about 2 minutes longer. Let cool to room temperature and strain through a fine-mesh sieve. Set aside.

2 To make the soup, in a saucepan over high heat, combine the chicken stock, radish, fish sauce, and pepper. Bring to a boil, then reduce the heat to maintain a gentle simmer.

3 Break off about 1 teaspoon of the pork and roll it into a tiny meatball. Repeat until all the pork is used. Drop the balls, a few at a time, into the simmering stock and cook for 1 minute. Add the rice and simmer until the rice is soft and the soup is slightly thickened, about 5 minutes.

4 Ladle the soup into warmed bowls and top with the cilantro, green onion, and garlic oil.

PORTUGAL
Chicken and Rice Soup

For this simple and comforting soup, the stock must be rich and flavorful, which is accomplished by reducing regular stock to concentrate the flavor. Portuguese cooks might add linguiça instead of chicken, or tiny rice-shaped pasta instead of rice.

5 cups (40 fl oz/1.25 l) reduced chicken stock (see above)

1 cup (7 oz/220 g) long-grain white rice

1 whole chicken breast, about 1 lb (500 g), boned, skinned, and cut into strips 1 inch (2.5 cm) long and ½ inch (12 mm) wide

¼ cup (2 fl oz/60 ml) fresh lemon juice

Salt and freshly ground pepper

6 tablespoons (⅓ oz/10 g) chopped fresh mint

MAKES 4–6 SERVINGS

1 In a small, heavy saucepan, combine 1 cup (8 fl oz/250 ml) of the chicken stock and 1 cup (8 fl oz/250 ml) water. Bring to a boil over high heat, stir in the rice, reduce the heat to low, cover, and simmer until all the liquid is absorbed, 20–25 minutes. Remove from the heat.

2 Pour the remaining 4 cups (32 fl oz/1 l) chicken stock into a heavy saucepan and bring to a simmer over medium heat. Add the chicken strips, reduce the heat to low, and cook very gently until tender and cooked through, 15–20 minutes.

3 Add the rice and lemon juice and season with salt and pepper. Heat briefly, then stir in the mint, ladle into warmed bowls, and serve at once.

Crab Risotto

The best rice varieties for risotto are the medium-grain Italian types, such as Arborio, Carnaroli, and Vialone Nano. As hot liquid is added, a little at a time, the grains swell and soften. In a perfect risotto, the grains are suspended in a creamy mass. Here the rice is combined with Dungeness crab. Dungeness connoisseurs cook their own crabs, as this recipe calls for. If you buy a cooked crab and order it cracked and cleaned, tell the fishmonger you want all of the shell pieces for use in the stock.

Fine sea salt and freshly ground pepper

1 live Dungeness crab, about 2 lb (1 kg)

2 cups (16 fl oz/500 ml) bottled clam juice

½ cup (4 fl oz/125 ml) dry white wine

1 large celery stalk, cut into 4 equal pieces

¼ yellow onion

5 tablespoons (2½ fl oz/75 ml) extra-virgin olive oil

1 cup (3 oz/90 g) thinly sliced leeks, white and pale green parts only

1½ cups (10½ oz/330 g) Arborio, Carnaroli, or Vialone Nano rice

2 tablespoons minced fresh flat-leaf (Italian) parsley

1 teaspoon grated lemon zest

MAKES 4 SERVINGS

1 In a large pot, bring 8 qt (8 l) water to a boil and add 3 tablespoons salt. Add the live crab and cover the pot. Boil for 20 minutes, then remove the crab with tongs and let cool.

2 Twist off the claws and legs, then lift off the hard top shell. Rinse the top shell and set it aside for the stock. Turn the crab over; lift off and discard the triangular tail flap. Pull off and discard the grayish feathery gills along both sides. With a heavy knife, quarter the body. If necessary, rinse the body pieces very quickly to remove the yellowish "butter."

3 Remove all the crabmeat from the quarters, then crack the legs and claws and remove the meat. Keep the meat in pieces as large as possible, and reserve all the shell pieces.

4 In a saucepan over medium heat, combine 4 cups (32 fl oz/1 l) water and the clam juice, wine, celery, onion, and crab shells. Bring to a simmer. Allow to simmer, uncovered, for 15 minutes. Place a fine-mesh sieve over a clean saucepan and strain the stock into the pan. Bring to a simmer over medium heat, then reduce to just below a simmer.

5 In a large saucepan over medium-low heat, warm 3 tablespoons of the olive oil. Add the leeks and stir to coat. Cook, stirring occasionally, until soft, 10–12 minutes. Add the rice and cook, stirring, until all the grains are hot. Begin adding the stock ½ cup (4 fl oz/125 ml) at a time, stirring often and adding more only when the previous addition has been absorbed. It should take about 20 minutes for the rice to become al dente and absorb most of the stock. (You may not need all of the stock.) The risotto should be creamy, neither soupy nor stiff, and the kernels should be tender yet firm in the center. Remove the risotto from the heat.

6 Set aside 4 attractive, large nuggets of crabmeat for garnish. Stir the remaining crabmeat into the rice along with the remaining 2 tablespoons olive oil, the parsley, and the lemon zest. Season with salt and pepper.

7 Spoon the risotto into warmed individual bowls, garnish each with a reserved crabmeat nugget, and serve at once.

Risotto Croquettes

These egg-shaped croquettes with a heart of molten mozzarella are a ubiquitous appetizer in Roman pizzerias, where they're known as *supplì al telefono—supplì* from the French word for surprise, *telefono* for the long cord the cheese forms when the croquette is bitten into.

For the tomato mixture

1½ oz (15 g) dried porcini mushrooms

1 tablespoon extra-virgin olive oil

¼ lb (125 g) ground (minced) lean beef

1 small yellow onion, finely chopped

1 can (14 oz/440 g) tomato purée

Salt

For the rice

Salt

2 cups (14 oz/440 g) Arborio rice

2 eggs, lightly beaten

2 tablespoons unsalted butter

2 tablespoons grated Parmigiano-Reggiano cheese

1 egg

1 cup (4 oz/125 g) fine dried bread crumbs

½ lb (250 g) fresh mozzarella cheese, cut to the size and shape of large sugar cubes (about 24 pieces)

Olive oil, preferably extra-virgin, for deep-frying

MAKES ABOUT
24 CROQUETTES

1 To make the tomato mixture, in a small bowl, combine the mushrooms with warm water to cover and let stand for 15 minutes to rehydrate. Drain, squeeze out the excess liquid, and chop finely. In a frying pan over medium heat, warm the olive oil. Add the beef, onion, and mushrooms and sauté until the meat is no longer red, about 10 minutes. Add the tomato purée and ½ teaspoon salt, bring to a boil, reduce the heat and simmer, uncovered, until reduced by one-third, about 20 minutes. Set aside to cool.

2 To make the rice, bring a large saucepan of water to a rapid boil. Add 1 tablespoon salt and the rice and cook, stirring occasionally, until the rice has softened but is still al dente, 10–12 minutes. Drain the rice and spread out on a large platter to cool slightly. Add the tomato mixture, eggs, butter, Parmigiano-Reggiano, and a pinch of salt. Using your hands, mix to combine. Let cool to room temperature.

3 Whisk the egg in a small, shallow bowl. Pour the bread crumbs into a second shallow bowl. To form each croquette, scoop up some rice and form it into the size and shape of an egg. Make a deep indentation, insert a piece of the mozzarella, and close the rice around it. Roll the ball in the egg and then the bread crumbs, coating evenly. Place on a large plate. Cover the plate and refrigerate for at least 1 hour or up to overnight.

4 Preheat the oven to 150°F (65°C) and put an ovenproof platter in it. Pour olive oil to a depth of at least 2 inches (5 cm) into a heavy saucepan or frying pan and heat to 325°F (165°C) on a deep-frying thermometer, or until a bit of rice dropped into the hot oil sizzles immediately on contact. Working in batches, fry the croquettes, turning as needed, until they form a crisp crust, 5–7 minutes. Using a slotted spoon, transfer to paper towels to drain, then to the oven to keep warm. Serve while the mozzarella core is hot.

Dolmas

No Greek meze table is complete without *dolmas*, the family of stuffed vine or cabbage leaves and vegetables such as tomatoes, eggplants (aubergines), and zucchini (courgettes). These popular rice-filled grape leaves are usually served at room temperature with lemon wedges or yogurt. One 8-ounce (250-g) jar of grape leaves should provide enough for filling and lining the pan.

1 cup (7 oz/220 g) long-grain white rice, preferably basmati

¼ cup (1½ oz/45 g) currants

¼ cup (1 oz/30 g) pine nuts (optional)

¾ cup (6 fl oz/180 ml) olive oil

2 cups (10 oz/315 g) finely chopped yellow onion

Salt

1 cup (3 oz/90 g) finely chopped green (spring) onions

1 teaspoon ground allspice

1 teaspoon ground cinnamon

½ cup (3 oz/90 g) peeled, seeded, chopped, and drained tomatoes, fresh or canned (optional)

½ cup (¾ oz/20 g) chopped fresh flat-leaf (Italian) parsley

¼ cup (⅓ oz/10 g) chopped fresh mint or dill

¾ cup (6 fl oz/180 ml) hot water

Freshly ground pepper

36 grape leaves preserved in brine, plus grape leaves for lining pan (optional)

2 cups (16 fl oz/500 ml) boiling water

Fresh lemon juice, plus lemon wedges for serving

MAKES 36 DOLMAS

1 Place the rice in a bowl, add cold water to cover, and let stand for 30 minutes. Place the currants in a small bowl, add hot water to cover, and let stand for 30 minutes until plumped. Drain the rice and currants and set aside.

2 Meanwhile, if using the pine nuts, preheat the oven to 350°F (180°C). Spread the nuts in a small pan and toast in the oven until fragrant, 6–8 minutes. Set aside.

3 In a large frying pan over medium heat, warm ½ cup (4 fl oz/120 ml) of the olive oil. Add the yellow onion and 1 teaspoon salt and sauté until softened, about 5 minutes. Add the green onions and sauté until softened, about 5 minutes longer. Add the allspice, cinnamon, and drained rice and cook, stirring, until the rice is opaque, about 4 minutes. Add the chopped tomatoes (if using), parsley, mint, drained currants, and hot water and cook, uncovered, until the water is absorbed and the rice is about half cooked, about 10 minutes. Stir in the pine nuts, if using. Season with salt and pepper. Let cool.

4 Rinse the grape leaves in cool water and cut off the stems. Working in batches, lay them out on a table, shiny side down. Place a tablespoonful of the rice filling near the stem end, fold the bottom end over the filling, then fold in the sides and roll up. Do not roll too tightly, as the rice will expand during cooking. Set aside, seam side down.

5 Select a baking pan or large, deep frying pan that will hold the stuffed grape leaves in a single layer and line it with grape leaves, if using. Arrange the stuffed grape leaves in the pan, seam side down. Place a heavy plate on top to keep them from unrolling while cooking, then pour the boiling water and the remaining ¼ cup (2 fl oz/60 ml) olive oil around the leaves. Cover and simmer gently over very low heat until the rice and leaves are tender, about 45 minutes. Remove from the heat and remove the plate. Sprinkle with a little lemon juice, let cool, then serve with lemon wedges.

Note: *Dolmas* can be refrigerated for up to 2 days. Bring to room temperature before serving.

Sticky Rice in Lotus Leaves

Raw grains of glutinous rice are whiter and less opalescent than common rice and when cooked release their starches to become softly sticky. It is rarely used plain. Instead, it is cooked with seasonings and flavorful ingredients to make fillings and savory snacks. Lotus leaves filled with sticky rice and "eight treasures"—which include ginkgo nuts, raisins, diced ham, red dates, dried shrimp, and sausage—is a favorite at celebration dinners. Scaled-down versions are enjoyed as dim sum treats.

1½ cups (10½ oz/330 g) glutinous rice, soaked in cold water to cover for 1 hour

3 dried black mushrooms, soaked in hot water to cover for 25 minutes and drained

2 Chinese sausages

¼ cup (1¼ oz/40 g) dried shrimp (prawns), soaked in hot water to cover for 25 minutes and drained

5 oz (155 g) boneless chicken thigh, cut into ½-inch (12-mm) cubes

¼ cup (1½ oz/45 g) raw peanuts

2 green (spring) onions, including tender green tops, chopped

2½ tablespoons light soy sauce

1½ tablespoons peanut oil

4 dried lotus leaves, soaked in cold water to cover for 1 hour

MAKES 4 PARCELS

1 Drain the rice and transfer it to a heatproof bowl. In a teakettle, bring 4 cups (32 fl oz/1 l) water to a boil. Pour over the rice. Let stand until cool.

2 Remove and discard the stems from the mushrooms and finely chop the caps.

3 Bring water to a simmer in a steamer base. Place the sausages on a heatproof plate in a steamer basket, set over the simmering water, cover, and steam until soft and plump, about 5 minutes. Remove from the steamer and let cool, then thinly slice.

4 Drain the rice and return it to the bowl. Add the mushrooms, sausages, shrimp, chicken, peanuts, green onions, soy sauce, and peanut oil. Stir until evenly distributed.

5 Drain the lotus leaves, which should now be soft and flexible, and pat dry. Fold each leaf in half and cut away the thick central stem and ribs. Lay the leaves on a flat work surface with the cut-stem area facing you. Divide the mixture evenly among the 4 leaves, piling it in the center. Working with 1 leaf at a time, fold the 2 outer edges over the filling, fold up the bottom, and fold over the top, enclosing the filling completely in a neat parcel. Place the leaf parcels, seam side down, in a steamer basket or steamer rack in which they fit snugly but not tightly.

6 Bring water to a simmer in the steamer base. Place the steamer basket over the simmering water, cover, and steam for about 40 minutes, replenishing the water as needed with boiling water to maintain the original level. To test for doneness, lift the top flap on a parcel; the rice should be partially translucent and tender.

7 Cut a cross in the top of each leaf to expose the filling and serve at once.

Rice Pudding with Almonds

4 cups (32 fl oz/1 l) milk

4 cups (32 fl oz/1 l) light (single) cream or half and half

½ cup (3½ oz/105 g) scented rice, preferably small-grain Gobinda Bhog, or brown basmati, thoroughly rinsed

1 cup (6 oz/185 g) light-colored jaggery or light brown sugar

4 green cardamom pods

½ teaspoon saffron threads, crushed

½ cup (3 oz/90 g) raisins

¼ cup (1 oz/30 g) sliced (flaked) almonds

Edible silver leaf (optional)

MAKES 6 SERVINGS

1 In a large, shallow saucepan over high heat, bring the milk and cream to a boil, stirring frequently to prevent scorching. Add the rice, reduce the heat to medium-low, and cook, stirring occasionally, until the liquid is reduced to the consistency of custard and the rice is soft and creamy, about 50 minutes. Add the sugar and mix well.

2 Pry open the cardamom pods and remove the seeds. Grind them to a powder, preferably in a mortar using a pestle. You can also wrap the seeds in plastic wrap and crush them with a mallet or rolling pin. Discard the cardamom pods. Add the cardamom, saffron, raisins, and almonds to the cooked rice mixture and mix well. Transfer to a bowl, let cool, then cover and refrigerate until chilled. Serve in small dessert bowls garnished with small squares of silver leaf, if using.

Coconut Rice Pudding

For the pudding

3 cups (24 fl oz/750 ml) milk

1 cup (8 fl oz/250 ml) canned coconut milk

1 cup (4 oz/125 g) sweetened shredded dried coconut, plus 2 tablespoons for garnish

½ cup (3½ oz/110 g) medium-grain white rice

2 egg yolks

1 tablespoon sugar

1 teaspoon vanilla extract

For the sauce

½ cup (4 fl oz/125 ml) heavy (double) cream

2 tablespoons sugar

½ vanilla bean, split lengthwise

1½ teaspoons ground espresso

3 oz (90 g) high-quality bittersweet chocolate, finely chopped

1 tablespoon unsalted butter

MAKES 4 SERVINGS

1 To make the pudding, in a heavy saucepan over medium heat, combine the milk, coconut milk, 1 cup coconut, and rice. Bring to a slow boil, reduce the heat to very low, and simmer, uncovered, stirring frequently, until the rice is very tender and all of the liquid is absorbed, about 1 hour.

2 In a small bowl, whisk together the yolks, sugar, and vanilla. Whisk in ½ cup (3½ fl oz/105 g) of the cooked rice. Stir this mixture back into the rice. The pudding can be served warm, at room temperature, or cold, but wait to make the sauce until just before serving.

3 To make the sauce, stir the cream and sugar together in a heavy saucepan. Scrape the seeds from the vanilla bean into the cream. Bring to a rolling boil over medium heat, remove from the heat, and stir in the coffee granules and chocolate. Stir until melted, about 1 minute. Whisk until shiny and smooth, then whisk in the butter.

4 Spoon the pudding into goblets and top with the sauce and shredded coconut. Serve at once.

Vegetable Couscous

Grain-like couscous is in fact a tiny semolina pasta. After cooking, it is garnished with vegetables, accompanied with spicy *harissa*, and served with grilled lamb, sautéed chicken, grilled *merguez* (a spicy North African lamb sausage), or all of the above.

For the harissa

6 oz (185 g) small dried red chiles such as árbol or bird's eye

4 cloves garlic

2 tablespoons ground cumin

Salt

1½ cups (12 fl oz/375 ml) extra-virgin olive oil

For the vegetables

8 small new potatoes

1 small head cauliflower

2 large carrots

2 tablespoons unsalted butter

2 tablespoons extra-virgin olive oil

2 yellow onions, chopped

2 cloves garlic, chopped

2 small dried red chiles such as árbol, seeded and crumbled

2 tablespoons ground turmeric

1 teaspoon ground cumin

1 teaspoon fresh thyme leaves

⅛ teaspoon saffron threads

Salt and freshly ground pepper

2 cups (16 fl oz/500 ml) vegetable or chicken stock

1 cup (5 oz/155 g) shelled English peas

For the couscous

3 cups (24 fl oz/750 ml) boiling water

2 cups (12 oz/375 g) couscous

1 tablespoon unsalted butter

Salt

¼ cup (⅓ oz/10 g) minced fresh mint

¼ cup (⅓ oz/10 g) minced fresh chives

¼ cup (⅓ oz/10 g) minced fresh tarragon

MAKES 4–6 SERVINGS

1 To make the *harissa*, with a mortar and pestle (or a blender), crush the chiles, including their seeds, into fine pieces. Add the garlic, cumin, 1 teaspoon salt, and 2 tablespoons of the olive oil. Continue to crush until a paste forms. Gradually work in the remaining olive oil to form a medium-thick sauce. Set aside.

2 To prepare the vegetables, halve the new potatoes and cut the cauliflower into florets. Peel the carrots and cut into 2-inch (5-cm) lengths. In a deep, heavy frying pan over medium heat, melt the butter with the olive oil. When the butter foams, add the onions and garlic and sauté until translucent, 2–3 minutes. Stir in the chiles, turmeric, cumin, thyme, saffron, ½ teaspoon salt, and ½ teaspoon pepper. Add the potatoes, cauliflower, and carrots and turn gently in the butter mixture, 1–2 minutes. Add the stock and stir, 1–2 minutes. Cover tightly, reduce the heat to low, and cook until the potatoes are almost tender, 15–20 minutes. Add the peas, cover again, and cook until the peas and potatoes are tender, 5–7 minutes longer. Remove from the heat and keep covered.

3 To make the couscous, in a large bowl, combine the boiling water, couscous, butter, and ½ teaspoon salt. Let stand until the water is absorbed, about 10 minutes. Turn into a fine-mesh sieve and press gently with a wooden spoon to remove excess water. Transfer to a bowl and, using a fork, gently fluff to separate the grains.

4 Just before serving, spoon 1 or 2 tablespoons of the hot stock from the vegetables into the *harissa* and stir to combine.

5 To serve, heap the couscous on a platter, spoon a little of the stock and a few vegetables over it, and sprinkle with a little of the mint, chives, and tarragon. Accompany with the remaining vegetables and their stock, the bowl of *harissa*, and the remaining herbs.

Tabbouleh

1 cup (8 fl oz/250 ml) boiling
water

½ cup (3 oz/90 g) fine bulgur

Leaves of 1 large bunch flat-leaf
(Italian) parsley

Leaves of 1 bunch spearmint

½ cup (2½ oz/75 g) red onion

2 cups (12 oz/375 g) cherry
tomatoes

Juice of 1 large lemon

2 tablespoons extra-virgin
olive oil

Salt and freshly ground pepper

MAKES 4 SERVINGS

1 In a large bowl, pour the boiling water over the bulgur.
Let stand for 30 minutes, uncovered, until the bulgur has
absorbed all the liquid and is softened.

2 Chop the parsley, mint, and onion. Add to the bulgur
and toss to combine.

3 Halve the tomatoes, place in a colander, and press lightly
to drain off some of their liquid and eliminate some seeds,
then add to the bulgur.

4 Pour the lemon juice and olive oil over the bulgur and
vegetables and mix well. Season with salt and pepper. Cover
and refrigerate for at least 2 hours or up to 24 hours
before serving.

Farro Salad

Farro, one of the world's oldest grains, has a brown skin and floury interior. Pearled
farro has had the outer skin polished off and cooks more quickly. When making this
summery salad, use squid no larger than your hand and take care not to overcook it.

1 cup (5 oz/155 g) pearled farro

1 lb (500 g) squid

2 cups (2 oz/60 g) tender
arugula (rocket) leaves

½ lb (250 g) cherry tomatoes,
quartered

⅓ cup (3 fl oz/80 ml) extra-virgin
olive oil

Juice of 1 lemon

Salt and freshly ground pepper

MAKES 4 SERVINGS

1 In a saucepan over high heat, bring 3 cups (24 fl oz/
750 ml) water to a boil. Add the farro, reduce the heat to low,
cover partially, and simmer until the farro is tender but still
firm, about 20 minutes. Drain well and set aside.

2 To clean each squid, pull the head and tentacles from
the body pouch. Discard the clinging innards. Cut off the
tentacles just below the eyes and discard the eye portion.
Squeeze the cut end of the tentacles to expel the hard beak
and discard. Pull the long, transparent quill from inside
the body pouch and discard. Remove and discard the gray
membrane covering the body pouch. Rinse the pouch and
tentacles under cold running water.

3 In a saucepan fitted with a steamer basket, bring 1 inch
(2.5 cm) of water to a boil. Add the squid, reduce to low,
cover, and steam until tender, 3–5 minutes. When cool
enough to handle, cut the pouches into ½-inch (12-mm)
rings and the tentacles into 1-inch (2.5-cm) sections.

4 Combine the farro, squid, arugula, and tomatoes in
a serving bowl. Add the olive oil and lemon juice and toss to
combine. Season with salt and pepper and serve at once.

ITALY
Tuscan Olive Oil

OLIVE VARIETIES

Dozens of olive varieties are grown throughout the world, each with its own size, shape, flavor, and use in the kitchen. Tuscan olives are strictly about oil. The five primary varieties are *moraiolo* and *correggiolo* (the two predominant ones), *frantoio* (from the Italian word for olive mill), plump *leccino*, and *pendolino*. The oils are blended much like wine grape juices. Capezzana, an estate-bottled Tuscan olive oil, is made from 60 percent *moraiolo* olives, 30 percent *frantoio*, 5 percent *leccino*, and 5 percent *pendolino* olives.

AUTHENTIC TUSCAN OLIVE OIL

Choosing the best-quality Tuscan olive oil is not always easy, as the labels can be deceiving. A homey-looking bottle with a *casalinga* (housewife) holding an olive branch on its old-fashioned label might well be a low-grade, industrially made oil. A bottle labeled *olio di oliva toscano* could mean that the bottler purchased olives from as far away as Spain or Greece and then pressed them in an industrial mill somewhere in Tuscany. The problem with imported olives is twofold: If they are not local varieties, they will differ in flavor from Tuscan olives. And more important, because olives begin to oxidize soon after they are picked, those that have traveled are less fresh than locally picked olives. For truly authentic *olio extra vergine di oliva toscano*, look for artisan-made Tuscan oils. Their labels will show the year of harvest and confirm that the olives were grown on the estate and pressed at the estate's own *frantoio* or a local nonindustrial mill.

Though winemaking is integral to the flow of Tuscan seasons, it takes awhile, sometimes a very long while, for the fruit to make the journey from *uva* (grapes) to a drinkable *vino*. By contrast, the olive harvest provides instant gratification, since the oil is at its very best just after it is pressed.

MAKING OLIVE OIL

HARVESTING THE OLIVES Olives are harvested using large, long-handled wooden rakes. The freshly picked olives are then whisked off to the mill in crates to be pressed within thirty-six hours.

PRESSING THE OLIVES Traditionally, oil was extracted by pressing the olives between granite millstones. Many nonindustrial mills now use a modern continuous-cycle system. The olives are conveyed up a belt, washed, and cut into a pulp. The resulting paste is kneaded and centrifugally "decanted" to separate it into solids, water, and oil.

DISCARDING THE SANSA *Sansa* is the dirty, brown residue of oil production, consisting primarily of ground pits and skin. It is piled outside the mill to be picked up by refineries that use chemical solvents to extract additional but inferior oil.

COLLECTING THE OIL At the tail end of the enormous machinery used to extract oil is a spout from which pure oil flows in a thin stream. The oil is then filtered and sent to an adjoining *orciaia* (olive oil storeroom) to rest in terra-cotta urns for several days before bottling.

Polenta with Beef Ragù

Polenta's indisputable domain is Italy's Veneto region in the north but the ground cornmeal is eaten throughout Italy. Sometimes it is cooked and cooled, then cut into thin slices, fried, and used like the bread in bruschetta. When still warm and soft, it's best heaped with a hearty sauce like this beef ragù with porcini mushrooms.

For the ragù

¼ cup (2 fl oz/60 ml) extra-virgin olive oil

1 yellow onion, finely chopped

1 large carrot, peeled and finely chopped

1 celery stalk, finely chopped

1 clove garlic, minced

3 fresh sage leaves

1½ lb (750 g) ground (minced) lean beef

Salt and freshly ground pepper

½ cup (4 fl oz/125 ml) dry white wine

1 bay leaf

1 can (14½ oz/455 g) crushed plum (Roma) tomatoes

3 oz (90 g) fresh porcini or cremini mushrooms, brushed clean and sliced

For the polenta

1⅔ cups (8½ oz/265 g) coarse-ground polenta

Freshly grated Parmigiano-Reggiano cheese for serving

MAKES 6 SERVINGS

1 To make the ragù, in a saucepan over medium heat, warm the olive oil. Add the onion, carrot, celery, and garlic and sauté until softened, about 15 minutes. Add the sage leaves and beef, and break up the meat with a wooden spoon. Season with pepper, then raise the heat to high and stir well. When the meat is evenly browned, add the wine and cook until the alcohol has evaporated, about 3 minutes. Stir in 1½ cups (12 fl oz/375 ml) cold water and the bay leaf. Bring to a boil, scraping the sides of the pan occasionally. Reduce the heat to low, partially cover, and simmer, stirring occasionally, until the meat has released all its juices, about 45 minutes. Season with salt and pepper. Stir in the tomatoes and mushrooms, return to a simmer, and cook over low heat until the sauce is a medium consistency, about 45 minutes longer. Adjust the seasoning if needed, set aside, and keep warm.

2 To make the polenta, in a heavy saucepan over high heat, bring 7 cups (56 fl oz/1.75 l) water to a boil. Add 2 teaspoons salt and pour in the polenta in a fine, steady stream, whisking constantly. Reduce the heat to medium. When the polenta begins to thicken, after about 5 minutes, reduce the heat to low. Cook, stirring constantly, until the polenta comes away easily from the sides of the pan, 30–40 minutes longer.

3 Divide the polenta among warmed individual bowls, ladle with a generous portion of the ragù, and serve at once. Pass the Parmigiano-Reggiano at the table.

MEXICO
Pork Tamales

For the filling

½ **white onion**

2 **cloves**

1½ **lb (750 g) boneless pork butt or shoulder, in large chunks**

4 **cloves garlic**

Sea salt

For the sauce

6 **ancho chiles, seeded**

½ **lb (250 g) tomatillos, husked and rinsed**

1 **white onion, coarsely chopped**

4 **cloves garlic**

¾ **teaspoon ground cumin**

⅛ **teaspoon ground allspice**

6 **tablespoons (3 fl oz/90 ml) safflower or canola oil**

2 **bay leaves**

Sea salt

For the tamales

50 **corn husks, rinsed**

⅔ **cup (5 oz/155 g) lard or vegetable shortening**

4 **cups (2½ lb/1.25 kg)** *masa harina* **for tamales**

1½ **teaspoons baking powder**

Sea salt

MAKES 40 SMALL TAMALES

1 To prepare the filling, stud the onion with the cloves and add it to a pot with the pork, the garlic, 1½ teaspoons salt, and water to cover. Bring to a boil, skimming off any foam. Reduce the heat, cover, and simmer for 1½–2 hours. Let cool. Remove the meat and reserve the broth, skimming off the fat. Finely shred the meat.

2 To make the sauce, in a bowl, soak the chiles in very hot water, 15–20 minutes. Drain, reserving the soaking water. In a saucepan, combine the tomatillos with water to cover and boil until soft, about 8 minutes. Drain. In a blender, combine the chiles, tomatillos, half of the chopped onion, the garlic, cumin, allspice, and ½ cup (4 fl oz/ 125 ml) of the chile soaking water. Blend until smooth.

3 In a deep, heavy frying pan over medium-high heat, warm the oil. Add the remaining chopped onion and sauté for 5 minutes. Add the chile purée and bay leaves. Reduce the heat to low and simmer uncovered, stirring occasionally, until the sauce begins to thicken, about 15 minutes. Stir in the meat, season with salt, and cook until thick and a little dry, about 20 minutes.

4 To make the tamales, soak the corn husks in very hot water until pliable, about 15 minutes. In a bowl, using an electric mixer, beat the lard until fluffy, about 5 minutes. Add the *masa harina*, the baking powder, and 1½ teaspoons salt and mix well. Reheat the broth and stir 3 cups (24 fl oz/ 750 ml) into the *masa harina* mixture, 1 cup (8 fl oz/250 ml) at a time, adding more broth if it is too dry. Beat for another 10–15 minutes until the *masa* (dough) is very light. It is ready when a spoonful floats in cold water.

5 Drain the husks and pat dry. Line the bottom of a steamer basket with a few husks and tear a few more into thin strips. Holding each husk in the palm of your hand, with the pointed end on your wrist, spread 1 tablespoon of the dough in the center of the upper half, leaving a margin on all sides. Put 1 teaspoon of filling in the center of the dough. Fold the sides of the husk over the filling, then fold up the pointed end. Tie closed with a strip of husk.

6 Stand the tamales in the steamer basket, folded end down, propping them around an inverted small funnel. Bring water to a boil in the bottom of the steamer pot and add the basket. Cover the tamales with corn husks and a kitchen towel, then place the lid on the steamer. Steam, without uncovering, for 1 hour, then remove one to check that the dough is firm. Serve hot.

PASTA AND NOODLES

Shapes and Strands
PASTA AND NOODLES AROUND THE WORLD

Ants climbing trees, Venus's navels, and swallowing clouds. Fat snails, wagon wheels, angel hair, and priests' hats. What else but the fanciful shapes of pasta and noodles could inspire cooks to give such unique names to their creations? Once enjoyed only by nobility, pasta has become an important staple, in one form or another, in kitchens throughout the world.

The ancient Etruscans, Greeks, Sicilians, Arabs, and Chinese have all been hailed as inventors of that basic dish, little pieces of dough boiled in water. While historians debate the matter, cooks rely on traditions reaching back centuries in both Europe and Asia. The term *pasta* generally refers to a wheat base; noodles can encompass a wide variety of starchy bases, such as rice, mung bean, buckwheat, and even root vegetables. In Italy, the hard semolina wheat of the hot southern provinces allowed cooks to cut intricate shapes and dry their pasta for long periods. From these Sicilian pastas, our modern, machine-extruded versions were developed. Meanwhile, Northern Italy's softer wheat lent itself to delicate, hand-rolled pastas that were best served fresh.

Sturdy wheat noodles originated in northern China and silken rice noodles in tropical countries. Buckwheat, a cold-climate grain, is the base for the firm, dark soba noodles of Japan and Korea. Adding egg to wheat dough creates lustrous pastas. In China, egg noodles join broth for hearty soups. In Italy's Emilia Romagna, fresh egg pasta is rolled and cut by hand into shapes such as fettuccine for serving with meat sauces. Italy's pasta dishes highlight local ingredients. Romans like tomato-rich meat sauce while Sardinians sprinkle pungent dried roe over their pasta. Southern Italians, surrounded by the sea, enjoy abundant sardines and anchovies in their sauces. Northern Italians grace their pasta simply with clear broth or creamy butter and freshly grated Parmigiano-Reggiano.

FILLED PASTAS

Northern Italians savor filled pastas. Bite-sized ravioli, tortellini, *agnolotti,* and cappelletti have fillings of meat, cheese, or full-flavored vegetables. Pasta sheets layered with ricotta, spicy sausage, meatballs, roasted vegetables, or pesto can be baked slowly into hearty lasagna. Filled and rolled cannelloni, topped with either tomato or béchamel sauce, is a popular dish hailing from Naples in the south.

In China, the round plumpness and silken wrappers of wontons give the dumplings their name, "swallowing clouds." With clear broth ladled over them, wontons are a popular fast food throughout Asia. In Cantonese dim sum teahouses, families also enjoy *cheong fun,* large sheets of steamed rice noodles wrapped around pork, shrimp (prawns), or beef and then drizzled with a sweet soy sauce.

SOUPS

Certain Italian pasta shapes were created specifically for soup. Small, square *quadrettini,* peppercorn-sized *acini di pepe,* and melon-seed *seme di melone* call for thin broths. Large tubes, shells, and wheels stand up to thicker soups, such as minestrone and *pasta e fagioli.*

In Asia, broth ladled over fresh noodles comes to the table for breakfast, lunch, and dinner. Many countries are famous for a particular noodle soup, from Japan's soba to Malaysia's *soto ayam,* and complex variations in noodles, broths, and toppings account for thousands of specialties in between. Japan's soup broths tend to be minimalist, perhaps mirin-sweetened shoyu broth, or dashi, the crystal-clear infusion of shaved bonito and wakame seaweed. Thick and chewy udon noodles provide a hearty base, while *somen,* thin, delicate strands, appears in lighter soups.

Farther south in Asia, cooks construct elaborate noodle dishes. Rich coconut milk, tart tamarind, golden turmeric root, warm spices, or ground peanuts flavor the broth of Southeast Asian noodle soups. The broth for Malaysian *laksa* boasts more than twenty ingredients, and shredded chicken, hard-boiled egg, fried shallots, julienned ginger flower, and a bouquet of fresh herbs are just some of the garnishes.

Thin vermicelli pasta, known as *sev* or *fideo,* was carried by Arabs from India to Spain. Today, many restaurants in Barcelona offer a *fideo*-based paella, but traveling on to Mexico, the delicate pasta became popular in brothy soups as well as *sopa seca,* a comforting dish in which the noodles have absorbed much of the flavorful stock.

COLD NOODLES

Asia's hot, humid summers have inspired refreshing cold noodle dishes. In Vietnam, thin rice vermicelli called *bun* are topped with finely shredded vegetables, grilled meats, and fresh herbs. In Japan, cooks ward off the heat by serving cold soba noodles on bamboo trays alongside a wasabi-spiked dipping sauce. In the Sichuan province of China, chilled sesame-flavored *dan dan* noodles are paired with julienned cucumber, and in Korea, *naeng myun* buckwheat noodles are combined with ice cubes and Asian pears in a tart, spicy broth.

FRIED NOODLES

Noodles take well to stir-frying and deep-frying. They can be served dry, tossed with a variety of fresh and cooked ingredients, or braised in a thick, flavorful sauce. Southeast Asian street vendors serve up quick, nutritious dishes using only a wok, two spatulas, and an array of ingredients. Bangkok's *pad thai* is perhaps the best-known of these, but variations on *mee goreng,* curry-infused Singapore noodles, Vietnam's *mi xao,* and silken ribbons of *chow fun* are enjoyed throughout the region.

After being shaped into bite-sized nests or platter-sized pillows, noodles can be deep-fried to a crisp texture. Flat, long *e-fu* noodles are boiled, fried, and dried for a chewy texture. Cooked and tossed with lobster, mushrooms, or perhaps yellow chives, *e-fu* are known as "long life noodles" and appear at Cantonese banquets for good luck.

Cellophane or glass noodles, enjoyed throughout Asia, turn transparent when cooked. Among these are the wide, flat *harusame* noodles in Japan and the fat, round *dang myun* in Korea, which are used for stir-fried *chap chae.*

DESSERTS

Eastern Europe's sweet kugel binds egg noodles with eggs, milk, sour cream, sugar, and cinnamon into a puddinglike dessert. Carrots, apples, raisins, almonds, orange zest, or vanilla may flavor the dish, and its texture may range from a creamy custard to a dense cake. In India, a vermicelli dessert known as *seviyan kheer* in the north and *semiya payasam* in the south features cardamom-infused milk, sliced nuts, raisins, and, for special meals, bits of silver leaf on the surface.

Ricotta Ravioli with Fresh Tomatoes

As its name implies, ricotta is made by "recooking" the whey left after making mozzarella or other cheeses. At some of Italy's most elegant restaurants, delicate *ricotta di bufala* is used to fill homemade ravioli, but cow's milk ricotta makes a fine substitution. The addition of ground cinnamon softens the tartness of the tomatoes.

For the filling

1¼ cups (10 oz/315 g) whole-milk ricotta cheese

½ cup (2 oz/60 g) Parmigiano-Reggiano cheese

1 egg

1½ teaspoons ground cinnamon

Salt and freshly ground pepper

For the pasta dough

3 cups (15 oz/470 g) all-purpose (plain) flour

Pinch of salt

4 eggs

2 teaspoons extra-virgin olive oil

For the sauce

¼ cup (2 fl oz/60 ml) extra-virgin olive oil

4 cloves garlic, crushed

1½ lb (750 g) plum (Roma) tomatoes, peeled and seeded, then coarsely chopped

Salt and freshly ground pepper

Handful of fresh basil leaves

Grated Parmigiano-Reggiano cheese for serving

MAKES 6 SERVINGS

1 To make the filling, in a bowl, stir together the cheeses, egg, and cinnamon. Season with salt and pepper.

2 To make the pasta dough, place the flour in a mound on a work surface and make a well in the center. Sprinkle with the salt. Break the eggs into the well, add the olive oil, and beat lightly with a fork. Swirl the egg mixture in a circular motion to incorporate the flour. When a rough mass forms, use both hands to work in enough of the remaining flour so the dough stops sticking to your fingers. On a clean, lightly floured surface, knead the dough until smooth and elastic, 6–8 minutes, adding flour if it is sticky. Wrap in plastic wrap and let rest for at least 20 minutes or up to 3 hours.

3 Unwrap the dough and cut it in half. Briefly knead each half, then, on a lightly floured work surface, press one half into a thick round. Roll it out with a floured rolling pin, turning and lightly dusting it with flour as you work, to form a thin, even round. Your hand should be visible through the dough when it is held up to the light. Place it on a lightly floured towel while rolling out the other half. Using a pizza cutter, cut the rounds into strips 3 inches (7.5 cm) wide.

4 Place heaping teaspoons of the filling along the upper half of the length of 1 strip, spacing them at 1½-inch (4-cm) intervals and leaving 1 inch (2.5 cm) of dough at each end. Brush around the filling with water, then fold the strip over the filling to enclose it. Seal each mound by pressing out any air. Using a fluted pastry wheel, cut 1½-inch (4-cm) filled squares. Repeat with the remaining strips and filling. Bring a large pot of water to a boil.

5 Meanwhile, to make the sauce, warm the olive oil in a frying pan over medium-low heat. Add the garlic and sauté until golden, about 1 minute. Add the tomatoes, raise the heat to medium, and bring to a simmer, stirring occasionally. Reduce the heat to low, season with salt and pepper, add the basil, and simmer until thickened into a light sauce, about 7 minutes. Keep warm.

6 Add 1 tablespoon salt and the ravioli to the boiling water and cook until al dente, 3–4 minutes; test a ravioli after 3 minutes. Drain and divide among individual bowls. Top with the sauce and serve at once with the Parmigiano-Reggiano.

Steamed Shrimp Dumplings

These delicate, open-faced dumplings resemble *siu mai,* a dim sum standard. The traditional filling includes ground (minced) pork and shrimp, but this version puts the accent on shrimp. Note that you will need a flat-bottomed steamer, such as a Chinese bamboo steamer, for this dish. You will also need a small amount of pork fat; ask a butcher for trimmings or reserve your own. The round, extra-thin *siu mai* wrappers are available in Chinese markets.

¾ lb (12 oz/375 g) large shrimp (prawns), peeled and deveined

1 oz (30 g) pork fat, diced

4 fresh water chestnuts, peeled and quartered

2 green (spring) onions, white and pale green parts only, sliced

3 fresh ginger slices, each ⅛ inch (3 mm) thick, peeled

1 large clove garlic, sliced

1 tablespoon dry sherry

1 tablespoon cornstarch (cornflour)

Fine sea salt

½ teaspoon sugar

½ teaspoon Asian sesame oil

1 egg white

30 *siu mai* wrappers, 3 inches (7.5 cm) in diameter

For the dipping sauce

½ cup (4 fl oz/125 ml) soy sauce

Chile oil

MAKES 6 SERVINGS

1 In a food processor, combine the shrimp, pork fat, water chestnuts, green onions, ginger, garlic, sherry, cornstarch, 1½ teaspoons salt, sugar, sesame oil, and egg white. Process until smooth.

2 Line a baking sheet with parchment (baking) paper. Work with 1 *siu mai* wrapper at a time and keep the others covered with a towel. Put about 1 tablespoon filling in the center of a wrapper, then cup the wrapper around the filling, pleating it like a cupcake liner. Keeping the bottom flat, wrap the thumb and index finger around the dumpling and press gently to flatten the pleats and adhere the wrapper to the filling. Set the dumpling on the baking sheet.

3 In a wok or steamer pot, pour in water to a depth of 1 inch (2.5 cm) and bring to a boil. Lightly oil the bottom of the steamer basket and arrange the dumplings inside, not touching. (You may need to steam them in 2 batches.) Top with the lid, and set the steamer over the boiling water. Reduce the heat to low and steam until the filling is firm and the wrapper is cooked, 10–20 minutes, replenishing the boiling water as needed.

4 While the dumplings steam, make the dipping sauce. In a small bowl, stir together the soy sauce with chile oil to taste.

5 Bring the dumplings to the table in the steamer basket and serve at once with the dipping sauce.

MEXICO
Three Chiles Pasta

The triumvirate of Mexican dried chiles, the ancho, pasilla, and guajillo, is used here to create an intensely flavored pasta dish that is served as a dry soup course. *Fideos*, very thin noodles coiled into an oval, is the most common form of pasta in Mexico.

¼ **white onion**

1 **tomato**

3 **cloves garlic, unpeeled**

2 **ancho chiles**

4 **pasilla chiles**

4 **guajillo chiles**

½ **teaspoon cumin seeds, toasted**

Sea salt and freshly ground pepper

2 **tablespoons safflower or canola oil**

14 oz (440 g) **dried** *fideos*

2 **cups (16 fl oz/500 ml) chicken stock**

¼ **cup (2 fl oz/60 ml)** *crema* **or crème fraîche**

¼ **cup (1½ oz/45 g) crumbled** *queso fresco*

MAKES 6 SERVINGS

1 Line a large, heavy frying pan with aluminum foil, shiny side up, and place over medium heat. Add the onion and cook, turning occasionally, until blackened in spots and softened. Transfer to a blender. Add the tomato to the pan and cook, turning, until the skin is blistered and begins to blacken and the interior softens. Transfer to the blender. Discard the foil and return the pan to medium heat. Add the unpeeled garlic and cook, turning, until softened and blackened. Let cool. Peel the cloves and add to the blender.

2 Clean the chiles with a damp cloth, then slit lengthwise and remove the seeds. Place the frying pan over medium heat. Add the chiles and, using a spatula, press down firmly on them for a few seconds. Turn and press for a few seconds longer. They should change color only slightly and start to give off their aroma. Place the chiles in a small bowl, add hot water to cover, and let soak for 10 minutes. Drain the chiles, then tear into pieces and add to the blender.

3 Add the cumin seeds to the blender and process until a smooth sauce forms, adding a tablespoon or so of water, if necessary. Pass through a sieve. Season with salt and pepper.

4 In a frying pan over medium-high heat, warm the oil. Add the *fideos*, breaking each coil into 3 parts, and stir and toss constantly until covered with oil and just beginning to turn golden brown. Add the sauce and cook, stirring often, for 5 minutes, reducing the heat when the sauce begins to bubble. Add the stock and stir until the sauce is absorbed into the pasta and the pasta is tender, about 5 minutes longer.

5 Scoop the *fideos* onto a warmed serving dish and top with the *crema* and *queso fresco*. Serve at once.

Pad Thai

Certain tastes—sweet, sour, salty, spicy, pickled—are always present in *pad thai*. One of the national dishes of Thailand, this tangle of noodles, shrimp, and seasonings also offers a trio of textures—crisp, crunchy, soft—in one dish. Be sure to choose the correct rice noodles, called *sen lek* in Thai. They are flat and roughly ¼ inch (6 mm) wide, about the size of linguine.

3 tablespoons vegetable oil

¼ lb (125 g) medium-sized shrimp (prawns), peeled and deveined

2 tablespoons chopped garlic

2 tablespoons chopped shallot

2 eggs

1 tablespoon small dried shrimp, chopped into ¼-inch (6-mm) pieces if large

1 tablespoon coarsely chopped preserved white radish

½ lb (250 g) dried flat rice noodles (see above), soaked in warm water for 20 minutes and drained

2 tablespoons sugar

3 tablespoons fish sauce

2 teaspoons tamarind concentrate mixed with 3 tablespoons water

2 tablespoons fresh lime juice

½ teaspoon red pepper flakes

½ lb (250 g) bean sprouts

2 green (spring) onions, including 1 inch (2.5 cm) of the tender green tops, cut into 1-inch (2.5-cm) lengths

½ cup (3 oz/90 g) coarsely chopped unsalted dry-roasted peanuts

For the garnish

Several fresh cilantro (fresh coriander) sprigs

1 fresh red chile, thinly sliced

1 lime, cut into wedges

MAKES 2–4 SERVINGS

1 Heat a wok over medium-high heat. When the pan is hot, add 1 tablespoon of the vegetable oil and swirl to coat the pan. When the oil is hot, add the fresh shrimp and toss and stir until they curl and turn bright orange-pink, about 30 seconds. Transfer to a bowl and set aside.

2 Add the remaining 2 tablespoons oil to the wok. When the oil is hot, add the garlic and shallot and stir-fry until golden brown, about 30 seconds. Raise the heat to high and crack the eggs into the wok. With the tip of a spatula, gently break up the egg yolks, but do not beat. Let them fry without stirring until they start to set, about 1 minute. Add the dried shrimp, preserved radish, and noodles and, using tongs or 2 spatulas, break up the eggs and toss everything together for about 1 minute. Add each of the following ingredients, one by one, tossing and stirring after each addition: sugar, fish sauce, tamarind water, lime juice, red pepper flakes, half of the bean sprouts, green onions, half of the peanuts, and reserved shrimp. Toss quickly and gently to coat each noodle strand, about 15 seconds. As soon as the strands begin to stick to one another, the noodles are cooked.

3 Transfer the *pad thai* to a platter and garnish with the remaining peanuts and bean sprouts, cilantro sprigs, chile slices, and lime wedges. Serve at once. Each diner squeezes a bit of lime juice over his or her serving.

Spicy Sesame Noodles

Although the origin of this iconic dish is unknown, regional versions and interpretations are found at Chinese restaurants everywhere. This recipe comes from a pan-Chinese restaurant in New York.

Sea salt

1 lb (500 g) fresh or dried Chinese egg noodles or dried linguine

4 tablespoons (2 fl oz/60 ml) Asian sesame oil, plus extra for cooking

¾ cup (7½ oz/235 g) creamy peanut butter

2 teaspoons tahini

2 tablespoons rice vinegar

1 tablespoon Asian chili oil or Hunan pepper sauce

1 jalapeño chile, halved and seeded

2–3 tablespoons grated fresh ginger

1 clove garlic, peeled and chopped

2 tablespoons sugar

Freshly ground white or black pepper

1 cup (8 fl oz/250 ml) brewed black tea or chicken stock, or as needed, at room temperature

1 English cucumber

3 small carrots

2 green (spring) onions, white and pale green parts only, thinly sliced

Fresh cilantro (fresh coriander) leaves for garnish (optional)

MAKES 6 SERVINGS

1   Bring a large pot of water to a boil. Generously salt the water, add the fresh noodles and a few drops of sesame oil, stir the noodles to prevent them from sticking, and cook until tender, about 3 minutes. (If using dried noodles, follow the timing on the package instructions.) Drain and rinse thoroughly under cold running water, then drain again. Transfer the noodles to a large bowl, add 2 tablespoons of the sesame oil, and toss to coat. Cover and refrigerate until chilled, at least 1 hour.

2   In a food processor or blender, combine the remaining 2 tablespoons sesame oil, 1 teaspoon sea salt, peanut butter, tahini, rice vinegar, chili oil, jalapeño, ginger, garlic, sugar, 1 teaspoon pepper, and 1 cup brewed tea. Process until smooth. Add more tea, if necessary, to make a sauce that is fluid enough to coat the noodles. Season with additional salt and pepper, if necessary.

3   Peel and seed the cucumber and cut into matchsticks 2 inches (5 cm) long. Peel the carrots and cut into 2-inch (5-cm) matchsticks.

4   Just before serving, add the sauce, cucumbers, carrots, and green onions to the noodles and toss to coat evenly. If the noodles are sticky, add a bit more tea and toss again. Serve at once, garnished with cilantro, if desired.

Herbed Spaetzle

In Germany, where these tender noodlelike dumplings originated, cooks use a special paddle and a sharp knife to drop shards of stiff dough expertly into boiling water. For this version, the consistency is that of drop biscuits, somewhere between a batter and a dough. The idea is to push the dough through the holes of a colander. Give spaetzle a home in soup, alongside roast meat, or under a stew rich with gravy, and choose herbs that will complement the other dishes on the menu.

1 cup (8 fl oz/250 ml) milk, plus extra if needed

2 eggs

1 tablespoon finely chopped fresh herbs (see above) such as sage or thyme leaves

⅛ teaspoon freshly grated nutmeg

Kosher salt or coarse sea salt

2¼ cups (11½ oz/360 g) all-purpose (plain) flour, plus extra if needed

2 tablespoons unsalted butter

Freshly ground white pepper

MAKES 4 SERVINGS

1 Bring a large pot of water to a boil. Ideally, the colander or steamer insert you use will sit above the water. If not, you might need a helper to hold it while you extrude the dough.

2 In a bowl, beat together the 1 cup milk, eggs, herbs, nutmeg, and ½ teaspoon salt until smooth. Add the 2¼ cups flour and stir to combine. Let the dough rest for 10 minutes. It should be fairly wet, like a thick pancake batter. If not, adjust accordingly with a little more milk or flour.

3 When the water is boiling, begin making the spaetzle: Place the butter in the bottom of a pan set over very low heat and allow it to melt; keep warm. Salt the water lightly and reduce the heat so that it boils gently.

4 Put about one-third of the dough into the colander or steamer insert. Holding it over the boiling water and using a rubber spatula or plastic pastry scraper, push down on the dough. Dribbles of dough should emerge from the bottom and drop into the water. Do not stir. Free-form "noodles" will take shape and rise to the top when done. Between batches, scrape the bottom of the colander to finish forming the noodles. Try to keep the water at a steady gentle bubble. If it boils too hard, the delicate spaetzle will disintegrate.

5 As the spaetzle rise to the top, lift them out of the water with a slotted spoon or wire skimmer, draining off as much water as possible. Transfer to the pan with the butter and stir gently. Cover to keep the spaetzle warm, but do not allow them to cook further. Repeat the process until all the spaetzle are boiled and tossed in butter.

6 Transfer the butter-coated spaetzle to a warmed bowl or individual plates and serve at once.

Orecchiette with Broccoli Rabe

Broccoli rabe is a favorite in the Southern Italian regions of Campania and Apulia. With its deep green florets, leaves, and stems, it looks like a broccoli cousin, but it's botanically closer to turnips. Here it's paired with orecchiette ("little ears") pasta. For an extra layer of flavor, add crumbled sausage or finely minced anchovies.

For the bread crumbs

1 tablespoon extra-virgin olive oil

½ cup (2 oz/60 g) fine dried bread crumbs

Fine sea salt

1½ lb (750 g) broccoli rabe

Fine sea salt

1 lb (500 g) orecchiette

⅓ cup (3 fl oz/80 ml) extra-virgin olive oil

4 large cloves garlic, minced

Red pepper flakes

MAKES 4–6 SERVINGS

1 To prepare the bread crumbs, in a small frying pan over medium-low heat, warm the olive oil. Add the bread crumbs and stir to coat. Season lightly with salt and cook, stirring often, until the crumbs are an even, deep golden brown, about 10 minutes. Pour onto a plate and set aside.

2 Bring a large pot of water to a boil. Meanwhile, trim the broccoli rabe, removing any dry ends and any stems that feel tough. (With broccoli rabe, the thick stems tend to be tender; it's the spindly stems that may need removing.)

3 Salt the boiling water, then add the broccoli rabe and cook, testing often, until the stems are just tender, 2–3 minutes. Using tongs, transfer to a sieve, then cool quickly under cold running water. Drain and squeeze gently to remove excess moisture. Chop coarsely and set aside.

4 Add the pasta to the boiling water, stir well, and cook until al dente, about 12 minutes, or according to the package directions.

5 While the pasta is cooking, in a large frying pan over medium-low heat, warm the olive oil. Add the garlic and red pepper flakes to taste and sauté briefly. Add the broccoli rabe and season with salt. Stir to coat with the seasonings. Cook until the broccoli rabe is hot throughout, about 2 minutes; keep warm.

6 When the pasta is ready, reserve 1 cup (8 fl oz/250 ml) of the pasta water. Drain the pasta and return it to the pot. Add the broccoli rabe and stir well over low heat to combine, moistening the pasta if necessary with some of the reserved pasta water. Divide the pasta among warmed bowls and sprinkle each portion with bread crumbs. Pass the remaining bread crumbs at the table.

Dried Pasta

ORECCHIETTE

Although this shape, called "little ears," originates in the south of Italy, it is also popular in Rome. The dough is made from either all hard-wheat flour, or half hard and half soft wheat, and water. Neither extruded nor rolled and cut, orecchiette represents a third technique of pasta making: rolling and poking. The dough is rolled into cylinders, cut into small pieces, then poked with a thumb and drawn against the work surface.

PENNE

Penna means "quill," and it is easy to see where bias-cut penne get their name. The short pasta can be found both smooth surfaced (*liscie*) and ridged (*rigate*). This versatile shape was almost certainly created in the Campania region, but penne are one of Italy's most popular all-purpose dried short pasta. They are often tossed with vegetable-based sauces and are obligatory in *penne all'arrabbiata,* a simple but delicious dish of tomatoes, garlic, chile, and parsley.

RIGATONI

A major player in the world of short formats, rigatoni are characterized by a large hole, ½ inch (12 mm) or more in diameter. Relatively thick and sturdy, they take about twice as long to cook as spaghetti and get their name from their surface striations—*riga* means "straight line." Rigatoni are well suited to sauces that combine solids and liquid, typified by the tomato sauce made with *la pagliata,* or veal intestines.

SPAGHETTI

When you tie up a package, you use *spago* (twine), and indeed spaghetti are nothing more than strings of hard-wheat flour and water. The king of pasta shapes, spaghetti can range in diameter from 1.7 to 2 millimeters (less than ¹⁄₁₆ inch). Any less and a second diminutive suffix turns it into *spaghettini*. Spaghetti is at its best with oil-based or relatively thin sauces that easily coat the long strands, such as *alle vongole* (with clams) or *pomodoro e basilico* (tomato and basil).

ORECCHIETTE

TORTELLONI

BUCATINI

CAPPELLETTI

PENNE

RIGATONI

SPAGHETTI

MALTAGLIATI

TORTELLONI

In Italy, ravioli are usually square and filled with a spinach and ricotta mixture, while *agnolotti*, usually semicircular, are filled with meat. Handmade stuffed pastas in less conventional shapes and extra-large sizes are called *tortelli* or *tortelloni*. A fluffy ricotta filling is perfect with the extra-tender pasta of *tortelloni*, though the form also lends itself to creative fillings, such as pear and cheese or radicchio and *speck*.

BUCATINI

Bucatini are thick spaghetti pierced down the middle by a narrow hole. What good is such a small hole? The risk with any thick shape is that the outside could cook to a mush while the inside remains crunchy. The hole allows the water to penetrate to the core so the pasta will cook evenly. In Italy, *bucatini* are almost always served *all'amatriciana* or *alla gricia*. Meant to be twirled like spaghetti, the strands fight back by hurling tomato sauce at the diner's shirt.

CAPPELLETTI

Christmas isn't Christmas without a full-bodied capon broth and plenty of small, meat-filled *cappelletti*. The name means "little hats," with specific reference to a type of floppy medieval hat. The shape is usually associated with the tortellini of the Emilia-Romagna region, where it originated. Technically the dough for *cappelletti* is a bit more robust and the meat filling varies. *Cappelletti* is usually found only in broth.

MALTAGLIATI

The neat rhomboids into which commercially made *maltagliati* are cut belie their name, which means "badly cut." There are two kinds of *maltagliati*: those cut neatly but on the bias, either manufactured or homemade, and those truer to their name, the scraps of any kind of pasta dough left over after ravioli, fettuccine, and lasagne have been cut into their uniform shapes. Both types of *maltagliati* can be cooked and sauced as for any short pasta shape.

Tagliatelle with Scallops and Favas

Freshly picked fava beans in their velvety pods first appear in UK farmers' markets in June. Brits eagerly take them home, shell the beans, and cook them briefly, then toss them into salads, purée them in creamy soups seasoned with sage, or add them to light pasta sauces like the one here. Bacon, a traditional British accompaniment for fava beans, enhances their sweetness. Pancetta may be substituted. It is important that the sauce be ready at the same time as the pasta.

1 cup (5 oz/155 g) fava (broad) beans, shelled

1 lb (500 g) bay scallops or sea scallops

Fine sea salt

9 oz (280 g) dried tagliatelle or fettuccine

8 tablespoons (4 fl oz/125 ml) extra-virgin olive oil

½ lb (250 g) lean bacon, diced

12 green (spring) onions, white and pale green parts only, thinly sliced

2 cloves garlic, finely chopped

Finely grated zest of 2 lemons

2 tablespoons fresh lemon juice

Freshly ground pepper

MAKES 4 SERVINGS

1 Bring a saucepan of water to a boil. Add the beans and boil until tender, 3–4 minutes. Drain and cool under cold running water. Pinch the end of each bean to slip it from the skin. Set the beans aside.

2 Bring a large pot of water to a boil. Meanwhile, remove the tough, white muscle from the side of each scallop. If using sea scallops, cut them into quarters. Set aside. Add 1 tablespoon salt and the pasta to the boiling water, stir, and cook until al dente, according to package directions.

3 While the pasta cooks, in a frying pan over high heat, warm 3 tablespoons of the olive oil. Add the scallops and sear for 1 minute on each side. Remove from the pan and set aside. Add 3 tablespoons oil to the pan and reduce the heat to medium. Add the bacon and cook, stirring frequently, until it just begins to turn crisp, about 5 minutes. Stir in the green onions and garlic and cook until they soften and become fragrant, about 1 minute. Add the beans, scallops, and lemon zest. Cook, stirring occasionally, until heated through, about 1 minute.

4 When the pasta is ready, drain and return to the pot. Add the remaining 2 tablespoons oil to the pasta and toss to coat. Add the lemon juice to the scallop mixture and season with salt and pepper. Add the mixture to the pasta, toss gently to combine, divide among warmed plates, and serve at once.

Seafood Noodles

According to legend, in the harbor town of Gandía, a fisherman was about to make a paella with the fish and shellfish he had just caught. Discovering he had no rice, he used pasta instead—and *fideuà* was born. Serve with crusty country bread.

½ lb (250 g) medium shrimp (prawns), peeled and shells reserved

1½ lb (750 g) fish heads and bones

12 large mussels

12 large clams

4 ripe tomatoes, about 1 lb (500 g) total weight, cored

Sea salt

½ teaspoon saffron threads

½ cup (4 fl oz/125 ml) olive oil

½ lb (250 g) grouper or other firm-fleshed fish fillets, cut into 1-inch (2.5-cm) cubes

1 large red bell pepper (capsicum), seeded and cut into ½-inch (12-mm) dice

½ lb (250 g) *fideos* or other short, thin macaroni

4 cloves garlic, minced

Handful of fresh flat-leaf (Italian) parsley leaves, minced

MAKES 4–6 SERVINGS

1 In a stockpot, bring 5 cups (40 fl oz/1.25 l) water to a boil. Add the reserved shrimp shells and the fish heads and bones to the water. Return to a boil, skimming off any foam. Reduce the heat and simmer gently, uncovered, until the liquid has reduced by one-third, about 30 minutes. Strain the stock into a bowl through a sieve lined with cheesecloth (muslin). Return the strained stock to the stockpot.

2 Scrub the mussels and clams, scraping the beards off the mussels. Pour 1 inch (2.5 cm) of water into a wide saucepan over medium-high heat. Add the mussels, discarding any that do not close to the touch, cover, and cook, shaking the pan occasionally, until they open, about 5 minutes. Using a slotted spoon, transfer the mussels to a bowl, discarding any that failed to open. Add the clams to the pan and cook the same way, then transfer to the bowl. Strain the cooking water through the lined sieve into the stockpot.

3 Halve the tomatoes and grate the flesh into a bowl. Discard the skins. Using a mortar and pestle, grind 1 teaspoon salt with the saffron until a deep yellow powder forms. Set aside.

4 In a 16-inch (40-cm) paella pan or wide, heavy frying pan over medium heat, warm the olive oil. Add the shrimp and cook, turning once, until opaque, about 1 minute. Using a slotted spoon, transfer to a bowl. Add the fish cubes to the pan and cook until opaque, about 2 minutes. Transfer to the bowl. Add the bell pepper to the pan and sauté until soft, about 2 minutes. Transfer to the bowl.

5 Add the macaroni, garlic, and parsley to the pan and fry until fragrant, about 30 seconds. Stir in the tomato pulp and sauté for 30 seconds longer. Add 4 cups (32 fl oz/1 l) of the fish stock and stir in the shrimp, fish, and bell peppers, and the ground saffron. Reduce the heat and simmer gently, without stirring. After 10 minutes, arrange the mussels and clams (in their shells) on the surface. Continue cooking until almost all of the stock is absorbed, about 10 minutes longer.

6 Turn off the heat and cover the pan with a clean kitchen towel. Let rest for 10 minutes to allow the flavors to mingle and the macaroni to absorb any remaining juices. Serve warm, not hot.

Spaghetti alla Carbonara

Dispute over the origin of this dish never ends. Did the *carbonari* (charcoal makers) invent it? Was it American GIs looking for a way to use their bacon and egg rations? Or does the name refer to the black flecks of pepper? Whatever the origin, the key is the technique: finding the precise point when the eggs, added raw to cooked spaghetti, are no longer liquid but not yet fully cooked. For variation, add red pepper flakes instead of black pepper, or wild asparagus instead of cured pork.

6 oz (185 g) *guanciale,* pancetta, or bacon, preferably in a single piece or in slices at least ¼ inch (6 mm) thick

1 tablespoon extra-virgin olive oil

Salt and freshly ground pepper

1 lb (500 g) spaghetti

¼ cup (1 oz/30 g) grated *pecorino romano* cheese

¼ cup (1 oz/30 g) grated Parmigiano-Reggiano cheese, plus extra as needed

2 eggs plus 1 egg yolk, at room temperature

MAKES 4–6 SERVINGS

1 If using *guanciale* or pancetta, cut it into strips about ¾ inch (2 cm) long by ¼ inch (6 mm) thick. If using commercially sliced bacon, which will be thinner than ¼ inch (6 mm), cut it into 1-inch (2.5-cm) pieces.

2 In a large frying pan over medium-low heat, combine the meat and olive oil and heat slowly until much of the fat is rendered and the meat has browned a little, about 15 minutes. It should take on an appealing color without becoming too crisp. Leave the meat and fat in the pan and cover to keep warm.

3 Bring a large pot of water to a boil. Add 1 tablespoon salt and the pasta to the boiling water, and stir for the first minute of cooking and occasionally thereafter. Cook until al dente, according to the package instructions.

4 Meanwhile, in a bowl, combine the cheeses. In another bowl, whisk together the 2 eggs and the additional yolk until well blended. Stir half the cheese mixture and several grinds of pepper into the eggs.

5 From this point on, timing and temperature are crucial. Put a large serving bowl in the sink and set a colander in the serving bowl. When the pasta is ready, pour it into the colander; the cooking water will warm the bowl. Lift out the colander and shake it a couple of times. Add the drained spaghetti to the pan with the meat and stir to coat the pasta with the fat. Reserve 1 cup (8 fl oz/250 ml) of the pasta water and pour the rest out. Transfer the pasta to the bowl and stir in the egg mixture, mixing vigorously to coat the pasta evenly. Add a splash of the reserved cooking water if the pasta seems a little dry. Add an extra handful of grated Parmigiano-Reggiano if it seems too wet. (If the eggs scramble, the bowl or the pasta was too hot; if they are runny, something was too cold. If the beaten eggs were at room temperature to start, the bowl warmed with hot water should provide just enough heat.)

6 Divide the pasta among warmed individual bowls and serve at once. Pass the remaining cheese at the table.

ITALY
Making Pasta

CHOOSING PASTA

The starting point for choosing a good dried pasta is the label. The best pasta is made in Italy of only semolina flour and water and has been extruded through *trafile di bronzo* (bronze dies), which gives it a rough surface that helps it absorb the sauce.

If dried pasta is bright yellow, it has probably been extruded through plastic or Teflon dies, which you should try to avoid for the best quality. Many artisanal or small pasta manufacturers, such as Latini and Benedetto Cavalieri, slowly dry their pasta at very low temperatures, which adds to the quality.

The world of pasta does not split neatly into industrial and homemade. Many shops selling fresh pasta rely on a method that falls somewhere between the two. Large machines are typically used to mix, extrude, and roll the dough, but it is often shaped and finished by hand.

WHO INVENTED PASTA?

Grain was first cultivated some nine thousand years ago. It was only a matter of time before someone thought to grind it into flour, mix it with water, shape it, and dry it.

Al-Idrisi, the Arab court geographer to Roger II of Sicily, reported in 1138 that the residents of Trabia, near Palermo, dried and exported strands of dough they called *itriya*, Arabic for "string." Records from Genoa dated 1244 and from the Anjou court in Naples dated 1295 show similar activity.

By the mid-fourteenth century, the Bolognese tradition of fresh pasta was under way. Then, in the 1830s, the modern age of dried commercial pasta began in Naples, along with the practice of cooking it al dente and serving it with a tomato sauce.

Experimentation with shapes began early. Dozens of antique pasta machines, as well as the shapes they made, are on display at the small pasta museum, the Museo Nazionale delle Paste Alimentari, near the Quirinal Palace.

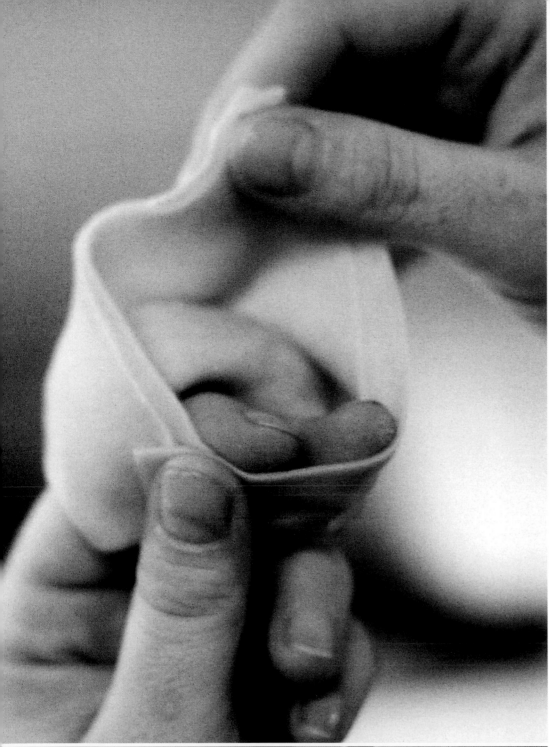

MAKING TORTELLONI

MIXING Equal amounts of soft-wheat and hard-wheat flours, a tiny pinch of salt, and whole eggs are mixed together by machine and then kneaded for about ten minutes. Water is added—just enough for the dough to form walnut-sized balls.

ROLLING The dough is shifted to a second compartment in the machine, from which it is extruded and spooled onto rollers. Sheets are cut from the spooled dough. They are passed through a second machine for rolling, emerging about three times longer and paper thin. Pieces of *speck* (smoke-cured pork) are put through a grinder and mixed with mascarpone and Parmigiano-Reggiano cheeses to make the filling.

FILLING AND SHAPING A pasta sheet is trimmed to a neat rectangle, brushed with egg yolk, and scored into squares. A dollop of filling is placed on each square, the squares are cut apart, each square is folded into a triangle, and the edges are pressed to seal. Finally, the two far points of the triangle are brought together, while the third point is curled outward like the peak of a soft cap.

PHILIPPINES
Chicken and Sausage Noodles

½ lb (250 g) dried rice vermicelli

2 tablespoons vegetable oil

Salt

2 tablespoons minced garlic

1 yellow onion, thinly sliced

2 celery stalks, thinly sliced

6 oz (185 g) boneless, skinless chicken breast, thinly sliced

2 Chinese sausages, sliced

1 carrot, peeled and julienned

1 small red bell pepper (capsicum), seeded and sliced

1 cup (3 oz/90 g) finely shredded cabbage

6 oz (185 g) large shrimp (prawns), peeled and deveined

2 tablespoons fish sauce

1 tablespoon soy sauce

½ cup (4 fl oz/125 ml) chicken stock

2 green (spring) onions, white and pale green parts, chopped

Fresh cilantro (fresh coriander)

1 lemon, cut into wedges

MAKES 6 SERVINGS

1 Soak the noodles in warm water for 15 minutes. Drain.

2 Heat a wok over medium-high heat. When the pan is hot, add the vegetable oil, 1 teaspoon salt, and the garlic and stir-fry until the garlic is light golden brown, about 1 minute. Add the yellow onion and celery and stir-fry until the vegetables soften and the onion is translucent, about 3 minutes. Add the chicken and sausage. Stir-fry until the chicken begins to turn opaque, about 2 minutes. Add the carrot, bell pepper, and cabbage and stir-fry for 1 minute. Add the shrimp and stir-fry until they turn bright orange-pink, 1–2 minutes. Sprinkle in the fish sauce and soy sauce and toss to mix well. Add the stock and toss again.

3 Add the noodles and, using tongs or 2 spatulas, toss with the vegetables until thoroughly mixed and the stock has been completely absorbed by the noodles, 3–5 minutes. Taste and adjust the seasonings with fish sauce and soy sauce, if necessary.

4 Transfer the noodle mixture to a large platter and top with the green onions and cilantro leaves. Garnish with the lemon wedges. Each diner adds a squeeze of lemon juice to his or her serving.

JAPAN
Soba Noodle Soup

2 boneless pork loin chops

2 tablespoons canola oil

1 tablespoon grated ginger

2 cloves garlic, thinly sliced

¼ yellow onion, finely chopped

1 tablespoon soy sauce

6 cups (48 fl oz/1.5 l) chicken stock

½ lb (250 g) dried soba noodles

4 button mushrooms, sliced

4 green (spring) onions, white and pale green parts only, sliced

Salt and freshly ground pepper

MAKES 4 SERVINGS

1 Cut the pork into slices ¼ inch (6 mm) thick. In a small frying pan over medium heat, warm the oil. When it is hot, add the pork and sauté until golden brown, about 4 minutes. Add the ginger, garlic, yellow onion, and soy sauce and sauté until the onion is translucent, about 2 minutes. Remove from the heat and set aside.

2 In a large saucepan over medium-high heat, bring the stock to a boil. Add the soba and stir to separate the noodles. Cook just until tender, about 5 minutes. Add the pork mixture, mushrooms, and green onions and cook for 1 minute to heat through. Season with salt and pepper. Ladle into individual bowls and serve.

Curried Fish Noodle Soup

Soup is common breakfast fare throughout Asia and each country has its favorite. In Burma it is *mohingha*—fish and noodles in a curried broth. For thin coconut milk, do not shake the can before opening. Spoon out the layers of thick cream and white milk, and use only the clear liquid bottom layer.

2 lb (1 kg) catfish fillets, cut into 1-inch (2.5-cm) cubes

Salt

½ teaspoon ground turmeric

2 lemongrass stalks, smashed

For the spice paste

3 yellow onions, cut into 1-inch (2.5-cm) pieces

1-inch (2.5-cm) piece fresh ginger, peeled and chopped

6 cloves garlic

1 lemongrass stalk, tender midsection only, chopped

2 fresh red chiles, seeded and roughly chopped

1 teaspoon dried shrimp paste

½ teaspoon ground turmeric

3 tablespoons peanut oil

4 cups (32 fl oz/1 l) thin coconut milk (see above)

1 cup (4 oz/125 g) thinly sliced bamboo shoot

2 tablespoons chickpea (garbanzo bean) flour mixed with ¼ cup (2 fl oz/60 ml) water to make a smooth paste

2 tablespoons fish sauce

2 tablespoons fresh lemon juice

¾ lb (375 g) thin fresh egg noodles or dried rice vermicelli

For the accompaniments

Vegetable oil for frying

4–6 shallots, thinly sliced

6 hard-boiled eggs, peeled and cut into wedges

2 lemons, cut into wedges

1 cup (1 oz/30 g) fresh cilantro (fresh coriander) leaves

1 white onion, finely sliced

MAKES 6 SERVINGS

1 Put the fish cubes in a bowl and toss with 1 teaspoon salt and the turmeric. Let stand for 15 minutes. Put the fish, the lemongrass, and 4 cups (32 fl oz/1 l) water into a saucepan and bring to a gentle boil. Reduce the heat and simmer for 5 minutes. Using a slotted spoon, transfer the fish to a bowl and set aside. Reserve the stock, discarding the lemongrass.

2 To make the spice paste, in a mortar or blender, combine the onions, ginger, garlic, lemongrass, chiles, shrimp paste, and turmeric and grind or process to a smooth paste.

3 In a large saucepan over medium-high heat, warm the peanut oil until it is almost smoking. Carefully add the spice paste (it will spatter in the hot oil), and stir immediately to incorporate. Reduce the heat, cover, and simmer gently, stirring occasionally. If the mixture seems too dry, stir in some water, re-cover, and simmer until the oil reappears at the edge of the paste. This should take 10–12 minutes total. Uncover, raise the heat to high, and add the reserved fish stock, thin coconut milk, and bamboo shoot. Bring to a boil, reduce the heat to low, and simmer, uncovered, until the bamboo shoot is tender, about 5 minutes. Raise the heat to high, add the chickpea paste, and stir until the stock begins to thicken, 1–2 minutes. Add the fish sauce and fish pieces and simmer for 5 minutes. Season with salt and the lemon juice. Remove from the heat and keep warm.

4 Meanwhile, if using egg noodles, bring a large saucepan of water to a boil. Add the noodles, stir, and boil until tender, about 2 minutes. Drain, rinse with warm water, and drain again. If using rice vermicelli, soak in warm water for 15 minutes, drain, then boil for 1 minute and drain.

5 Pour vegetable oil to a depth of 1 inch (2.5 cm) into a frying pan and heat to 325°F (165°C) on a deep-frying thermometer. Add the shallots and fry until golden brown, about 5 minutes. Transfer to paper towels to drain. Let cool.

6 Arrange the fried shallots and other accompaniments on a platter. Divide the noodles among individual bowls. Ladle the hot soup over the noodles and serve at once. Diners add lemon juice and accompaniments as desired.

Pho Beef Noodle Soup

Many Vietnamese begin the day with *pho*, a fragrant health tonic. Simple but time-consuming to prepare, it is often taken at a street stall, where one has a wide choice of meats to add: sliced raw beef, brisket, flank steak, tripe, tendon, meatballs, or *dac biet*, a mixture. For cool contrast, there are raw vegetables and herbs—bean sprouts, basil, mint, coriander, saw-leaf herb—to toss in as well. If you can find fresh rice noodles, omit the soaking and simply warm them through in boiling water.

For the beef stock

3 lb (1.5 kg) oxtails, chopped into 2-inch (5-cm) pieces

2–3 lb (1–1.5 kg) beef brisket

4-inch (10-cm) piece fresh ginger, cut into 4 equal pieces, crushed

10 shallots, unpeeled

1 lb (500 g) daikon, cut into 2-inch (5-cm) chunks

2 carrots, each cut into thirds

7 star anise

5 cloves

2 cinnamon sticks

3 tablespoons fish sauce, or to taste

2 teaspoons sugar, or to taste

½ lb (250 g) beef sirloin, wrapped in plastic wrap and placed in the freezer for 1 hour

Leaves from ½ bunch fresh cilantro (fresh coriander)

½ bunch fresh Thai basil

12 fresh saw-leaf herb sprigs

2 limes, cut into wedges

½ lb (250 g) flat dried rice noodles, ¼ inch (6 mm) wide, soaked in warm water for 20 minutes

1 white onion, thinly sliced

3 green (spring) onions, including 1 inch (2.5 cm) of the tender green tops, thinly sliced

1 lb (500 g) bean sprouts

MAKES 6 SERVINGS

1 To make the stock, fill a large stockpot with water and bring to a boil. Add the oxtails and brisket, return to a boil, and boil for 3 minutes. Pour off the water, then add 4 qt (4 l) fresh water to the pot and bring to a boil.

2 Meanwhile, place a dry frying pan over high heat and add the ginger and shallots. Char them, turning occasionally to color evenly, 2–3 minutes. Transfer to the stockpot, along with the daikon, carrots, star anise, cloves, and cinnamon sticks. Return to a boil, reduce the heat to a gentle simmer, cover partially, and cook for 1½ hours. Remove the brisket and set aside to cool. Continue to simmer the stock until richly fragrant and light amber, about 1 hour longer.

3 Cut the brisket across the grain into thin slices. Set aside. When the stock is done, strain it through a sieve and skim off the fat. Discard the oxtails or reserve for another use. Return the stock to the stockpot and season with the fish sauce and sugar. Bring to a gentle simmer and maintain.

4 Remove the partially frozen beef from the freezer and cut at an angle into paper-thin slices as wide as possible. Arrange on a platter. On a separate platter, arrange the cilantro leaves, basil, saw-leaf herb sprigs, and lime wedges.

5 Drain the noodles. Bring a large saucepan of water to a boil. Warm 6 deep soup bowls with ladlefuls of the hot water. Drop the noodles into the pot, stir well, and cook until just tender, 1–2 minutes. Drain. Pour off the water from the soup bowls and divide the noodles evenly among them. Put a few slices of the cooked brisket into each bowl. Top with some of the white onion slices, a sprinkle of green onions, and a handful of the bean sprouts. Ladle hot stock into each bowl. Serve with the platters of beef and herbs. Each diner takes a few herbs and a little beef and squeezes lime juice over the top.

FAGIOLO ZOLFINO DEL PRATOM

Lentilles Roses
4,90€/kg

LEGUMES

Out of the Pod

LEGUMES AROUND THE WORLD

Legumes and the seeds that emerge from them—either eaten fresh or harvested and dried—are among the most nutritious staples of the world pantry. Simple to cook and beautiful in their range of shapes and colors, peas and beans readily absorb aromatic spices and herbs. They reveal rustic cooking at its most comforting while highlighting distinct regional flavors.

Known as pulses in many parts of the world, the edible seeds of leguminous plants—peas, beans, and lentils—were once largely viewed as the food of the poor. Easy to cook in a hearth's embers and as fortifying as they are filling, regionally diverse pulses fueled the world's farmers for centuries. Chickpeas (garbanzo beans) flourished throughout the Middle East, thriving on the region's long, hot growing season. Beans, along with squash and maize, were one of the important Three Sisters of Native American agriculture. These returned to Europe with the early explorers of the New World and were readily adopted into the local cuisines. In India, where pulses prevail, more than fifty varieties of lentils alone are grown throughout the subcontinent. The impact of these various

elements remains in evidence. Spiced chickpea paste in the Middle East, pinto beans with rice in the Americas, simmered white beans with olive oil in Italy, curried mung beans in India, sweetened red beans in Asia, and pigeon peas simmered in coconut milk in Africa—all are enjoyed today in ways remarkably similar to traditional dishes. And as pulses have long surpassed their humble origins, cooks all over are now searching for heritage beans to work into their dishes, with the result that old varieties have become more widely available. Bearing evocative names—scarlet runner, goat's eye, black valentine, red nightfall, and butterscotch calypso are just a few of the varieties currently being grown and dried—a colorful array of pulses returns to the kitchen.

MIDDLE EAST

Chickpeas were first cultivated in Turkey over five thousand years ago. Pounded until smooth with sesame paste and garlic and then swirled with olive oil, chickpeas become hummus, a spread eaten with warm pita bread as a light meal or snack. Dried fava or broad beans are also popular, especially when married with lemon and garlic to make a favorite breakfast dish, *ful medames,* served with bread and eggs. Lentils also appear in a wide variety of Middle Eastern dishes, often cooked with rice, cracked wheat, or other grains, much like a pilaf.

AMERICAS

From Mexico, the origin of many of the most familiar bean varieties, come two basic ways of eating beans. *Frijoles de la olla,* or pot beans, refers to the round-bellied bean crock that was traditionally the favored vessel for simmering either pinto or black beans. *Frijoles refritos,* or refried beans, take on silky richness when mashed and cooked a second time with garlic and pork fat. Flavored with a *sofrito* of onions, garlic, and bell peppers (capsicums) and then served with corn tortillas, beans are an ancient staple from the tip of Chile to the islands of the Caribbean.

Boston's early colonists learned to bake beans from the area's indigenous tribes, though molasses and pork trimmings soon replaced the original flavorings of maple syrup and bear fat. Chuck wagons heading west were infamous for their regular servings of beans, and the many versions of chili in Denver, San Antonio, and Santa Fe attest to endless ways of dressing up pinto beans in a hearty stew with Mexican spices. Flat, thin pigeon peas were carried by slaves from their native Africa through the Caribbean and then on to the American South. Red beans and rice, black-eyed pea soup with ham bone, and a New Year's bowl of hopping John are other bean dishes still popular throughout the South.

EUROPE

The people of Tuscany were especially taken with the New World's beans and soon became known as *mangiafagioli,* or bean eaters, for their love of starchy fava beans and creamy, white cannelloni. Drizzled with olive oil, stirred into soups, or mashed and spread on slices of grilled bread, beans appear on the Tuscan table in myriad forms. Other special beans of northern Italy include speckled *borlotti,* buttery yellow *zolfini,* and opalescent *sorani.* In the warmer climate of southern Italy, *ceci,* or chickpeas, found favor.

French cooks have claimed the green *lentille du Puy* as their own. These tiny lentils keep their shape well when stewed with lamb, served alongside sausages or salt cod, added to soup with spring potatoes, or tossed with vinaigrette for a substantial salad. A hearty specialty in the southwest of France, cassoulet depends on cooking *haricot blanc* beans to perfect tenderness with a rich mix of pork, goose, Toulouse sausages, and duck confit. In Provence, each family boasts its own version of *soupe au pistou,* a soup made with dried flageolet beans and fresh vegetables that is finished at the table with an intensely aromatic pestolike purée of basil, garlic, and olive oil.

INDIA

Pulses play a central role in the day-to-day cooking of India, where their high protein content is especially valuable in the prevalent vegetarian diet. A peek into any Indian kitchen will reveal neat containers of red, yellow, black, white, and green pulses. *Dal,* Sanskrit for "split," refers to the dried, hulled, and split pulse itself as well as to a simple everyday dish made from lentils, chickpeas, mung beans, or kidney beans. Turmeric gives *dal* its distinctive golden tint, and spices fried in oil and drizzled over the dish before serving add complex flavors.

One of the most popular dishes, especially in northern India, is *channa bhatura,* a classic pairing of spicy chickpeas with plenty of fried, puffed bread. Chickpeas, which are also known regionally as *chole,* Bengal *gram,* or *kabuli chana,* appear in a variety of curries with other ingredients such as potatoes, chopped greens, eggplant (aubergine), tomatoes, tamarind, and yogurt.

EAST ASIA

In East Asia, beans nearly always appear in sweets. Sprinkled with palm sugar, topped with peanuts or sesame seeds, and served with sticky rice, adzuki beans in particular are much appreciated in China and Japan and throughout Southeast Asia. Malaysians make *ais kacang,* Filipinos create *halo halo,* and the Vietnamese serve *che*—all snacks that highlight the small red beans in colorful concoctions with layers of shaved ice and favorite toppings such as coconut milk, ice cream, condensed milk, lotus seeds, corn kernels, grass jelly, or fresh tropical fruit. At the end of formal Chinese banquets, a small bowl of slightly sweetened red bean soup might be served to close the meal. From Tokyo, Japan, to Kota Bharu, Malaysia, red bean paste adds color and sweetness at the center of steamed buns, cookies, crepes, *mochi,* moon cakes, and a multitude of other confections.

Cuban Black Bean Soup

Integral to this traditional Cuban soup is *sofrito*, a mixture of onions, garlic, bell peppers, chiles, herbs, spices, and sometimes ham.

2 cups (14 oz/440 g) dried black beans

2 bay leaves

For the sofrito

¾ cup (6 fl oz/180 ml) extra-virgin olive oil

2 red bell peppers (capsicums), seeded and chopped

2 large white onions, chopped

8 cloves garlic, chopped

2 tablespoons dried oregano

1½ tablespoons ground cumin

Sea salt

1 tablespoon sugar

1 tablespoon sherry vinegar, or more to taste

2 tablespoons dry sherry, or more to taste

1 red onion, finely diced, for garnish

½ cup (½ oz/15 g) fresh cilantro (fresh coriander) leaves, for garnish

MAKES 6 SERVINGS

1 Pick over the beans, discarding any grit or misshapen beans. Rinse well, place in a large bowl, and add water to cover generously. Let soak for at least 4 hours or up to overnight. (Alternatively, for a quick soak, bring the beans and water to a rapid simmer and cook for 2 minutes. Remove from the heat, cover, and let stand for 1 hour.) Drain the beans and place in a large pot with the bay leaves and 4 qt (4 l) water. Bring to a boil, reduce the heat to low, and simmer, stirring occasionally and adding hot water if the beans become exposed, until tender, about 2 hours.

2 Meanwhile, to make the *sofrito*, in a large frying pan over medium heat, warm the olive oil. Add the bell peppers and sauté until they begin to soften, about 5 minutes. Add the white onions and sauté until tender and translucent, 10–12 minutes. Add the garlic, oregano, cumin, and 1½ tablespoons salt and sauté until the garlic is fragrant, about 2 minutes. Let cool slightly. Transfer to a blender or food processor and purée until smooth, 2–3 minutes.

3 Stir the *sofrito* and sugar into the beans and simmer until the flavors are combined, 20–30 minutes. Stir in the 1 tablespoon vinegar and 2 tablespoons dry sherry. Taste the soup and adjust the seasonings with vinegar, dry sherry, and salt. Serve the soup warm, ladled into bowls and garnished with the red onion and cilantro.

Red Bean Pancakes

In China, red beans boiled with sugar are used in a sweet dessert soup or as a stuffing for sweet pastries, such as these sugar-dusted pancakes.

1 egg

½ cup (2½ oz/75 g) all-purpose (plain) flour

3 tablespoons cornstarch (cornflour)

2 tablespoons vegetable oil, plus 2–3 teaspoons

2 teaspoons Asian sesame oil

6 oz (185 g) sweetened red beans or red bean paste

1 tablespoon confectioners' (icing) sugar

MAKES 8–10 SERVINGS

1 In a food processor, combine the egg and 1 cup (8 fl oz/ 250 ml) water and process briefly to blend. Add the flour, cornstarch, and 2 tablespoons vegetable oil and process until a thin batter forms. Let stand for 10 minutes.

2 Place a heavy, nonstick frying pan over medium-high heat. When it is hot, add ½ teaspoon each vegetable and sesame oil and swirl to coat the pan.

3 Pour one-fifth of the batter into the pan and tilt the pan to spread the batter evenly over the bottom. Cook over medium-high heat until set on the bottom, about 30 seconds. Carefully spread one-fifth of the red beans across the center of the pancake, then fold the sides and ends over it to form a rectangle. Using a flat spatula, press on the rectangle to spread the filling evenly. Cook for 20 seconds to brown the underside, then turn and cook, again pressing gently, to brown the other side, about 30 seconds. Transfer the pancake to a plate and repeat with the remaining batter, filling, and vegetable and sesame oils.

4 Cut the pancakes into slices ¾ inch (2 cm) wide, arrange on a serving platter, and dust with the sugar. Serve warm or at room temperature.

Sausage and Red Bean Soup

Creamy red beans are favored for this hearty Cajun dish, but it would also be delicious with black beans, Great Northerns, black-eyed peas, or pintos. You might also stop before puréeing the beans, adding the reserved ham at that point, for the traditional red beans and steamed rice. It's also fine to substitute chicken or vegetable stock, to replace the andouille with another lean smoked sausage, or to forgo the meat. Serve with a side of corn bread (page 32) and a bottle of hot sauce.

1 lb (500 g) dried red kidney beans

1 meaty ham bone, about 1 lb (500 g), trimmed of fat

1 yellow onion, chopped

1 celery stalk, chopped

2 cloves garlic, chopped

1 large bay leaf

½ teaspoon dried thyme

1 teaspoon Tabasco, or to taste

Sea salt and freshly ground pepper

½ lb (250 g) andouille or other lean smoked sausage, cut into slices ¼ inch (6 mm) thick

Chopped green (spring) onions, including the tender green parts, for garnish

MAKES 6–8 SERVINGS

1 Pick over the beans, discarding any grit or misshapen beans. Rinse well, place in a large bowl, and add water to cover generously. Let soak overnight. (Alternatively, for a quick soak, bring the beans and water to a rapid simmer and cook for 2 minutes. Remove from the heat, cover, and let stand for 1 hour.)

2 In a large pot, combine the ham bone and 6 cups (48 fl oz/ 1.5 l) water and bring to a boil. Reduce the heat to medium-low and cook at a lively simmer for 1 hour, skimming frequently to remove any foam that rises to the surface.

3 Remove the pot from the heat. Carefully lift the ham bone from the pot and set aside to cool. Remove the meat from the bone, discarding any fat. Set the meat aside. Skim off any fat from the surface of the stock. Return the bone to the stock.

4 Drain the beans and add to the stock along with the yellow onion, celery, garlic, bay leaf, and thyme. Bring to a boil, reduce the heat to low, cover, and simmer, stirring frequently, until the beans are tender, about 2 hours.

5 Remove and discard the ham bone and bay leaf and let the soup cool slightly. Scoop out 3 cups (21 oz/655 g) of the beans with a little liquid and place in a blender. Process until smooth, then return the purée to the pot. Cut the reserved ham into bite-sized pieces and add to the pot. Season with the Tabasco, salt, and pepper.

6 In a large frying pan over medium-high heat, brown the andouille slices on both sides, about 2 minutes per side. Remove from the heat.

7 Ladle the soup into warmed bowls. Top each serving with several slices of andouille and a sprinkle of green onions. Serve at once.

Louisiana Charcuterie

ANDOUILLE

For the king of Louisiana sausages, a long casing is stuffed with lean chunks of ham, seasoned with salt and pepper, and slow-smoked into a dense link the size of a wiener or a rolling pin, depending on its maker. Andouille (pronounced on-DOO-ee) is the premier ingredient in gumbos and jambalayas and a traditional accompaniment for red beans. It is also tasty grilled with a sweet-hot dip of pepper jelly (page 32), or cradled in French bread and topped with creamy red beans.

BOUDIN

For white boudin (BOO-dan), the pride of Cajun country, minced green (spring) onions, rice, and seasonings are stuffed into casings with finely ground pork. It is prepared with great care at gas stations, convenience stores, and small groceries, wrapped in butcher paper and presented with a pack of saltines. Tourist information centers offer maps of the Boudin Trail. Black or red boudin is a blood sausage prepared mainly by home cooks.

HAM

In the South, a baked ham is the symbol of abundance and hospitality. A roasted fresh ham, an interesting alternative, has a flavor more like pork roast and a drier texture produced by curing the meat overnight in a Cajun-style rub of coarse salt, pepper, and spices. After Sunday dinner, chunks of ham are sure to appear in everything from scrambled eggs to smothered cabbage. And no cook would dream of wasting the bone, which lends smoky depth to a pot of beans.

TASSO

Lean Cajun-style tasso (TOSS-oh) ham is very dry and dense. Smoke-cured in chunks, rubbed with salt, pepper, filé (ground sassafras leaves), and spices, it has a tough consistency that tenderizes when stewed, so tasso is used primarily as a flavoring for slow-pot foods, such as beans and gumbo. It is a fine addition to jambalaya, evoking the air-cured Spanish-style ham that was most likely used in the original version.

ANDOUILLE

PICKLED PORK

CRACKLINS

FRESH SAUSAGES

BOUDIN

HAM

TASSO

HOGSHEAD CHEESE

PICKLED PORK

Also known as pickle meat, pieces of fresh pork are cured for several days in vinegar seasoned with salt, garlic, mustard seeds, peppercorns, bay leaves, and allspice. Reminiscent of corned beef, it is used to flavor red beans and vegetables. In the local spirit of "everything but the oink," various cuts of pork are preserved in a similar brew and presented in large jars at country barrooms, where patrons who are so inclined may snack on pickled pig's feet, lips, or snouts.

CRACKLINS

Fried pork rinds have achieved unlikely popularity because they add desired crunch to low-carb diets, but the authentic version is a world away from the Styrofoam-like snack sold in plastic bags. Real cracklins, known in French Louisiana as *gratons*, are made by frying strips of pork skin in boiling oil until they curl, then seasoning them with salt and at least two kinds of pepper. They are also crumbled into batter for corn bread.

FRESH SAUSAGES

Pork sausage seasons Cajun rice dressings, stuffed bell peppers (capsicums), and meat loaf. Common varieties are scented with anise, flecked with green (spring) onion, or, in the case of the brick red "hot sausage," supercharged with cayenne. In casings, they soak up the highly spiced water at a seafood boil or add substance to a pot of beans. Simmered in red gravy, a link joins a meatball atop pasta for the local Sicilian special known as "spaghetti with a ball and bat."

HOGSHEAD CHEESE

Hogshead cheese is an ugly name for chopped pork in a stiff and spicy aspic seasoned with cayenne pepper and green (spring) onions. In bygone days it was made with hog jowls, hence the name, but now it is more likely to contain shreds from the meaty shoulder, or butt, roast. It is often chilled in small loaf pans, so a slice fits comfortably on a saltine. Like much of Louisiana charcuterie, it tastes much better than it sounds.

Bruschetta with White Beans

White beans are a staple of the Italian diet. Nothing does greater justice to the sharp, fruity flavor of freshly pressed olive oil than a slice of toasted bread smothered with warm beans and generously doused with the pungent, new oil. White kidney beans or Great Northern beans can be substituted for cannellinis.

2 cups (14 oz/440 g) dried cannellini beans

8 tablespoons (4 fl oz/125 ml) extra-virgin olive oil

3 cloves garlic

1 fresh sage sprig

6–8 peppercorns

Salt and freshly ground pepper

4 slices coarse country bread, about ¾ inch (2 cm) thick

MAKES 4 SERVINGS

1 Pick over the beans, discarding any grit or misshapen beans. Rinse well, place in a large bowl, and add water to cover generously. Let soak overnight. (Alternatively, for a quick soak, bring the beans and water to a rapid simmer and cook for 2 minutes. Remove from the heat, cover, and let stand for 1 hour.)

2 Drain the beans, rinse well, and place in a large pot. Add 8 cups (64 fl oz/2 l) water, 2 tablespoons of the olive oil, the garlic, sage, and peppercorns, cover, and bring to a simmer over medium heat. Reduce the heat so that the water simmers very gently and cook until the skins of the beans are tender and the interiors are soft, about 2 hours. Season with salt three-fourths of the way through the cooking time. Remove the beans from the heat and let cool slightly in their cooking water.

3 Preheat the oven to 375°F (190°C). Arrange the bread slices in a single layer on a baking sheet and bake until golden, 3–5 minutes.

4 Divide the toasts among individual plates. Ladle a generous amount of beans and a bit of the cooking water on each toast. Drizzle abundantly with some of the remaining olive oil, season with salt and pepper, and serve.

Spicy Pinto Beans

A bowl of these beans can be a healthy and tasty light meal by itself—perhaps with a green salad and a few hot tortillas—or they can be served as a side dish. When buying beans, look for so-called new crop beans. The older beans are, the longer they need to cook. In Mexico, cooks seldom soak their beans before cooking them, considering it an unnecessary step.

1 cup (7 oz/220 g) dried pinto beans

3 tablespoons safflower or canola oil

1 white onion, finely chopped

1 clove garlic, minced

Sea salt

3 serrano chiles

½ lb (250 g) ripe tomatoes, simmered in water until tender and drained, or 1 can (14½ oz/ 455 g) diced tomatoes, undrained

2 cups (12 oz/375 g) canned nopales, well rinsed and diced

2 large fresh epazote sprigs

MAKES 4 SERVINGS

1 Pick over the beans, discarding any grit or misshapen beans. Rinse well, place in a large pot, and add water to cover generously. Bring to a boil, then reduce the heat until the water is barely simmering.

2 In a small frying pan over medium heat, warm 1 tablespoon of the oil. Add half of the onion and sauté until softened, about 4 minutes. Stir in the garlic and cook for 1 minute. Add the onion and garlic to the simmering beans and continue to cook, partially covered, until the beans are just tender, about 2 hours. Stir occasionally and add hot water as needed to keep the water level at 1 inch (2.5 cm) above the beans.

3 Add 1 teaspoon salt and continue to cook until the beans are soft, about 40 minutes longer. Drain the beans, reserving ½ cup (4 fl oz/125 ml) of the bean broth. Set the beans and broth aside.

4 Meanwhile, in a frying pan over medium heat, warm the remaining 2 tablespoons oil. Add the remaining chopped onion and the chiles and sauté until the onion is translucent, about 3 minutes. Leaving the onion in the pan, transfer the chiles to a blender. Add the tomatoes and blend to a slightly textured purée. Mix the purée into the onion and cook over medium-high heat, stirring often, until the sauce is reduced, about 5 minutes.

5 Add the nopales and epazote, and season with salt. Reduce the heat to medium and, when the mixture starts to boil, stir in the beans and reserved broth and simmer for about 5 minutes to heat through. Transfer to a warmed serving dish and serve at once.

Chicken and Chickpea Soup

6 cups (48 fl oz/1.5 l) chicken stock

1 skinless, bone-in whole chicken breast

1 fresh mint sprig

1 tablespoon safflower or canola oil

½ large white onion, chopped

1 large carrot, peeled and diced

2 cloves garlic, chopped

1 chipotle chile in adobo, finely chopped

1 fresh epazote sprig

Salt and freshly ground pepper

1 can (15 oz/470 g) chickpeas (garbanzo beans)

1 avocado, preferably Hass

1 lime, cut into 6 wedges

MAKES 6 SERVINGS

1 In a saucepan over medium heat, bring the stock, chicken, and mint to a simmer and cook, partially covered, until the chicken is opaque throughout, about 15 minutes. Carefully lift the chicken and mint from the pan, reserving the stock. Discard the mint and let the chicken cool, then remove the chicken meat from the bones. Discard the bones and shred the meat. Set the meat and stock aside.

2 In a large saucepan over medium heat, warm the oil. Add the onion and carrot and sauté until the onion is translucent, about 5 minutes. Add the garlic and sauté for 1 minute. Pour in the stock and add the chile, epazote, ½ teaspoon salt, and ½ teaspoon pepper. Bring to a simmer, cover, and cook for 20 minutes. Rinse the chickpeas, add them to the soup, and simmer, uncovered, for 10 minutes longer. Add the shredded chicken and heat through.

3 Ladle the soup into warmed bowls, top with diced avocado, and pass the lime wedges at the table.

Spicy Hummus with Pita

1 cup (6 oz/185 g) dried chickpeas (garbanzo beans)

½ teaspoon baking soda (bicarbonate of soda)

1 clove garlic, crushed

Juice of 2 lemons

3 tablespoons tahini

Sea salt

Extra-virgin olive oil for drizzling

½ teaspoon paprika

6 pita breads, homemade (page 25) or purchased

MAKES 6 SERVINGS

1 Pick over the chickpeas; discard any grit or misshapen chickpeas. Rinse, place in a bowl, and add water to cover generously. Let soak overnight.

2 Drain the chickpeas and place in a saucepan. Add water to cover and bring to a boil. Boil for 10 minutes, reduce the heat to medium-low, add the baking soda, and cook until the chickpeas are meltingly soft, about 50 minutes.

3 Drain the chickpeas, reserving the cooking water. Place the chickpeas in a food processor, add the garlic, and purée. Add the lemon juice, the tahini, and 4 tablespoons of the cooking water. Season with salt. Pulse twice and check the consistency. If necessary, add more cooking water until the mixture forms a creamy paste. It will thicken as it cools. Taste and adjust the seasoning. Transfer to a serving bowl, drizzle with olive oil, and sprinkle with the paprika. Set aside.

4 Preheat the broiler (grill). Arrange the pita breads on a baking sheet and toast until slightly crisp, 1–2 minutes per side. Serve warm alongside the hummus.

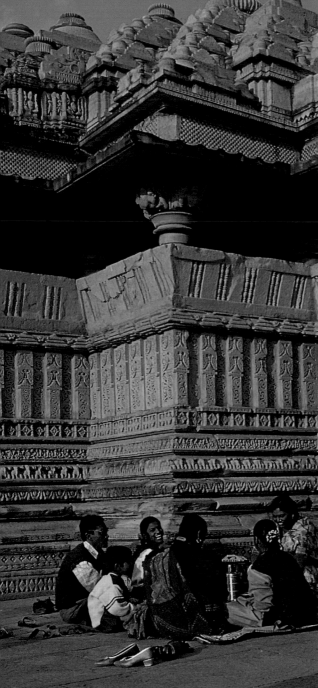

SPAIN
Chickpea, Tomato, and Chorizo Salad

For the vinaigrette

6 tablespoons (3 fl oz/90 ml) extra-virgin olive oil

2 tablespoons red wine vinegar

1 clove garlic, finely chopped

Fine sea salt and freshly ground black pepper

2 red bell peppers (capsicums)

1 lb (500 g) tomatoes, peeled

1 small red onion, diced

1 cup (1 oz/30 g) flat-leaf (Italian) parsley leaves, coarsely chopped, plus extra for garnish

2 cans (15 oz/470 g each) chickpeas (garbanzo beans)

Pinch of cayenne pepper

Sea salt and freshly ground black pepper

1 tablespoon olive oil

½ lb (250 g) Spanish chorizo

MAKES 4 SERVINGS

1 To make the vinaigrette, in a large bowl, whisk together the olive oil, vinegar, and garlic. Season with salt and black pepper. Set aside.

2 Preheat the broiler (grill). Quarter and seed the bell peppers and place them skin side up in a small roasting pan. Broil (grill) until the skin blisters and blackens, about 5 minutes. Transfer to a small bowl, cover, and let cool.

3 Peel the bell peppers, cut into large dice, and add to the vinaigrette. Dice the tomatoes and add to the peppers along with the onion and parsley. Rinse the chickpeas, add to the salad, and stir to combine. Season with cayenne, salt, and black pepper.

4 In a large frying pan over medium heat, warm the olive oil. Cut the chorizo into half moons, add to the hot oil, and fry until crisp, 2–3 minutes on each side. Transfer to paper towels to drain.

5 Add the chorizo to the salad and toss to combine. Taste and adjust the seasonings. Garnish with parsley and serve at once.

INDIA
Curried Chickpeas

¼ cup (2 fl oz/60 ml) olive oil

1 teaspoon cumin seeds

2 yellow onions, finely chopped

1 teaspoon grated ginger

2 teaspoons ground coriander

½ teaspoon ground turmeric

½–1 teaspoon cayenne pepper

2 tomatoes, finely chopped

3 cups (21 oz/655 g) canned chickpeas (garbanzo beans)

2 teaspoons tomato paste

1 teaspoon fresh lemon juice

½ cup (4 fl oz/125 ml) water

1 teaspoon garam masala

¼ cup (⅓ oz/10 g) chopped fresh cilantro (fresh coriander)

MAKES 6 SERVINGS

1 In a large frying pan over medium-high heat, warm the oil. When it is hot, add the cumin seeds and cook, stirring, until they darken, about 15 seconds. Add the onions and cook, stirring occasionally, until light brown, about 10 minutes. Add the ginger, coriander, turmeric, cayenne pepper to taste, and tomatoes. Cook, stirring occasionally, until the tomatoes begin to brown, about 6 minutes.

2 Rinse the chickpeas and add to the pan along with the tomato paste, lemon juice, and ½ cup (4 fl oz/125 ml) water. Mix well and bring to a boil. Reduce the heat to low, cover, and simmer until the flavors are blended, about 5 minutes. Taste and adjust the seasonings. Transfer to a warmed serving dish, sprinkle with the garam masala and cilantro, and serve at once.

Winemaking follows the rhythm of the year, beginning in the depths of winter when the vines are pruned and cared for, continuing through the summer when the grapes ripen, and culminating in autumn when, in a burst of activity, the grapes are finally harvested and crushed.

Making Spanish Wine

THE HARVEST

The moment of the harvest depends on a variety of factors: climate and altitude, grape varietal, and whether the grapes are red or white. Grapes may also be left on the vine longer than usual to concentrate their natural sugars in the sun, as in the case of some *moscatels*. Once they are ready, the grapes are cut from the vines in bunches and transported to the winery as quickly as possible, where they begin their transformation.

CATALAN WINE DYNASTIES

The story of Catalan wine is one of history, tradition, and economic influence. Nobody knows this better than the dynasties that have dominated *el vi català* over time—in some cases for hundreds of years. Some of the most important names in Catalan wine are families that have built up powerful businesses around their own vineyards and cellars. The Torres family of the Penedès is known throughout the world as the creators of a great wine empire. Another preeminent name is Raventós, the influential family behind the Codorníu label, whose *cava* is one of the most popular in Spain. The family bottled its first sparkling wines in the 1870s, many of which they sent off to royalty in Madrid. The Ferrer family of Freixenet, another well-known, highly regarded sparkling wine producer, also boasts a company history that goes back to the nineteenth century. Finally, the Gramona family represents another Penedès wine dynasty that has recently shot to fame as a producer of up-to-date wines like Gessami, Chardonnay, Más Escorpí, and the ice wine Vi de Gel.

MAKING WINE

CRUSH AND EXTRACTING Once harvested, the grapes are destemmed and crushed, and then the juice is extracted in a press, though red grapes are sometimes left whole to ferment. The traditional method of pressing with the feet is now quite rare, although it is occasionally seen in rural settings.

FERMENTING Next, the juice undergoes fermentation, the process by which the sugars in the grape juice are converted into alcohol by the yeasts occurring on the grape skins. This is usually done in stainless-steel vats and takes around fifteen days, after which the wine is cloudy. It is then left to settle until it is clear.

RACKING AND BOTTLING At the end of fermentation, wine is usually "racked," or poured off from the tanks and separated from the sediment that settles at the bottom. This allows the wine to breathe. Racking may occur several times before the wine is ready to bottle. It is then filtered, bottled, and ready for aging or selling.

FRANCE
Warm Lentils with Vinaigrette

Tiny French lentils are served many ways: tossed with a vinaigrette or dressed with truffle shavings as a side dish, combined with aromatics for a cold-weather soup, or simmered with sausages for a one-dish meal. Here they get just a hint of cream.

1 cup (7 oz/220 g) Puy lentils

½ cup (4 fl oz/125 ml) dry white wine

½ carrot, peeled and chopped

½ celery stalk, chopped

1 bay leaf

3 or 4 fresh thyme sprigs

3 shallots, chopped

2 cloves garlic, chopped

3 tablespoons chopped fresh flat-leaf (Italian) parsley

Salt and freshly ground pepper

2 tablespoons heavy (double) cream, or to taste

1 teaspoon sherry vinegar

MAKES 4–6 SERVINGS

1 Pick over the lentils, discarding any grit or misshapen lentils. Rinse well, place in a large saucepan, and add 4 cups (32 fl oz/1 l) water. Add the wine, carrot, celery, bay leaf, thyme, half of the shallots, and half of the garlic. Bring to a boil, reduce the heat to medium-low, cover, and simmer until the lentils are just tender but not mushy and have absorbed most of the liquid, 30–35 minutes.

2 Drain the lentils, reserving about 2 tablespoons of the cooking liquid. Place the lentils and reserved liquid in a serving bowl. Add the remaining shallots and garlic and the parsley to the hot lentils and toss to combine. Season with salt and pepper, and stir in the 2 tablespoons cream and 1 teaspoon vinegar. Taste and adjust the seasonings. Serve warm or at room temperature.

INDIA
Delhi-Style Dal

Side-dish *dals* are generally soupy. They are best served in small bowls and eaten with a spoon. For extra flavor, top with a little *usli ghee* just before serving.

1½ cups (10½ oz/330 g) pink, red, or yellow lentils

½ teaspoon ground turmeric

Salt

1 tomato, finely chopped

3 tablespoons vegetable oil

1 teaspoon cumin seeds

1 yellow onion, finely chopped

4 cloves garlic, thinly sliced

½ teaspoon cayenne pepper

1 teaspoon garam masala

¼ cup (⅓ oz/10 g) finely chopped fresh cilantro (fresh coriander)

MAKES 4 SERVINGS

1 Pick over the lentils, removing any grit or misshapen lentils. Rinse well, place in a deep pot, and add the turmeric and 4 cups (32 fl oz/1 l) water. Bring to a boil, reduce the heat to low, and simmer, uncovered, until the lentils are tender, about 25 minutes for pink or red lentils and 40 minutes for yellow. Stir in 1½ teaspoons salt and the tomato and cook until the tomato is soft, about 5 minutes. Keep warm.

2 In a small frying pan over medium-high heat, warm the oil. Add the cumin seeds and sauté until they turn very dark, about 30 seconds. Add the onion and garlic and sauté until light golden, about 6 minutes. Stir in the cayenne and garam masala, then pour the mixture into the lentils. Add the cilantro and mix well. Taste and adjust the seasonings. Serve at once.

VEGETABLES

The Garden's Harvest

VEGETABLES AROUND THE WORLD

For travelers, a visit to a produce market is an inspiring way to learn about the local cuisine. Farmers in Provence set up their vegetables under the shade of plane trees, as they have for centuries, while market women navigate the canals of Bangkok, their boats piled high with produce. Small or large, markets boast fresh, flavorful vegetables at their most colorful and alluring.

Centuries of international trade have spread regional vegetables to nearly every corner of the world. Vegetables from Southeast Asia and China are readily available in the West while those native to the Americas, including potatoes, tomatoes, corn, chiles, and a multitude of squashes, are now integral to the cuisines of Asia, Europe, and Africa. Regional dishes encompass an astonishing variety of tastes and techniques—from tender braised leeks in Paris to dry-cooked cauliflower in Mumbai to spicy stir-fried long beans in Chengdu. Even the bright, beloved medley of bell peppers (capsicums), zucchini (courgettes), eggplant (aubergine), and tomatoes reveals variations from region to region. *Briami,* a layered Greek casserole, is cooked slowly then sprinkled with fronds

of dill or fennel. The famed ratatouille of Provence and the baked, stuffed vegetables of Turkey, Lebanon, and Iran each highlight the silken texture of this iconic quartet. Hard squashes, such as butternut, kabocha, acorn, and the aptly named turban, offer similar versatility. Simmered in dashi broth to make a popular Japanese stew, curried in coconut milk with Thai spices, or puréed into a creamy soup with Washington apples, squashes absorb flavors both subtle and vibrant. With their long vegetarian traditions, cooks in India, Thailand, China, and Japan have created extensive menus based on vegetables. And as meatless traditions spread beyond their ancient capitals, vegetables are leaving behind their side-dish status to take center stage at Western meals.

SALADS

Bringing vegetables to the table uncooked and simply garnished is the purest way to enjoy them. In Europe and North America, a dedicated salad course has become standard for formal meals. This can take the minimalist French form of mesclun tossed with just a glimmer of olive oil or the *salata horiatiki* of Greece, a country salad exuberantly garnished with olives, tomatoes, cucumbers, and cubes of feta cheese. Composed arrangements such as Niçoise salad and informal potato salads studded with crunchy lardons, mint leaves, or sweet-sour pickles are other ways of serving chilled vegetables during the sultry months of summer.

In tropical Asia and the hot-dry Middle East, chopped and barely seasoned vegetables provide a refreshing counterpoint to main dishes. Mediterranean raw vegetable salads include Tunisian carrots flavored with cumin, young radishes brightened with lemon juice, and ripe tomatoes generously sprinkled with cilantro (fresh coriander) leaves. In Japan, *sunomono* encompasses an entire class of cold salads that combine vegetables with a vinaigrette of shoyu, mirin, rice vinegar, and sesame oil. Cooked vegetables mixed with *aemono*, a light, sweet sesame- or walnut-based sauce, help clear the palate between courses at the Japanese table.

In Vietnam, Thailand, Laos, and Cambodia, meals often require a large platter of young greens such as watercress, baby mustard, water cabbage, or spring lettuce arranged alongside an abundance of fresh herbs, especially cilantro (fresh coriander), mint, holy basil, and dill. Wrapped into bite-sized bundles to accompany rice or stirred into soups, they contribute to the complex flavors of Southeast Asian dishes.

GREENS

Cooked greens are also important in every cuisine. Kale in the colcannon of Ireland, sautéed chard in Italy, stir-fried bok choy in China, and the meaty, long-cooked collards of the American South are just a few of the ways greens are integral to daily meals. They are easy to cook and nourishing for the body. Seasonal greens range from the first tender nettle leaves of spring to the hardy, pleasantly bitter escarole of winter. Humble, sturdy cabbage is iconic in dishes such as Germany's sauerkraut, Poland's bulgur-filled *golabki* rolls, and India's wide, shimmering ribbons sprinkled with black mustard seeds.

ROOTS AND TUBERS

Native to the high slopes of the Peruvian Andes, potatoes are now harvested in thousands of varieties. Markets regularly stock thin fingerlings, tiny red-skinned potatoes, deep-hued Delta blues, and buttery Yukon golds along with hefty russet Burbanks. Whether deep-fried into crisp fries or baked beneath a melting layer of grated cheese, potatoes provide comforting accompaniment to daily fare. Sweet potatoes, yams, and their starchier Latin American cousins, *batatas,* are favorites when baked or roasted in embers, whipped into a silken purée, or simmered in a spicy curry sauce.

Beets, turnips, parsnips, and rutabagas (swedes) are staples in eastern Europe, where an array of pickles, soups, and chopped salads come to the table year-round. Other important tubers in world cuisines include taro and cassava, also known as manioc or yucca. Simply boiled or steamed, they are the foundations of meals in the Pacific Islands, West Indies, and Africa.

MUSHROOMS

More than any other plant, mushrooms are unique to their environment. Growing only in specific places, beneath the red pines of Japan or at the root of oak trees in the southwest of France, wild mushrooms have proven nearly impossible to cultivate. Japanese matsutake, the golden chanterelles of France, and the deeply fragrant porcini of Italy still draw families out for annual foraging expeditions after spring rains.

Mushrooms thrive in Japan's humid climate. Of the nearly 4,000 varieties that grow on the islands, shiitake, enoki, and oyster are among the most familiar. Throughout Asia, cone-shaped straw mushrooms grow in rice fields after the grain has been harvested. Tree ear mushrooms add crunchy texture to numerous dishes, while dried mushrooms, much preferred among Chinese cooks, develop a firm, meaty texture that holds up well to stir-frying and long braising.

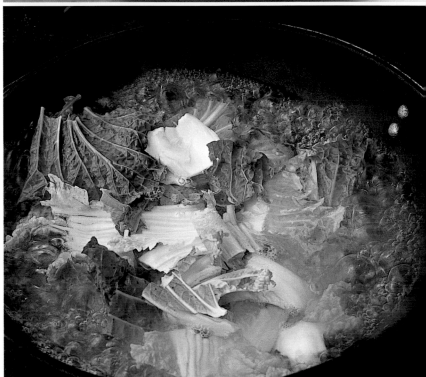

GREECE
Spinach and Feta Rolls

Here, spanikopita—the spinach, feta, and filo-pastry pie that is one of Greece's most popular exports—is made into individual servings, ideal for an elegant appetizer.

Sea salt and freshly ground pepper

4 lb (2 kg) spinach (about 4 bunches), rinsed well and tough stems removed

¼ cup (2 fl oz/60 ml) extra-virgin olive oil

1 large yellow onion, chopped

¾ cup (1 oz/30 g) chopped fresh flat-leaf (Italian) parsley

¼ cup (⅓ oz/10 g) chopped fresh dill

3 green (spring) onions, white and pale green parts, minced

½ cup (2½ oz/75 g) pine nuts

½ lb (250 g) feta, crumbled

6 sheets filo pastry, each about 12 by 18 inches (30 by 45 cm), thawed overnight in the refrigerator if frozen

4 tablespoons (2 oz/60 g) unsalted butter, melted

MAKES 6 SERVINGS

1 Bring a large pot of water to a boil. Generously salt the water, add the spinach, and stir until wilted, about 1 minute. Transfer to a colander and rinse with cold water, then squeeze out the excess moisture. Roughly chop the spinach, place it in a large bowl, and set aside.

2 In a frying pan over medium-high heat, warm the olive oil. Add the yellow onion and cook until transparent and lightly browned, 6–8 minutes. Stir in the parsley, dill, and green onions and season with salt and pepper. Combine with the spinach. Place the pine nuts in a dry frying pan over medium heat and toast, shaking the pan occasionally, until fragrant and golden, 5–7 minutes. Add the pine nuts and the feta to the spinach mixture and toss to combine.

3 Preheat the oven to 375°F (190°C). Have ready a rimmed baking sheet lined with parchment (baking) paper. Cut the filo sheets in half lengthwise, stack them between sheets of parchment paper, and cover with a damp kitchen towel. Working with 1 half sheet at a time, brush lightly with butter. Add a spoonful of filling to one end, leaving a ½-inch (12-mm) border at the edges. Fold the sides of the filo sheet over onto the filling, then roll into a cylinder. Place on the baking sheet, seam side down. Cut 2 diagonal slits in the top of each roll and lightly brush with the remaining butter. Bake until golden, 20–25 minutes. Serve warm.

SPAIN
Spinach with Raisins and Pine Nuts

¼ cup (1½ oz/45 g) raisins

3 tablespoons olive oil

1 small yellow onion, chopped

3 oz (90 g) serrano ham, chopped (optional)

2 lb (1 kg) spinach, rinsed well and tough stems removed

¼ cup (1½ oz/45 g) pine nuts, toasted

Salt and freshly ground pepper

MAKES 4 SERVINGS

1 In a bowl, combine the raisins with hot water to cover. Let stand until plump, about 30 minutes. Drain and set aside.

2 In a large frying pan over medium heat, warm the olive oil. Add the onion and the ham, if using, and sauté until the onion is tender, 8–10 minutes. Add the spinach and stir until it is wilted, 2–3 minutes. Stir in the raisins and the pine nuts and season with salt and pepper. Transfer to a warmed serving dish and serve at once.

CHINA
Chinese Greens with Oyster Sauce

Chinese greens belong to the cabbage family of green vegetables. Their flavor and bitterness can be more pronounced than in common cabbages. Petite bok choy, sold as "baby" or "Shanghai" bok choy, is milder and more tender than full-grown.

1 bunch Chinese greens such as Chinese broccoli or bok choy, about 10 oz (315 g)

2 cups (16 fl oz/500 ml) chicken stock or water

Salt

1 tablespoon vegetable oil

3½ tablespoons oyster sauce

MAKES 4 SERVINGS

1 If using Chinese broccoli, cut off the hard stems and discard any large, tough leaves. Cut the stems in half crosswise. If using baby bok choy, trim the ends and slit each head in half lengthwise. For large bok choy, trim the ends, separate the leaves and stems, and cut the stems into 4-inch (10-cm) lengths.

2 In a wok or saucepan, bring the stock to a boil. Add 1 teaspoon salt and the oil. Add the greens and boil, uncovered, until crisp-tender, about 2½ minutes for Chinese broccoli or 1½ minutes for baby bok choy. If using large bok choy, cook the stems first for 2 minutes, then add the leaves and cook for 20 seconds. Transfer the greens to a serving plate, reserve 1½ tablespoons of the cooking liquid, and pour off the rest.

3 Place the wok over medium heat and add the reserved cooking liquid and the oyster sauce. Warm gently until almost boiling. Pour over the greens and serve at once.

ITALY
Greens with Garlic

Green leafy vegetables are an integral part of the Italian diet, especially in the winter, when spinach, broccoli rabe, and wild greens are at their best. Boiled then sautéed with garlic and chile, as here, they are known as *strascinata* (literally, "dragged").

1 lb (500 g) broccoli rabe or other leafy green vegetable

Salt

2 tablespoons extra-virgin olive oil

2 cloves garlic, chopped

1 small dried red chile, cut into pieces, or ½ teaspoon red pepper flakes

MAKES 4–6 SERVINGS

1 Pick over the greens carefully, discarding any yellow leaves. Trim away any tough stems. Rinse well.

2 Bring a large pot of water to a boil. Add 1 tablespoon salt and the greens and boil until crisp-tender, 6–8 minutes. Transfer the greens to a colander but do not press or squeeze them; they should stay fairly wet.

3 In a large frying pan over medium-high heat, warm the olive oil. When it is hot, add the garlic and chile and cook, stirring occasionally, about 2 minutes. Add the greens, reduce the heat to medium, and sauté until all the water from the greens has evaporated, 7–10 minutes. Transfer to a warmed dish and serve at once.

Italian Greens

BROCCOLO ROMANESCO

The Roman variety of what in Italian is properly called *cavolo broccolo romanesco* is found principally in the winter. It looks like a chartreuse cauliflower with pointed florets, but the taste is nearer broccoli. The florets are delicious simply boiled or steamed and dressed with olive oil and a squeeze of lemon, or deep-fried as part of a *fritto misto*. They can also be boiled and sautéed, as for *cicoria* and *broccoletti*, or served on pasta.

CICORIA SELVATICA

Gathered in the countryside in the cool months, wild chicory grows in exuberant heads with lots of curly, saw-toothed leaves. The flavor ranges from pleasantly bitter to very bitter indeed. The leaves are rinsed and trimmed like spinach, then dropped into a pot of boiling salted water and cooked until tender. People with strong palates will eat boiled chicory cold with olive oil and lemon juice, but most prefer to sauté the boiled greens with garlic and chile (see page 136).

MISTICANZA ROMANA

The term *misticanza* is applied to an assortment of greens, from mild combinations that recall Provençal mesclun to banal bags of ready-made salads to robust blends of spiky, hairy wild things that must be boiled to be edible. To connoisseurs, however, *la misticanza romana* is a wild salad of considerable character and charm. Gathered in the countryside in wintertime, the mix will vary. It is usually dressed with only vinegar and olive oil.

LATTUGA ROMANA

American Caesar salad is creeping onto Italian menus—and no wonder, with such tender and flavorful romaine (cos) lettuce. In Rome, it is called simply *lattuga* (lettuce). In the vernacular of the Roman vegetable market, the generic term for salad greens is *insalata* rather than *lattuga*, which is reserved for romaine only. It is used like any salad green, but unlike other lettuces, it can also be cooked as an addition to *la vignarola* (stewed spring vegetables) or braised on its own.

BROCCOLO ROMANESCO

BROCCOLETTI

RUGHETTA SELVATICA

SPINACI

CICORIA SELVATICA

MISTICANZA ROMANA

LATTUGA ROMANA

PUNTARELLE

BROCCOLETTI

Broccoletti are not exactly the same thing as broccoli rabe (*cime di rapa* or *broccoletti di rapa*) but the slight differences don't matter. Available principally in the cooler months, it is like broccoli whose leaves have grown and whose florets have shrunk. Greengrocers carefully trim off the tough ends, then peel and split the remaining stems. *Broccoletti* make an excellent addition to pasta, or they can be served as a side dish, boiled and dressed with olive oil and lemon juice.

RUGHETTA SELVATICA

In Italian it is *ruchetta*; in Rome it is *rughetta selvatica*. Although best translated as "wild arugula," a truly analogous plant may not exist. Available all year, *rughetta* has a bitter, peppery flavor. Despite the name, most *rughetta selvatica* is cultivated, but sharp eyes will find it growing even in the city. It's often mixed with cherry tomatoes or with green (spring) onions and Parmigiano-Reggiano, but is also delicious solo.

SPINACI

People who think they don't like spinach should not give up until they have tasted it in Italy. Mainly available in winter, it reaches the market young and tender, enticingly pink at the base, the smallest leaves almost emerald. Whole leaves are usually steamed and served with butter or with lemon and olive oil. They can also be sautéed with raisins and pine nuts. Spinach is an essential ingredient in classic ravioli when mixed with ricotta. The smallest leaves are sold for salads.

PUNTARELLE

With the first warm weather, the stalks of *puntarelle*, a type of Catalonian chicory, grow woody, and won't be seen again until the first chill of autumn. Preparation begins with the special cut. The outer leaves and tough bases of the hollow stalks are removed. Each stalk is then carefully peeled and split lengthwise into several strips. *Puntarelle* are typically served with a dressing made with anchovy and garlic.

Beet, Avocado, and Fennel Salad

Chefs love golden beets and pink-and-white-striped Chioggia beets because they don't "bleed" their color as red beets do, making artful composed salads possible. In this one, crisp fennel and creamy avocado provide textural contrast with the beets, and thin shavings of ricotta salata add a salty counterpoint. This firm, white sheep's milk cheese from southern Italy is made by salting, pressing, and briefly aging ricotta.

4 beets, preferably golden or Chioggia, about 1 lb (500 g) total weight without greens

For the vinaigrette

1½ tablespoons fresh lemon juice

1 shallot, finely minced

Sea salt and freshly ground pepper

¼ cup (2 fl oz/60 ml) extra-virgin olive oil

1 small fennel bulb

1½ oz (45 g) wedge ricotta salata or feta cheese

½ large avocado

1 tablespoon minced fresh flat-leaf (Italian) parsley

MAKES 4 SERVINGS

1 Preheat the oven to 400°F (200°C). If the greens are still attached to the beets, cut them off, leaving 1 inch (2.5 cm) of the stem attached. Leave the roots attached as well. Put the beets in a baking dish and add water to a depth of ¼ inch (6 mm). Cover with aluminum foil and bake until the beets are tender when pierced with a knife, about 1 hour. Let cool. Peel the beets and trim the roots, then let cool completely.

2 To prepare the vinaigrette, in a small bowl, combine the lemon juice, shallot, and a generous pinch of salt. Let stand for 30 minutes. Whisk in the olive oil. Season with pepper. Taste and adjust the seasoning.

3 Cut the beets into very thin slices. Put them in a bowl and toss gently with about one-third of the vinaigrette, taking care not to break up the slices. Make a thin bed of the beets on a large platter or divide among individual plates.

4 Cut off the stems and feathery tops and any bruised outer stalks from the fennel bulb, then halve lengthwise. Slice each half crosswise into paper-thin slices. Put the fennel in a bowl, add about one-half of the remaining vinaigrette, and toss to coat. Scatter the fennel over the beets. Shave the ricotta salata (or crumble the feta) evenly over the fennel.

5 Scoop the avocado flesh from the peel in one piece. Put the avocado half cut side down on a work surface and thinly slice crosswise. Arrange the avocado slices on top of the salad. Drizzle with as much of the remaining vinaigrette as desired, then top with the parsley. Serve at once.

Beet and Cabbage Borscht

Recipes for borscht have always varied, depending on their origin—the Ukraine, Poland, or Russia—as well as the cook's preferences. Some borschts are a cornucopia of vegetables; contemporary versions might use chicken stock rather than beef, or even be vegetarian. This soup begins with a rich broth made from beef marrow bones, which is customary in eastern European cooking.

For the broth

3 lb (1.5 kg) beef marrow bones

Sea salt

2½ lb (1.25 kg) brisket, trimmed of excess fat

2 cups (14 oz/440 g) canned whole plum (Roma) tomatoes

1 large yellow onion, quartered

2 celery stalks, cut into 6-inch (15-cm) pieces

1 teaspoon black peppercorns

1 bay leaf

1½ lb (750 g) red beets

2 tablespoons apple cider vinegar, plus ¼ cup (2 fl oz/ 60 ml), or to taste

Sea salt and freshly ground pepper

½ small green cabbage, thinly sliced

½ large yellow onion, diced

1 celery stalk, diced

2 carrots, peeled and thinly sliced

2 tablespoons chopped fresh dill, plus extra for garnish

1 tablespoon sugar, or to taste

Sour cream for garnish

MAKES 10–12 SERVINGS

1 Place the bones in a large soup pot with 4 qt (4 l) water and 1 tablespoon salt. Bring to a boil, reduce the heat to low, cover partially, and simmer, frequently skimming the foam from the surface, about 1 hour. Carefully remove the bones from the pot and discard. Add the brisket, tomatoes and their liquid, onion, celery, peppercorns, and bay leaf. Bring to a boil, reduce the heat to low, cover partially, and simmer until the brisket is fork-tender, about 2 hours.

2 Transfer the brisket to a bowl. Strain the broth into a separate bowl, pressing on the solids to extract all the liquid. Discard the solids. Cover the bowls of brisket and broth and refrigerate until the broth is chilled, for at least 4 hours or up to overnight.

3 If the greens are still attached to the beets, remove them. Cut the beets into halves or quarters. Bring a saucepan with 2 qt (2 l) water to a boil. Add the beets, 2 tablespoons apple cider vinegar, and 1 tablespoon salt, cover, and return to a boil, then reduce the heat to medium-low and simmer until the beets are very tender, about 1 hour, adding more water if necessary to cover the beets. Let the beets cool in their cooking liquid.

4 Skim the fat from the surface of the chilled beef broth and pour into a soup pot over medium heat. Cut the meat into ¼-inch (6-mm) cubes, add to the broth, and heat until warm, about 10 minutes. Add the cabbage, onion, and celery and simmer until tender, about 20 minutes.

5 Remove the beets from their cooking liquid and strain the liquid through a sieve into the soup pot. Slip off the skins and shred the beets on the large holes of a grater. Add the shredded beets to the soup pot along with the carrots and 2 tablespoons dill. Simmer over medium-low heat until the carrots are tender, about 15 minutes. Stir in the ¼ cup (2 fl oz/60 ml) vinegar and 1 tablespoon sugar, and season with salt and pepper. Taste the soup and adjust the seasonings with vinegar and/or sugar.

6 Ladle the borscht into warmed individual bowls. Garnish each bowl with a dollop of sour cream and a sprinkling of dill. Serve at once.

Brussels Sprouts with Bacon

The oft-maligned Brussels sprout has a distinct, nutty flavor that comes through in the simple preparations of skilled cooks. They are also enhanced by stronger flavors such as bacon and balsamic vinegar, as in this preparation.

6 slices bacon

2 tablespoons white balsamic vinegar or balsamic vinegar

½ teaspoon Dijon mustard

1 clove garlic, minced

1 teaspoon chopped fresh thyme

½ cup (4 fl oz/125 ml) extra-virgin olive oil

Sea salt and freshly ground pepper

1½ lb (750 g) Brussels sprouts

2 tablespoons unsalted butter

MAKES 6 SERVINGS

1 In a frying pan over medium-low heat, fry the bacon slices, turning occasionally, until crisp, 7–8 minutes. Transfer to paper towels to drain.

2 Meanwhile, in a small bowl, whisk together the vinegar, mustard, garlic, and thyme. Whisking constantly, pour in the olive oil in a slow, steady stream. Season with salt and pepper.

3 Remove the outer leaves from each Brussels sprout and discard any that are blemished. Continue to remove the leaves, using a small, sharp knife to cut away the core. In a large saucepan over medium heat, melt the butter. Add the Brussels sprout leaves and ½ cup (4 fl oz/125 ml) water, cover, raise the heat to high, and bring to a boil. Reduce the heat to medium-low and steam the leaves until bright green and tender, about 7 minutes, adding more water if needed. Drain and transfer to a serving bowl.

4 Crumble the bacon and add it to the olive oil mixture. Drizzle over the Brussels sprout leaves and toss to coat. Season with salt and pepper and serve at once.

Poached Leeks with Vinaigrette

Pairing this naturally sweet member of the onion family with a classic mustard vinaigrette has proven to be a perfect marriage. French cooks bind the long, slender vegetables together in a bundle, to maintain their cylindrical shape.

12 small to medium leeks, 2½–3 lb (1.25–1.5 kg) total weight

Sea salt and freshly ground pepper

2 tablespoons sherry vinegar

2 teaspoons Dijon mustard

6 tablespoons (3 fl oz/90 ml) extra-virgin olive oil

¼ cup (1½ oz/45 g) cherry tomatoes, halved or quartered (optional)

2 tablespoons chopped fresh chives

1 tablespoon chopped fresh tarragon

1 tablespoon chopped fresh flat-leaf (Italian) parsley

MAKES 6 SERVINGS

1 Trim off the root end of each leek and the dark green tops, leaving about 2 inches (5 cm) of the paler green parts. Remove any discolored outer leaves, halve each stalk lengthwise, then rinse the dirt from between the layers by fanning them out but not separating them. Using kitchen string, tie the stalks into 3 bundles of 4 leeks each.

2 Bring a large pot of water to a boil. Salt the water, add the leeks, cover, and cook until they are just tender when pierced with a knife, 7–9 minutes. Drain, cut off the strings, and arrange on individual plates.

3 In a small bowl, whisk together a pinch of salt and the vinegar until the salt dissolves, then whisk in the mustard. Slowly pour in the olive oil while whisking constantly. Season with pepper, then taste and adjust the seasoning.

4 Garnish the leeks with the cherry tomatoes, if using. Drizzle with the vinaigrette and sprinkle with the chives, tarragon, and parsley. Serve warm, at room temperature, or slightly chilled.

Leek and Zucchini Frittata

8 eggs, beaten

Salt and freshly ground pepper

2 tablespoons unsalted butter

3 tablespoons extra-virgin olive oil

3 leeks, white and pale green parts only, sliced crosswise into rings

1 lb (500 g) zucchini (courgettes), halved lengthwise and thinly sliced

Handful of fresh basil leaves

MAKES 4 SERVINGS

1 Preheat the broiler (grill). In a bowl, lightly beat the eggs just until blended. Season with salt and pepper.

2 In a large ovenproof frying pan over medium heat, melt the butter with the olive oil. Add the leeks and sauté until they begin to soften, about 3 minutes. Add the zucchini and sauté until lightly golden, 5–8 minutes, adding the basil leaves toward the end of cooking. Distribute the vegetables and basil evenly over the bottom of the pan, then pour the eggs over the top. Reduce the heat to low and cook slowly, occasionally running a spatula along the sides of the pan to keep the frittata from sticking, until the sides and bottom are set but the center is still loose, about 5 minutes.

3 Slip the pan under the broiler and cook until the top is firm and lightly golden, about 3 minutes. Serve warm or at room temperature.

French Onion Soup

This hearty soup captures the very essence of Paris. It gained its fame as the classic middle-of-the-night restorative during the heyday of Les Halles, the former wholesale food market. It is still served in establishments big and small throughout France.

3 tablespoons unsalted butter

1 tablespoon canola oil

2½ lb (1.25 kg) yellow onions, thinly sliced

Pinch of sugar

Salt and freshly ground pepper

2 cups (16 fl oz/500 ml) light red or dry white wine

8 cups (64 fl oz/2 l) beef stock

1 bay leaf

6 thick slices coarse country bread, each 1½ inches (4 cm) thick

3 cups (12 oz/375 g) shredded Comté or Gruyère cheese

MAKES 6 SERVINGS

1 In a large, heavy pot over medium-low heat, melt the butter with the oil. Add the onions and sugar, and season with salt and pepper. Cover and cook, stirring occasionally, until the onions are meltingly soft, golden, and lightly caramelized, 25–30 minutes.

2 Add the wine, raise the heat to high, and cook until the liquid is reduced by about half, 8–10 minutes. Add the stock and bay leaf, reduce the heat to medium-low, and simmer, uncovered, until the soup is dark and fully flavored, about 45 minutes. If the liquid is evaporating too quickly and the soup tastes too strong, add a little water, then cover the pot and continue cooking.

3 Preheat the oven to 400°F (200°C). Arrange the bread slices on a baking sheet and toast, turning once, until golden, 3–5 minutes per side. Set aside.

4 Remove the bay leaf from the soup and discard. Ladle the hot soup into ovenproof soup bowls arranged on a baking sheet. Place a piece of toast on top of the soup in each bowl and sprinkle with the cheese. Bake until the cheese melts and the toasts are lightly browned around the edges, 10–15 minutes. Serve at once.

Sweet and Sour Onions

Romans have had a taste for sweet and sour since ancient times, when honey, grape must, or sweet wine provided the sweet, and vinegar or *garum* (a fish sauce) the sour. These onions, cooked until golden brown and tender, are ubiquitous in the colder months, complementing simply prepared meat dishes.

1 lb (500 g) small, flat onions such as Cipolline or Borettana, or small boiling onions

2 tablespoons extra-virgin olive oil

¼ cup (2 oz/60 g) sugar

Salt

½ cup (4 fl oz/125 ml) white wine vinegar

½ cup (4 fl oz/125 ml) dry white wine

MAKES 2–4 SERVINGS

1 Cut off the root end of each onion and remove the papery skin and the outer layer if it is blemished. Alternatively, bring a pot of water to a boil. Add the onions, boil for 1 minute, drain, and immerse in cold water to cool. Cut off the root ends, then squeeze each onion to slip it from its skin. Rinse to remove any residual skin or dirt.

2 Place the onions in a single layer in a heavy saucepan or deep frying pan. Drizzle with the oil, sprinkle with the sugar and ¼ teaspoon salt, and add the vinegar, wine, and ½ cup (4 fl oz/125 ml) water. Stir just to mix.

3 Place the pan over medium heat and bring to a boil. Reduce the heat to medium-low and simmer, uncovered, until much of the liquid has evaporated and a thick sauce remains in the pan, about 1 hour. The onions should be quite tender and golden brown. Transfer to a serving bowl and serve warm or at room temperature.

Note: The onions will keep nicely, tightly covered, in the refrigerator for a few days.

Pickled Red Onions

1 habanero chile

2 small red onions, thinly sliced

⅓ cup (3 fl oz/80 ml) fresh lime juice

2 cloves garlic, slightly smashed

⅛ teaspoon dried oregano, preferably Mexican

Sea salt and freshly ground pepper

MAKES ABOUT 2 CUPS
(7 OZ/220 G)

1 Using tongs, roast the chile over the flames of a gas-stove burner, turning it occasionally, until the skin is blackened and blistered. Alternatively, roast it under a preheated broiler (grill). Set aside.

2 Place the onion slices in a heatproof bowl and add boiling water to cover. Let soak, 2–3 minutes. Drain the onions, transfer to a small bowl, and toss with the lime juice, garlic, oregano, 1 teaspoon salt, and ¼ teaspoon pepper. Bury the chile in the bottom of the onions. Let marinate for 1 hour; stir occasionally so that all of the onions come into contact with the chile. Remove the habanero or place it atop the onions as a garnish, and serve.

Note: The onions will keep for 2 weeks, covered, in the refrigerator.

Stir-Fried Long Beans

Long beans, also known as yard-long beans, can be 18 inches (45 cm) or more in length. Most are dark green, but a pale green variety sometimes turns up in Asian markets. There you'll also find jars of the Thai roasted chile paste and fish sauce called for in this recipe, as well as Thai basil, which has a more anise-like perfume than Mediterranean basil.

Fine sea salt

1 lb (500 g) long beans, ends trimmed, cut into 4-inch (10-cm) lengths

1½ tablespoons peanut oil

1½ tablespoons Thai roasted chile paste

1 tablespoon Thai or Vietnamese fish sauce

⅓ cup (⅓ oz/10 g) fresh Thai basil leaves

MAKES 4 SERVINGS

1 Bring a large pot of water to a boil. Salt the water, then add the long beans and cook until barely tender, about 3 minutes. Drain and rinse with cold water to stop the cooking. Thoroughly pat dry.

2 Heat a wok or large frying pan over medium-high heat. Add the peanut oil and swirl to coat the bottom. Add the beans and the chile paste and stir-fry until the beans are coated with the seasoning. (The chile paste will clump at first but will eventually dissolve and coat the beans nicely.) If the beans are still a little underdone, add 1–2 tablespoons water, cover, and let them steam until they are done to your taste. Uncover and sprinkle with the fish sauce.

3 Remove from the heat, add the basil, and toss to distribute. Transfer to a warmed serving dish and serve at once.

Asian Vegetables

ASIAN HERBS

Many Western supermarkets stock Thai basil and cilantro (fresh coriander), but smart shoppers go to Asian markets for the best selection of Asian herbs. Among the favorites are kaffir lime leaf, kari leaf, shiso, and *rau ram*. Kaffir lime leaves have a citrus fragrance that enlivens Thai soups. Kari leaf, or curry leaf, adds aroma to south Indian dishes. Japanese shiso has a minty taste, and *rau ram*, eaten raw, adds its grassy taste to salads.

BOK CHOY

The most typical bok choy has snowy white stems, a bulbous base, and deep green leaves. It is cut up and added to stir-fries, chow mein, wonton soup, and other dishes in which its mildly bitter flavor is appreciated. Shanghai bok choy, a petite member of the family, has pale green, cupped stems and slightly darker green leaves. It is increasingly a favorite, even in non-Asian kitchens, for its shapeliness and mild flavor. Cooks halve it and steam it or add it to soups.

LONG BEANS

Long beans—also known as yard-long beans or asparagus beans—are unrelated to Western green beans. They are a cousin of black-eyed peas but long beans are always eaten in the pod, not shelled. They have a more intense taste and chewier texture than Blue Lake beans or *haricots verts* and are often stir-fried. The plants perform best in warm climates, where it is said that you can practically watch them grow.

DAIKON

A long, white, relatively mild type of radish, daikon is increasingly available in Western supermarkets. The name is Japanese, but daikon is also regularly used in kitchens throughout Asia, and is especially common in Korea. Daikon may be simmered in soups and stews, or pickled, as for kimchi. Chefs who blend the cuisines of East and West often use it in salads.

ASIAN HERBS

ASIAN EGGPLANT

LEMONGRASS

SOYBEANS

BOK CHOY

LONG BEANS

DAIKON

BITTER MELON

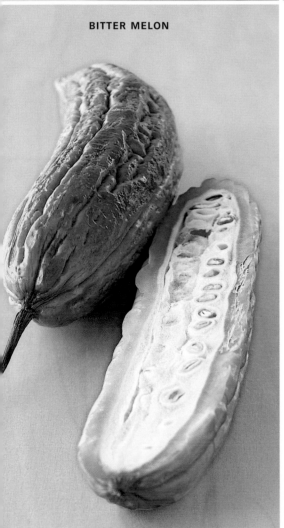

ASIAN EGGPLANT

Asian markets carry eggplants (aubergines) of remarkable variety. Some are elongated and much more slender than the Western globe eggplant. Others are small, white, and round and about the size of an egg, providing a clue to the source of the vegetable's name. Some Asian eggplants are pale green or streaked with green and white. Others range from pale lavender to purple to almost black. The elongated ones may be used interchangeably in recipes.

LEMONGRASS

An essential seasoning in Southeast Asian restaurants and an increasingly popular aromatic among non-Asian chefs, lemongrass lends a sprightly citrus flavor to soups, sauces, and braised dishes. Resembling a long, woody green (spring) onion, it must be trimmed of its coarse leafy tops and tough exterior, then thinly sliced or smashed to release its aroma. Western cooks use it to flavor everything from scallops to sorbet.

SOYBEANS

Known as *edamame* in Japanese, soybeans in the pod have become enormously popular, with supermarkets now stocking them in the freezer or refrigerated case, precooked and packaged. In summer, you might find them fresh at farmers' markets or in specialty-produce stores. Fresh soybeans resemble sugar snap peas but are soft and fuzzy. The beans inside are shiny with a nutty flavor. Japanese restaurants boil the whole beans in salted water and serve them as a snack.

BITTER MELON

The name speaks the truth. Bitter melon, which looks like a ridged, warty cucumber, is indeed bitter, due to the presence of quinine. For Westerners, it is an acquired taste, but Chinese diners appreciate its cooling nature. The melon is usually seeded, with the surrounding seed membrane removed, but not peeled. Typically, it is cooked with pungent ingredients such as chiles and salted black beans.

Pea Soup

In nineteenth-century London, soup made from dried peas was sold from street barrows. The peas were cooked into a thick soup that not only was filling but also helped fend off the damp chill. The soup was known as London Particular after the famously dense, sulfurous smog that enveloped the city. To this day, very thick fog is called a "pea souper." Hearty, old-fashioned winter pea soups such as this recipe are made with split peas, while lighter versions use English peas.

1 cup (7 oz/220 g) yellow or green split peas

2 tablespoons sunflower oil

¼ lb (125 g) bacon, finely diced

1 yellow onion, coarsely diced

1 clove garlic, coarsely chopped

1 carrot, peeled and coarsely diced

2 celery stalks, coarsely diced

Leaves of 1 fresh flat-leaf (Italian) parsley sprig, plus extra for garnish (optional)

Sea salt and freshly ground pepper

MAKES 4 SERVINGS

1 Pick over the peas, discarding any grit or misshapen peas. Rinse well, place in a large bowl, and add water to cover generously. Let soak for at least 12 hours or up to overnight.

2 In a large saucepan over low heat, warm the sunflower oil. Add the bacon and cook, stirring frequently, until it releases its fat, about 3 minutes. Add the onion, garlic, carrot, and celery and cook, stirring occasionally, until soft, about 10 minutes.

3 Drain the peas and add to the pan along with the parsley leaves and 7 cups (56 fl oz/1.75 l) water. Bring to a boil, reduce the heat to low, cover partially, and simmer until the peas are meltingly soft, about 2 hours. Halfway through the cooking time, add about 2½ cups (20 fl oz/625 ml) water to replenish the cooking liquid.

4 Purée the soup with an immersion blender or transfer to a food processor and purée. Strain the puréed soup through a coarse-mesh sieve into a clean saucepan. Gently reheat over medium-low heat, stirring occasionally and diluting with water if it is too thick. Season with salt and pepper.

5 Ladle the soup into warmed bowls, garnish with parsley leaves if desired, and serve at once.

Peas with Basil

Fresh peas are one example of the premium Italians put on seasonal ingredients. For most of the year, *piselli* tend to be absent from menus and markets. In spring, however, they abound. They are sold still in their pods, heaped in baskets at farmers' markets and the *fruttivendolo* (greengrocer), though some vendors sell small quantities that they have shucked while passing the time between customers.

4 lb (2 kg) fresh peas in their pods

6 tablespoons (3 fl oz/90 ml) extra-virgin olive oil

1 yellow onion, chopped

1 teaspoon sugar

Salt and freshly ground pepper

Handful of fresh basil leaves

MAKES 4 SERVINGS

1 Shell the peas into a bowl and set aside. You should have about 4 cups (1¼ lb/625 g) shelled peas.

2 In a heavy saucepan over low heat, warm the olive oil. Add the onion and sauté until softened and translucent but not browned, about 10 minutes. Add the peas and stir. Pour in just enough water to cover the peas, cover the pan, and cook until soft but not mushy, 7–10 minutes. Add the sugar, season with salt and pepper, and stir in the basil. Continue cooking until the peas are tender but still firm, about 5 minutes longer. Serve at once.

Peas with Paneer

Matar paneer, like tandoori chicken and lamb with spinach, is an Indian classic. The city of Varanasi, in northern India, is famous for its vegetarian cuisine, and this dish of peas and braised cheese in a spicy tomato sauce is the jewel in its crown.

3 tablespoons vegetable oil

2 teaspoons cumin seeds

2 yellow onions, finely chopped

2 tablespoons ground coriander

1 teaspoon ground turmeric

3 fresh hot green chiles such as serrano, minced

1 tablespoon peeled and grated fresh ginger

3 large tomatoes, puréed

Salt

2 cups (10 oz/315 g) fresh or thawed frozen green peas

2 cups (10 oz/315 g) fried paneer cubes (page 315)

1 teaspoon garam masala

¼ cup (⅓ oz/10 g) chopped fresh cilantro (fresh coriander)

MAKES 6 SERVINGS

1 In a frying pan over medium-high heat, warm the oil. When hot, add the cumin and cook, stirring, until it darkens, about 15 seconds. Add the onions and cook, stirring occasionally, until lightly browned, about 8 minutes. Stir in the coriander, turmeric, chiles, and ginger and cook, stirring, until the ginger is lightly fried, about 2 minutes.

2 Add the tomatoes and 1½ teaspoons salt and cook, about 5 minutes. Add 2 cups (16 fl oz/500 ml) water and the peas. Bring the sauce to a boil, reduce the heat to low, cover, and simmer gently until the peas are cooked, about 5 minutes.

3 Add the paneer and cook until it absorbs some of the moisture and puffs slightly, about 5 minutes. Add the garam masala, half of the chopped cilantro, and the thawed frozen peas, if using. Increase the heat to medium and cook until the peas are heated through, about 3 minutes. Sprinkle with the remaining cilantro and serve at once.

Grilled Asparagus

Grilled asparagus is a particularly successful match for the orange-flavored olive oils increasingly found on market shelves. The tender asparagus spears are blanched first, then seared on a hot grill and topped off with shaved Parmigiano-Reggiano.

2 lb (1 kg) asparagus

Sea salt

Ice water

1 tablespoon extra-virgin olive oil

1½ teaspoons orange-flavored olive oil

Wedge of Parmigiano-Reggiano cheese

MAKES 4 SERVINGS

1 Snap off the tough ends of the asparagus spears. Bring a large pot of water to a boil. Salt the water, then add the asparagus. Boil just until the spears lose their raw taste, about 2 minutes for medium-sized spears. Transfer to a bowl of ice water, then drain and pat dry.

2 Prepare a charcoal or gas grill for direct grilling over high heat. If the grill rack is adjustable, position it about 3 inches (7.5 cm) from the fire. Brush the asparagus spears with the extra-virgin olive oil and season with salt. Place them on the grill rack, laying them across the bars. Cook until blistered and lightly charred, then turn and cook until blistered and charred on the other side, 1–2 minutes per side.

3 Transfer to a platter. Drizzle with the orange olive oil and toss gently. Thinly shave 2 oz (60 g) of the cheese over the asparagus. Toss again gently and serve at once.

Asparagus with Egg and Parmesan

Thick-stalked cultivated asparagus is used for this Florentine dish, which, though meatless, is considered substantial enough to be offered as a main course in some restaurants. Serve it with a salad of baby lettuces and country bread.

20 medium- to thick-stalked asparagus spears, about 1 lb (500 g) total weight

2 tablespoons unsalted butter

4 extra-large eggs

Salt and freshly ground pepper

½ cup (2 oz/60 g) freshly grated Parmigiano-Reggiano cheese

MAKES 4 SERVINGS

1 Bring a large pot of water to a boil. Snap off the tough end from each asparagus spear. Using a vegetable peeler, remove the tough outer skin of each spear to within about 2 inches (5 cm) of the tip.

2 Divide the spears into 4 equal bunches and tie each with kitchen string. Add the bundles, tips up, to the boiling water and cook until tender but firm, 4–6 minutes. Drain, remove the strings, and arrange the spears on individual plates.

3 In a large frying pan over medium heat, melt the butter. Break each egg into the pan, taking care not to puncture the yolk or overlap the whites. Cook for 2 minutes, then season with salt and pepper. Add 2 tablespoons water to the pan, cover, and cook until the whites are solid but the yolks are still runny, about 2 minutes. Drape 1 egg over each serving of asparagus. Sprinkle with the cheese and serve at once.

Zucchini and Corn Timbales

3 small zucchini (courgettes), trimmed

2½ cups (15 oz/470 g) fresh or briefly thawed frozen corn kernels

5 eggs

1 tablespoon sugar

1 tablespoon all-purpose (plain) flour

1 tablespoon heavy (double) cream

Sea salt

½ teaspoon dried thyme

Hot water

For the sauce

4 poblano chiles

4 tablespoons (2 oz/60 g) unsalted butter

½ white onion, finely chopped

3 cups (24 fl oz/750 ml) milk, scalded

¼ cup (1½ oz/45 g) all-purpose (plain) flour

Sea salt and freshly ground pepper

MAKES 6 SERVINGS

1 Preheat the oven to 350°F (180°C). Butter six 1-cup (8-fl oz/250-ml) timbale molds or ramekins and set aside.

2 Using a vegetable peeler, remove long, narrow strips of peel from 1 zucchini. Cut each strip into 3-inch (7.5-cm) lengths. You will need 12 pieces. Bring a small saucepan of water to a boil, add the zucchini pieces, and cook for 2 minutes. Drain, rinse, and lay out on a plate.

3 In a blender or food processor, combine the corn kernels and ½ cup (4 fl oz/125 ml) water. Add the eggs, sugar, flour, cream, and 1 teaspoon salt, and blend well. Set aside. Using the largest holes on a grater, grate all 3 zucchini and measure out 1 cup (5 oz/155 g). Sprinkle with salt, toss well, and let stand, about 10 minutes. Squeeze the zucchini in a kitchen towel, then stir it into the corn mixture along with the thyme. Divide the mixture among the molds.

4 Place the molds in a baking pan, not touching. Pour in hot water to reach halfway up the sides of the molds. Bake until a knife inserted into the middle of a timbale comes out oily but clean, about 45 minutes.

5 To make the sauce, preheat the broiler (grill). Place the chiles on a baking sheet and roast, turning occasionally, until they are evenly blistered and blackened, 6–8 minutes. Set aside to cool. Peel off the charred skins. Slit the chiles open and remove the seeds and veins. In a saucepan over medium heat, melt 1 tablespoon of the butter. Add the onion and sauté until translucent, 4–5 minutes. Transfer to a blender along with the chiles and ½ cup (4 fl oz/125 ml) of the hot milk. Purée until very smooth. In a frying pan over medium-low heat, melt the remaining 3 tablespoons butter. Sprinkle in the flour and stir, about 2 minutes. Add 1 cup (8 fl oz/250 ml) of the hot milk and whisk until smooth. Stir in the remaining 1½ cups (12 fl oz/375 ml) milk and the puréed chiles. Cook, stirring frequently, until the sauce is reduced and thickened, about 4 minutes. Season with salt and pepper. Keep warm.

6 Remove the timbales from the pan and let cool slightly. Run a knife around the inside of each, place a plate on top, and turn the timbale out onto the plate. For the garnish, arrange 2 zucchini pieces in curls on top of each timbale. Spoon the sauce around the timbales and serve at once.

ITALY

Zucchini with Almonds and Pecorino

This simple dish can be served either as a first course or as a side dish for an Italian-inspired summer meal, such as grilled steaks drizzled with olive oil.

6 zucchini (courgettes), about 1½ lb (750 g) total weight

¼ cup (2 fl oz/60 ml) extra-virgin olive oil

¼ cup (1 oz/30 g) sliced (flaked) almonds

Sea salt and freshly ground pepper

Wedge of pecorino romano cheese

MAKES 4 SERVINGS

1 Trim the ends from each zucchini and then cut them lengthwise into slices ⅛ inch (3 mm) thick. Cut each slice into matchsticks about 2 inches (5 cm) long.

2 Divide the olive oil between 2 frying pans and place over high heat. When the oil is hot, add the almonds, dividing them between the pans, and cook, stirring constantly, until golden brown, about 2 minutes. Divide the zucchini between the pans, turn off the heat, and toss to coat with the hot oil until the zucchini is warmed through, about 30 seconds. Season with salt and pepper. Transfer to a small serving platter and top with shavings of the pecorino romano. Serve at once.

TURKEY

Zucchini Fritters

Although these fritters are at their best when hot, in many Turkish cafés they are served at room temperature accompanied by *tzatziki*, the popular yogurt-cucumber sauce. Traditionally part of the *meze* course, they also make a nice side dish.

1 lb (500 g) small zucchini (courgettes), coarsely grated

Salt and freshly ground pepper

½ lb (250 g) feta cheese, or equal parts feta and kasseri or ricotta salata

6 green (spring) onions, white and pale green parts only, minced

½ cup (½ oz/15 g) chopped fresh dill

¼ cup (⅓ oz/10 g) chopped fresh flat-leaf (Italian) parsley

¼ cup (⅓ oz/10 g) chopped fresh mint

3 eggs, lightly beaten

1 cup (5 oz/155 g) all-purpose (plain) flour

Peanut oil for frying

MAKES 4 SERVINGS

1 Place the zucchini in a colander. Sprinkle lightly with salt, toss well, and let stand for 30 minutes. Squeeze the zucchini in a kitchen towel to remove the excess liquid. Transfer to a bowl. Crumble the cheese over the zucchini and add the green onions, dill, parsley, mint, eggs, and flour. Season with salt and pepper. Stir to mix well.

2 Pour peanut oil to a depth of ¼ inch (6 mm) into a deep frying pan and heat over medium-high heat. When the oil is hot, drop spoonfuls of the batter into the oil, being careful not to crowd the pan. Fry, turning once, until nicely browned on both sides, 2–3 minutes per side. Using a slotted spoon, transfer to paper towels to drain. Arrange the fritters on a warmed platter and serve at once.

Pecorino Toscano

FOGLIA DI NOCE

Cheese makers refer to pecorino aged under walnut leaves as being *fermentato*, or fermented. This version of sheep's milk cheese is made by placing a three-month-old pecorino in an old wine barrel, surrounding it with walnut leaves, and aging it for at least another forty days. The piquant cheese is easy to spot at the market since withered walnut leaves are usually still pressed onto the surface of the rind. It is more costly than a traditionally made pecorino.

ERBOLINO

One of the up-and-coming varieties of herbed, fresh pecorino, *erbolino* is flavored with garlic, red pepper flakes, parsley, and rosemary. Soft herbed cheeses are best in the springtime, when the sheep feed on abundant spring grasses and produce large quantities of flavorful milk. *Erbolino* makes a good *stuzzichino* (snack), cut into cubes and eaten alone or sliced into thin wedges and served with crisp, crackerlike *schiacciata*.

PECORINO BLU

Blue cheeses are made by exposing cheeses to molds that form blue or green veins throughout, giving them an intense flavor and scent. Gorgonzola, from the town of the same name near Milan, is Italy's most famous Italian *blu*. Fattoria Corzano e Paterno's *pecorino blu* is made by curdling sheep's milk in a particular way, then adding to it the same penicillin culture used to make Gorgonzola. The result is an unusual, elegant dessert cheese.

PECORINO DI FOSSA

The making of this cheese is mysterious enough to pique the interest of even the most skeptical. During August, rounds of specially selected three- to four-month-old pecorino are wrapped in white cotton and sealed in deep earthen *fosse* (pits), with walls covered in hay and wild grasses, for one hundred days. When the pit is opened, the cloth is covered in a fine mold, and the cheese that emerges is spicy and pungent.

FOGLIA DI NOCE

PECORINO STAGIONATO

PECORINO GRAN RISERVA

BUCCIA DI ROSPO

ERBOLINO

PECORINO BLU

PECORINO DI FOSSA

PECORINO FRESCO DOLCE

PECORINO STAGIONATO

Just how *stagionato* (aged) an aged pecorino will be depends on the *caseificio* (cheese dairy). Typically, a *pecorino stagionato* spends about nine months in the cheese cellar, during which time each cheese is turned periodically and may be rubbed with *la morchia* (olive oil dregs) and covered in *cenere* (ash). Ash is said to help draw humidity out of the cheese, so that once it is fully aged, its consistency will allow the cheese to be cut easily into thin shavings.

PECORINO GRAN RISERVA

This artisan cheese maker's premier aged pecorino may spend up to eighteen months in the cellar before being sent to market. The structure of this cheese causes it to cut rather unevenly, not unlike Parmigiano-Reggiano, which is aged for even longer. A glass of full-bodied red wine, a wedge of *pecorino gran riserva*, and a bit of chestnut honey, quince paste, or fig jam make a lovely end to an elegant meal.

BUCCIA DI ROSPO

Only one cheese maker, Fattoria Corzano e Paterno, makes this cheese, poetically named *buccia di rospo* (toad's skin) for its warty surface. Like many delicacies, it was born of error—in this case when excess humidity in the cheese cellar caused a pecorino to ferment under its rind. The resulting cheese is creamier than most pecorinos and has a slightly acrid odor and full flavor. *Buccia di rospo* has been compared with the sharp, buttery Taleggio of Lombardy.

PECORINO FRESCO DOLCE

After *marzolino* (the super-fresh, soft cheese made in spring with sheep's milk), *pecorino fresco* is the least aged of all pecorinos. It has a pale, smooth rind, a creamy interior, and a delicate, nutty flavor referred to as *dolce*, which translates as "sweet," but in this context means only lightly salted. As pecorino ages, it becomes more *saporito*, literally "flavorful," though in Tuscany the word denotes a pleasant saltiness.

Corn Salad

The influence of the Choctaws is evident in this traditional Cajun stir-fry, a casual farmhouse jumble that is much more than the sum of its parts. Also known as *maquechoux*, it is a specialty throughout southeast Louisiana, where every cook has a favorite version. Some include cream, bacon, ham, or shellfish. Fresh sweet corn, however, is essential. In this version, fresh flavors and bright colors are free to shine.

6 ears corn, husked

3 tablespoons unsalted butter

1 yellow onion, chopped

1 green bell pepper (capsicum), seeded and chopped

2 ripe tomatoes, peeled, seeded, and chopped

Sea salt and freshly ground black pepper

Cayenne pepper

MAKES 4–6 SERVINGS

1 In a large, shallow bowl, stand each ear of corn upright, stem end down. Using a large knife, slice downward to remove all the kernels. Then, using the back of the knife, scrape the cob downward in the same fashion, releasing the creamy "milk." Discard the cobs and set the corn kernels and their milk aside.

2 In a large frying pan over medium heat, melt the butter. Add the onion and bell pepper and sauté until very tender and lightly browned, 10–15 minutes. Add the tomatoes and the corn kernels and their milk and stir just until the kernels are crisp-tender, 2–3 minutes. Season well with salt, black pepper, and cayenne. Spoon into a warmed serving bowl and serve at once.

Corn with Chipotle-Lime Butter

Little known outside the Mexican community until the 1990s, chipotle chiles, which are dried and smoked jalapeños, have become a huge crossover hit in the United States. Canned chipotles in adobo sauce—whole chiles preserved with tomato, vinegar, and spices—can be found in Mexican markets and most supermarkets. Paired with butter and lime, the chiles lend a zesty flavor to corn on the cob. Store leftover chipotles in the refrigerator in an airtight glass jar.

For the butter

½ cup (4 oz/125 g) unsalted butter, at room temperature

3 tablespoons minced fresh cilantro (fresh coriander)

1 tablespoon grated lime zest

1 chipotle chile in adobo sauce, finely minced

Sea salt

6 large ears corn, yellow or white, husked

MAKES 6 SERVINGS

1 In a bowl, combine the butter, cilantro, lime zest, and chipotle chile and stir until smooth. Season with salt and set aside.

2 Bring a large pot of water to a boil. Add the corn, cover, and remove from the heat. Let stand for 5 minutes.

3 Remove the corn and place on a kitchen towel to drain briefly, then transfer to a serving platter. Slather with the seasoned butter and serve at once.

Provençal Tomato Tart

For the pastry

1½ cups (7½ oz/235 g) all-purpose (plain) flour

2 tablespoons freshly grated Parmesan cheese

1 tablespoon fresh rosemary leaves

Sea salt and freshly ground pepper

½ cup (4 oz/125 g) chilled unsalted butter

3 tablespoons ice water

For the filling

¼ lb (125 g) fresh goat cheese

3 tablespoons chopped fresh basil, plus 1 sprig for garnish

Freshly ground pepper

4 ripe tomatoes, cut into slices ¼ inch (6 mm) thick

Extra-virgin olive oil for drizzling

Coarse sea salt for sprinkling

MAKES 6 SERVINGS

1 To make the pastry, in a food processor, combine the flour, Parmesan, rosemary, ½ teaspoon salt, and ¼ teaspoon pepper and process for about 30 seconds. Cut the butter into 8 pieces and distribute evenly over the flour mixture. Pulse about 10 times, or until the mixture resembles coarse meal. Sprinkle the ice water over the surface and pulse about 7 more times. (The dough will still appear rather loose, but should hold together when pressed between your fingers.) Shape the dough into a disk ¾ inch (2 cm) thick, wrap tightly in plastic wrap, and refrigerate for at least 30 minutes or up to overnight.

2 Preheat the oven to 425°F (220°C). On a lightly floured work surface, roll out the dough into a round about 12 inches (30 cm) in diameter and ⅛ inch (3 mm) thick. Wrap the round loosely around the pin, then carefully unroll it into a 9- or 10-inch (23- or 25-cm) tart pan with a removable bottom, allowing the excess to drape over the sides. Press the pastry gently into the bottom and sides of the pan, then roll the pin across the top of the pan, trimming off the excess dough.

3 Prick the pastry evenly over the bottom with a fork, then line with a sheet of parchment (baking) paper. Fill the pastry with pie weights or dried beans and bake until set, about 8 minutes. Remove the pie weights and parchment, return the pastry to the oven, and continue to bake until tender and golden, 8–12 minutes longer. Transfer to a wire rack and let cool to room temperature.

4 To prepare the filling, in a food processor, combine the goat cheese, 2 tablespoons of the chopped basil, and ¼ teaspoon pepper. Process until smooth, about 30 seconds.

5 Spread the cheese mixture evenly over the cooled crust. Beginning at the outer edge, arrange the tomato slices in slightly overlapping concentric circles. Drizzle lightly with olive oil and sprinkle with coarse salt, pepper, and the remaining 1 tablespoon chopped basil. Garnish with the basil sprig and serve at once.

Cherry Tomato–Goat Cheese Tartlets

Heirloom tomatoes—with such intriguing names as Extra Eros Zlatolaska, Banana Legs, and Radiator Charlie's Mortgage Lifter—come in myriad shapes and colors. Rather than how well they travel or how long a shelf life they might have, they are grown for their incomparable flavor, which is showcased in these tartlets.

20–25 fresh basil leaves, cut into thin strips

2 cloves garlic, finely minced

2 cups (12 oz/375 g) mixed small heirloom or cherry tomatoes, halved

¼ cup (2 fl oz/60 ml) extra-virgin olive oil, plus extra for drizzling

Sea salt

1 sheet good-quality frozen puff pastry, about 10 by 12 inches (25 by 30 cm), partially thawed

5 oz (155 g) fresh goat cheese

About ½ cup (4 fl oz/125 ml) milk

1 large red heirloom tomato such as black krim, brandywine, or purple Cherokee

1 large yellow or white heirloom tomato such as Hugh's or great white

6 green zebra tomatoes or other medium tomatoes, quartered

MAKES 6 SERVINGS

1 Preheat the oven to 400°F (200°C). In a small bowl, combine two-thirds of the basil strips, the garlic, and the halved small tomatoes. Add the ¼ cup (2 fl oz/60 ml) olive oil, season with salt, and toss gently. Set aside.

2 Place the puff pastry on a lightly floured work surface. Cut the sheet into 6 rectangles, each about 4 by 5 inches (10 by 13 cm). Place the rectangles on a baking sheet and prick them all over with a fork to prevent the pastry from rising. Bake until light golden brown, 10–12 minutes. Remove from the oven and let stand on the baking sheet. Leave the oven on.

3 Meanwhile, in a small bowl, using a fork, mash the goat cheese. Slowly pour in the milk, stirring until the mixture is smooth but not runny. (You may not need all of the milk.)

4 Cut the large tomatoes into slices ½ inch (12 mm) thick and season with salt. Gently spread 1 heaping tablespoon of the goat cheese mixture onto each pastry rectangle. Using only the large, center tomato slices, place a slice on each tart. Return the pan to the oven and bake until the tomatoes are warmed through, about 5 minutes.

5 Place the tarts on individual plates. Season the quartered tomatoes with salt and divide evenly among the tarts. Top each tart with a mound of the tomato and basil mixture. Drizzle with the olive oil. Scatter the reserved basil strips around each plate and serve at once.

Tomato and Basil Bruschetta

It seems, and is, so simple—garlic-rubbed toast with raw tomato on top—but like many of Italy's favorite foods, *bruschetta al pomodoro* brings you face to face with the brilliance of basic ingredients.

1 large or 2 medium ripe tomatoes, or about 16 cherry tomatoes

About 16 fresh basil leaves

4 slices coarse country bread, about ½ inch (12 mm) thick

2 cloves garlic, peeled and left whole

Salt

2–4 tablespoons (1–2 fl oz/ 30–60 ml) extra-virgin olive oil

MAKES 2 SERVINGS

1 Core the tomatoes and cut into slices ¼ inch (6 mm) thick. If using cherry tomatoes, cut them in half. Tear any large basil leaves into pieces; leave the smaller leaves whole.

2 Preheat the oven to 375°F (190°C). Arrange the bread slices on a baking sheet and bake until golden, 3–4 minutes.

3 Rub a garlic clove vigorously over one side of each slice of toasted bread. (The rough surface of the bread will shred the garlic.) Divide the bread, garlic side up, between 2 plates. Arrange the tomatoes in a single layer on the bread. If you are using cherry tomatoes, squash the halves, cut side down, into the bread. Sprinkle with salt and drizzle with the olive oil. Distribute the basil evenly on top. Serve at once.

Gazpacho

11 slices day-old coarse country white bread, about 10 oz (315 g) total weight, crusts removed

2 tablespoons sherry vinegar

3 lb (1.5 kg) ripe tomatoes, peeled and seeded

½ yellow onion, cut into chunks

1 cucumber, peeled, halved, seeded, and cut into chunks

1 red bell pepper (capsicum), seeded and cut into chunks

1 cup (8 fl oz/250 ml) extra-virgin olive oil

Sea salt

For the garnish

1 small cucumber, peeled, halved, seeded, and diced

1 red bell pepper (capsicum), seeded and diced

2 hard-boiled eggs, chopped

2 slices serrano ham, finely chopped

MAKES 6–8 SERVINGS

1 Place 9 slices of the bread in a food processor and spoon the vinegar over them. Add the tomatoes, onion, cucumber and bell pepper chunks, ⅔ cup (5 fl oz/160 ml) of the olive oil, and 1 cup (8 fl oz/250 ml) water, and pulse until smooth for a thick gazpacho. For a thinner gazpacho, add more water and pulse again. Season with salt and more vinegar, if desired. Cover and refrigerate until well chilled, for at least 2 hours or up to 4 hours.

2 Cut the remaining 2 bread slices into ½-inch (12-mm) cubes. In a frying pan over medium-high heat, warm the remaining ⅓ cup (3 fl oz/90 ml) olive oil. Add the bread cubes and fry, stirring often, until golden brown on all sides, about 3 minutes. Transfer to paper towels to drain.

3 Just before serving, transfer the gazpacho to a serving bowl and add a handful of ice cubes. Place the diced cucumber, diced bell pepper, hard-boiled eggs, ham, and fried bread cubes in small bowls. Pass the bowls at the table for diners to garnish their soup as desired.

Purée of Artichoke Soup

Like many French soups and stocks, this one calls for a *bouquet garni*—a bundle of aromatic herbs that seasons the soup and is then easily discarded. To make one, place 2-inch (5-cm) pieces of celery stalk, a few sprigs each of flat-leaf (Italian) parsley and thyme, a bay leaf, and 8 to 10 peppercorns onto an 8-inch (20-cm) square of cheesecloth (muslin). Bring up the corners and tie with kitchen string.

For the cèpe butter

1 tablespoon small pieces dried cèpe mushrooms

Boiling water

1 small clove garlic

Salt

4 tablespoons (2 oz/60 g) unsalted butter, at room temperature

For the soup

1 tablespoon white wine vinegar, or juice of ½ lemon

4 large or 5 or 6 medium artichokes, about 2½ lb (1.25 kg) total weight

1 tablespoon unsalted butter

3 tablespoons extra-virgin olive oil

4 or 5 shallots, 2½–3 oz (75–90 g) total weight, chopped

2 cloves garlic, chopped

½ cup (4 fl oz/125 ml) dry white wine

2 cups (16 fl oz/500 ml) chicken stock

1 *bouquet garni* (see above)

Salt and freshly ground pepper

MAKES 4–6 SERVINGS

1 To make the cèpe butter, in a small bowl, combine the mushrooms with boiling water to cover. Let soak, covered, 30–60 minutes. Drain well, squeezing out the excess liquid. In a small food processor, crush the garlic with a pinch of salt. Add the mushrooms and process to mix, then work in the butter. Transfer to a bowl and refrigerate.

2 Fill a large bowl with water and add the vinegar. Working with 1 artichoke at a time, cut off the stem flush with the bottom, then peel and slice the stem and add to the vinegar water. Snap off the tough outer leaves, placing them in a saucepan, until you reach the pale, tender inner leaves. Cut the top one-third off the artichoke, removing the pointed tips of the leaves. Quarter the artichoke lengthwise and cut out the fuzzy choke. Add the quarters to the vinegar water.

3 Add 5 cups (40 fl oz/1.25 l) water to the saucepan and cook, uncovered, until the water is green and flavored, 10–15 minutes. Strain through a fine-mesh sieve into a measuring pitcher. Discard the leaves and set the cooking water aside. You should have about 4 cups (32 fl oz/1 l).

4 Drain the artichokes and slice into uniform pieces. In a large, heavy saucepan over medium-high heat, melt the butter with the olive oil. Add the shallots and garlic and sauté until softened, 3–5 minutes. Add the artichokes and sauté until half-cooked, about 5 minutes.

5 Add the wine and cook until reduced to 1–2 tablespoons. Add the reserved water, stock, and *bouquet garni*. Bring to a boil, reduce the heat to medium, and cook until the artichokes are tender enough to purée, 10–15 minutes.

6 Remove and discard the *bouquet garni*. Using a slotted spoon, transfer the artichokes to a food processor, add a small amount of the cooking liquid, and purée until smooth. Return the purée to the saucepan (straining it through a fine-mesh sieve for the smoothest soup) and stir to combine with the cooking liquid. Season with salt and pepper.

7 Ladle into bowls, top each portion with ½–1 teaspoon of the cèpe butter, and serve at once.

Braised Artichokes

This dish is remarkable for three things: the mystique of the *carciofo romanesco* (Roman globe artichoke), the special way it is cut, and the mintlike *mentuccia* (Roman for *nepitella*, or calamint). If you don't have access to Roman artichokes, buy the most tender artichokes available and aggressively remove the inedible parts.

Juice of ½ lemon

4 young, tender artichokes

3 tablespoons fresh *nepitella* (calamint), peppermint, pennyroyal, flat-leaf (Italian) parsley leaves, or a combination

1 clove garlic (optional)

4 tablespoons (2 fl oz/60 ml) extra-virgin olive oil, or as needed

Salt

½ cup (4 fl oz/125 ml) dry white wine, or as needed

MAKES 4 SERVINGS

1 Fill a bowl with water and add the lemon juice. Working with 1 artichoke at a time, trim off the base of the stem, leaving about 2 inches (5 cm) attached, then peel the stem's dark outer layer. Snap off the tough outer leaves until you reach the pale, tender inner leaves. Hold the artichoke in one hand and a small, sharp knife in the other. Rest the artichoke against the knife blade without pressing and turn the artichoke against the blade. Then cut about ½ inch (12 mm) off the top. Add the trimmed artichoke to the water.

2 Finely chop together the herb(s) and the garlic, if using. Transfer to a small bowl, add 2 tablespoons of the olive oil and ¼ teaspoon salt, and mix well.

3 Using an apple corer or your fingers (if the artichoke is very tender), remove some of the choke from the center of each artichoke to create a small cavity. Put 2 spoonfuls of the herb mixture into each, reserving the rest. Choose a heavy pot large enough to hold the artichokes snugly in a single layer and tall enough to accommodate the stems, and place the artichokes in it, stems up. Sprinkle the remaining herb mixture over the artichokes, then drizzle with 2 or more tablespoons olive oil. Place over medium heat and brown lightly on the bottom, about 5 minutes.

4 Pour in the wine to a depth of not more than ½ inch (12 mm). Cover the pot and place over medium heat, preferably with a flame diffuser. When the liquid boils, reduce the heat to low. Put a kitchen towel over the top of the pot, keeping its edges away from the burner, and cover with the lid. (This will draw off moisture so the artichokes will not taste boiled.) Weight the lid to keep it as tight as possible. Cook the artichokes until quite tender, up to 40 minutes depending on how young the artichokes are. Check the level of the liquid 2 or 3 times, adding wine as needed to maintain the level.

5 When the artichokes are tender, uncover and let any liquid evaporate. Continue cooking in the oil that remains in the pan, 3–5 minutes. Transfer the artichokes to a serving plate and pour any oil in the pot over the artichokes. Serve warm or at room temperature.

ITALY
Roman Artichokes

ARTICHOKE VARIETIES

Carciofo alla giudia achieves its greatest glory in late winter and early spring with the arrival of the Romanesco artichoke, a globe variety harvested around Rome. It is even better if it's also a *cimarolo*, from the *cima* (top) of the plant's main stem. *Cimaroli* are larger than the artichokes from the side branches, and the top is slightly flattened. During most of winter, Rome's markets offer delicious, albeit smaller, specimens from warmer regions.

FRITTI

Rome has a mass addiction to deep-frying. Morsels of food, some in *pastella* (batter), some in bread crumbs, and some thrown naked into the hot oil, are served in various combinations at every level of the restaurant hierarchy. Bars, *rosticcerie*, *friggitorie* (fry shops), and pizzerias serve *supplì* (page 67), and *arancini* (rice balls). A typical *fritti* lineup will feature, in addition to artichokes, batter-dipped zucchini (courgette) flowers filled with mozzarella and anchovies, nutmeg-scented potato croquettes, and crisp zucchini spears. It is usually a good idea to skip the fried snacks at neighborhood pizzerias and order them instead at gourmet shops or fine restaurants.

Perhaps the most famous dish of the Roman Jewish repertory is *carciofo alla giudia*, a deep-fried and pressed artichoke that looks like a flower dipped in bronze. The petals are crisp and the heart is tender. There is no batter or flour. The expert preparation ensures that every bit of the treat is edible.

MAKING CARCIOFI ALLA GIUDIA

TRIMMING One of the most enviable skills of the Roman cook or greengrocer is the ability to trim a raw artichoke into a neat ball atop a smooth stem, all edible. The outer leaves are pulled off, and the stem is peeled. The artichoke is then rolled against a blade to remove the tips of the outer layer. Finally, the center leaves and choke are dug out, and the artichoke is placed in water.

FRYING The damp artichokes are tossed vigorously with salt and pepper before being dropped into a deep pot of hot (330°–350°F/170°–180°C) olive oil for about 20 minutes, then drained head down. Just before serving, the fried artichokes are dropped into fresh hot oil for a brief second fry.

PRESSING After the second fry, each artichoke is pressed gently, head down, between perforated metal disks to drain off the last drops of oil. This gives the artichoke its characteristic flowerlike shape. From there, it goes directly to the plate, alone or as part of a *fritto misto*.

Curried Cauliflower Stew

A favorite of Indian children, *gobhi masala* is a delicately spiced cauliflower stew, the seasoning of which varies by region. In this recipe from Madhya Pradesh, the cauliflower is braised in a rich coconut sauce with Moghul spices. Indian cooks use the whole cauliflower—leaves and all—which adds depth to the sauce.

1 head cauliflower, about 2 lb (1 kg)

3 tablespoons *usli ghee* or vegetable oil

2 cassia leaves

1 cinnamon stick

1 teaspoon cumin seeds

1 yellow onion, finely chopped

1 tablespoon grated ginger

1 tablespoon ground coriander

½–1 teaspoon cayenne pepper

Salt

2 tomatoes, finely chopped

1 tablespoon tomato paste

1 cup (8 fl oz/250 ml) coconut milk or light (single) cream

1 boiling potato, peeled and cut into 1-inch (2.5-cm) pieces

1 teaspoon garam masala

½ cup (¾ oz/20 g) chopped fresh cilantro (fresh coriander)

MAKES 6 SERVINGS

1 Separate the cauliflower into florets and cut them into 2-inch (5-cm) pieces. Peel the stem and cut it crosswise into slices ⅛ inch (3 mm) thick. Chop the tender leaves into 2-inch (5-cm) pieces. Set aside.

2 In a large saucepan over medium heat, warm the *usli ghee*. Add the cassia leaves, cinnamon, and cumin and let sizzle for 30 seconds. Add the onion and cook, stirring occasionally, until light brown, about 3 minutes. Stir in the ginger, ground coriander, cayenne pepper to taste, 1½ teaspoons salt, tomatoes, tomato paste, ½ cup (4 fl oz/ 125 ml) of the coconut milk, and ½ cup (4 fl oz/125 ml) water. Add the cauliflower and potato, mix gently, and bring to a boil. Reduce the heat to low, cover, and cook until the vegetables are tender, 17–18 minutes.

3 Uncover and add the remaining ½ cup (4 fl oz/125 ml) coconut milk, the garam masala, and half of the cilantro. Mix well. Transfer to a warmed serving dish, sprinkle with the remaining cilantro, and serve at once.

Roasted Cauliflower

2 tablespoons capers

1 head cauliflower, about 1 lb (500 g), cored and cut into 1-inch (2.5-cm) florets

½ cup (3 oz/90 g) golden raisins (sultanas)

¼ cup (2 fl oz/60 ml) extra-virgin olive oil

Salt and freshly ground pepper

2 tablespoons finely chopped fresh flat-leaf (Italian) parsley

MAKES 4 SERVINGS

1 Preheat the oven to 400°F (200°C). If using salt-packed capers, rinse and pat dry with a paper towel. Combine the cauliflower florets, raisins, and capers on a rimmed baking sheet. Drizzle with the olive oil, sprinkle with salt and pepper, and toss to coat. Spread in an even layer. Roast, stirring occasionally, until golden brown, 20–25 minutes.

2 Transfer to a serving bowl. Sprinkle with 1 tablespoon of the parsley and toss to combine. Sprinkle the remaining parsley over the top. Serve warm or at room temperature.

Caramelized Root Vegetables

1½ lb (750 g) mixed root vegetables such as carrots, parsnips, turnips, rutabagas, sweet potatoes, and/or salsify

¼ cup (2 fl oz/60 ml) extra-virgin olive oil

¼ cup (2 fl oz/60 ml) maple syrup

Sea salt and freshly ground pepper

2 tablespoons unsalted butter, cut into small pieces

MAKES 4 SERVINGS

1 Preheat the oven to 400°F (200°C). Peel the root vegetables. Cut long, slender vegetables such as carrots and parsnips on the diagonal into 2-inch (5-cm) pieces. Cut the turnips and other round vegetables into 2-inch (5-cm) chunks. Place on a rimmed baking sheet. Drizzle with the olive oil and maple syrup, sprinkle with salt and pepper, and toss to coat with the seasoning. Spread the vegetables out in a single layer and scatter the butter pieces on top.

2 Roast the vegetables, turning them occasionally, until tender and golden brown, about 30 minutes. Transfer to a warmed serving bowl and serve at once.

MEXICO

Baked Sweet Potatoes

Sweet potatoes were a significant part of the pre-Hispanic diet but now are more apt to be found made into candies, such as the famous *camotes* of Puebla, or steam-baked and sold by vendors for a nourishing morning or evening snack.

4 sweet potatoes, well scrubbed

¾ cup (5 oz/155 g) firmly packed brown sugar or chopped *piloncillo*

⅓ cup (3 fl oz/80 ml) fresh lime juice

⅓ cup (3 fl oz/80 ml) fresh orange juice

1½ teaspoons ground cinnamon

½ teaspoon ground allspice

4 tablespoons (2 oz/60 g) unsalted butter (optional)

Sea salt and freshly ground pepper

MAKES 4 SERVINGS

1 Preheat the oven to 400°F (200°C). Poke a few holes in the top of each sweet potato and place the potatoes on a baking sheet. Bake until soft to the touch, about 45 minutes.

2 Just before the sweet potatoes are ready, in a saucepan, stir together the brown sugar, lime and orange juices, cinnamon, and allspice. Place over low heat and cook, stirring, until the sugar dissolves and the mixture is syrupy, about 3 minutes.

3 Place the potatoes in a serving dish and let cool slightly. Slit each potato lengthwise and lightly mash the flesh inside with a fork, adding 1 tablespoon butter if desired. Pour an equal amount of the syrup into each opening, season with salt and pepper, and squish the syrup into the flesh, letting it puddle in the dish. Serve at once.

Root Vegetable Crisps

Most London pubs sell packets of crisps or nuts, but stylish bars serve their own vegetable crisps, bread sticks, and marinated olives. The crisps are made from finely sliced root vegetables, such as potatoes, parsnips, and celery root, and are tossed in sea salt. Some are flavored with a dusting of chili powder or chopped fresh thyme.

1 large parsnip, peeled

1 russet potato, peeled

1 small celery root (celeriac), peeled and halved lengthwise

1 large red beet, peeled

Sunflower oil for deep-frying

Sea salt

MAKES 6 SERVINGS

1 Cut the parsnip lengthwise into slices slightly thinner than a coin. Place the slices in a bowl of water. Repeat for the potato, celery root, and beet, placing the slices of each vegetable into separate bowls of water. Set aside to soak, about 20 minutes, to remove the excess starch.

2 Pour sunflower oil to a depth of 4 inches (10 cm) into a large, heavy frying pan, and heat over medium-high heat to 375°F (190°C) on a deep-frying thermometer. Drain the vegetable slices and thoroughly pat dry. Carefully place a handful of parsnip slices in the hot oil and fry until golden and crisp, about 3 minutes. Using a slotted spoon, transfer to a wire rack lined with paper towels to drain. When the oil returns to 375°F (190°C), fry the remaining parsnip slices. Fry the potato slices, then the celery root slices, and finally the beet slices in the same way, letting the oil return to 375°F (190°C) before adding each batch to the pan. The potato slices will cook in 3 minutes; the celery root and beet slices will cook in 4 minutes and will crinkle slightly and will not become crisp until they begin to cool. Place the crisps in a bowl and season with salt. Serve at once.

BELGIUM
Pommes Frites

Though they're known as French fries or *pommes frites*, the deep-fried potatoes that both France and Belgium are famous for may have originated in Belgium. Sidewalk vendors of the mid-nineteenth century reportedly began frying cut potatoes in vats of hot fat. Some say it was horse fat, and that it still makes the best fries, but this recipe calls for canola oil. For the best flavor, melt a piece of beef suet in the oil.

6–8 russet or other baking potatoes, about 2 lb (1 kg) total weight

Sea salt

Canola or olive oil for deep-frying

2–3 oz (60–90 g) beef suet (optional)

MAKES 6 SERVINGS

1 Peel the potatoes if desired. Cut into thin julienne for shoestring potatoes, batons ¼–½ inch (6–12 mm) thick for standard French fries, or ovals ⅛–¼ inch (3–6 mm) thick for *pommes soufflées*. Place the potatoes in a large bowl of salted water and let stand for at least 1 hour or up to 3 hours. If desired, change the water once to remove the excess starch. Drain the potatoes and pat dry.

2 Pour oil to a depth of 4–5 inches (10–13 cm) into a deep, heavy frying pan or a heavy saucepan. Add the beef suet, if using, to the cold oil and heat over medium heat to 325°F (165°C) on a deep-frying thermometer. Working in batches, add the potatoes, being careful not to crowd the pan. Fry the potatoes, stirring once or twice, until almost tender but still pale and waxy, about 2 minutes for the shoestring cut, 3–4 minutes for the ovals, 6–8 minutes for the batons. Using a slotted spoon, transfer the potatoes to paper towels to drain. Let stand for at least 5 minutes or up to 3 hours.

3 Just before serving, reheat the oil to 375°F (190°C). Again working in batches, fry the potatoes until golden brown, about 1 minute for the shoestring cut, 1–2 minutes for the batons and the ovals. Transfer to fresh paper towels to drain. Season with salt and serve hot.

Potato Gratin

This potato gratin is simplicity itself: no cheese topping or onions, just potatoes, butter, and cream, with a bit of garlic. The recipe originated in the Dauphiné, a region of mountains, forests, and pasturelands that lies between the Savoy, with its alpine lakes and snowy peaks, and Provence, home to sunshine and lavender. In bistros, this homey gratin is often served next to roasted meat or poultry.

3–5 cloves garlic, chopped

3½–4 lb (1.75–2 kg) russet potatoes, peeled

Salt and freshly ground pepper

1 cup (8 fl oz/250 ml) heavy (double) cream

4 tablespoons (2 oz/60 g) unsalted butter, cut into bits

1 tablespoon chopped fresh chives

1 tablespoon chopped fresh flat-leaf (Italian) parsley

MAKES 4–6 SERVINGS

1 Preheat the oven to 375°F (190°C). Butter a 3-qt (3-l) baking dish about 3½ inches (9 cm) deep. Sprinkle about half of the garlic over the bottom and sides of the dish.

2 Cut the potatoes into slices about ⅛ inch (3 mm) thick. Arrange a layer of slightly overlapping slices in the dish, season with salt and pepper, and pour a few spoonfuls of cream over them. Sprinkle lightly with some of the garlic. Continue layering until all the potatoes and garlic are used. Top with the remaining cream and dot with the butter.

3 Bake the potatoes until they are very tender, have absorbed all of the cream, and are golden brown on top, 1–1½ hours, raising the heat to 400°F (200°C) for the last 10–15 minutes to develop a crust.

4 Serve directly from the dish, sprinkling each portion with some of the chives and parsley.

Roasted Fingerling Potatoes

Fingerling potatoes are thin-skinned, dense, and waxy, and they cook quickly because they're small. Roasted with fresh herbs and garlic, they brown beautifully and perfume the kitchen as they cook. Small garlic cloves alongside the potatoes will probably be too caramelized to eat, but larger cloves should be soft and creamy.

1½ lb (750 g) fingerling potatoes or other waxy potatoes

2 tablespoons extra-virgin olive oil

Sea salt

1 head garlic

Leaves of 1 fresh rosemary sprig, about 6 inches (15 cm) long

MAKES 4 SERVINGS

1 Preheat the oven to 425°F (220°C). In a large bowl, toss the potatoes with the olive oil to coat. Spread them in a single layer in a roasting pan or large frying pan. Season with salt.

2 Break the garlic into individual cloves but do not peel them. Scatter the cloves and rosemary leaves around the potatoes. Bake, stirring once or twice, until the potatoes are nicely browned and easily pierced with a knife, about 30 minutes. Serve at once.

Wild Mushroom Tartlets

¼ oz (7 g) *each* dried cèpe and dried morel mushrooms

½ cup (4 fl oz/125 ml) chicken or vegetable stock, heated

4 tablespoons (2 oz/60 g) unsalted butter, or as needed

2 shallots, chopped

2 cloves garlic, chopped

3–4 oz (90–125 g) mixed fresh mushrooms such as chanterelle, fairy ring, and wood blewit, brushed clean, tough stems removed, and caps coarsely chopped

¼ lb (125 g) fresh white mushrooms, brushed clean and thinly sliced

1½ tablespoons all-purpose (plain) flour

¼ cup (2 fl oz/60 ml) heavy (double) cream

Pinch of cayenne pepper

Pinch of freshly grated nutmeg

Salt

1 or 2 slices dry-cured ham such as Bayonne or prosciutto, diced

¼ cup (2 fl oz/60 ml) Port

14 oz (440 g) good-quality puff pastry, homemade or thawed from frozen

1 egg yolk mixed with 1 tablespoon whole milk

MAKES 4 SERVINGS

1 In a small bowl, combine the dried mushrooms and hot stock. Cover and let soak, 30–60 minutes. Drain through a sieve lined with cheesecloth (muslin), pressing against the mushrooms and reserving the stock. Coarsely chop the mushrooms and set aside.

2 In a heavy nonstick frying pan over medium heat, melt 2 tablespoons of the butter. Add the shallots and garlic and sauté until softened, 1–2 minutes. Working in 2 batches, add the fresh mixed and white mushrooms. Raise the heat and sauté until browned, 3–5 minutes, adding butter if they stick. Combine the sautéed and rehydrated mushrooms in the pan and sauté, about 2 minutes. Transfer to a bowl.

3 Melt 1 tablespoon of the butter in the pan over medium heat. Sprinkle in the flour and cook, whisking, until lightly browned, 1–2 minutes. Whisk in the reserved stock and cook, stirring, until it thickens, 1–2 minutes. Whisk in the cream. Stir in the mushrooms and season with the cayenne, the nutmeg, and salt. Cook, stirring, until the mixture is bound together and almost no liquid remains, 2–3 minutes. Transfer to a bowl and set aside.

4 Wipe out the pan and return it to medium heat. Add the remaining 1 tablespoon butter and the ham, and cook, stirring, for 1 minute. Add the Port, bring to a boil, and reduce to a glaze (about 1 tablespoon), 3–4 minutes. Pour over the mushrooms, cover, and refrigerate for at least 2 hours or up to overnight.

5 Preheat the oven to 400°F (200°C). Lightly butter four 4-inch (10-cm) tartlet pans. On a lightly floured surface, roll out two-thirds of the puff pastry into a 12-inch (30-cm) square about ⅛ inch (3 mm) thick. Using a 6-inch (15-cm) cardboard circle as a guide, cut out 4 rounds. Place each into a pan, patting it firmly into the bottom and up the sides, leaving an overhang of about ¼ inch (6 mm). Divide the filling among the pans, heaping it slightly in the center.

6 Roll out the remaining pastry into a 10-inch (25-cm) square about ⅛ inch (3 mm) thick. Using a 5-inch (13-cm) cardboard circle as a guide, cut out 4 rounds. Lay each over a filled tartlet. Fold the overhanging pastry onto the top round, crimping with your fingers to seal. Cut a few small slits in the top of each tartlet. Brush with the egg mixture.

7 Bake until lightly golden, 20–30 minutes. Transfer to a wire rack to cool briefly. Remove the tartlets from their pans and serve warm or at room temperature.

Stuffed Black Mushrooms

The Chinese name of this dish, *xianggu roubing*, translates as "a long and happy marriage." Naturally it is often included on the banquet menu at weddings. To make a vegetarian dish, a spicy mix of mashed bean curd or eggplant (aubergine) can be substituted for the shrimp and pork stuffing. A vegetarian version of oyster sauce is sold in well-stocked Asian grocery stores.

12 dried black mushrooms, each 1½ inches (4 cm) in diameter and about 1½ oz (45 g), soaked in 1½ cups (12 fl oz/375 ml) hot water for 25 minutes

For the stuffing

1 tablespoon dried shrimp (prawns), soaked in ½ cup (4 fl oz/125 ml) hot water for 25 minutes

7 oz (220 g) pork tenderloin, minced

1 large egg white

2 teaspoons light soy sauce

1 teaspoon rice wine

½ teaspoon peeled and grated fresh ginger

1 teaspoon cornstarch (cornflour)

½ teaspoon superfine (caster) sugar

Salt

½ cup (4 fl oz/125 ml) vegetable oil

1½ tablespoons oyster sauce

½ teaspoon superfine (caster) sugar

1½ teaspoons cornstarch (cornflour) dissolved in 1 tablespoon water

MAKES 4–6 SERVINGS

1 Drain the mushrooms, reserving the soaking water. Trim off the stems as close as possible to the undersides of the mushroom caps and discard. Set the caps aside.

2 To prepare the stuffing, drain the shrimp, reserving the soaking water. In a food processor, finely chop the shrimp. Add two-thirds of the pork along with the egg white, soy sauce, rice wine, ginger, cornstarch, sugar, and ¼ teaspoon salt. Process to a smooth paste. Add the remaining pork and process briefly to mix without pulverizing.

3 Scoop up spoonfuls of the paste and form into balls, making 12 in all. Press 1 ball into the underside of each mushroom cap, smoothing the edges.

4 In a wok over medium-high heat, warm the oil. When it is hot, add the mushrooms, stuffing side down, and fry until the stuffing is golden brown, about 1 minute. Transfer the mushrooms to a plate and pour off the oil from the wok.

5 In the wok, combine the 2 cups (16 fl oz/500 ml) of the reserved soaking water, the oyster sauce, and sugar. Bring to a boil, stirring constantly. Return the mushrooms, stuffing side up, to the wok, reduce the heat to medium-low, and simmer, uncovered, until the mushrooms are tender, about 25 minutes. Using a slotted spoon, transfer the mushrooms to a serving plate.

6 Strain the sauce in the wok through a fine-mesh sieve into a small saucepan and bring to a boil. Reduce the heat to medium-high and boil until reduced to about ⅔ cup (5 fl oz/160 ml), about 7 minutes. Add the cornstarch mixture and stir until lightly thickened, about 1 minute. Spoon the sauce over the mushrooms and serve at once.

Mushroom Empanadas

For these empanadas, which are like oversized quesadillas, homemade corn tortillas are folded over and sealed around a flavorful filling of mushrooms and Mexican cheese, then browned on a hot grill.

For the filling

2 tablespoons unsalted butter or safflower oil

1 white onion, finely chopped

1 serrano chile, finely chopped

6 cloves garlic, minced

¾ lb (375 g) fresh mushrooms, preferably portobello or porcini, brushed clean and coarsely chopped

2 tablespoons finely chopped fresh epazote (optional)

Sea salt and freshly ground pepper

For the tortillas

1 lb (500 g) freshly prepared *tortilla masa* or 1¾ cups *masa harina* for tortillas

Sea salt

1 cup (8 fl oz/250 ml) plus 2 tablespoons warm water, if using *masa harina*

1½ cups (6 oz/185 g) shredded *quesillo de Oaxaca*, Muenster, or mozzarella cheese (optional)

1 cup (8 fl oz/250 ml) tomatillo salsa, homemade or purchased

MAKES 4–6 SERVINGS

1 To prepare the filling, in a frying pan over high heat, melt the butter. Add the onion and chile and sauté until the onion is translucent, about 30 seconds. Add the garlic and continue to sauté for a few seconds. Add the mushrooms and cook, stirring occasionally, about 4 minutes. When the mushrooms begin to release their liquid, stir in the epazote (if using), ½ teaspoon salt, and ½ teaspoon pepper, then immediately remove from the heat. Let cool.

2 To make the tortillas, if using fresh *masa*, put it in a bowl and knead with 1 teaspoon salt, adding a little warm water, if needed, to make a soft dough. If using *masa harina*, put it in a bowl, add the warm water, and mix with your hands; let rest for 5 minutes, then add 1 teaspoon salt and knead for 1 minute. Shape into balls 1½ inches (4 cm) in diameter, then cover with a damp kitchen towel. Put 2 sheets of heavy plastic inside a tortilla press. Working with 1 masa ball at a time, place it between the plastic sheets and press firmly to make a tortilla 6–7 inches (15–18 cm) in diameter, rotating the dough if needed.

3 Remove the top piece of plastic and sprinkle 1 tablespoon of the shredded cheese, if using, in the lower half of the tortilla, keeping the edges free. Spoon on some of the mushroom filling. Fold the other half of the tortilla over the filling and press the edges together to seal. Lift the empanada off of the bottom piece of plastic.

4 Preheat the oven to 200°F (95°C). Heat a *comal*, griddle, or large, heavy frying pan over medium-high heat. Gently lay each empanada on the hot surface and cook until it starts to brown, about 1 minute. Turn and brown the other side. Transfer to an ovenproof platter and keep warm in the oven. Repeat with the remaining tortillas and filling. Serve warm with the salsa on the side.

Sichuan Spicy Eggplant

The Sichuanese say that, to be at its best, this popular dish should be made with unpeeled eggplant, to give it a purple color, and be loaded with garlic. Surprisingly, the taste is strong but not overpowering. Several species of garlic-flavored plants grow in Sichuan, and local cooks use them all without restraint.

4 Asian (slender) eggplants (aubergines), or 1 or 2 globe eggplants, about 1 lb (500 g) total weight

Salt

¼ lb (125 g) coarsely ground (minced) pork

1 tablespoon hot bean sauce

1 cup (8 fl oz/250 ml) vegetable oil

¼ cup (1 oz/30 g) chopped garlic

2 tablespoons peeled and grated fresh ginger

2 tablespoons light soy sauce

1 tablespoon hoisin sauce

1 teaspoon black vinegar

1 teaspoon superfine (caster) sugar

2 teaspoons cornstarch (cornflour) dissolved in ⅓ cup (3 fl oz/80 ml) chicken stock or water

½ cup (1½ oz/45 g) chopped green (spring) onion, including tender green tops

2 teaspoons Asian sesame oil

½ teaspoon Sichuan peppercorns, crushed (optional)

1–2 tablespoons chopped fresh cilantro (fresh coriander)

MAKES 4–6 SERVINGS

1 If using Asian eggplants, trim them and cut into strips 2 inches (5 cm) long by ¾ inch (2 cm) wide by ¼ inch (6 mm) thick. If using globe eggplants, trim them and cut into slices ⅓ inch (9 mm) thick, then cut the slices in half. Place the eggplant pieces in a colander and sprinkle with 1 tablespoon salt. Let stand to draw off the bitter juices, about 30 minutes. Rinse thoroughly under cold running water, drain, and pat dry.

2 In a bowl, combine the pork and hot bean sauce, mixing well. Set aside.

3 In a wok over high heat, warm the vegetable oil until the surface ripples. Add the eggplant pieces and cook, about 1 minute. Reduce the heat slightly and continue to cook until the pieces are browned but still retain their shape, 5–6 minutes. Place the colander over a bowl. Pour the eggplant and oil into the colander and let drain for at least 30 minutes or up to 4 hours.

4 Return the wok to high heat and add 1 tablespoon of the strained oil. Add the pork, garlic, and ginger and stir-fry until the pork is cooked and lightly colored, 1½–2 minutes. Return the eggplant to the wok and add the soy sauce, hoisin sauce, black vinegar, and sugar. Cook, stirring carefully, about 30 seconds. (The eggplant will begin to break up at this stage.) Add the cornstarch mixture and simmer, stirring slowly, until lightly thickened, about 40 seconds.

5 Stir in the green onion and sesame oil. Taste and adjust the seasoning with salt. Transfer to a warmed serving plate, sprinkle with the Sichuan peppercorns (if using) and cilantro, and serve at once.

Grilled Eggplant with Peppers

All summer, Italian markets are filled with an array of beautiful eggplants and peppers, trucked in from nearby farms. This recipe pairs the two vegetables because they both do well on the grill and are happy partners—passed with good bread and perhaps slices of *mozzarella di bufala*—at *terrazzo* parties, but don't hesitate to prepare them separately. Both also make an excellent side dish.

2 cloves garlic

About ½ cup (½ oz/15 g) fresh flat-leaf (Italian) parsley leaves

½ cup (4 fl oz/125 ml) extra-virgin olive oil, or as needed

2 teaspoons red wine vinegar

3 red or yellow bell peppers (capsicums)

1 medium-large eggplant (aubergine), preferably light skinned and round, cut crosswise into slices ½ inch (1 cm) thick

2 tablespoons extra-virgin olive oil

1 teaspoon chopped fresh herbs such as oregano, Italian (flat-leaf) parsley, or basil (optional)

Salt

½ teaspoon red pepper flakes (optional)

MAKES 6 SERVINGS

1 Prepare a charcoal or gas grill for direct grilling over medium-high heat. Finely chop together the garlic and parsley leaves. Transfer to a bowl, add the ½ cup (4 fl oz/ 125 ml) olive oil and the vinegar, and mix well. Set aside.

2 Lay the bell peppers on the grill rack about 8 inches (20 cm) above the fire. Grill the peppers, turning as needed, until the skin is evenly blistered and blackened and the flesh is soft but not burned, about 10 minutes. Working in batches if necessary, grill the eggplant slices, turning once, until both sides are seared with grill marks and are tender, about 6 minutes total. (The timing will depend on the intensity of the heat.) Transfer the peppers to a paper bag and set aside to cool. Set the eggplant slices aside to cool.

3 Peel the charred skins from the peppers. Cut each bell pepper in half lengthwise and discard the seeds, ribs, and stem. Slice lengthwise into strips about ⅜ inch (1 cm) wide. Put the pepper strips in a small bowl, drizzle with the 2 tablespoons olive oil, and sprinkle with the chopped herbs, if using.

4 Layer the eggplant slices tightly in a straight-sided glass or ceramic serving dish, topping each layer with the olive oil-parsley mixture, salt, and red pepper flakes, if using. If the eggplant seems dry, add more oil. Serve at room temperature alongside the peppers.

Note: The grilled vegetables can be covered and left at room temperature for up to 1 hour or kept in the refrigerator for up to 3 days.

Ancho Chiles with Chicken Picadillo

Traditionally, it is the poblano chile that is stuffed to create the classic chile relleno. If the same chile is prepared in its dried form—the rich, chocolate-sweet ancho chile—a very different dish results. Serve with white rice, black beans, or both.

For the picadillo

½ cup (4 fl oz/120 ml) olive oil

1 cup (5 oz/155 g) finely chopped white onion

2 tablespoons minced garlic

2 lb (1 kg) ripe plum (Roma) tomatoes, finely chopped

¼ teaspoon dried thyme

2 bay leaves

½ cup (3 oz/90 g) raisins

2 lb (1 kg) boneless, skinless chicken thighs, finely chopped

Sea salt

¼ cup (2 oz/60 g) capers

½ cup (2½ oz/75 g) green olives, pitted and chopped

½ cup (3 oz/90 g) slivered blanched almonds

¼ cup (⅓ oz/10 g) each firmly packed finely chopped fresh cilantro (fresh coriander) and fresh flat-leaf (Italian) parsley

Leaves of 6 fresh mint sprigs, finely chopped

For the chiles

8 large ancho chiles

¼ lb (125 g) *piloncillo*, grated, or ½ cup (3½ oz/105 g) firmly packed dark brown sugar

½-inch (12-mm) piece true cinnamon bark

⅔ cup (5 fl oz/160 ml) cider vinegar

Sea salt

For the sauce

2 cups (16 fl oz/500 ml) *crema*

½ cup (2½ oz/75 g) finely chopped white onion

Sea salt

¼ cup (⅓ oz/10 g) firmly packed finely chopped fresh cilantro (fresh coriander)

MAKES 4 SERVINGS

1 To make the picadillo, in a large saucepan over medium heat, warm ¼ cup (2 fl oz/60 ml) of the olive oil. Add the onion and sauté until translucent, about 2 minutes. Add the garlic and cook, about 1 minute. Stir in the tomatoes, thyme, and bay leaves and simmer until the mixture begins to dry out, about 15 minutes. Add the raisins and cook until the flavors are melded and any excess liquid is absorbed, about 10 minutes longer.

2 In a large frying pan over medium-high heat, warm the remaining ¼ cup (2 fl oz/60 ml) olive oil and heat until smoking. Add the chicken and cook, stirring constantly, until lightly browned, about 4 minutes. Salt lightly, then pour in the tomato sauce and cook, stirring occasionally, about 5 minutes. Rinse the capers and add to the pan along with the olives, almonds, cilantro, parsley, and mint. Set aside.

3 To prepare the chiles, leaving the stem end intact, make a lengthwise slit in each chile and remove the seeds and veins, taking care not to break the walls. In a small saucepan, combine the *piloncillo*, cinnamon, vinegar, ½ teaspoon salt, and 4 cups (32 fl oz/1 l) water. Bring to a boil, stirring to dissolve the sugar. Reduce the heat to medium and simmer, about 5 minutes. Add the chiles, cover, and remove the pan from the heat. Let the chiles soak until soft, 15–20 minutes. Transfer to paper towels to drain.

4 Preheat the oven to 350°F (180°C). Carefully stuff the chiles with the picadillo and place them, just touching, in a baking dish. Cover and bake until heated through, about 15 minutes.

5 Meanwhile, to prepare the sauce, in a small saucepan over low heat, combine the *crema*, onion, and ½ teaspoon salt, bring to a bare simmer, and cook, 4–5 minutes. Strain, add the cilantro, and keep warm. Arrange the chiles on individual plates, drizzle the sauce over them, and serve at once.

ITALY

Peperonata

This side dish is a quintessential warm-weather gem, as bright and colorful on the palate as it is on the plate. It pairs well with panfried chicken or veal scaloppine.

1 lb (500 g) red bell peppers (capsicums), seeded

¼ cup (2 fl oz/60 ml) extra-virgin olive oil

1 red onion, halved and thinly sliced crosswise

2 bay leaves

3 tomatoes, peeled, seeded, and coarsely chopped

Salt and freshly ground pepper

MAKES 4 SERVINGS

1 Cut the bell peppers into 2-inch (5-cm) squares. In a saucepan over low heat, combine the peppers, olive oil, onion, and bay leaves and cook, stirring often, until the vegetables are softened and have released their juices, about 15 minutes.

2 Add the tomatoes, season with salt and pepper, and simmer gently until the vegetables are soft, about 5 minutes. Remove and discard the bay leaves. Serve the peperonata warm or chilled.

Note: The success of this dish largely depends on using ripe, seasonal tomatoes. If ripe tomatoes are unavailable, substitute canned whole plum (Roma) tomatoes.

GREECE

Green Pepper and Sausage Ragout

The *loukanika* sausage traditionally used for this rustic stew is subtly seasoned with orange zest, marjoram, coriander, and allspice. Add these aromatics to the stew if you can find only Italian sausage. Serve with white beans and crusty bread.

4 tablespoons (2 fl oz/60 ml) olive oil

1 lb (500 g) Greek *loukanika* or Italian sweet sausages, sliced ¾ inch (2 cm) thick

1 lb (500 g) long sweet green peppers (capsicums), seeded and cut lengthwise into 1-inch (2.5-cm) strips

1 lb (500 g) tomatoes, peeled, seeded and chopped

1 tablespoon dried oregano

¼ teaspoon ground allspice (optional)

½ teaspoon ground coriander (optional)

2 teaspoons grated orange zest (optional)

Salt and freshly ground pepper

MAKES 4 SERVINGS

1 In a large sauté pan over high heat, warm 2 tablespoons of the olive oil. Add the sausages and brown on all sides, about 5 minutes. Using a slotted spoon, transfer the sausages to a plate and set aside.

2 Add the remaining 2 tablespoons oil to the pan and reduce the heat to medium. Add the peppers and sauté until softened, 5–8 minutes, then return the sausages to the pan along with the tomatoes. Stir to combine. If using Italian sausage, add the allspice, coriander, and orange zest. Reduce the heat to low, cover, and simmer until the flavors have blended and the sauce has thickened, 15–20 minutes. Season with salt and pepper. Serve hot.

SEAFOOD

From the Sea

SEAFOOD AROUND THE WORLD

Oceans and rivers shape our world, and from their waters flow an abundance of fish and shellfish. Global traditions for serving seafood have been handed down through the centuries. Italian families prepare up to thirteen dishes of seafood for the Feast of the Seven Fishes on Christmas Eve, and a whole fish brought to the table in China ensures prosperity and abundance.

The red *rascasse* and gilt-headed sea bream of the Mediterranean Sea, the oysters of New Orleans, and the grass carp of China's West Lake are the stuff of legends—examples of special, highly local fish and shellfish that become celebrated in their native regions. Fish range widely in their flavor and texture. Delicate, flaky sole, for instance, requires different treatment than rich, fatty mackerel or firm, meaty mahi-mahi. Still, cooks around the world seem to agree that the best way to enjoy fresh seafood is with minimal gilding. Virtually every country has its version of grilled or fried seafood served with nothing but a wedge of lemon. Japanese and French cuisines, in particular, exemplify subtle approaches to seafood. Salmon gently poached in court bouillon,

trout sautéed in butter with a sprinkling of toasted almonds, and shimmering slices of tuna arranged on hand-pressed rice strive for minimalist perfection. Eating seafood raw or barely cooked is another much-loved way to showcase fish and shellfish. Sushi and sashimi have become popular fare far beyond Japan's borders. Along the southern coast of France, diners enjoy platters of *fruits de mer* served on ice, and in cities around the world, seafood aficionados can find raw bars for slurping oysters from the half shell. In Spain and Mexico and throughout South America, there are endless variations on ceviche, a refreshing dish in which lime juice rather than heat "cooks" fish and shrimp (prawns). But preparations for seafood are as diverse as the fish in the sea.

SALTWATER FISH

Large, firm-fleshed saltwater fish rank among the most desired of seafood. But along with tuna, mahi-mahi, swordfish, black cod, and sea bass, small fish have regained favor among chefs and diners. Giant shoals of herring, sardines, anchovies, and smelt move through the world's oceans. Every year, the smelt runs of New England and Canada's maritime provinces mark the arrival of spring. Northern and eastern Europeans are especially fond of herring. The extensive spreads of Swedish smorgasbord and Russian *zakuska* highlight its many incarnations: pickled in vinegar, smothered in sour cream, smoked over alder wood, stewed with tomatoes, coiled around olives. Dill, bay leaves, mustard sauce, and parsley are typical seasonings for these strongly flavored, fatty fish. Farther south, grilled sardines and anchovies are enjoyed all along the coastline from Spain to Greece.

Resourceful Mediterranean fishermen created such stews as the celebrated bouillabaisse of Marseille. Family recipes for Italy's *zuppa di pesce* were carried by immigrants all the way to California, where it was transformed into San Francisco's cioppino. Simpler tomato-based seafood soups appear in nearly every region of the world.

In India, aficionados seek specialties from Kerala, Goa, and the Bengali region. In the south, fish curries are flavored with a unique variety of tamarind and simmered for hours in an earthenware *chatti*. In the Bengal region, seafood from the Ganges Delta comes to the table cooked in spicy yogurt, covered in a curry redolent with mustard seeds, stewed with vegetables, or wrapped in banana leaves. The kingfisher reigns supreme in tiny Goa, which draws from colonial Portuguese traditions in dishes such as *recheiado* and *caldeirada*, a stew flavored with wine. The shimmering white, diamond-shaped pomfret is prized for its delicate flesh throughout the subcontinent.

Cooks in Veracruz, a narrow state along Mexico's eastern coastline, like to incorporate seafood, epazote (an herb similar to oregano), and dried chiles into local versions of tacos, enchiladas, and *tortas*. Classic Veracruz dishes include *caldo de siete mares* (soup of the seven seas) and *arroz a la tumbada*, which features fish, shrimp, clams, and squid tossed together with rice and tomatoes.

FRESHWATER FISH

Catfish, tilapia, and channel fish, which thrive in Southeast Asia's rivers and canals, might be stirred into spicy-tart soups, grilled in a cloak of banana leaves, or fried and served with green mango salad.

Catfish is appreciated wherever America's Mississippi River flows. Its breaded and fried fillets are a cornerstone of southern cooking.

In China, whole carp steamed with sliced ham and black mushrooms is a classic preparation. Fish balls and cakes made from pike or perch appear in noodle soups at the hawker stalls of Malaysia, Singapore, and Thailand. On the other side of the world, Jewish cooks follow tradition by making gefilte fish with the same types of fish. Other freshwater fish such as trout and salmon travel annually up the rivers of northern Europe and North America. Grilled right over a campfire or cured to silky smoothness, they command many loyal followers.

SHELLFISH

More than any other seafood, oysters develop flavors from their home waters. Brittany's Belon, Japan's Kumamoto, New York's Blue Point, Washington's Olympia—the finest are named after their origins.

Shellfish tend to divide along hot and cold lines. Black mussels abound in Canada, while green-lipped mussels thrive in Southeast Asia. Crabs and lobsters also vary depending on location. The large Dungeness crabs of America's Pacific Northwest, the blue crabs from Maryland's Chesapeake Bay, and the meaty, black-tipped claws of the stone crabs of Florida reveal the range of varieties in just one country.

Shrimp, abundant in the Gulf of Mexico and the Indian Ocean, hold up well to robust spices like Mexico's chipotle chile, India's diverse curries, and Southeast Asia's ubiquitous garlic, lemongrass, and chile paste. Shrimp is a key ingredient in dim sum specialties including delicately pleated *har gau* and shrimp and chive dumpling.

DRIED FISH

We now value freshness above all in seafood, but ancient methods for preserving fish linger in popular dishes to this day. Pickled herring, smoked salmon, and dried cod continue to delight our palates. Dried shrimp appear repeatedly in Chinese recipes, and dried bonito flavors dashi, the essential Japanese clear broth.

Perhaps the most renowned of dried fish is salted cod. Salt cod fritters appear on the menus of every continent. The fish was long a staple in northern Europe, and its importance along early sea trade routes can be tracked by even a short list of favorite dishes: Provence's *brandade de morue,* Newfoundland's salt cod chowder, Jamaica's saltfish sautéed with ackee, and *bacalao a la Vizcaina,* a classic Basque dish with tomatoes and peppers now served on feast days in Mexico.

Baked Fish with Sorrel

Béarnaise is among the "mother sauces" of French cuisine, important in its own right and a base for other sauces, such as this one with sorrel. Delicate, almost lemony sorrel leaves melt into a purée when heated. Cream helps stabilize this sauce.

8 tablespoons (4 oz/125 g) unsalted butter, plus 3 tablespoons

¼ cup (2 fl oz/60 ml) dry white wine

1 tablespoon white wine vinegar

½ shallot, chopped

1 teaspoon chopped fresh tarragon

1 small bunch sorrel, about ½ oz (15 g)

2 egg yolks

2 tablespoons heavy (double) cream

Pinch of cayenne pepper

Salt and freshly ground black pepper

1 carrot, peeled

1 celery stalk

½ leek, including tender green part

¼ English (hothouse) cucumber

2 shallots, chopped

2 cloves garlic, chopped

6 whiting, flounder, or salmon fillets, 5–6 oz (155–185 g) each

Juice of ¼ lemon, or to taste

1 bay leaf

2 teaspoons chopped fresh lemon thyme or English thyme

1–2 teaspoons chopped fresh chives

MAKES 6 SERVINGS

1 Cut 2 tablespoons of the butter into 6 pieces and refrigerate. In a small saucepan over low heat, melt 6 tablespoons (3 oz/90 g) of the butter and leave over low heat until it becomes clear and separates, 1–2 minutes. Skim off any foam from the surface and carefully pour the clear, golden liquid into a bowl, leaving the milky solids behind. Set the melted butter aside. Discard the solids.

2 In a small saucepan over medium-high heat, combine the wine, vinegar, ½ chopped shallot, tarragon, and 1 tablespoon water. Bring to a boil and cook until reduced to about 1 tablespoon, about 3 minutes. Strain through a fine-mesh sieve into a bowl, pressing on the solids to extract all the liquid. Let cool, 2–3 minutes. Discard the solids.

3 Remove the center rib from each sorrel leaf and discard. Coarsely chop the leaves. In a heatproof bowl, whisk the egg yolks. Add the warm wine mixture and whisk until slightly thickened. Set the bowl over (but not touching) barely simmering water. Add the chilled butter pieces and whisk constantly until the mixture thickens slightly. Whisk in the reserved melted butter 1–2 tablespoons at a time, whisking continuously to emulsify, until the mixture has thickened. Whisk in the cream and then the sorrel. Add the cayenne and season with salt. Keep warm over the water and serve within 30 minutes. Whisk occasionally to keep a skin from forming.

4 Preheat the oven to 375°F (190°C). Finely julienne the carrot, celery, leek, and cucumber. In a small, heavy nonstick frying pan over medium heat, melt the remaining 3 tablespoons butter. Add the 2 chopped shallots and the garlic and sauté until softened, about 5 minutes. Sprinkle half of the shallots and garlic in the bottom of a baking dish large enough to hold the fish in a single layer without touching. Arrange the fish on top and sprinkle with the lemon juice. Top with the remaining shallots and garlic. Surround with the vegetables, bay leaf, and thyme. Season with salt and pepper. Cover the dish and bake until the fish is opaque at the center, about 10 minutes.

5 To serve, divide the fish and vegetables among individual plates. Top with some of the sauce and sprinkle with the chives and black pepper. Pass the remaining sauce in a bowl at the table.

Slow-Cooked Salmon and Lentils

Baking salmon at a low temperature produces a creamy, moist interior. Fillets of wild king salmon, a West Coast species with a high fat content, lend themselves well to this method, although you can also substitute farmed salmon. Here, the fillets are placed on a bed of buttery lentils and topped with an herb-shallot butter. Look for small French green lentils for this dish, not the larger brown type, which don't hold their shape as well. Lentils vary widely in their cooking times, so test often.

For the herb butter

2 tablespoons unsalted butter, at room temperature

1 small shallot, finely minced

2 teaspoons minced fresh flat-leaf (Italian) parsley

1½ teaspoons Dijon mustard

Sea salt and freshly ground pepper

For the lentils

3½ tablespoons unsalted butter

½ large yellow onion, minced

½ large carrot, peeled and diced

1 small inner celery stalk, diced

2 cloves garlic, minced

3 cups (24 fl oz/750 ml) light chicken stock, or equal parts canned reduced-sodium broth and water

1 large fresh thyme sprig

1 cup (7 oz/220 g) French green lentils, picked over and rinsed

Sea salt and freshly ground pepper

1½ tablespoons minced fresh flat-leaf (Italian) parsley

4 king salmon fillets, about 6 oz (185 g) each, skin removed

Sea salt and freshly ground pepper

MAKES 4 SERVINGS

1 Preheat the oven to 300°F (150°C). Butter a baking dish large enough to hold the salmon in one layer.

2 To make the herb butter, in a bowl, combine the butter, shallot, parsley, and mustard and mix with a spoon until smooth. Season with salt and pepper.

3 To make the lentils, in a frying pan over medium-low heat, melt 2 tablespoons of the butter. Add the onion, carrot, celery, and garlic and sauté until softened, about 20 minutes. Meanwhile, in a saucepan over medium heat, combine the stock and thyme and bring to a simmer. Add the lentils, cover partially, adjust the heat to maintain a simmer, and cook until tender, 20–25 minutes. Remove from the heat and discard the thyme sprig. Using a slotted spoon, add the lentils to the vegetables along with a few tablespoons of their liquid. Season with salt and pepper, stir well, then cover and simmer until the lentils have absorbed the liquid, about 10 minutes. Add more liquid if needed. Keep warm over low heat.

4 Season the salmon fillets on both sides with salt and pepper, then place in the prepared baking dish. Bake until the fish just flakes, 20–25 minutes.

5 Remove the lentils from the heat. Add the parsley and the remaining 1½ tablespoons butter and stir until the butter melts. Divide the lentils among warmed individual plates. Top with the salmon fillets, and top each fillet with herb butter, spreading it evenly. Serve at once.

Blini with Salmon

Buckwheat flour provides a distinctive nutty taste to these traditional Russian pancakes, but since it can be hard to find, it can be replaced with whole-wheat (wholemeal) flour. Blini are typically accompanied by salt herring, caviar, or smoked salmon, as this recipe calls for. Sour cream is a suitable substitute for crème fraîche.

For the blini

½ cup (2½ oz/75 g) all-purpose (plain) flour

¼ cup (1½ oz/45 g) buckwheat flour

½ teaspoon rapid-rise yeast

½ cup (4 fl oz/125 ml) milk

1 egg, separated

1 tablespoon unsalted butter, melted

1 tablespoon sour cream

Sea salt

4 teaspoons sunflower oil or clarified unsalted butter

¾ cup (6 oz/185 g) crème fraîche

13 oz (410 g) thinly sliced smoked salmon

6 chives, coarsely snipped

Freshly ground pepper (optional)

4 lemon wedges

MAKES 4 SERVINGS

1 To prepare the blini, warm a large bowl by filling it with hot water, draining it, and wiping it dry. In the bowl, combine the all-purpose and buckwheat flours and the yeast. In a saucepan over medium heat, warm the milk just until small bubbles appear along the edge of the pan, but do not let it come to a boil. Slowly pour the milk into the dry ingredients, beating constantly with a wooden spoon to form a smooth batter. Cover with plastic wrap and let rise in a warm place until doubled in bulk, about 2 hours.

2 In a bowl, beat together the egg yolk, melted butter, sour cream, and a pinch of salt. Add to the risen batter and, using the wooden spoon, beat until combined. In a small bowl, whisk the egg white until stiff peaks form, then fold into the batter. Cover with plastic wrap and let stand, about 30 minutes.

3 Preheat the oven to 125°F (52°C). In a large nonstick frying pan over medium-high heat, warm 1 teaspoon of the sunflower oil. When it is hot, working in batches, drop tablespoonfuls of the batter into the pan, allowing 1½ inches (4 cm) between each blini. Cook until the blini are puffed and golden brown and tiny bubbles appear on the surface, about 2 minutes. Using a spatula, turn the blini and cook until golden brown on the second side, about 2 minutes. Transfer to an ovenproof plate and keep warm in the oven. Cook the remaining blini, using 1 teaspoon of oil for each batch. You should have about 16 blini.

4 Divide the blini among individual plates. To serve, place a heaping tablespoonful of crème fraîche on each plate, setting it partially on the warm blini. Divide the salmon among the plates, setting it atop the blini. Garnish each plate with chives, a light grinding of pepper (if using), and a lemon wedge. Serve at once.

Sea Bass with Black Beans and Ginger

This dish gets its flavor from ginger, fermented black beans—soybeans that have been dried, salted, and fermented until black—and dried mandarin peel. The latter is sold in powdered form in Asian markets. You may substitute dried tangerine peel and grind it in a spice grinder or with a mortar and pestle. Rinse the black beans gently to remove the excess salt before cooking with them. Serve the dish with steamed rice and stir-fried baby bok choy or other Chinese greens.

1 tablespoon sunflower oil

2 cloves garlic, peeled

2 tablespoons fermented black beans (see above), rinsed and chopped

2 tablespoons oyster sauce

1 tablespoon Chinese rice wine or dry sherry

1 tablespoon Asian sesame oil

¼ teaspoon corn oil

1 tablespoon sugar

1 tablespoon ground dried mandarin peel or dried tangerine peel (see above)

1½ teaspoons cornstarch (cornflour) dissolved in 3 tablespoons cold water

2 green (spring) onions, white and pale green parts only, thinly sliced on the diagonal

1 small red or green chile such as serrano, thinly sliced

½-inch (12-mm) piece fresh ginger, peeled and finely shredded

4 striped sea bass fillets, 6–8 oz (185–250 g) each

MAKES 4 SERVINGS

1 In a small saucepan over low heat, warm the sunflower oil. Add the garlic and cook, about 1 minute; do not let the garlic brown. Add the black beans and cook gently until the beans are infused with the garlic oil, about 2 minutes. Remove from the heat and stir in the oyster sauce, rice wine, sesame oil, corn oil, sugar, and ground mandarin peel. Bring to a boil over medium-high heat, reduce the heat to low, and simmer very gently until the flavors come together, about 10 minutes. Add the cornstarch mixture, stir vigorously, and simmer until thickened into a sauce, about 2 minutes. Pour the sauce into a nonreactive bowl and let cool, about 30 minutes.

2 Stir the green onions, chile, and ginger into the sauce. Add the fish fillets to the sauce and marinate, about 10 minutes. Place 2 of the fillets, skin side down, in a single layer on a sheet of aluminum foil. Spoon half of the sauce over the fillets, turn to coat in the sauce, and arrange skin side down. Seal the foil tightly. Repeat with the 2 remaining fillets. Place the foil packets in separate compartments of a bamboo steamer or other steamer rack and cover tightly.

3 Pour water into a wok or other pan and bring to a boil. Place the steamer over the wok, and cook until the fish is opaque throughout and flakes when tested with a knife, about 12 minutes. Carefully remove the packets from the steamer. Gently unwrap and divide the fillets and the sauce between warmed plates. Serve at once.

Fish Pie

This pie is a classic example of what the British refer to as "nursery food"—sophisticated comfort food for adults, who will find the seafood filling in a luscious sauce, topped with creamy mashed potatoes, very satisfying.

For the topping

2 lb (1 kg) Yukon gold potatoes, peeled and cut into large chunks

Sea salt and freshly ground pepper

⅓ cup (3 oz/90 g) unsalted butter, at room temperature

⅓ cup (3 fl oz/80 ml) milk

For the filling

½ lb (250 g) fresh haddock or cod fillets, skin removed

1 cup (8 fl oz/250 ml) milk

⅔ cup (5 fl oz/160 ml) heavy (double) cream

5 whole peppercorns

3 flat-leaf (Italian) parsley sprigs

1 bay leaf

1½ lb (750 g) smoked haddock or cod fillets, skin removed

1 tablespoon unsalted butter

2 tablespoons all-purpose (plain) flour

⅔ cup (5 fl oz/160 ml) dry vermouth such as Noilly Prat

2 tablespoons fresh lemon juice

½ lb (250 g) *each* raw shrimp (prawns) and bay or sea scallops

MAKES 6 SERVINGS

1 To prepare the topping, place the potato chunks in a saucepan with cold water to cover generously and salt the water. Bring to a boil and cook until the potatoes are tender when pierced, about 20 minutes. Drain, cover with a towel, and let dry, about 5 minutes. Pass the potatoes through a ricer or mash in a bowl with a potato masher. Add the butter and beat until smooth. Pour in the milk and again beat until smooth. Season with salt and pepper.

2 To prepare the filling, in a wide nonreactive saucepan over medium heat, combine the fresh fish fillets, milk, cream, peppercorns, parsley, and bay leaf. Bring to a simmer and cook until the fish flakes when tested at the thickest part, 5–8 minutes. Transfer the fillets to a shallow bowl. Immerse the smoked fish fillets in the milk mixture, bring to a simmer over medium heat, and cook until the fish flakes, about 3 minutes. Transfer the fillets to the bowl. Strain the milk mixture and reserve. As the fish cools, add any liquid in the bowl to the strained milk.

3 In a saucepan over low heat, melt the butter. Add the flour and cook, stirring constantly, until blended with the butter, about 2 minutes. Stir in the vermouth, raise the heat to medium-high, and boil until the mixture is thick and smooth, about 2 minutes. Slowly add the strained milk, stirring constantly, and cook until a thick sauce forms, about 6 minutes. Reduce the heat and simmer until the flour has lost its raw taste, about 5 minutes. Remove from the heat, stir in the lemon juice, and season with salt and pepper.

4 Preheat the oven to 375°F (190°C). Break the fish into large flakes, discarding any bones, and place in a large bowl. Peel and devein the shrimp and remove any muscle from the scallops; cut into bite-sized pieces as necessary. Add to the fish. Pour in the sauce and stir gently. Transfer the filling to a 9-inch (23-cm) square baking dish about 3 inches (7.5 cm) deep or divide among six 1½-cup (12-fl oz/375-ml) baking dishes. Top with the potato mixture, spreading it to cover. Using a fork, fluff the potatoes to create a textured surface.

5 Bake until the topping is golden and the filling is bubbling, about 30 minutes for individual pies or 50 minutes for a single pie. Serve at once.

British Seafood

EELS

This serpentine fish makes its tenacious voyage from the Sargasso Sea to London's rivers and estuaries before being caught on its journey homeward to spawn. The adult eel is sold live and prized for its delicate, richly flavored flesh. Pie-and-mash shops have been preparing it two ways for more than a century: cold and jellied with malt vinegar and bread and butter, and hot and stewed with a vivid green parsley sauce. It is also excellent smoked, served with horseradish.

ENGLISH BROWN SHRIMP

Not to be confused with the American shellfish of the same name (known in London as prawns) these tiny delicacies are gray when alive, but take on a pinkish brown hue when briefly boiled. Traditionally served "potted" in butter spiced with mace, nutmeg, and cayenne, they are sublime with crusty bread. Shrimp can also be added to creamy sauces, enveloped in mayonnaise, or turned into a shrimp bisque.

EUROPEAN LOBSTER

An essential element of the British "season" (along with Wimbledon, the Ascot races, and opera alfresco at Glyndebourne) the king of crustacea is caught between April and October and sold live. Its dark blue carapace and claws, which turn scarlet when cooked, yield dense, sweet white flesh. The liver enriches sauces, and the precious coral (eggs) makes a savory butter. Lobster is served cold, with herbed mayonnaise or lemon, or hot, drizzled with butter or sauce.

COD

Once so prolific in the North Atlantic that a thriving fishing port was located on the Thames estuary, cod stocks have declined in recent years, making it scarce and expensive. As green or gray as the sea, it has pearly flesh that separates into firm, moist flakes, making it suitable for poaching, roasting, marinating, or salting, and perfect in a fish pie. Deep-fried in batter, cod forms half of Londoners' favorite takeaway: fish and chips.

EELS

DOVER SOLE

BROWN CRAB

MACKEREL

ENGLISH BROWN SHRIMP

EUROPEAN LOBSTER

COD

WHITSTABLE OYSTERS

DOVER SOLE

Formerly a mainstay of English fish cookery, the exquisitely flavored Dover sole, from the cold waters of the North Sea, has become a luxury. A small flatfish with both eyes on one side of its head, it is half sepia and half cream, with dark patches. The firm but delicate flesh is best prepared simply: grilled with a savory butter, or accompanied by a delicate hollandaise sauce or *beurre blanc*. Sole is superb cooked on the bone or, once filleted, pan-fried, poached, or steamed.

BROWN CRAB

One of the finest crustaceans in British waters, the brown crab is abundant and inexpensive. Often sold boiled, the crab is best presented as simply as possible: cold, with mayonnaise, lemon, and brown bread and butter. Fishmongers often sell prepared crab, separating white claw meat from brown body meat and mixing the latter with English mustard, chopped hard-boiled egg, and mayonnaise before piling it back in the shell.

MACKEREL

This handsome fish has a svelte body cloaked in brilliant colors: shimmering metallic green-blue on top and silvery white on the underbelly. The smaller specimens are best grilled or barbecued, while the larger are best stuffed and baked. All sizes benefit from being served with a piquant sauce or accompaniment to offset their richness. Gooseberry sauce is a classic choice, as is mustard butter. Mackerel is also delicious smoked, either hot or cold.

WHITSTABLE OYSTERS

Contrary to their current elevated status, oysters were once bought by the barrel and made into stews and fritters. Famed since Dickens's time, the south-coast Whitstable oyster is opened just before eating and consumed live to savor the briny juice and capture the elusive flavor. Raw oysters might be dressed with shallot vinegar or lemon. Grilled oysters are often bathed in cream, sprinkled with Parmesan, and dotted with butter.

Sardines in Vinaigrette

Escabeche, or pickling in vinegar and spices, is one of the oldest means of preserving food, and the technique has persisted in contemporary Portuguese and Spanish cuisine. Although originally used for meat and game, the preparation works well with any oily, strong-flavored fish, such as these fresh sardines.

2 cups (10 oz/315 g) all-purpose (plain) flour

Salt and freshly ground pepper

2 lb (1 kg) sardines, filleted

Equal parts olive and sunflower oil for frying

6 tablespoons (3 fl oz/90 ml) olive oil

2 bay leaves

12 whole peppercorns

3 cloves garlic, crushed

1 teaspoon pimentón or sweet paprika

1 cup (8 fl oz/250 ml) white wine vinegar

MAKES 6 SERVINGS

1 Place the flour on a plate or in a shallow bowl, season with salt and pepper, and stir to combine. Lightly dredge the filleted sardines in the flour, shaking off any excess.

2 Pour the olive and sunflower oils to a depth of 1 inch (2.5 cm) into a large, heavy-bottomed frying pan and heat over high heat until smoking hot. Working in batches, fry the sardines, turning once, until golden brown, about 2 minutes per side. Transfer to a heatproof ceramic dish. When all the sardines are cooked, sprinkle them with salt and set aside.

3 Clean the frying pan and add the 6 tablespoons olive oil. Warm the oil over medium heat until hot. Add the bay leaves, peppercorns, and garlic and sauté until the garlic is lightly browned, about 3 minutes. Remove from the heat, add the pimentón, and stir once or twice to combine. Add the vinegar and 1 cup (8 fl oz/ 250 ml) water, return to medium heat, and simmer until reduced by one-fourth, about 5 minutes.

4 Pour the contents of the frying pan over the sardines and gently shake the dish to ensure that the vinegar mixture is evenly distributed. Set aside and let cool. The sardines can be served at once, but will be better after a day or two in the refrigerator, where they will keep, tightly covered, for up to 5 days. Bring to room temperature before serving.

Miso-Marinated Black Cod

This remarkably flavorful black cod warrants being served solo on a plate, with just the caramelized exterior set against the glistening snow-white flesh underneath.

½ **cup (4 fl oz/125 ml) mirin**

⅓ **cup (3 fl oz/80 ml) sake**

1 **cup (8 oz/250 g) white miso**

½ **cup (4 oz/125 g) sugar**

4 **black cod fillets, about 6 oz (185 g) each, patted dry**

MAKES 4 SERVINGS

1 In a saucepan over medium heat, combine the mirin and sake and simmer to evaporate the alcohol, about 1 minute. Add the miso and sugar and stir until smooth. Bring to a simmer and cook, stirring constantly, until the sugar dissolves, about 3 minutes. Set aside to cool.

2 Reserve 3 tablespoons of the marinade in an airtight container in the refrigerator. Pour half of the remaining miso marinade into a shallow nonreactive dish large enough to hold the fillets in a single layer. Add the fillets and pour the remaining marinade over the fish. Cover and refrigerate for at least 2 days or up to 3 days.

3 Preheat the broiler (grill). Remove the reserved marinade from the refrigerator and bring to room temperature.

4 Remove the cod fillets from their marinade and lightly wipe off any excess with paper towels. Discard the marinade. Arrange the fillets in a single layer, not touching, on a baking sheet. Broil (grill) 8 inches (20 cm) from the heat source until the fish is caramelized and a rich brown color, about 10 minutes. Remove from the oven, turn the fillets over, and broil just until the flesh flakes easily, 3–5 minutes longer. Divide the fillets among warmed individual plates. Drizzle with the reserved marinade and serve.

Tandoori Fish

The delicate marinade used for this dish is infused with ginger, garlic, and *ajowan* (the seeds of the thymol plant, a close relative of cumin and caraway) for a wonderful flavor. This recipe calls for sour cream instead of the traditional yogurt, as it lends a buttery flavor and appealing sheen.

2 salmon fillets, 12–14 oz (375–440 g) total weight

1 teaspoon fresh lemon juice

1 teaspoon minced garlic

1 teaspoon fresh ginger, peeled and minced

½ teaspoon garam masala

½ teaspoon *ajowan* seeds (see above), bruised, or ½ teaspoon dried thyme

¼ teaspoon cayenne pepper

Salt

1 tablespoon sour cream

1 tablespoon *usli ghee* or olive oil

1 Lay the fish in a shallow nonreactive dish. In a cup, combine the lemon juice, garlic, ginger, garam masala, *ajowan*, cayenne, and ½ teaspoon salt. Rub the spice mixture all over the fish. Coat the fillets with the sour cream, cover, and let marinate for 30 minutes at room temperature or for 3 hours in the refrigerator.

2 Prepare a charcoal or gas grill for direct grilling over medium-high heat or preheat a broiler. Brush the fillets with some of the *usli ghee*. Place on the grill rack or a broiler pan and grill 5 inches (13 cm) from the heat source, turning just once and basting from time to time with more *usli ghee*, until the fish is barely opaque, about 6 minutes total if using a grill or about 7 minutes if using a broiler. Transfer to a warmed platter and serve at once.

MAKES 2 SERVINGS

Fish Tacos

1½ lb (750 g) red snapper or other firm white-fleshed fish fillets

Sea salt and freshly ground pepper

¾ cup (4 oz/125 g) all-purpose (plain) flour

¼ cup (2 oz/60 ml) corn or safflower oil

2 cups (16 fl oz/500 ml) fresh salsa, homemade or purchased

10 corn tortillas, homemade or purchased, warmed

1 cup (3 oz/90 g) chopped cabbage

2 limes, quartered

1 Season both sides of each fish fillet with salt and a generous amount of pepper. Spread the flour on a plate and dip the fish in it, coating evenly and shaking off any excess.

2 In a large frying pan over medium-high heat, warm the oil until it is hot but not smoking. Add the fish fillets and fry, turning once, until golden on both sides, about 1 minute total. Transfer to paper towels to drain. While the fillets are still hot, shred them with a fork. Put the salsa in a bowl and stir in the fish.

3 To assemble the tacos, place some fish on each tortilla, add a bit of the cabbage, and fold to enclose loosely. Serve at once with the limes on the side.

MAKES 10 TACOS

Spicy Fish Cakes

This snack food is readily available from street hawkers in Thailand. Many versions exist, but this one, made with kaffir lime leaves, is a favorite. You can substitute the zest of 1 lime for the leaves, but the unique perfumy character of the kaffir lime will be missing. They can also be accompanied by Sriracha sauce instead of the relish.

For the cucumber relish

½ cup (4 fl oz/125 ml) rice vinegar

¼ cup (2 oz/60 g) sugar

Salt

½ English (hothouse) cucumber, peeled

½ carrot, peeled

1 large shallot, or ¼ red onion, thinly sliced

3 Fresno or serrano chiles, seeded (if desired) and finely chopped

Fresh cilantro (fresh coriander) leaves

¼ cup (1½ oz/45 g) chopped unsalted dry-roasted peanuts

For the fish cakes

1 lb (500 g) whitefish fillets, finely ground

1 tablespoon roasted chile paste or red curry paste

1 tablespoon fish sauce

1 tablespoon cornstarch (cornflour)

2 oz (60 g) green beans, ends trimmed and beans thinly sliced

6 kaffir lime leaves, spines removed and leaves finely slivered

Salt

Peanut oil for deep-frying

MAKES 6 SERVINGS

1 To make the relish, in a small saucepan over medium heat, combine the vinegar, sugar, and 1 teaspoon salt. Bring to a gentle boil, stirring to dissolve the sugar and salt. Remove from the heat and set aside to cool. Cut the cucumber and carrot in half lengthwise and then again in half lengthwise. Cut each piece crosswise into thin slices. Just before serving, in a bowl, gently toss the cucumber, carrot, shallot, and chiles in the vinegar mixture. Garnish with cilantro leaves and the peanuts.

2 To prepare the fish cakes, in a bowl, combine the fish, chile paste, fish sauce, cornstarch, green beans, lime leaves, and ½ teaspoon salt. Knead the mixture for 1 minute. Divide into 20 balls and then flatten each into a patty about 2 inches (5 cm) in diameter and ½ inch (12 mm) thick.

3 Pour oil to a depth of 1 inch (2.5 cm) into a heavy frying pan and heat over medium-high heat to 375°F (190°C) on a deep-frying thermometer. Slip a few patties into the hot oil and fry on the first side until golden brown, about 2 minutes. Turn and fry on the second side until golden, about 2 minutes longer. Transfer to paper towels to drain. Arrange on a platter and serve at once with the relish on the side.

Salt Cod Fritters

Boneless salt cod—*bacalhau* in Portuguese and *bacaloa* in Spanish—originated in the time of Columbus, with Portuguese fishermen preserving it by gutting, filleting, and salting it while at sea and then sun-drying it once they were home.

½ lb (250 g) boneless salt cod

2 boiling potatoes, about 10 oz (315 g) total weight

2 tablespoons olive oil

1 small yellow onion, minced

2 cloves garlic, finely minced

2 eggs, lightly beaten

3 tablespoons *each* chopped fresh flat-leaf (Italian) parsley and fresh cilantro (fresh coriander)

Pinch of cayenne pepper

Freshly ground black pepper

Milk, if needed

Olive oil for deep-frying

MAKES 6–8 SERVINGS

1 Place the fish in a bowl with cold water to cover. Cover and refrigerate 24 hours, changing the water every 8 hours.

2 Drain the fish and place in a saucepan with water to cover. Bring to a simmer and cook until tender, 10–15 minutes. Drain and let cool. Flake it, removing any skin and bones. Pulse in a food processor until finely shredded.

3 Place the potatoes in a saucepan with water to cover, bring to a boil, and cook until tender, 20–30 minutes. Drain and let cool. Peel and mash the potatoes. Add the cod. In a small frying pan over medium heat, warm the oil. Add the onion and sauté until tender, about 8 minutes. Add the garlic and sauté for 2 minutes. Stir into the cod mixture. Fold in the eggs, parsley, and cilantro. Season with the cayenne and black pepper. Form into 1-inch (2.5-cm) balls.

4 Pour oil to a depth of 2 inches (5 cm) into a deep, heavy frying pan and heat to 375°F (190°C) on a deep-frying thermometer. Add the balls in batches, and fry until golden, about 4 minutes. Drain on paper towels and serve at once.

Florentine Salt Cod

2 lb (1 kg) boneless salt cod

3 tablespoons extra-virgin olive oil, plus extra for frying

3 cloves garlic, crushed

All-purpose (plain) flour for dredging

2 cups (12 oz/375 g) canned crushed plum (Roma) tomatoes

1 tablespoon finely chopped fresh flat-leaf (Italian) parsley

Freshly ground pepper

MAKES 6 SERVINGS

1 Place the fish in a bowl with cold water to cover. Cover and refrigerate, changing the water every 8 hours, for 36–48 hours. Drain, remove any skin and errant bones, and pat dry. Cut into pieces 2½ by 5 inches (6 by 13 cm).

2 Pour olive oil to a depth of about ½ inch (12 mm) into a frying pan over low heat. Add the garlic and sauté, about 2 minutes. Discard the garlic. Raise the heat to medium and heat the oil until hot but not smoking. Dredge the fish and place in a single layer in the pan. Cook, turning once, until opaque, about 6 minutes. Transfer to paper towels to drain.

3 Discard the oil, wipe out the pan, add the 3 tablespoons olive oil, and return to medium heat. Add the tomatoes and parsley and cover with the fish. Reduce the heat to medium-low and cook, occasionally spooning the tomatoes over the fish, about 10 minutes. Season with pepper and serve.

Oysters en Brochette

4 sturdy rosemary branches, or 4 bamboo skewers, each 12 inches (30 cm) long

8 thin slices French bread, toasted and buttered, or 8 buttered toast points

Unsalted butter as needed

6–8 thin slices best-quality bacon

12–16 oysters, shucked

¼ lemon

Freshly ground white or black pepper

MAKES 4 SERVINGS

1 If using rosemary sprigs for skewers, strip off most of the leaves, leaving about 2 inches (5 cm) of leaves at the top. Soak the rosemary branches or bamboo skewers in water to cover, about 30 minutes. Preheat the broiler (grill), or prepare a charcoal or gas grill for direct grilling over high heat.

2 Cut the bacon in half crosswise. In a small frying pan over medium-high heat, fry the bacon until lightly browned but still flexible, about 3 minutes on each side. Transfer to paper towels to drain.

3 Place the oysters on a plate, squeeze the lemon juice over them, and season with pepper. Wrap each oyster in a piece of the bacon, and thread 3 or 4 oysters onto each skewer. Arrange the skewers on the grill rack about 5 inches (13 cm) from the fire and grill, turning once, until the bacon is crisp but the oysters are still plump and juicy, 3–4 minutes per side. Alternatively, arrange on a broiler pan and broil (grill), turning once, 3–4 minutes per side.

4 Divide the bread among individual plates, top with the oysters, and serve at once.

Gulf Coast Seafood

BACKYARD SEAFOOD FRY

Along the coast of the Gulf of Mexico, a backyard seafood fry is considered down-home entertaining at its best, promising tall tales, an abundance of decadent foods, and hands-on dining. In Louisiana, the kettle is stocked with fresh soft-shell crabs, plump oysters, or Gulf shrimp (prawns). Farm-raised catfish is also popular, though aficionados swear by wild "flathead cat" from the Mississippi River. Thick batters or elaborate coatings are rare. Southern-fried seafood is simply dusted with cornmeal or corn flour, usually seasoned with plenty of salt and black pepper plus a bit of cayenne, then fried in hot peanut oil.

The main dish of fried seafood is typically accompanied by a regular cast of side dishes, such as crispy hush puppies, tangy coleslaw, creamy potato salad, fresh buttered corn on the cob, and cheese grits spiked with plenty of cayenne pepper. Ice chests are stocked with bottles of locally brewed beer and root beer. Large pitchers are filled with frosty cold lemonade and sweetened iced tea, and desserts range from juicy peach cobbler to chilled wedges of watermelon.

OYSTERS ON THE MENU

Great old New Orleans oyster bars include Acme Oyster House and Felix's in the French Quarter, The Pearl in the Central Business District, and Casamento's Uptown. Other good choices are Mandina's in Mid-City and Cooter Brown's or Franky and Johnny's Uptown.

Belly up to the bar for fresh oysters. A cool dozen will be presented in moments by expert shuckers at classic seafood houses and oyster bars all along the coast, where several generations of locals have enjoyed their oysters raw or cooked—whether fried, broiled, barbecued, or stewed.

SHUCKING OYSTERS

OPENING THE SHELL First, scrub the oysters with a stiff brush under cold running water. Using a rubber mitt made for shucking or a tough work glove to protect your hand, place an oyster in the palm of one hand. Using a proper oyster knife (never a kitchen knife, which is too flexible and almost certain to cause injury), gently insert the blade into the gap between the top and bottom halves at the hinge end. Pointing the blade away from you, in case the knife slips, firmly twist the handle until the halves separate.

RELEASING THE OYSTER Gently slide the blade between the two shells to sever the adductor muscle that connects them near the hinge. Discard the shallow top shell. Finally, work the blade under the oyster to release it from the muscle that connects it to the bottom shell, taking care not to cut into the meat or lose the briny "liquor."

SERVING Use the knife to scrape away any bits of debris clinging to the shell or the meat. Serve the oysters in their bottom shells, atop a bed of ice.

Steamed Mussels with Aioli

¼ teaspoon powdered saffron, preferably saffron threads pounded in a mortar

1 cup (8 fl oz/250 ml) dry white wine

For the aioli

2 cloves garlic

Sea salt

1 egg yolk, at room temperature

½ cup (4 fl oz/125 ml) extra-virgin olive oil

1 small fennel bulb

¼ cup (2 fl oz/60 ml) extra-virgin olive oil

¾ cup (4 oz/125 g) minced shallot

4 lb (2 kg) mussels, well scrubbed and beards removed

2 long orange zest strips

¼ cup (⅓ oz/10 g) chopped fresh flat-leaf (Italian) parsley

MAKES 4 SERVINGS

1 In a small bowl, combine the saffron and wine and let steep for 30 minutes.

2 To make the aioli, in a mortar, combine the garlic cloves with a pinch of salt and pound to a paste with a pestle. Set aside. Put the egg yolk in a small bowl, add a few drops of warm water, and whisk lightly. Begin whisking in the olive oil slowly—drop by drop at first, then a little faster as it begins to emulsify. Whisk in the garlic paste. Taste and adjust the seasoning with more salt if needed.

3 Remove the stems, feathery tops, and any bruised outer stalks from the fennel bulb, then cut the bulb into ¼-inch (6-mm) dice. In a large pot over medium-low heat, warm the olive oil. Add the fennel and shallot and sauté until the fennel is softened, 12–15 minutes. Discard any mussels that do not close to the touch; add the rest to the pot along with the saffron mixture and the orange zest. Raise the heat to high and bring to a boil. Boil, uncovered, about 1 minute. Cover and cook until the mussels open, shaking the pot occasionally, 3–4 minutes.

4 Whisk enough of the pan juices into the aioli to make a sauce you can drizzle. Transfer the mussels and their juices to a serving bowl, discarding any mussels that failed to open. Discard the orange zest and drizzle the mussels with the aioli. Garnish with the parsley and serve at once.

Mussels with Garlic Butter

French mussels are farmed along the Atlantic coast, south of Brittany, and in the Mediterranean near Marseilles. An ancient method is used: oak poles are stuck into the sand of the shallow coastal waters and the mussels attach themselves to the poles naturally, where they grow to maturity. In this recipe, green garlic butter, similar to what flavors escargots, perfumes the mollusks.

Salt

3 lb (1.5 kg) mussels, well scrubbed and beards removed

2 shallots, chopped

2 cups (16 fl oz/500 ml) dry white wine

3–4 slices day-old coarse country bread, torn into large pieces

For the garlic butter

5 cloves garlic, chopped

1 bunch fresh flat-leaf (Italian) parsley, about 6 oz (185 g)

½ cup (4 oz/125 g) unsalted butter, at room temperature

2 green (spring) onions, white and pale green parts only, thinly sliced

2 tablespoons coarsely chopped fresh tarragon

2 tablespoons pastis or anise-flavored liqueur

2 tablespoons extra-virgin olive oil

Juice of ½ lemon, or to taste

1–2 tablespoons heavy (double) cream

Salt and freshly ground pepper

Lemon wedges for serving

MAKES 6 SERVINGS

1 In a large bowl, combine 4 cups (32 fl oz/1 l) water with 3 tablespoons salt and stir to dissolve the salt. Add the mussels and let stand for about 1 hour to rid them of any sand, then drain well. Place the mussels in a clean bowl and refrigerate, uncovered, for up to 1 day.

2 Preheat the oven to 375°F (190°C). Arrange the mussels in a single layer in a shallow baking pan, discarding any that do not close to the touch, and add the shallots and wine. Cover the pan with aluminum foil and bake just until the shells open, about 10 minutes. Remove from the oven and let cool in the pan. Remove the mussels from the wine, discarding any that failed to open, and discard the wine. Raise the oven temperature to 400°F (200°C).

3 In a food processor, process the bread until it forms coarse crumbs. Measure out 1 cup (2 oz/60 g) and set aside; reserve the remainder for another use.

4 To make the garlic butter, in the food processor, process the garlic until puréed, then add the parsley and process to a finely minced mixture. Cut the butter into 3 or 4 pieces and add to the parsley mixture along with the green onions, tarragon, and pastis. Process until combined. Add the olive oil, lemon juice, and enough cream to create a soft, fluffy mixture. Season with salt and pepper.

5 Working with 1 mussel at a time, pull off and discard the top shell and run a small, sharp knife around the mussel to loosen it from the bottom shell. Lay the mussels in their shells in a single layer in the baking pan. Spoon an equal amount of the garlic butter onto each mussel and sprinkle the crumbs generously on top.

6 Return the mussels to the oven and bake until the tops are sizzling, the butter is melted and fragrant, and the crumbs are crisp, 8–10 minutes. Transfer to a platter and serve at once, with the lemon wedges on the side.

Manhattan Clam Chowder

People have strong preferences for either the New England cream-based clam chowder or the Manhattan tomato-based version. Some believe that Rhode Islanders were the first to add tomatoes to what was likely a French-Canadian invention, others that the Manhattan version descended from chowders sold at Coney Island food stands. A likelier theory is that it was the creation of fishmonger William H. Winters, who owned the original Fulton Fish Market in the early 1900s.

12 quahog clams, or 18–24 littleneck or cherrystone clams, well scrubbed

6 slices bacon, chopped

1 large yellow onion, diced

4 cloves garlic, chopped

3 celery stalks, finely diced

2 carrots, peeled and finely diced

1 bay leaf

1 teaspoon *each* dried thyme, oregano, and basil

¼ teaspoon red pepper flakes

2 cups (14 oz/440 g) canned whole tomatoes, drained and crushed

¾ lb (375 g) russet potatoes, peeled and diced

¾ cup (6 fl oz/180 ml) bottled clam juice

Sea salt and freshly ground black pepper

¼ lb (125 g) bay scallops

20–22 manila clams, well scrubbed

¼ cup (⅓ oz/10 g) finely chopped fresh flat-leaf (Italian) parsley, plus extra for garnish

1–2 tablespoons fresh lemon juice

MAKES 6 SERVINGS

1 Place the quahog or littleneck clams in a wide saucepan, discarding any that do not close to the touch. Add 2 cups (16 fl oz/500 ml) water, bring to a boil, cover, and steam just until the clams open, 8–10 minutes. Transfer the clams to a bowl, discarding any that failed to open, and reserve the clam broth in the pot. When the clams are cool enough to handle, remove the clam meat and chop, then set aside. Strain the broth through a fine-mesh sieve lined with a double layer of cheesecloth (muslin) and set aside. Discard the solids.

2 In a soup pot over high heat, fry the bacon, stirring occasionally, until it is lightly browned, 5–6 minutes. Add the onion and garlic, reduce the heat to low, and cook, stirring occasionally, until the onion is translucent, about 5 minutes. Add the celery, carrots, bay leaf, thyme, oregano, basil, and red pepper flakes and cook until the vegetables begin to soften, about 5 minutes. Add the tomatoes, return to a simmer, and cook until they break down, about 10 minutes. Add the potatoes, clam juice, and reserved broth, return to a simmer, and cook until the potatoes are just tender, 8–10 minutes. Taste and adjust the seasoning with salt and black pepper. (The soup can be prepared up to this point, cooled to room temperature, and refrigerated for up to 1 day. Refrigerate the reserved chopped clams separately. Before serving, reheat the soup gently over medium heat.)

3 Just before serving, add the scallops and the manila clams in their shells, discarding any that do not close to the touch. Cook over medium heat until the clams open and the scallops are opaque, 4–5 minutes. Discard any clams that failed to open, and stir in the ¼ cup (⅓ oz/10 g) parsley and reserved chopped clams. Do not allow the soup to simmer or the clams will toughen. Stir in the lemon juice to taste.

4 Divide the chowder among warmed individual bowls, garnish with parsley, and serve at once.

Linguine with Clams

Many types of clams are harvested all over Italy; the thumbnail-sized, sweet-tasting *vongole veraci* are considered the best for this dish. To capture all of their flavorful juices, the clams are cooked in their shells right in the sauce. Be sure to provide bowls in which to discard the shells.

3 lb (1.5 kg) small hard-shell clams, soaked in cool water for 30 minutes and well scrubbed

2 large cloves garlic, finely chopped

1 small dried red chile, crushed, or 1 pinch of red pepper flakes

⅓ cup (3 fl oz/80 ml) olive oil

¼ cup (⅓ oz/10 g) finely chopped fresh flat-leaf (Italian) parsley

½ cup (4 fl oz/125 ml) dry white wine

1 lb (500 g) linguine or spaghetti

Salt

MAKES 4–6 SERVINGS

1 Discard any clams that do not close to the touch. In a large saucepan over medium heat, warm the garlic and the chile in the olive oil until the garlic is golden, about 1 minute. Stir in the parsley. Add the clams and wine, cover, and cook over medium heat, shaking the pan occasionally, until the clams open, about 5 minutes. Discard any clams that fail to open.

2 Meanwhile, bring a large pot of salted water to a boil. Add the pasta and cook, stirring frequently, until al dente. Drain, reserving a ladleful of the cooking water.

3 Transfer the pasta to a warmed serving bowl. Add the clams and their juice and stir and toss well. Add a little of the cooking water if the pasta seems too dry. Serve at once.

CHINA
Deep-Fried Crab

For the dipping sauce

⅓ cup (2½ oz/75 g) firmly packed light brown sugar

½ teaspoon tamarind concentrate

1½ tablespoons thick soy sauce

For the crab balls

7 oz (220 g) fresh crabmeat

2½ oz (75 g) ground (minced) fat pork such as pork butt

⅓ cup (2 oz/60 g) finely chopped water chestnuts

1 tablespoon chopped green (spring) onion, white part only

1 slice white bread, crusts removed and roughly chopped

1 egg white

1 tablespoon tapioca starch

Salt and ground white pepper

Sunflower oil for deep-frying

MAKES 18–20 BALLS

1 To prepare the sauce, in a saucepan over medium heat, combine the sugar and ½ cup (4 fl oz/125 ml) water, bring to a simmer, and cook until the syrup is golden brown and reduced by half, about 10 minutes. Stir in the tamarind and soy sauce. Pour into small dishes and set aside.

2 To prepare the crab balls, in a food processor, combine the crabmeat and pork and process to form a smooth paste. Add the water chestnuts, green onion, bread, egg white, tapioca starch, ½ teaspoon salt, and ½ teaspoon pepper, and process until smooth. The mixture will be soft and moist but will result in light-textured balls. If it is too moist to work with, add a little tapioca starch.

3 Pour the oil to a depth of 2 inches (5 cm) into a wok, and heat over medium-high heat to 375°F (190°C) on a deep-frying thermometer. Using a tablespoon, scoop up balls of the crab mixture and carefully drop them into the oil. Do not crowd the pan. Fry, turning as needed, until evenly golden brown, about 1½ minutes. Transfer to paper towels to drain. Serve at once with the dipping sauce.

UNITED KINGDOM
Spicy Crab Salad

3 cups (18 oz/560 g) fresh lump crabmeat

1 Thai chile, finely diced

Finely grated zest and juice of 2 limes

2 tablespoons coarsely chopped fresh mint

2 tablespoons mayonnaise

Salt and freshly ground pepper

6 tablespoons (3 fl oz/90 ml) extra-virgin olive oil

1 small red onion

2 hearts of romaine (cos) lettuce

2 bunches watercress, trimmed into sprigs

3 avocados

MAKES 6 SERVINGS

1 Place the crabmeat in a bowl and pat dry. Add the chile, lime zest, juice of 1 lime, mint, and mayonnaise. Stir gently to combine. Season with salt, cover, and refrigerate.

2 To make the dressing, in a small bowl, whisk together the olive oil and 2 tablespoons of the lime juice. Season with salt and pepper and set aside.

3 Halve the onion lengthwise, peel, then slice thinly. Set aside one-fourth for garnish. Tear the lettuce leaves into a large bowl, and add the remaining onion and the watercress. Drizzle with the dressing and toss. Halve each avocado and remove the pit. Using a large spoon, scoop out the flesh from each half in one piece. Discard the peel. Divide the greens among 6 plates. Top each with an avocado half. Spoon one-sixth of the crabmeat mixture onto each avocado half. Garnish with the reserved onion and serve.

MEXICO
Shrimp with Orange and Tequila

6 tablespoons (3 oz/90 g) unsalted butter

2 tablespoons finely chopped white onion

2 cloves garlic

16 large shrimp (prawns), peeled and deveined

1 chipotle chile in adobo, or 2 serrano chiles, finely chopped

Very narrow strips of zest from 1 orange

¼ cup (2 fl oz/60 ml) *tequila reposado*

3 tablespoons minced fresh cilantro (fresh coriander)

Sea salt

MAKES 4 SERVINGS

 In a frying pan over medium heat, melt the butter. Add the onion and sauté until translucent, 3–4 minutes. Add the garlic and shrimp and cook, stirring frequently, until the shrimp turn pink and begin to curl, 4–5 minutes. Add the chile and the orange zest. Stir briefly to mix.

2 Pour the tequila over the shrimp, carefully ignite with a long match, and let the flames burn out. Add the cilantro, season with salt, and serve at once.

INDIA
Spicy Grilled Shrimp

This simple dish showcases Goa's succulent shrimp. Rubbed with fiery-hot *richeiado* spice paste then pan-grilled, they accompany tropical cocktails such as Goa's *fenni*—fermented coconut or cashew fruit juice—which is also used in the dish.

1 lb (500 g) jumbo or large shrimp (prawns)

For the spice paste

1 tablespoon minced garlic

1 tablespoon grated ginger

2 teaspoons cayenne pepper

1 teaspoon ground black pepper

1 teaspoon ground cumin

½ teaspoon ground cinnamon

¼ teaspoon ground cloves

¼ teaspoon ground turmeric

2 tablespoons *fenni* or gin

1 teaspoon dark brown sugar

2 tablespoons mustard or olive oil

1 tablespoon fresh lemon juice

MAKES 2 SERVINGS

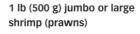 Peel and devein the shrimp, leaving the tails intact, and place the shrimp in a shallow nonreactive dish. To prepare the spice paste, in a small bowl, combine the garlic, ginger, cayenne, black pepper, cumin, cinnamon, cloves, turmeric, *fenni,* and sugar. Rub the paste evenly over the shrimp. Let stand at room temperature, about 30 minutes.

2 In a large frying pan over high heat, warm the oil. When it is very hot, add the shrimp and cook, tossing, until they turn pink and curl, about 5 minutes. Sprinkle with the lemon juice. Serve at once.

Shrimp with Garlic and Parsley

Along with paella and grilled fish, griddled shrimp are a fixture on the menu of nearly every beach restaurant up and down the Mediterranean coast from the Costa Brava to Alicante. *La plancha,* a kind of griddle, is arguably the Spanish cook's favorite tool.

24 large shrimp (prawns) in the shell, about 1½ lb (750 g) total weight

Salt and freshly ground pepper

Olive oil for drizzling

4 cloves garlic, minced

Handful of fresh flat-leaf (Italian) parsley leaves, minced

MAKES 4 SERVINGS

1 Place the shrimp in a bowl, season with salt and pepper, and drizzle generously with olive oil.

2 Heat a griddle or a large frying pan over high heat. It is ready when a drop of water on the surface sizzles and evaporates instantly. Place the shrimp on the hot surface and cook, turning once, until they are opaque throughout and the shells begin to brown, about 5 minutes per side. Sprinkle the garlic and parsley over the shrimp. Cook, without stirring, about 30 seconds, then turn again. Transfer to a warmed platter and serve at once.

Fried Shrimp with Tamarind

¾ lb (375 g) shrimp (prawns) in the shell

2 teaspoons tamarind concentrate mixed in ½ cup (4 fl oz/125 ml) water

3 tablespoons peanut oil or vegetable oil, or as needed

½ teaspoon salt

1 teaspoon sugar

3 green (spring) onions, including tender green tops, cut into 1½-inch (4-cm) lengths

MAKES 6 SERVINGS

1 Rinse the shrimp well and pat dry. Cut into the shells with a sharp knife to devein. Put the shrimp in a bowl with the tamarind water and let stand, turning occasionally, about 30 minutes.

2 Place a wok or large frying pan over medium-high heat. Add the oil and salt and swirl to coat the pan. When the oil starts to smoke, remove the shrimp from the tamarind water, reserving the liquid, and place as many as will fit in a single layer in the pan. Fry in the hot oil, undisturbed, until the bottoms are browned and crusty, about 1 minute. Turn and fry on the second side until browned and a bright orange-pink, about 1 minute longer. Using a slotted spoon, transfer to paper towels to drain. Keep warm. Fry the remaining shrimp the same way, using more oil if needed.

3 Pour the reserved tamarind water into the pan and add the sugar. Boil briskly until it forms a glaze, about 1 minute. Return the shrimp to the pan along with the green onions and cook, stirring constantly, until the shrimp are coated with the glaze. Transfer to a serving dish and serve at once.

Spanish Seafood

DORADA

The *dorada* is distinguished from similar species of fish by a small golden patch just above the eyes; hence, the English name, gilthead bream. (*Dorada* means "golden.") It is the classic choice for roasting whole in the oven, either *a la sal* (encased in salt) or on a bed of potatoes and onions. Once expensive, it is now more affordable, thanks to the rise of *piscifactorias* (fish farms) along the Mediterranean coast.

ESCÓRPORA

The *escórpora*, or scorpion fish, is a common sight in the fish markets of Barcelona and other Mediterranean cities (such as Marseilles, where it is used in bouillabaisse). *Scorpaena scrofa* is an unprepossessing creature, red and covered with fierce-looking spines that are poisonous to the touch, even when the fish is dead. A rockfish that lives close to the shoreline, the *escórpora* is valued for its rich flavor and gelatinous flesh and is considered vital to any good fish stock.

SARDINES

Few smells are more evocative than that of fresh sardines grilling over an open fire. These small, silvery fish are at their best from June to September, when they are fat and meaty. The food fiesta *sardinada popular*, in Calella on the coast near Girona, is a grand celebration (usually in mid-May) of grilled sardines served with the classic tomato-rubbed bread and washed down with plenty of wine.

BOQUERONES

Anchovies marinated in olive oil, parsley, and vinegar, or *boquerones en vinagre*, are regularly seen in tapas bars. They are also served deep-fried, either whole or in fillets. But most commonly they are salted and canned in olive oil, then eaten as a snack on toast, in salads, or as a topping for savory *coques* (flatbreads). The most prestigious salted anchovy preparations in Spain, those of L'Escala near Girona, raise this humble fish to the level of a true delicacy.

LANGOSTINOS

CALAMARS

MUSCLOS

GAMBES

DORADA

ESCÓRPORA

SARDINES

BOQUERONES

ORADA / DORÁDA
5'70 €/Kg

LANGOSTINOS

Langostinos (also referred to as Dublin Bay prawns) are often confused with their undersea cousins, *gambes* (shrimp/prawns). They are paler in color and have a more delicate flavor and firmer, meatier texture. The Spanish regard *langostinos* as superior to shrimp and are prepared to pay a much higher price for them at the market—especially during the holidays, when they are traditionally prepared. They are often served cold, with *allioli* on the side.

GAMBES

Juicy and bursting with the flavor of the sea, *gambes*, or shrimp (prawns), are cooked *a la plancha* (on a griddle, page 218) or *a la brasa* (over coals), or are briefly fried in olive oil. Eat them Spanish style: first snap off their heads and suck out the juices, then peel off the shell from the rest of the body. For the best of the best, seek out the shrimp of Palamós and Roses, two small coastal towns north of Barcelona.

CALAMARS

Calamars a la romana, battered and deep-fried squid rings, is the classic Spanish treatment for this popular seafood. Squid are also commonly cooked *a la plancha*, simmered with potatoes and onions, or, in the Empordá, stuffed with ham, egg, and an almond *picada*. In upscale restaurants, it is usual to see the designation *de pote*, meaning that the squid has been caught by the hook-and-line method and not the invasive commercial techniques that damage the flesh.

MUSCLOS

Spanish *musclos*, or mussels, come mainly from the cool waters of Galicia, where they are farmed in the estuaries of the Rias Baixas. They typically find their way into some type of rice dish, or sometimes they are prepared *a la plancha* and tossed with parsley and garlic. A popular tapa presents the cold, cooked mussel in its shell, dressed with a vinegary *pipirrana* of diced red and green bell pepper (capsicum) and tomato.

Scallops in Red Curry

Unlike the more common Thai curry, or *gaeng*, which generally has the consistency of soup and is served in a bowl, *choo chee* curry uses less coconut milk, resulting in a thicker sauce, and is served on a plate. If you're using canned coconut milk, open it without shaking the can, then scrape the thick mass off the top—that is the coconut cream. The opaque white layer in the middle is the coconut milk.

½ cup (4 fl oz/125 ml) coconut cream (see above)

1 tablespoon Thai red curry paste, homemade or purchased, or as needed

1 tablespoon palm sugar or brown sugar, or as needed

1–2 tablespoons fish sauce

1 cup (8 fl oz/250 ml) coconut milk (see above)

10 kaffir lime leaves, spines removed

1 tablespoon vegetable oil

¾ lb (375 g) sea scallops, patted dry

Handful of fresh Thai basil leaves, plus sprigs for garnish

1 fresh red chile, seeded and finely sliced

MAKES 4 SERVINGS

1 In a wok or saucepan over medium-high heat, bring the coconut cream to a gentle boil. Adjust the heat to maintain a gentle boil and cook, stirring constantly, until tiny beads of oil appear on the surface, 5–8 minutes. Add the 1 tablespoon curry paste and fry gently, stirring constantly, for about 2 minutes. Add the 1 tablespoon sugar and 1 tablespoon fish sauce and stir for a few seconds. Add the coconut milk and lime leaves and bring to a boil. Reduce the heat to medium-low and simmer, stirring occasionally, about 5 minutes.

2 Meanwhile, in a frying pan over medium-high heat, warm the vegetable oil. When the oil is hot, add as many scallops as will fit in a single layer. Let brown, undisturbed, about 1 minute. Turn them over and brown on the second side, about 1 minute. Transfer to a plate. Repeat with the remaining scallops.

3 When the sauce thickens to a creamy consistency, taste and adjust the seasoning with curry paste, palm sugar, and fish sauce. Add the scallops and basil leaves and stir to heat through. Transfer to a serving platter and garnish with the chile slices and basil sprigs.

Scallop Ceviche

1 lb (500 g) bay scallops

½ cup (4 fl oz/125 ml) fresh lime juice, plus extra if needed

1 ripe tomato, diced

1 tablespoon finely chopped fresh cilantro (fresh coriander)

1 serrano chile, minced

⅓ cup (3 fl oz/80 ml) extra-virgin olive oil

3 avocados

Sea salt

MAKES 6 SERVINGS

1 Put the scallops in a nonreactive bowl and toss with the ½ cup (4 fl oz/125 ml) lime juice. Cover and let marinate at room temperature, 10–15 minutes.

2 Drain the scallops and stir in the tomato, cilantro, chile, and oil. Halve the avocados and discard the pits. With a small melon baller, spoon out balls of the avocado flesh, or make cross-hatched cuts through the flesh and scoop out the resulting cubes. Add the avocado to the ceviche and toss gently. Season with salt and, if needed, more lime juice. Serve at once.

Scallops with Bacon and Radicchio

For this dish, delicate bay scallops are seared quickly to retain their sweet, nutty flavor and served with juicy tomatoes, crunchy radicchio, and a simplified basil pesto.

For the pesto

2 cups (2 oz/60 g) loosely packed fresh basil leaves

2 cloves garlic

½ cup (4 fl oz/125 ml) extra-virgin olive oil

2 tablespoons unsalted butter

¼ lb (2 oz) bacon, cut into strips ¼ inch (6 mm) wide

2 lb (1 kg) bay scallops, patted dry

1–2 heads radicchio, cored and cut into thin strips

2 large tomatoes, peeled and seeded, then finely diced

MAKES 6–8 SERVINGS

1 To prepare the pesto, put the basil and garlic in a food processor and process to chop very finely. Add the olive oil and process to form a paste that still has some texture. Set aside.

2 In a large frying pan over medium heat, melt the butter and heat until golden. Add the bacon and sauté until golden brown, 2–3 minutes. Transfer to a small plate. Raise the heat to medium-high, add the scallops, and cook, turning once, until golden, about 2 minutes per side. Add the pesto and bacon and toss quickly to coat the scallops. Add the radicchio and mix well. Divide among warmed individual plates, top with the tomatoes, and serve at once.

POULTRY

Birds of a Feather

POULTRY AROUND THE WORLD

A whole chicken, turkey, goose, or duck symbolizes celebration and prosperity around the world. Roasted to perfectly brown crispness or unveiled from layers of moist lotus leaves, a bird at the center of the dinner table unites everyone gathered in a moment of gustatory awe. Fortunately, members of the poultry family are equally comfortable in the casual garb of everyday dishes.

Poultry's versatility—its ability to absorb flavorings from Tuscan rosemary to Indian curries, its adaptability to the roasting pan, the simmering soup pot, or the glowing coals—has made it the cornerstone of daily fare across cultures. Hunting in forests and meadows for pheasant, partridge, grouse, woodcock, or squab was once the primary way to bring birds to the table. Today, domesticated poultry, including quail and Cornish game hens, have taken their place. Turkey has associations ranging from the humble sandwich to the centerpiece of many feasts, but chicken is perhaps the most universal of all meats. Sichuan cooks like slicing chicken meat thin for stir-frying with peanuts and tongue-numbing peppercorns and chiles. American southerners memorize

their sacred family recipes for the perfect fried chicken, while Indians debate the ideal ratio of butter, tomatoes, and almonds for their much-loved dish, *murgh makhani.* In fact, chicken and turkey are so popular, so interchangeable, that it's difficult to imagine a time when they were confined, respectively, to the Old and New Worlds. Arabs and Asians had long been sharing their pigeon pies, *tagines,* and aromatic curries, but it wasn't until colonists disembarked in the Americas with clucking chickens under their arms and ships returned to Europe with exotic turkeys that recipes began incorporating both and that the birds' popularity began to spread. To this day, rubbed with myriad seasonings, birds continue to bring new, vibrant flavors into kitchens everywhere.

CHICKEN

In China, a plainly cooked whole chicken is de rigueur at wedding and holiday banquets. More elaborate versions include five-spice powder or orange peel, but the simplest of all, Hainan chicken, is the best known in Asia. In Malaysia and Singapore, where everyone has a passionate opinion on which hawker stall is the best, the dish goes simply by the name chicken rice. It begins with a high-quality bird, involves barely poaching the meat in clear stock followed by dips in ice-cold water, and then ends with a plate of pandanus-infused rice and a trio of sauces based on thick soy, red chile, and ginger. Chickens also play important roles in China's medicinal cooking, especially the famed black-skinned bird known as *wu gu ji,* whose gaminess is highly prized for making full-flavored, restorative broths.

Another famous chicken is France's *poulet de Bresse.* Raised on pastureland, fed local grains and milk, and patriotically colored with a red comb, white feathers, and astonishingly blue feet, Bresse chickens are highly prized for their firm, flavorful meat. French chefs boast hundreds of traditional ways of cooking chicken—it was Henry IV who originally promised a chicken in every pot—and they carefully codify their recipes. In Italy, simplicity reigns. Roasted whole with just a couple of lemons inside or pressed beneath a brick with a few sprigs of rosemary, Italian chicken dishes make full use of the country's olive oil. Eastern European Jews serve slow-simmered chicken soup, perhaps ladled over matzo balls, and render chicken fat into schmalz for cooking and flavoring a wide variety of dishes.

The national dish of Ethiopia, *doro wat,* highlights chicken in a sauce based on spiced butter and a fiery seasoning paste. On the opposite coast of Africa, *poulet yassa,* a Senegalese specialty, calls for marinating chicken with lemon juice and generous amounts of thinly sliced onions. Eaten over rice, this stew is a favorite throughout West Africa.

In Jamaica, jerk chicken spotlights the island's native allspice tree. Its warmly flavored berries marry with scotch bonnets in an aromatic rub. The best versions, grilled over an open pit of allspice wood and draped with allspice leaves, absorb layers of flavor. Jerk stands dot the island, and the dish has followed Jamaican immigrants as they've resettled in other countries. Other meats, such as pork and fish, find their way into the pit, but jerk chicken is the most popular incarnation of Jamaica's national dish.

DUCK

The distinct fat layer of the Pekin or Long Island duck is desired by the Chinese for roasting to papery crispness, while Western cooks look for Muscovy ducks with lean, rich meat. A hybrid is the prized Moulard, with its large, meaty breast lobes, known as *magret*.

Gascony, in the southwest of France, is famous for a hearty cuisine based on duck and goose. Luxurious duck confit and foie gras hail from this region, but local cooks take care to use every part of the bird. Gizzards are cured in salt, then sliced thinly and tossed with frisée for a filling salad. The skin becomes *grattons*, leftover meat is packed into rillettes, and the bones are roasted for making stock.

Peking duck is perhaps the most famed of Chinese preparations. Lacquered with glaze and roasted to a distinctive mahogany color, the whole duck is served in a formal, three-course banquet. Its crisp skin is carved tableside and wrapped in pancakes with scallions, cucumber, and hoisin sauce. The meat appears, stir-fried, in the second course. The bones are the base for a soup that then closes the meal. Roast duck is also served throughout Asia in a bowl of soup with egg noodles, shiitake mushrooms, bamboo shoots, or greens.

TURKEY

In addition to Thanksgiving celebrations, turkey stars in mole, one of Mexico's signature dishes. A centerpiece of holiday feasts, mole takes on regional variations, from golden yellow through shades of herbal greens and chile reds to the deep black of a Oaxacan mole. The complex flavors derive from the richness of nuts and seeds, the warmth of spices like cinnamon and clove, the smokiness of dried chiles, and balancing notes of chocolate. The turkey is cooked separately and combined with the sauce just before the dish is served.

GAME BIRDS

In Europe, currants, elderberries, quince, and other seasonal fruits balance the stronger flavor of game birds. In the Middle East, pigeon and quail are stuffed with couscous or glazed with pomegranate molasses. Flaky layers of filo dough encase cinnamon-infused pigeon meat and whole almonds in *bisteeya*, a Moroccan sweet-savory pie. In China and Southeast Asia, quail is a favorite from banquet tables to street stalls. Dipped in five-spice salt or drizzled with fresh lime juice, the tiny birds are eaten while still hot and crisp.

Chicken Tomatillo Enchiladas

This recipe comes from Xochimilco, where, long before the Spanish conquest, the Aztecs were raising vegetables, chiles, and herbs on floating gardens encircling Tenochtitlán, their island capital.

For the chicken

2 lb (1 kg) chicken breasts

¼ white onion

1 head garlic, halved crosswise

Sea salt

For the sauce

3 lb (1.5 kg) tomatillos, husked and rinsed

9 serrano chiles

3 cloves garlic, chopped

¼ cup (2 fl oz/60 ml) safflower or canola oil

Sea salt

For the enchiladas

⅓ cup (3 fl oz/80 ml) safflower or canola oil

18 corn tortillas, homemade or purchased

1 cup (8 fl oz/250 ml) *crema*

1 white onion, thinly sliced

1 cup (5 oz/155 g) crumbled *queso fresco*

MAKES 6 SERVINGS

1 To prepare the chicken, place it in a saucepan with the onion, garlic, and 1 tablespoon salt and add water to cover. Bring to a boil, reduce the heat to medium, cover, and simmer until the chicken is cooked through, 20–25 minutes. Let cool, then lift out the chicken, reserving the broth for another use. (The chicken can be wrapped and refrigerated for up to 1 day before continuing.) Discard the skin and bones and shred the meat with your fingers. There should be 4 cups (1½ lb/750 g) chicken.

2 To prepare the sauce, in a saucepan, combine the tomatillos and chiles with water to cover. Bring to a boil and cook until tender, 10–15 minutes, then drain. Adding them in batches, place the tomatillos and chiles in a blender along with the garlic and process to form a smooth sauce.

3 In a frying pan over medium-high heat, warm the oil until it begins to smoke. Add the sauce and fry, stirring constantly, until bubbling. Reduce the heat to low and cook until the sauce starts to thicken, about 5 minutes. Add 1 tablespoon salt; taste and add salt if needed so that the sauce is highly seasoned. You should have 3 cups (24 fl oz/ 750 ml) of sauce. Add some of the reserved chicken broth if needed. Keep warm.

4 Preheat the oven to 350°F (180°C). To make the enchiladas, in a frying pan over medium-high heat, heat the oil until sizzling hot. Using tongs, quickly pass each tortilla through the oil to soften, then drain on paper towels. Dip each tortilla briefly in the warm sauce and set on a plate. Put a large spoonful of shredded chicken near one edge, roll up the tortilla, and place, seam side down, in a baking dish. Cover with the remaining sauce and bake until thoroughly heated, about 10 minutes. Remove the enchiladas from the oven and top with the *crema*, onion slices, and crumbled cheese and serve at once.

Chicken Tikka Masala

Indian food is so loved by the British that it is now regarded as an essential part of the national diet. The British developed a taste for curried dishes in the eighteenth century, but it was not until the 1970s that Indian restaurants began to influence how the British ate. One of the most popular dishes, a uniquely British invention, is chicken tikka masala, succulent cubes of chicken breast bathed in a sweet, spicy sauce. Serve with white rice and warm pita breads (page 25).

For the marinade

¼ cup (2 oz/60 g) plain whole-milk yogurt

Juice of 1½ limes

2 teaspoons peeled and finely chopped fresh ginger

1 teaspoon cumin

1 teaspoon garam masala

2 teaspoons paprika

4 boneless, skinless chicken breast halves, about 4 oz (125 g) each, cut into 1-inch (2.5-cm) cubes

Sea salt

5 tablespoons (2½ fl oz/75 ml) sunflower oil

1 small yellow onion, finely diced

1 clove garlic, finely chopped

1 teaspoon peeled and chopped fresh ginger

5 green cardamom pods

1 teaspoon ground cumin

1 teaspoon ground coriander

½ teaspoon ground turmeric

½ teaspoon ground chile

1 lb (500 g) tomatoes, peeled, seeded, and diced

1 jalapeño chile, thinly sliced

½ cup (4 fl oz/125 ml) heavy (double) cream

¼ teaspoon garam masala

Juice of ½ lemon

MAKES 4 SERVINGS

1 To prepare the marinade, in a nonreactive bowl, stir together the yogurt, lime juice, ginger, cumin, garam masala, and paprika.

2 Add the chicken cubes to the marinade and stir to coat. Cover and refrigerate for at least 1 hour or up to 7 hours.

3 Preheat the broiler (grill). Line a broiler pan with aluminum foil. Remove the chicken cubes from the marinade, shaking off the excess, and place on a plate. Season with salt, drizzle with 2 tablespoons of the sunflower oil, and toss to coat. Arrange the chicken in a single layer on the prepared pan. Broil (grill), turning once, until browned, about 3 minutes per side. Alternatively, heat a stove-top grill pan over medium-high heat, add the chicken in a single layer, and cook, turning once, until browned, about 3 minutes per side. Set aside.

4 In a saucepan over medium heat, warm the remaining 3 tablespoons sunflower oil. Add the onion, garlic, and ginger and cook, stirring frequently, until the onion is soft, 4–5 minutes. Add the cardamom, cumin, coriander, turmeric, and ground chile and cook, stirring constantly, about 2 minutes. Add the tomatoes and cook, stirring frequently, until the oil separates from the tomato mixture, 5–8 minutes. Add the chile, cream, and ½ cup (4 fl oz/125 ml) water, bring to a boil, reduce the heat to low, and simmer until the mixture forms a creamy sauce, 8–10 minutes. Stir in the cooked chicken and the garam masala, season with salt, and simmer until the chicken is heated through, 8–10 minutes. Stir in the lemon juice and serve at once.

Chicken and Vegetable Potpie

This version of the classic chicken potpie has a biscuit topping—pastry and mashed potatoes being the popular alternatives—and is served straight from the frying pan. Both are in keeping with the dish's rustic New England character.

For the filling

8 tablespoons (4 oz/125 g) unsalted butter

½ lb (250 g) fresh button mushrooms, thinly sliced

2 carrots, peeled and diced

1 yellow onion, chopped

1 small red bell pepper (capsicum), seeded and diced

Salt and freshly ground black pepper

1 clove garlic, minced

1 teaspoon chopped fresh thyme

1¼ lb (625 g) boneless, skinless chicken breasts or thighs, cut into bite-sized pieces

¼ cup (1½ oz/45 g) all-purpose (plain) flour

2 cups (16 fl oz/500 ml) chicken stock

1 cup (8 fl oz/250 ml) heavy (double) cream

1 cup (5 oz/155 g) fresh or frozen peas

2 tablespoons dry sherry

2 tablespoons chopped fresh chives

2 tablespoons chopped fresh flat-leaf (Italian) parsley

For the topping

1 cup (5 oz/155 g) all-purpose (plain) flour

1 tablespoon sugar

2 teaspoons baking powder

½ teaspoon salt

Pinch of ground cayenne pepper

5 tablespoons (2½ oz/75 g) unsalted butter, chilled, cut into ½-inch (12-mm) pieces

½ cup (4 fl oz/125 ml) buttermilk

MAKES 6 SERVINGS

1 To make the filling, in an ovenproof frying pan 11 inches (28 cm) in diameter and 2½ inches (6 cm) deep, melt 2 tablespoons of the butter over medium heat. Add the mushrooms, carrots, onion, and bell pepper and season with salt and black pepper. Cook, stirring occasionally, until barely tender, about 10 minutes. Add the garlic and thyme and cook, stirring, until fragrant, about 1 minute. Transfer to a large plate.

2 Raise the heat to medium-high and add another 2 tablespoons butter to the frying pan. When the butter melts, add the chicken and season with salt and black pepper. Cook, stirring often, until the chicken is lightly browned and barely cooked through, about 4 minutes. Transfer it to the plate with the vegetables.

3 Reduce the heat to medium-low and melt the remaining 4 tablespoons (2 oz/60 g) butter in the pan. Add the flour and whisk until bubbling but not browned, about 1 minute, scraping up any browned bits on the pan bottom. Pour in the stock and the cream, raise the heat to medium-high, and bring to a boil. Reduce the heat to low and simmer, stirring occasionally, until thickened, about 3 minutes. Add the reserved vegetables and chicken and the peas, sherry, chives, and parsley. Season with salt and black pepper. Turn off the heat, cover, and set aside. (You may refrigerate the filling for up to 6 hours. Uncover and reheat gently, stirring frequently, while making the topping.)

4 Preheat the oven to 400°F (200°C). To make the biscuit topping, in a bowl, whisk together the flour, sugar, baking powder, salt, and cayenne pepper. Using a pastry cutter, cut in the butter until the pieces are no larger than peas. Add the buttermilk and stir gently to form a soft dough.

5 Uncover the filling. Bring to a boil over medium-high heat, stirring occasionally, about 3 minutes. Reduce the heat to medium-low. Using 2 tablespoons, drop small amounts of the dough onto the filling to cover almost completely. Transfer to the oven and bake until the topping is lightly browned and a toothpick inserted into it comes out clean, about 25 minutes. Serve at once.

Braised Chicken with Shallots

The Alsace is a land of orchards and grain fields, of medieval villages and storybook castles, of sauerkraut and beer. It includes stretches of both the Rhine River and the Vosges Mountains, and is home to some of the best white wines in France, including parchment-dry Rieslings that Parisians cook with and pour at the table. In this recipe, Alsatian Riesling becomes the base for a sauce enriched with cream and seasoned with tarragon, an herb more fully established in the French pantry than in any other.

4½ lb (2.25 kg) chicken pieces, preferably legs with thighs attached

Salt and freshly ground pepper

3 tablespoons extra-virgin olive oil

6–8 shallots, about ½ lb (250 g) total weight, chopped

3 cloves garlic, chopped

1 bottle (750 ml) full-bodied white wine such as Riesling

3 tablespoons small pieces dried mushrooms such as chanterelle, cèpe, or fairy ring

2 cups (16 fl oz/500 ml) chicken stock

2 tablespoons coarsely chopped fresh tarragon

¾ cup (6 fl oz/180 ml) heavy (double) cream

A few drops fresh lemon juice (optional)

2 tablespoons chopped fresh chives

1–2 tablespoons chopped fresh chervil

MAKES 4–6 SERVINGS

1 Preheat the oven to 350°F (180°C). Rinse the chicken pieces and pat dry. Season with salt and pepper, then rub with the olive oil. In a large, heavy nonstick pan over medium-high heat, brown the chicken in batches, turning occasionally, 10–15 minutes per batch. Transfer to a platter.

2 Pour off all but 1 tablespoon of fat from the pan and place over medium heat. Add the shallots and garlic and sauté until softened, about 5 minutes. Add the wine, raise the heat to high, bring to a boil, and cook until reduced by half, 10–15 minutes. Stir in the mushrooms, stock, and half of the tarragon. Pour the sauce into a roasting pan at least 4 inches (10 cm) deep and large enough to hold the chicken in a single layer. Arrange the chicken on the sauce.

3 Bake the chicken until opaque throughout when pierced with a knife, 35–40 minutes. Raise the heat to 400°F (200°C) and continue baking until the edges of the skin are crisp, about 5 minutes longer. Transfer the chicken to a deep platter and cover loosely with aluminum foil to keep warm.

4 Spoon off any fat from the sauce. Place the pan over high heat, bring the sauce to a boil, and cook, stirring, until reduced by about half, 7–8 minutes. Stir in the cream. Taste and adjust the seasoning with salt and pepper and with lemon juice, if using. Pour the sauce over the chicken and sprinkle with the chives, chervil, and remaining tarragon. Serve at once.

FRANCE
Making Champagne

CHAMPAGNE LABELS DEMYSTIFIED

The terms *brut non-dosé*, *brut*, *demi-sec*, and *doux* mean "bone dry," "dry," "off-dry," and "sweet," respectively. The phrase *blanc de blancs* denotes that a wine was made entirely from white Chardonnay grapes. *Blanc de noirs* means it was made entirely from red Pinot Noir and Pinot Meunier grapes.

Most Champagne is nonvintage (NV), that is, blended from wines that balance the qualities of different years' harvests. Likewise, most Champagne is made by large producers that purchase their grapes. Such a producer is called a *négociant-manipulant*. By contrast a *récoltant-manipulant* or *propriétaire-récoltant* is a small producer that grows its own grapes. These are often high-quality, artisanal wines. Bottles with a vintage year on the label must be made entirely of grapes from a single year's high-quality harvest. These are *millésime*, or vintage Champagnes, and they are aged longer than NV wines. The finest Champagnes come from a limited number of villages designated *grand cru* (grand growth) or *premier cru* (first growth).

The famed sparkling wines of the Champagne region are the product of a more involved process than that used for making still wines. They begin in Champagne's soil, take form through a series of steps in the winery, and are perfected in damp chalk cellars originally built by the Romans.

AGING SUR LATTES

In underground chalk halls, bottles of Champagne are stacked ten feet (3 meters) high, in rows that can extend for more than two-thirds of a mile (1 kilometer). Here, the wines are aging *sur lattes* (on boards) after a second fermentation in the bottle. Once a blend has been determined, the young wine is bottled and a mixture of sugar and yeast is added. Fermentation begins, and then the bottle is sealed with a cap and put to rest for at least fifteen months.

MAKING CHAMPAGNE

CRUSH AND FIRST FERMENTATION After harvest, the grapes are crushed and the juice is transferred to stainless-steel vats. Yeast is added and the first fermentation begins.

BLENDING AND SECOND FERMENTATION After the blend is determined, the wine is bottled, a mixture of yeast and sugar is added, and a second fermentation begins. At this point, carbon dioxide bubbles are trapped in the bottle. The bottles are given a few shakes, or *poignetage*, to stir up the yeast and enrich the wine, and the bottles are aged *sur lattes*.

RIDDLING The bottles are placed at an angle. Each bottle is given a periodic series of twists, known as riddling, to encourage sediment to collect in the bottle's neck.

DISGORGEMENT AND DOSAGE Cellar workers make sure all sediment has settled. Then, in a process known as disgorgement, the tops of the bottles are flash-frozen; the solidified sediment flies out when the bottles are briefly uncapped. A *dosage* of new wine and sugar is added, and the wine is readied for shipment or further aging.

Braised Spicy Ginger Chicken

Ginger, garlic, chiles, vinegar, and Sichuan pepper are the typically exuberant flavors of the landlocked province of Hunan. The city of Dong'an, the reputed birthplace of this dish, is on its southern border.

For the sauce

½ cup (4 fl oz/125 ml) chicken stock or water

1½ tablespoons light soy sauce

1 tablespoon black vinegar

2 teaspoons chile oil

1 tablespoon superfine (caster) sugar

14 oz (440 g) boneless chicken thighs, cut into ¾-inch (2-cm) cubes

1 tablespoon dark soy sauce

1 tablespoon cornstarch (cornflour)

Peanut oil for deep-frying

¾ cup (2½ oz/75 g) chopped green (spring) onion, including tender green tops

1 fresh hot red chile, seeded and sliced

1 tablespoon peeled and grated fresh ginger

1 tablespoon crushed garlic

Salt

Ground white pepper or Sichuan pepper

MAKES 4 SERVINGS

1 To make the sauce, in a small bowl, stir together the stock, light soy sauce, vinegar, chile oil, and sugar. Set aside.

2 In a nonreactive bowl, combine the chicken, dark soy sauce, and cornstarch and mix well. Let stand for at least 15 minutes.

3 Pour oil to a depth of 1 inch (2.5 cm) into a wok, and heat to 360°F (182°C) on a deep-frying thermometer, or until a small cube of bread dropped in turns golden within a few seconds. Carefully add the chicken to the hot oil, stir to separate the pieces, and fry until golden brown, about 1½ minutes. Transfer to a rack over paper towels to drain.

4 Pour off all but 2 tablespoons of the oil and return the wok to high heat. Add the green onion, chile, ginger, and garlic and stir-fry until partially wilted, about 30 seconds. Return the chicken to the wok and stir-fry until the ingredients are evenly mixed, about 30 seconds. Pour in the sauce and stir until well mixed, about 10 seconds. Reduce the heat to medium-low, cover, and simmer gently until the chicken is tender and the flavors are well blended, about 4 minutes. Season with salt and pepper. Serve at once.

Braised Chicken with Pancetta

Deep and spicy Italian red wine complements winter stews and braises such as this one, especially when tomato sauce is involved. Serve this dish with a creamy polenta, such as the one on page 76.

½ oz (15 g) dried porcini mushrooms

Hot water

1 chicken, about 3½ lb (1.75 g), cut into 8 serving pieces (2 wings, 2 legs, 2 thighs, 2 breasts)

Sea salt and freshly ground pepper

1 tablespoon extra-virgin olive oil

3 oz (90 g) pancetta, minced

2 large cloves garlic, minced

1 tablespoon minced fresh sage

½ cup (4 fl oz/125 ml) hearty, spicy red wine such as Barbera d'Asti

1 can (14½ oz/455 g) plum (Roma) tomatoes with juice, puréed in a blender

1½ tablespoons minced fresh flat-leaf (Italian) parsley

MAKES 4 SERVINGS

1 Place the mushrooms in a small bowl, add ¾ cup (6 fl oz/180 ml) hot water, and let soak until softened. Drain through a fine-mesh sieve lined with cheesecloth (muslin), pressing against the mushrooms and reserving the soaking liquid. Chop the mushrooms and set aside.

2 Rinse the chicken pieces and pat dry. Season with salt and pepper. Heat a large frying pan over medium-high until hot. Add the olive oil and swirl to coat the bottom. When the oil is almost smoking, add the chicken in one layer, skin side down. Reduce the heat to medium and cook until browned, about 8 minutes. Turn and cook until browned on the second side, about 8 minutes longer. Transfer to a platter and pour off all but 1 tablespoon fat.

3 Place the pan over medium-low heat and add the pancetta. Sauté until the pancetta crisps, about 1 minute. Add the garlic and sage and sauté for about 1 minute. Add the wine and simmer briefly, scraping the browned bits from the pan bottom. Add the tomatoes, mushrooms, and reserved soaking liquid. Bring to a simmer, adjust the heat to maintain a gentle simmer, and cook, uncovered, about 15 minutes. Add a little water if the sauce is too dry.

4 Preheat the oven to 200°F (95°C). Return the chicken to the pan, cover, and simmer gently, turning it once in the sauce, until tender, about 15 minutes. As the pieces are done, transfer them to a heatproof serving platter kept in the oven. (The breasts may be done first.) If the sauce seems thin, raise the heat to high and simmer until thickened. Spoon the sauce over the chicken and garnish with the parsley. Serve at once.

Chicken Curry

Enjoyed by Indonesians and Malaysians alike, the original version of this traditional ritual feast dish has become obscured through the cross-cultural sharing of recipes. For the thin coconut milk it calls for, do not shake the can before opening. Spoon out the creamy top layer and milky middle layer and use only the clear lower layer.

1 small chicken, about 3½ lb (1.75 kg), cut into serving pieces

Juice of 1 lemon

For the spice paste

1 tablespoon coriander seeds

1½ teaspoons cumin seeds

½ teaspoon fennel seeds

½ teaspoon whole white peppercorns

6 candlenuts or blanched almonds, soaked in water for 10 minutes and drained

6 large shallots, quartered

4 cloves garlic, quartered

1-inch (2.5-cm) piece fresh ginger, peeled and coarsely chopped

4 slices fresh galangal, peeled and chopped, or 2 slices dried galangal

2–3 tablespoons vegetable oil

2 lemongrass stalks, tender midsection only, smashed and cut in half

2 *salam* leaves, bay leaves or curry leaves

2 kaffir lime leaves, spines removed

2 cups (16 fl oz/500 ml) thin coconut milk

2 teaspoons palm sugar or dark brown sugar

1 teaspoon tamarind concentrate mixed in ¼ cup (2 fl oz/60 ml) water

Salt

2 tablespoons fresh lemon juice

Vegetable oil for frying

4–6 shallots, thinly sliced

MAKES 4 SERVINGS

1 Rinse the chicken pieces and pat dry. Place in a large nonreactive bowl and rub with the lemon juice. Set aside.

2 To prepare the spice paste, in a small, dry frying pan over medium heat, toast the coriander, cumin, and fennel seeds and the white peppercorns until fragrant, 1–2 minutes. Transfer to a mortar or spice grinder and grind to a fine powder. Transfer to a blender and add the candlenuts, shallots, garlic, ginger, and galangal. Process to form a smooth paste. If necessary, add 2–3 tablespoons water to facilitate the blending.

3 Preheat a wok or Dutch oven over medium-high heat. When the pan is hot, add 2 tablespoons of the vegetable oil and swirl to coat the pan. When the oil is hot but not smoking, add the spice paste and cook, stirring, until the oil and paste are emulsified, about 3 minutes. Reduce the heat to medium-low and simmer gently, stirring frequently, until the paste is fragrant, dry, and a light khaki color, 5–7 minutes. Do not allow the paste to brown.

4 Add the chicken pieces and lemongrass and fry together, stirring often, until the chicken is nicely coated with the spice paste, about 5 minutes. Add the *salam* leaves, lime leaves, coconut milk, sugar, and tamarind water. Raise the heat to high and bring the mixture to a boil. Reduce the heat to medium and boil gently uncovered, stirring occasionally, until the chicken is cooked through and the sauce has thickened and has an oily surface, about 20 minutes. Spoon off the excess surface oil. Add the lemon juice and season with salt.

5 Meanwhile, pour vegetable oil to a depth of about 1 inch (2.5 cm) into a small frying pan, and heat over medium heat to 325°F (165°C) on a deep-frying thermometer. Add the shallots and fry until light golden brown, about 5 minutes, reducing the heat if they color too quickly. Transfer to paper towels to drain and let cool.

6 Transfer the chicken to a serving dish and garnish with the fried shallots. Serve at once.

Vietnamese Five-Spice Chicken

This Vietnamese dish gets its flavor from five-spice powder, which is used primarily in Vietnamese and southern Chinese cooking. Despite its name, the seasoning mixture doesn't always contain five spices. It typically includes star anise, cassia (a type of cinnamon), fennel, cloves, Sichuan peppercorns, and sometimes ginger and/or cardamom. Look for it in Asian markets and well-stocked supermarkets.

6 cloves garlic, sliced

1 large shallot, coarsely chopped

1 tablespoon peeled and minced fresh ginger

4 teaspoons sugar

¼ cup (2 fl oz/60 ml) soy sauce

¼ cup (2 fl oz/60 ml) Thai or Vietnamese fish sauce

½ teaspoon five-spice powder (see above)

Freshly ground pepper

1 chicken, about 3 lb (1.5 kg), cut into 8 serving pieces (2 wings, 2 legs, 2 thighs, 2 breasts), plus 2 extra wings

MAKES 4 SERVINGS

1 To prepare the marinade, in a small food processor, combine the garlic, shallot, ginger, and sugar and process to form a paste. Alternatively, combine the ingredients on a cutting board and, using a large, sharp knife, mince to a paste. Transfer to a small bowl and whisk in the soy sauce, fish sauce, five-spice powder, and several grinds of pepper.

2 Rinse the chicken pieces and pat dry. Place in a shallow nonreactive dish, pour the marinade over the pieces, and turn to coat. Cover and refrigerate, turning the chicken several times in the marinade, 8–12 hours. Bring to room temperature before cooking.

3 Prepare a charcoal or gas grill for direct grilling over medium heat. Remove the chicken pieces from the marinade, reserving the marinade, and place skin side down on the grill rack directly over the heat source. Grill until nicely browned, 11–12 minutes, basting once or twice with the marinade. Turn, baste again, and grill until the juices run clear when a thigh is pierced with a knife, 11–12 minutes longer. Do not baste during the final 10 minutes.

4 Remove the chicken pieces from the grill, let cool slightly, then cut each breast in half crosswise. Serve at once.

Grilled Chicken Kebabs

1 large yellow onion, chopped

4 cloves garlic, minced

¼ cup (2 fl oz/60 ml) fresh lemon juice

1 tablespoon paprika

1 tablespoon chopped fresh thyme

½ teaspoon cayenne pepper

Freshly ground black pepper

1 cup (8 oz/250 g) plain yogurt

1½ lb (750 g) boneless, skinless chicken breasts or thighs, cut into 1-inch (2.5-cm) cubes

Olive oil for brushing

Salt

MAKES 4 SERVINGS

1 To prepare the marinade, in a food processor, combine the onion, garlic, lemon juice, paprika, thyme, cayenne, and ½ teaspoon black pepper. Pulse to mix. Add the yogurt and pulse again to mix.

2 Place the chicken cubes in a nonreactive bowl, pour the marinade over the cubes, and stir to coat. Cover and refrigerate, about 8 hours.

3 If using bamboo skewers, soak them in water to cover, about 30 minutes. Prepare a charcoal or gas grill for direct grilling over medium heat, or preheat a broiler (grill). Remove the chicken from the marinade, reserving the marinade, and thread onto skewers. Brush with olive oil and sprinkle with salt and black pepper. Place the skewers on the grill rack or a broiler pan and grill, turning and basting once with the reserved marinade, until the chicken is no longer pink in the center, 4–5 minutes per side for breast meat and 5–6 minutes per side for thigh meat. Transfer to warmed individual plates and serve at once.

Chicken with Pepper-Lime Sauce

1 teaspoon whole peppercorns

6 cloves garlic, quartered

¼ cup (2 fl oz/60 ml) mushroom soy sauce

2 tablespoons sugar

1 tablespoon vegetable oil

Coarse salt

2 small chickens, 2½ lb (1.25 kg) each, halved

Fresh cilantro (fresh coriander) sprigs

For the dip

1 tablespoon ground peppercorns

1½ teaspoons coarse salt or sea salt

2 limes, halved

MAKES 4 SERVINGS

1 To prepare the marinade, in a mortar using a pestle, coarsely grind the peppercorns. Add the garlic and crush to a coarse paste. Transfer to a bowl and stir in the mushroom soy sauce, sugar, vegetable oil, and 1 teaspoon coarse salt.

2 Rinse the chicken halves and pat dry. Place the halves in a large, shallow baking dish, pour the marinade over the chicken, and turn to coat. Cover and refrigerate for at least 1 hour or up to overnight.

3 Prepare a charcoal or gas grill for direct grilling over medium heat. Place the chicken halves, skin side down, on the grill rack about 4 inches (10 cm) from the fire and grill until the skin is nicely charred, about 15 minutes. Turn and grill until charred on the second side and the juices run clear when a thigh is pierced with a knife, 10–15 minutes longer. Transfer to a cutting board and cut into serving pieces. Arrange on a platter and garnish with cilantro sprigs.

4 To prepare the dip, divide the pepper and salt among 4 dipping saucers. Squeeze ½ lime into each and stir until the salt dissolves. The dip can also be poured over the chicken rather than dipped into.

Roast Chicken with Lemon

It is one thing to say that simplicity is the essence of the Tuscan kitchen. It is quite another to taste the extraordinary deliciousness that can come from just one chicken, two lemons, and a pinch of salt and pepper.

1 chicken, about 3½ lb (1.75 kg), neck and giblets removed

2 tablespoons extra-virgin olive oil

Salt and freshly ground pepper

2 small lemons

MAKES 4 SERVINGS

1 Preheat the oven to 375°F (190°C). Rinse the chicken inside and out and pat dry. Rub the outside of the chicken with the olive oil, then sprinkle the skin and cavity with salt and pepper. Stuff the cavity with the 2 whole lemons. Tuck the wings behind the back. Draw the drumsticks together and tie tightly with kitchen string.

2 Lightly oil a shallow roasting pan large enough to hold the chicken comfortably. Place the chicken, breast side up, in the pan and roast, basting occasionally with the juices, until it is deep golden brown and the juices run clear when a thigh is pierced with a knife, about 1¼ hours. An instant-read thermometer inserted into the thickest part of a thigh away from the bone should register 165°F (74°C).

3 Transfer the chicken to a carving board and set the roasting pan aside. Remove the lemons from the cavity and set aside. Loosely tent the chicken with aluminum foil and let rest, about 10 minutes.

4 When the lemons are cool enough to handle, cut them in half and squeeze the juice into the roasting pan. Discard the lemons. Add 3 tablespoons water to the juices in the pan. Place over high heat and cook until reduced by one-third, about 2 minutes.

5 Remove the string, carve the chicken, and arrange on a warmed serving platter. Pour the pan juices over the chicken and serve at once.

Five Flavor Chicken

The expressive names of Sichuanese dishes reflect their flavor characteristics. This dish, often called "strange flavor chicken," is one in which sweet, sour, hot, salty, and spicy blend with no single flavor predominating. Sichuan pepper, made from the tiny, red-brown berries of the prickly ash tree, is native to the central provinces of China. It adds an appealing flavor wherever it is used.

For the sauce

2 tablespoons very finely minced green (spring) onion, including tender green tops

1 tablespoon peeled and grated fresh ginger

1 tablespoon very finely chopped garlic

1 tablespoon sesame paste

2½ tablespoons light soy sauce

5–6 teaspoons Asian sesame oil

1 tablespoon red vinegar

1 tablespoon vegetable oil

2–3 teaspoons chile oil

2½ teaspoons superfine (caster) sugar

½ teaspoon ground Sichuan pepper (optional)

2 whole chicken legs (drumsticks and thighs)

1 tablespoon light soy sauce

Vegetable oil for deep-frying

MAKES 4 SERVINGS

1 To make the sauce, in a bowl, beat together the green onion, ginger, garlic, sesame paste, soy sauce, sesame oil, vinegar, vegetable and chile oils, sugar, pepper (if using), and 2 tablespoons water until a thin, creamy sauce forms. Set aside.

2 Bring water to a simmer in a steamer base. Place the chicken legs on a steamer rack over the water, cover, and steam until tender and the juices run clear when a thigh is pierced with a knife, about 25 minutes. Remove the chicken and let cool, about 5 minutes. Brush lightly with the soy sauce and let stand, uncovered, about 20 minutes.

3 Pour the oil to a depth of 3 inches (7.5 cm) into a wok, and heat over medium-high heat to 360°F (182°C) on a deep-frying thermometer, or until a small cube of bread dropped into it begins to turn golden within a few seconds. Carefully add the chicken to the hot oil and fry until the skin is amber and glossy, about 2 minutes. Gently lift out the chicken, holding it over the pan for a moment to drain. Let cool, about 5 minutes or until just warmer than room temperature.

4 Remove the meat from the bones and cut into bite-sized strips. Arrange in a pile on a platter. Spoon half of the sauce over the chicken and pass the remainder in a bowl at the table.

Chicken and Ham Croquettes

This dish has its roots in the cooking of a less prosperous time in Europe, when meat was a luxury. In Spain as elsewhere, the leftovers from Sunday's dinner would find their way into Monday's. Nowadays, these fried morsels are on the menu of nearly every tapas bar in Spain. They also make a tasty midday snack.

3 tablespoons olive oil, plus extra for frying

3 tablespoons all-purpose (plain) flour

1½ cups (12 fl oz/375 ml) milk

1½ cups (12 fl oz/375 ml) chicken stock

⅓ cup (2 oz/60 g) finely chopped cooked chicken meat

⅓ cup (2 oz/60 g) finely chopped serrano or other salt-cured ham

Pinch of freshly grated nutmeg

Salt and freshly ground pepper

1 cup (4 oz/125 g) fine dried bread crumbs

2 large eggs

MAKES 4–5 SERVINGS

1 In a small, heavy-bottomed saucepan over low heat, combine the 3 tablespoons olive oil and the flour. Cook, stirring constantly, until the flour has absorbed all the oil, 2–3 minutes. Add the milk and stock, little by little, stirring constantly and using a whisk to smooth out any lumps. Cook the sauce, continuing to stir, until smooth and thick, 10–15 minutes. Remove from the heat, stir in the chicken, ham, and nutmeg, and season with salt and pepper.

2 Pour the mixture into a metal baking pan and let cool to room temperature. Cover with plastic wrap and refrigerate overnight; the mixture will congeal into a thick paste.

3 Put the bread crumbs in a shallow bowl. In a second bowl, lightly beat the eggs. Using a spoon and your hands, form the chilled paste into short logs about 2 inches (5 cm) long and about 1 inch (2.5 cm) in diameter. Roll them once in the bread crumbs, then in the beaten eggs, and then again in the bread crumbs, making sure each croquette is thoroughly coated.

4 Pour olive oil to a depth of 1 inch (2.5 cm) into a large frying pan over medium-high heat and heat until very hot. Add the croquettes a few at a time and fry, turning once, until golden brown, about 3 minutes. Transfer to paper towels to drain. Serve at once.

Whatever venue you choose for taking an aperitif in Spain, you will find something there to eat with it: a small plate of cured sardines or sliced chorizo, slices of Manchego cheese, a slim wedge of tortilla española, or crunchy, sweet whole garlic cloves.

SPAIN

Tapas

A wide variety of tapas—little dishes to accompany drinks—are served all over Spain. Standard tapa fare tends toward tangy, bite-sized concoctions of cured or pickled foods, such as pickled baby onions, wild mushrooms marinated in oil, slices of cured tuna roe, or crostini with a wide variety of toppings. The offerings also vary by locale: Galician bars, for example, might feature such regional small dishes as *pulpo a feira* (octopus with paprika and olive oil) and tuna-stuffed empanadas. Some tapas bars offer just a few trademark selections while others design a miniature feast each day. Updated *cerveserias*—stylish "beer halls"—cheerfully mix and match local food and drink traditions with whatever takes their fancy.

Catalonia's complex relationship with the rest of Spain extends to its eating—and its snacking. When Barcelonans snack, they do it differently. *Raciones* (medium-sized servings) of sliced sausage and hams; *entrepans* stuffed with fresh cheese and anchovies; bowls of olives and nuts; or tomato-rubbed bread are alternatives to the typical Spanish repertoire. Basque-style bars keep trays of *pintxos* (snacks) on the bar to be eaten at will and paid for later. The favorite drinks are dry red Rioja wine or cider, served in the flat-bottomed glasses typical of the Basque country.

The newest wave in snacking is called the *tapa de autor*. Chefs at chic venues delight in creating miniature dishes that reflect their individual interests in fusion food and contemporary trends, resulting in such upscale nibbles as duck liver with hibiscus-flower syrup and tuna sashimi pizza.

TAPAS SAMPLER

Boquerones en Vinagre Fresh anchovies are filleted, cured in vinegar and salt, and dressed with olive oil, minced garlic, and parsley. The tangy vinegar marinade makes them the perfect foil for a glass of cold Manzanilla or other fine dry sherry.

Patatas Bravas Deep-fried potato chunks served with a spicy sauce, *patatas bravas* ("brave potatoes") are popular with students, probably because they're both inexpensive and tasty. But they are also a midday favorite of working people, who often wash them down with a glass of red wine.

Caracoles A bowlful of fresh snails are a thing of beauty. Caracoles might be roasted *a la llauna* (in a special tin pan) or cooked in a simple sauce with garlic, red bell pepper (capsicum), and perhaps a little blood sausage and a hint of chile.

Croquetas These golden croquettes, with a crispy crumb coating and a meltingly tender interior, are traditionally made with ham, chicken or a combination of the two. More forward-looking tapas bars include inventive fillings based on ingredients like wild mushrooms, shrimp (prawns), and spinach.

Jamón Ibérico Cured ham from the Iberian pig hails from the western regions of Andalusia and Extremadura. It is served in small slices cut directly from the ham at the moment of ordering and makes a delicious tapa with beer, a glass of good red wine, or a cava.

Berberechos These tiny clams, farmed in Galician estuaries and almost always canned in their own juices, are a traditional accompaniment to the midday glass of vermouth. They are usually eaten by sprinkling them with a squeeze of lemon, then spearing them with a toothpick.

Olives – 2⁵⁰
Almonds – 2⁵⁰
Caperberries – 2⁵⁰
Maize Kernels – 2⁵⁰
Pickled chillies – N/A
Tortilla – 3
Manchego – 3⁵⁰
Babaganoush – 3
Piquillo Peppers – 3
Pimentos de Padron – 3⁵⁰
Boquerones – 3⁵⁰
Sardinas – 3⁵⁰
Grilled chorizo – 3⁵⁰
Jamon Iberico – 12
Syrian lentils 3 houmous 3
white asparagus 3
Soup 4⁵⁰

INDONESIA
Fried Chicken with Lime and Coconut

For this dish, commonly served on festive occasions, the chicken is first braised in coconut juice and a few spices, then is deep-fried until the skin is crisp and flavorful. Alternatively, the chicken can be grilled over hot coals for about ten minutes.

1 chicken, 3½ lb (1.75 kg), quartered or cut into serving pieces

Juice of 2 limes

For the spice paste

6 whole peppercorns

4 red Fresno or jalapeño chiles, seeded and quartered

2 large shallots, quartered

3 cloves garlic, quartered

1 green coconut, or 2 cups (16 fl oz/500 ml) frozen coconut juice, thawed

1 lemongrass stalk, tender midsection only, smashed

5 kaffir lime leaves, spines removed

1 *salam* leaf, bay leaf, or curry leaf

Salt and freshly ground pepper

Vegetable oil for deep-frying

MAKES 4 SERVINGS

1 Rinse the chicken pieces and pat dry. Rub the chicken with the lime juice and set aside. To prepare the spice paste, in a mortar, pound the peppercorns. Add the chiles, shallots, and garlic and pound to form a smooth paste. Alternatively, process in a blender, adding a few tablespoons of water to facilitate the blending.

2 If using the coconut, soak it in water, about 1 minute. Using an ice pick, puncture one or two of the three brown dots. Pour the juice into a bowl. You will need 2 cups (16 fl oz/ 500 ml). If you have less, use water to make up the difference.

3 Put the spice paste in a wok or large, heavy pot. Add the chicken pieces, coconut juice, lemongrass, lime leaves, *salam* leaf, 1 teaspoon salt, and several grinds of pepper. Bring to a boil, reduce the heat to medium, cover, and boil gently, about 20 minutes. Remove the chicken, drain well, and transfer to a plate. (If desired, to prepare a sauce, strain the cooking liquid and spoon off any fat from the surface. Return it to a clean saucepan and boil over medium-high heat until reduced to a light sauce consistency. Keep warm.)

4 Pour the oil to a depth of about 2 inches (5 cm) into a wok or heavy, deep frying pan over medium-high heat, and heat to 350°F (180°C) on a deep-frying thermometer. Pat the chicken dry and sprinkle with 1 teaspoon salt. When the oil is ready, add half of the chicken pieces and deep-fry, turning as needed, until golden brown on all sides, about 5 minutes total. Transfer to paper towels to drain. Repeat with the remaining chicken. Arrange on a platter and serve at once. If using the sauce, pass it in a small bowl at the table.

Southern Fried Chicken

Ask nearly anyone in the United States to name the quintessential dish of "the South" and fried chicken will invariably be the answer. Every cook in the region claims to have the ultimate recipe for this centerpiece of the southern Sunday dinner, but all agree that a crisp crust and a moist interior are nonnegotiable.

1 chicken, 4 lb (2 kg), cut into 8 serving pieces (2 wings, 2 legs, 2 thighs, 2 breasts)

½ cup (4 oz/125 g) kosher salt

¼ cup (2 oz/60 g) sugar

2 cups (16 fl oz/500 ml) buttermilk

1 egg, beaten

1 teaspoon Tabasco sauce or other hot-pepper sauce

1 cup (5 oz/155 g) yellow cornmeal

2 cups (10 oz/315 g) all-purpose (plain) flour

1 teaspoon paprika

1 teaspoon celery seed

1 teaspoon garlic powder

1 teaspoon onion powder

Salt and freshly ground pepper

2½ cups (1¼ lb/625 g) solid vegetable shortening (vegetable lard)

MAKES 4 SERVINGS

1 Rinse the chicken pieces and pat dry. In a large nonreactive bowl, combine 8 cups (64 fl oz/2 l) water, the kosher salt, and the sugar and stir to dissolve. Place the chicken pieces in the brine and weight down with a small plate to immerse completely. Cover and refrigerate for at least 12 hours or up to 24 hours.

2 In a bowl, mix together the buttermilk, egg, and Tabasco sauce. Remove the chicken from the brine, place in the buttermilk mixture, and turn to coat evenly. Let stand, about 15 minutes.

3 In a shallow baking dish, stir together the cornmeal, flour, paprika, celery seed, garlic powder, onion powder, 1 teaspoon salt, and 1 teaspoon pepper. Working with 1 piece at a time, remove the chicken from the buttermilk mixture and allow the excess to drip away. Dredge in the seasoned flour and place on a large baking sheet. Let stand, about 10 minutes. Dip each piece in the buttermilk mixture a second time and dredge in the seasoned flour again. Return to the baking sheet.

4 In a large, deep frying pan over medium-high heat, melt the shortening and heat to 365°F (185°C) on a deep-frying thermometer. Place the chicken, skin side down, in the pan, arranging the dark meat pieces in the center and the white meat along the sides. Allow the pieces to touch slightly, but do not crowd the pan. Reduce the heat to medium and cook until the chicken is golden brown on the first side, about 12 minutes. Turn, cover, and cook, about 10 minutes. Uncover, turn the chicken once more, and cook until the skin is crisp and the meat is cooked through, 8–10 minutes longer. Transfer to paper towels to drain. The chicken can be served hot or at room temperature, or can be chilled in the refrigerator and eaten cold.

MEXICO
Turkey Mole

Both the turkey and the mole for this dish can be made in advance—in fact, the flavors mellow if the mole rests overnight—making it popular for fiestas. For flavorful lard, look for a butcher shop that renders its own or substitute safflower oil.

1 whole turkey breast, 6–8 lb (3–4 kg), halved

6 cloves garlic

1 white onion, thickly sliced

Sea salt

For the mole

12 ancho chiles

15 dried pasilla chiles

15 cascabel chiles

7 tablespoons (1½ oz/45 g) sesame seeds

8 tablespoons (4 oz/125 g) flavorful lard (see above) or (4 fl oz/125 ml) safflower oil

6 tomatillos, husked, rinsed, and quartered

1 white onion, finely chopped

2 cloves garlic, minced

¼ teaspoon aniseeds

¼ teaspoon ground cumin

1 day-old corn tortilla

1 slice day-old French bread

25 almonds

30 peanuts

2 tablespoons raisins

About ½-inch (12-mm) piece true cinnamon bark

3 cloves

1 disk Mexican chocolate, about 1½ oz (45 g), broken into chunks

1 teaspoon sugar

Sea salt

MAKES 10–12 SERVINGS

1 In a large pot, bring the turkey, garlic, onion, salt to taste, and water to cover to a slow boil, skimming off any foam. Reduce the heat and simmer, about 30 minutes. Remove the turkey, strain the broth, and refrigerate. (Skim the fat from the broth before using.)

2 To make the mole, seed and devein the chiles, reserving 1½ tablespoons seeds from each type. Toast the seeds in a heavy frying pan over medium heat until golden; transfer to a dish. Toast the sesame seeds lightly, set 2 tablespoons aside, and add the rest to the chile seeds.

3 In a frying pan over medium heat, warm 2 tablespoons of the lard. Add the tomatillos and onion and cook until browned, 10–15 minutes. Add the garlic and cook until soft, 3–4 minutes. Stir in the aniseeds and cumin. Transfer to a blender and process to a smooth paste. Wipe out the pan, add 2 tablespoons lard, and warm over medium-high heat until shimmering. Fry the tortilla, turning once; drain on paper towels. Fry the bread, turning once; drain on paper towels. In batches, fry the almonds, peanuts, raisins, cinnamon, and cloves for a few seconds each; drain on paper towels. Add to the blender along with the toasted chile seeds, 1 cup (8 fl oz/250 ml) of the broth, and the tomatillos. Process to a thick paste. Set aside.

4 Add the remaining lard to the pan over medium heat. Fry the chiles in batches until blistered, tossing constantly. Transfer to a bowl, add hot water to cover, and soak, about 30 minutes. Drain and tear into pieces. Purée in the blender with ½–1 cup (4–8 fl oz/125–250 ml) of the broth.

5 Pour off all but 1 tablespoon fat in the pan. Place over medium-high heat, add the tomatillo paste, reduce the heat, and simmer, stirring, about 3 minutes. Stir in the puréed chiles and cook for several minutes. Add the chocolate and sugar, stirring to melt. Stir in 4 cups (32 fl oz/1 l) of the broth and simmer, about 2 minutes. Season with salt.

6 Add the turkey. Simmer, turning occasionally and basting often, until a thermometer inserted into the thickest part registers 150–155°F (66–68°C), about 45 minutes. Let stand, 10–15 minutes. Lift out the turkey, scraping off the sauce, and slice thickly. Arrange on a platter and top with the mole. Sprinkle with the reserved sesame seeds and serve.

Seared Duck with Pomegranate

Wilted spinach, cinnamon-spiced duck breasts, and a sweet-and-sour pomegranate molasses—this dish exemplifies a style of European cuisine that marries Spanish, North African, and Middle Eastern influences. Pomegranate molasses has no ready substitute, but may be replaced with slightly sweetened tamarind syrup.

4 skin-on, boneless duck breasts, about 6 oz (185 g) each, rinsed and patted dry

⅛ teaspoon ground cinnamon

Sea salt and freshly ground pepper

1 small clove garlic, finely chopped

3 tablespoons pomegranate molasses

1 teaspoon honey (optional)

For the spinach

1 tablespoon olive oil

4 green (spring) onions, white and pale green parts only, thinly sliced

1 lb (500 g) baby spinach leaves, stems removed

Sea salt and freshly ground pepper

MAKES 4 SERVINGS

1 Trim any sinews from the duck breasts. Using a sharp knife, score the skin of each breast in a crosshatch pattern, taking care not to cut through to the meat. In a small bowl, stir together the cinnamon, 1 teaspoon salt, and a grinding of pepper. Rub the seasonings onto the duck breasts, especially the skin. Place the breasts on a plate, cover with plastic wrap, and refrigerate, about 2 hours.

2 Preheat the oven to 175°F (80°C). Select an ovenproof dish large enough to hold the duck breasts in a single layer and place it in the oven.

3 Set a frying pan over low heat and place the duck breasts in the pan, skin side down. Cook until the fat begins to render, about 3 minutes. Raise the heat to medium and cook until crisp and golden, about 5 minutes. Turn and cook until the meat is firm but still pinkish red when cut into with a sharp knife, about 5 minutes longer. Transfer the duck breasts to the warmed dish in the oven.

4 Pour off all but 1 tablespoon of the fat from the pan. Add the garlic and stir off the heat for about 45 seconds. When the pan has cooled slightly, place it over low heat, stir in the pomegranate molasses and 6 tablespoons (3 fl oz/ 90 ml) water, and cook until reduced slightly, about 1 minute. Season with salt and pepper. The molasses is tart, so if you prefer a sweeter sauce, stir in the honey. Set aside.

5 To cook the spinach, in a wide saucepan over high heat, warm the olive oil. Add the green onions and cook, stirring occasionally, until softened, 2–3 minutes. Add the spinach to the pan, one handful at a time, and stir until wilted. When all the spinach is wilted, season with salt and pepper.

6 To serve, reheat the sauce over medium heat. Slice each duck breast at an angle into 3 or 4 pieces and place on warmed individual plates. Add any accumulated juices in the dish to the sauce, raise the heat to high, bring to a boil, and pour over the breasts, dividing evenly. Spoon the spinach alongside the duck and serve at once.

Roast Duck Legs with Turnips

This recipe has the rich, slow-cooked flavor of a traditional French confit but with less fat. Tender young turnips and their greens are an ideal accompaniment. Unless the turnips have lush leaves, you will need to purchase a second bunch of greens.

Sea salt and freshly ground black pepper

4 juniper berries

12 whole black peppercorns

4 duck legs, about 2 lb (1 kg) total weight, rinsed and patted dry

½ bunch fresh thyme

1 lb (500 g) turnip greens, thick stems removed

1 lb (500 g) turnips, thickly peeled and cut into wedges ½ inch (12 mm) wide

1 large clove garlic, minced

Pinch of red pepper flakes

Red wine vinegar

MAKES 4 SERVINGS

1 Preheat the oven to 300°F (150°C). In a mortar, combine ¾ teaspoon salt, the juniper berries, and the black peppercorns and crush with a pestle until finely ground. Season the duck legs evenly with the mixture. Place a flat rack in a roasting pan. Divide the thyme sprigs into 4 equal bunches and place the bunches on the rack in 4 well-spaced mounds. Top each mound with a duck leg, skin side up.

2 Roast the duck legs, about 1½ hours, then pour off and reserve the fat from the pan. Continue roasting the duck until the skin is browned and crisp, about 1 hour longer, basting twice with the reserved fat during the final hour.

3 Meanwhile, bring a large pot of water to a boil. Salt the water, then add the turnip greens and cook just until tender, about 5 minutes. Drain and cool quickly under running cold water. Squeeze dry and chop coarsely.

4 About 20 minutes before the duck is ready, heat 1 tablespoon of the reserved duck fat in a frying pan over medium heat. Add the turnips, season with salt and black pepper, and toss to coat with the fat. Cook uncovered, tossing occasionally, until the turnips are tender and nicely colored, 15–20 minutes.

5 In another frying pan over medium-low heat, warm 1½ tablespoons of the reserved duck fat. Add the garlic and red pepper flakes and sauté briefly. Add the turnip greens and cook, stirring, until heated through. Season with salt and vinegar.

6 Remove the duck from the oven and discard the thyme sprigs. Arrange the duck, turnips, and turnip greens on a large platter and serve at once.

Duck with Port and Figs

6 skin-on, boneless duck breast halves, about 7 oz (220 g) each, rinsed and patted dry

2 cups (16 fl oz/500 ml) Port

Sea salt and freshly ground pepper

8–10 fresh basil leaves, torn or finely chopped

2–3 tablespoons unsalted butter

8 fresh figs, such as black Mission, about ¾ lb (375 g) total weight, halved lengthwise

½ cup (4 fl oz/125 ml) dry red wine such as Côtes-du-Rhône

2 cups (16 fl oz/500 ml) chicken or beef stock, or a combination

MAKES 6 SERVINGS

1 Using a sharp knife, score the skin of each duck breast in a crosshatch pattern, taking care not to cut through to the meat. Drizzle both sides with 2–3 tablespoons of the Port. Season with salt and pepper, then press the basil into both sides. Let stand at room temperature for 30 minutes. Meanwhile, pour the remaining Port into a saucepan and bring to a boil over medium-high heat. Reduce the heat to medium-low and cook until reduced to ¼ cup (2 fl oz/60 ml), 10–15 minutes. Transfer to a bowl and set aside.

2 In a large frying pan over medium-high heat, melt the butter. Add the figs and cook on both sides until softened, about 2 minutes. Transfer to a plate and keep warm. Place the duck breasts, skin side down, in the pan and cook over until browned, about 4 minutes. Turn and cook on the other side until browned. Transfer to a plate and keep warm.

3 Pour the pan juices into a bowl; set aside. Pour the red wine into the pan, bring to a boil over high heat, and cook, stirring, until reduced to 2 tablespoons, about 5 minutes. Meanwhile, spoon off any fat from the juices in the bowl. Add to the pan along with the stock and cook until reduced to ¼ cup (2 fl oz/60 ml), about 5 minutes. Stir in the reduced Port and figs.

4 Slice the duck breasts and arrange on individual plates. Spoon the sauce and figs over the duck and serve at once.

Red Duck Curry

½ cup (4 fl oz/125 ml) coconut cream (see note)

3 tablespoons red curry paste

1–2 tablespoons brown sugar

1–2 tablespoons fish sauce

½ Chinese roast duck

2½ cups (20 fl oz/625 ml) coconut milk (see note)

8 kaffir lime leaves

1 cup (6 oz/185 g) cubed pineapple (1-inch/2.5-cm cubes)

8 cherry tomatoes, halved

1 cup (1 oz/30 g) Thai basil

MAKES 4 SERVINGS

1 In a wok over medium heat, combine the coconut cream and curry paste and cook, stirring, until beads of oil appear on the surface, 5–8 minutes. Chop the duck into small pieces and add to the pan along with the sugar and fish sauce. Add the coconut milk and lime leaves, bring to a boil, then reduce the heat to medium-low. Simmer for 5 minutes.

2 Add the pineapple, tomatoes, and basil leaves and stir just until the basil leaves are wilted. Transfer to a serving dish. Serve hot or at room temperature.

Note: For coconut cream, open the can of coconut milk without shaking it and skim the cream off the top. Then spoon out the creamy layer of coconut milk underneath, leaving behind the thin coconut milk below that.

MEAT

On the Farm

MEAT AROUND THE WORLD

A visit to a butcher shop or charcuterie in any part of the world, whether Spain, France, India, or China, will suggest the dishes most integral to the local cuisine. Trimmed lamb chops, perfectly formed sausages, veal breasts ready for stuffing, halal mutton for layering in *biryani,* and fatty pork minced by hand—these are the foundations of special dishes in various cuisines.

Ambitious dinner hosts might carve a standing rib roast, a pork tenderloin stuffed with apples, or a sugar-glazed ham. In China and Japan, meat arrives at the table cut into bite-sized pieces for eating with chopsticks. In much of India and Southeast Asia, where foods are eaten with the fingers or with only a spoon and fork, meat is also served in small pieces or cooked until it falls off the bone. Once minced or ground, meats become endlessly versatile. The best French butchers are also masters of charcuterie. In their shops, meat lovers will find sausages, country pâté, and truffle-studded terrines. French colonists brought charcuterie to Vietnam, where the techniques were adapted to local ingredients in preparations such as *cha lua,* a sausage seasoned with fish sauce and

wrapped in banana leaves. Other specialties include slightly sweet *lap cheong,* a cured sausage popular in China, and *sai ua,* a northern Thai sausage infused with shallots, lemongrass, kaffir lime, and chiles. In the United States, schools of barbecue claim loyal followers. Exacting combinations of rubs, wood smoking, basting, grilling, and saucing determine regional flavors, which are further influenced by each pit master's secret recipe. Kansas City has its ribs slathered with a thick, sweet sauce, North Carolina its pulled pork sandwiches, and Texas its brisket infused with mesquite. The open grill of South Africa's *braai* and Australia's barbie are as important for anchoring social gatherings as they are for imparting much-appreciated smokiness and char to local game.

Meatballs, a time-honored way of stretching meat, appear in favorite dishes in every cuisine. They are formed into large rounds for lion's heads, one of Shanghai's classic dishes; rolled small for serving with Swedish lingonberries; ladled with marinara sauce over Italian spaghetti; and stirred into broth for Mexico's *sopa de albóndigas.* In Asia, meatballs might contain a sprinkling of potato starch to give them a distinctive resilient texture, and in Mediterranean countries, ground meat is mixed with bulgur and shaped into *kofte.*

The use of shanks, heads, tails, and organ meats once distinguished the food of the poor. While the wealthy preferred whole roasts or buttery meat pies, families of lesser means depended on stews and soups to make their meat go further. Stewing also tenderized tougher cuts and made efficient use of the hearth's heat. Today, though, we enjoy stews for their complex flavors. No matter the cut, meat—when braised with wine, enriched with coconut milk, or married with dried fruit and nuts—readily absorbs the world's various flavors.

BEEF

Though unknown in the western hemisphere until Europeans unloaded their live cargo onto the shores of North and South America, cattle ranches soon stretched across the vast prairies of the United States and the fertile pampas of Argentina. The culture of cowboys and gauchos gave rise to traditions of simply prepared steaks, from a strip steak topped with only butter to slices of *carne asada con chimichurri.*

Stories of Mongol horsemen searing meat on their shields over an open fire or simmering soup in their helmets attempt to explain the origins of such crowd-pleasing dishes as grilled Korean *bulgogi,* Japanese *sukiyaki,* and Chinese hot pot. In Vietnam, *pho bo,* a soup highlighting various cuts of beef over rice noodles, and *bo nhung dam,* a festive meal with seven courses of beef, are both legacies of the far-reaching Mongols. Beef was prohibited in Japan until the nineteenth century, but the country has since perfected its own special brand of luxury beef. Known as *kobe,* the meat comes from Wagyu cattle whose flesh, with the help of daily massages and a diet richly spiked with sake, has become famous for its tenderness and generous marbling.

Skirt and flank steaks, from a tough muscle across the belly, turn succulent when sliced thinly and cooked quickly, making them popular for fajitas and stir-fries. Brisket, a muscle over the front legs,

is meltingly tender when cured and smoked or cooked in slow, moist heat. With this humble cut, Jewish immigrants in the United States perfected corned beef and pastrami, deli meats that, when piled onto slices of rye bread, are a must-have for any visitor to New York City.

PORK

Pale, succulent pork is the king of meats in China. In fact, the Chinese word for *meat* and for *pork* is one and the same. Ground or minced pork lies at the heart of many of the country's famous buns, rolls, and dumplings. Throughout Asia, weddings require the roasting of a suckling pig. In Hawaii, celebrations often feature whole pigs cooked overnight in *imu* pits between hot volcanic rocks and fresh ti leaves.

Dry curing transforms the leg and belly meat of pigs into legendary specialties: Italy's prosciutto and pancetta plus the fine-textured hams of Bayonne, Serrano, Yunnan, and West Virginia. From the acorns that fatten the pigs to the mountain air in the curing sheds, the landscape infuses these meats with unique, local flavor.

LAMB

The cuisines of the Middle East and Mediterranean regions draw heavily from lamb. In Greece, lamb plays an important role in religious feasts. After returning from midnight mass on the eve of Easter, *mageritsa* is served to break the long Lenten fast. Made from the organs of the same spring lamb being spit-roasted for Easter dinner, it is a soothing soup flavored with lemon and dill. Middle Eastern street food includes kebabs of lamb marinated in garlicky yogurt, grilled, and then wrapped in lavash bread. Finely ground lamb flavored with pine nuts and fragrant cinnamon fills tartlets, flatbreads, and filo pastry rolls in Arabic-influenced kitchens from Spain across Northern Africa to Afghanistan.

More than any other, Moghul cuisine centered on lamb. Prohibited from eating pork, discouraged from preparing beef by neighboring Hindus, and located far from the shores of the Indian Ocean, Moghul rulers enjoyed a different rich and lavish dish of lamb every day of the year. Kashmiri *aab gosht,* lamb cooked in milk with cardamom and cinnamon, and Lucknowi *nalli korma,* lamb shanks simmered to tenderness in an almond-thickened sauce, are two hallmarks of northern India's rich culinary tradition.

FRANCE
Steak Frites

Hangar steak—*onglet* in French parlance—is the classic cut for *steak frites* in Parisian bistros. It has a rich, meaty flavor but must be cooked no more than medium-rare or it toughens. Remember that the correct timing depends on the thickness of the steak, not on its weight. Serve with *frites* (page 174).

4–6 hangar steaks, 8–12 oz (250–375 g) each, trimmed of most fat and lightly marbled if possible, at room temperature

Sea salt and freshly ground pepper

Olive oil for brushing

3 tablespoons unsalted butter

12 shallots, about ¾ lb (375 g) total weight, thinly sliced

¾ cup (6 fl oz/180 ml) dry red wine

1 cup (8 fl oz/250 ml) beef stock

MAKES 4–6 SERVINGS

1 Pat the steaks dry with paper towels. Season with salt and pepper, and brush lightly with olive oil.

2 Heat a large, heavy nonstick frying pan over high heat until very hot. Cook the steaks until browned and slightly crusty on the first side, 45–60 seconds. Turn and repeat on the second side, 45–60 seconds. Reduce the heat to medium-high and cook the steaks, 2–4 minutes longer on each side. To test for doneness, press your finger firmly against one of the steaks; the rarer the meat, the more soft and fleshy it will feel. If desired, make a small cut in the meat to check the color. Transfer the steaks to a platter and cover loosely with aluminum foil. (The steaks will continue to cook slowly as they rest.)

3 Reduce the heat to medium-low. Melt 1½ tablespoons of the butter in the pan. Add the shallots and sauté until golden brown, 5–7 minutes. Add the wine, raise the heat to high, and cook, stirring, until the liquid is almost evaporated, 5–6 minutes. Add the stock and cook until the shallots are very tender and the liquid is reduced to a flavorful sauce, 5–6 minutes. Remove from the heat and whisk in the remaining 1½ tablespoons butter.

4 Transfer the steaks along with any accumulated juices to individual plates. Spoon the shallots and sauce over the steaks. Serve at once.

Steak Chimichurri

⅓ cup (3 fl oz/80 ml) olive oil

⅓ cup (3 fl oz/80 ml) sherry vinegar

3 tablespoons fresh oregano leaves

½ cup (½ oz/15 g) coarsely chopped fresh flat-leaf (Italian) parsley

7 cloves garlic, coarsely chopped

Red pepper flakes

4 T-bone steaks, each about 1 inch (2.5 cm) thick

Salt

MAKES 4 SERVINGS

1 In a food processor, combine the oil, vinegar, oregano, parsley, and garlic, and process until finely chopped and well combined. Pour into a shallow nonreactive dish large enough to hold the steaks in a single layer, and stir in the red pepper flakes. Season the steaks with salt, add to the marinade, and turn to coat. Let stand at room temperature, about 10 minutes.

2 Meanwhile, prepare a charcoal or gas grill for direct-heat grilling over high heat and oil the grill rack. Or, preheat a broiler (grill). Remove the steaks from the marinade, reserving the marinade. Place the steaks on the grill rack, or put them on a baking sheet and place under the broiler. Brush the steaks with the remaining marinade. Cook, carefully turning once, about 8 minutes total for medium-rare, or until done to your liking. Serve at once.

Shaking Beef

Although the sound of the sizzling oil coupled with the rapid shaking of the pan gave birth to the name of this dish, it may be more appropriate to call it sautéed beef with lots of sweet garlic sauce. It's served atop a simple watercress salad.

6 cloves garlic, chopped

1 tablespoon fish sauce

1 tablespoon sugar

Salt

3 tablespoons vegetable oil

¾ lb (375 g) beef sirloin, cut into 1-inch (2.5-cm) cubes

For the salad

1 small red onion, thinly sliced

1½ teaspoons distilled white vinegar

1½ teaspoons Japanese-style soy sauce

1½ teaspoons olive oil

½ teaspoon sugar

Salt and freshly ground pepper

1 bunch watercress, tough stems removed

MAKES 4–6 SERVINGS

1 In a nonreactive bowl, stir together half of the garlic, the fish sauce, sugar, ¼ teaspoon salt, and 1 tablespoon of the vegetable oil. Add the beef and turn to coat well. Cover and let stand for at least 30 minutes at room temperature or refrigerate for up to 2 hours.

2 To make the salad, in a bowl, toss together the onion and vinegar and set aside, about 5 minutes. In a small bowl, stir together the soy sauce, olive oil, sugar, ¼ teaspoon salt, and ¼ teaspoon pepper. Add to the onion and mix well. Add the watercress, toss, and arrange on a platter.

3 Heat a wok or frying pan over high heat. Add the remaining 2 tablespoons oil and swirl to coat the pan. When the oil is hot, add the remaining garlic and stir-fry until lightly browned, about 1 minute. Add the beef in a single layer and cook, undisturbed, until seared, about 1 minute. Turn the meat over to sear on the second side, about 1 minute, then cook about 3 minutes longer. The meat should be medium-rare. Arrange the beef on top of the watercress salad and serve at once.

Wine-Braised Short Ribs

Short ribs become tender and succulent when braised slowly with a small amount of liquid. This basic braise invites variation: substitute oxtails for the short ribs; add some chopped peeled tomato to the sautéed vegetables; or toss in a few dried porcini mushrooms. The ribs can release a good amount of fat, so skim the sauce carefully. Serve with mashed potatoes.

4 lb (2 kg) beef short ribs, cut into 3-inch (7.5-cm) lengths

Sea salt and freshly ground pepper

1 tablespoon olive oil

⅓ lb (5 oz/155 g) small fresh white mushrooms, brushed clean, trimmed, and quartered

½ large yellow onion, minced

1 large carrot, peeled and finely diced

1 large celery stalk, finely diced

1 tablespoon minced fresh thyme

1 cup (8 fl oz/250 ml) dry white wine

2 tablespoons minced fresh flat-leaf (Italian) parsley

MAKES 4 SERVINGS

1 Preheat the oven to 300°F (150°C). Season the ribs with salt and pepper. In a large, heavy frying pan over high heat, warm the olive oil, swirling to coat the bottom. When the oil is hot, add the meat, reduce the heat to medium, and brown well on all sides, about 25 minutes total. As the ribs are done, transfer them in a single layer to a large baking dish.

2 Pour off all but 2 tablespoons of the fat in the pan and return to medium heat. Add the mushrooms, onion, carrot, celery, and thyme. Season with salt and pepper and cook, stirring occasionally, until the vegetables are softened, about 10 minutes. Transfer to the baking dish and return the empty pan to high heat. Add the wine and simmer until reduced by half, scraping up any browned bits on the pan bottom. Add to the baking dish along with 1 cup (8 fl oz/250 ml) water. Cover tightly and bake until the ribs are fork-tender, 2½–3 hours. Turn off the oven.

3 Transfer the ribs to an ovenproof serving platter, cover with aluminum foil, and place in the warm oven. Pour the contents of the baking dish into a large measuring pitcher and let settle, about 5 minutes, then skim off as much surface fat as possible. Pour the remainder into a frying pan and reheat to serve as a sauce, simmering over high heat to thicken and concentrate the sauce if needed. Taste and adjust the seasoning. Pour the sauce over the ribs and garnish with the parsley. Serve at once.

Braised Brisket Tsimmes

Traditional Jewish Sabbath observances prohibit the use of an oven, so brisket, which benefits from long, slow cooking, was placed in the oven by sundown on Friday and left to cook in the residual heat until the next day. Brisket with sweet potatoes and fruit, in this case, prunes, is called a *tsimmes* (SIM-eez), a Yiddish word referring to a number of ingredients cooked in one pot. Serve with egg noodles, noodle kugel, or potato pancakes.

1 brisket, 4–5 lb (2–2.5 kg)

1 teaspoon Hungarian paprika

Sea salt and freshly ground black pepper

4 tablespoons (2 fl oz/60 ml) canola oil

3 large yellow onions, chopped

4 cloves garlic, chopped

½ teaspoon ground allspice

¼ teaspoon red pepper flakes

2 cups (16 fl oz/500 ml) red wine

2 cups (14 oz/440 g) canned crushed tomatoes

2 bay leaves

2 sprigs fresh thyme

1 sprig fresh rosemary

2 lb (1 kg) orange-fleshed sweet potatoes or yams, peeled and cut crosswise into 1-inch (2.5-cm) rounds

6–8 small carrots, peeled and cut into 1½-inch (4-cm) pieces

½ lb (250 g) pitted prunes

¼ cup (⅓ oz/10 g) chopped fresh flat-leaf (Italian) parsley for garnish

MAKES 8 SERVINGS

1   Trim the brisket of excess fat, then rinse and pat dry. Rub the meat on all sides with the paprika and season generously with salt and black pepper. In a large Dutch oven over medium-high heat, warm 2 tablespoons of the oil. Add the brisket and sear on all sides until deep brown, about 4 minutes per side. Transfer to a plate and set aside.

2   Preheat the oven to 350°F (180°C). In the same pot over medium heat, warm the remaining 2 tablespoons oil. Add the onions and cook, stirring occasionally, until golden brown and tender, 10–15 minutes. Add the garlic, allspice, and red pepper flakes and sauté until the garlic is fragrant, about 2 minutes. Return the brisket to the pot, fat side up. Pour in the wine, the tomatoes, and 4 cups (32 fl oz/1 l) water. Add the bay leaves and the thyme and rosemary sprigs. Cover, place in the oven, and cook, basting often with the sauce in the pot, until the meat breaks apart easily when pierced with a fork, about 3 hours.

3   Remove from the oven and add the sweet potatoes, carrots, and prunes. Cover and continue to cook until the vegetables are soft, about 1 hour. Remove the pot from the oven and let cool to room temperature, then refrigerate for at least 4 hours or up to overnight.

4   Preheat the oven to 350°F (180°C). Remove the pot from the refrigerator and skim the fat from the surface of the liquid. Transfer the meat to a cutting board and cut across the grain into slices ½ inch (12 mm) thick. Return the meat to the pot, cover, place in the oven, and cook until heated through, about 30 minutes. Arrange the brisket and vegetables on a warmed platter and spoon the sauce over the top. Garnish with the parsley and serve at once.

UNITED KINGDOM
Bangers and Mash with Onion Gravy

Sausages roasted until mahogany brown and served with mashed potatoes and onion gravy are a favorite in British eateries. The British sausage became known as a banger around World War I, probably because it spluttered as it fried. Along with minced pork or beef (or both), the sausages contain bread crumbs, which gives them a soft consistency and a mild flavor.

2 lb (1 kg) good-quality bangers or pork sausages

1 tablespoon sunflower oil

For the mash

2 lb (1 kg) Yukon gold potatoes

Sea salt and freshly ground pepper

⅓ cup (3 fl oz/80 ml) milk

2 tablespoons unsalted butter

For the gravy

2 tablespoons unsalted butter

1 tablespoon olive oil

2 red onions, halved and finely sliced

1½ teaspoons all-purpose (plain) flour

1 teaspoon red wine vinegar

1 cup (8 fl oz/250 ml) full-bodied red wine, such as Shiraz

1 cup (8 fl oz/250 ml) chicken or beef stock

Sea salt and freshly ground pepper

MAKES 4 SERVINGS

1   Preheat the oven to 400°F (200°C). Place the sausages in a roasting pan, drizzle with the oil, toss to coat, and spread out in a single layer. Bake, turning them after 15 minutes, until evenly colored, about 30 minutes.

2   Meanwhile, to make the mash, peel the potatoes and cut them into large chunks. Place in a saucepan with water to cover, salt the water, and bring to a boil over medium heat. Continue to cook until the potatoes are tender when pierced with a knife, about 15 minutes. Drain, cover with a kitchen towel, and let stand until dry, about 5 minutes. In the same pan, combine the milk and butter, and bring to a boil over medium-high heat. Remove from the heat and set aside. Pass the potatoes through a ricer or place in a bowl and mash with a potato masher. Add the hot milk mixture and beat until smooth. Season with salt and pepper.

3   To make the gravy, in a wide, shallow nonreactive saucepan over medium-low heat, melt the butter with the olive oil. Add the onions and cook, stirring frequently, until the onions are meltingly soft, about 20 minutes. Stir in the flour and cook until lightly colored, 2–3 minutes. Stir in the vinegar and cook until evaporated. Stir in the red wine and stock, raise the heat to bring to a boil, reduce the heat to low, and simmer until a rich sauce forms, about 10 minutes. Season with salt and pepper.

4   Divide the sausages and mash among individual plates. Spoon some gravy over the top and serve at once. Pass the remaining gravy at the table.

On a warm summer evening, many a London street is filled with the murmuring of voices and the clinking of glasses. These are the sounds of the pub, an institution so integral to London life that few could imagine the city without it.

London Pubs

The pub, as licensed public houses are affectionately known, is there for everyone. It is a place to meet up for a quick drink after work, to enjoy an informal meal, or to linger quietly over a pint of beer. There are no rules about what you can drink. A gin and tonic, a nonalcoholic ginger beer, or a glass of wine is served as often as a pint of beer.

London has around 5,500 pubs that vary greatly in style from the cozy mews pub to the hip-and-happening gastropub. The British often worry that pub culture is in decline, but modern pubs are following a long tradition of adapting to the needs of the day. Fifteenth-century London was filled with coaching inns, taverns, and ale houses, each serving a different purpose. Taverns, for example, were visited for their fine French wines and port, which was drunk in vast quantities when the wine trade was interrupted by war with France. The tavern's modern descendant is the wine bar.

Coaching inns resembled hotels. Arrayed along the highways of Britain, they offered accommodation, food, drink, and stabling, as well as a good source of news from the mail coaches. Only one has survived in London—the George Inn on Borough High Street in Southwark, established in the 1540s during the reign of Henry VIII. Here, you can linger over a fruity, dry ale in much the same way inn patron William Shakespeare might have done. Southwark was a wild place in the playwright's day. Beyond the reach of city ordinances, it was awash in theaters, brothels, and bear rings. Coaching inns went into decline with the arrival of railways in the nineteenth century.

Ale houses are widely regarded as the direct ancestor of the public house. As their name implies, they served ale, a brew made from fermented grain. In the early fifteenth century, hops were added to this brew to help preserve it. From that time, ale (unhopped) became beer (hopped). Technically, the word *beer* refers to all drinks that have been fermented with grain and seasoned with hops. The English, however, rarely apply this term to lager, porter, or stout.

Londoners have always drunk beers from all over England, including their own London brews. London Porter, a black, heavily hopped, and highly alcoholic beer, was created in London in the 1720s. It was exported to Ireland, where Arthur Guinness produced his own version, which by the beginning of the eighteenth century was sold to Londoners as Guinness. Today, barely a handful of London breweries remain. Many traditional London beers are "bitters," an English term for a well-hopped ale with a deep bitterness and a mild acidity.

Different pubs offer different selections. The choices are influenced by the brewery that owns the pub. (Independently owned pubs are known as freehouses.) The Guinea, a small mews pub in Mayfair, for instance, belongs to the Young's estate and serves cask-conditioned, dry Young's Bitter or Young's Special. The Churchill Arms is a Fuller's pub, so customers can choose from an array of Fuller's beers, from the flowery Chiswick Bitter to the more complex London Pride.

Thai Meatballs with Lemongrass

These simplified Thai meatballs are served as canapés on lettuce leaves with an aromatic dipping sauce. The recipe can easily be doubled for a large party.

For the sauce

1 lemongrass stalk

2 tablespoons sugar

½ teaspoon red pepper flakes

¼ cup (2 fl oz/60 ml) boiling water

2½ tablespoons white wine vinegar

For the meatballs

½ bunch fresh cilantro (fresh coriander), including stems, finely chopped

2 green (spring) onions, white and pale green parts only, finely chopped

1 clove garlic, finely chopped

Finely grated zest of 1 lemon

Finely ground black pepper

Pinch of freshly grated nutmeg

½ egg, lightly beaten

1½ teaspoons Thai fish sauce

6 oz (185 g) ground (minced) pork

All-purpose (plain) flour for coating

3 tablespoons sunflower oil

16 small Bibb lettuce leaves

MAKES 6–8 SERVINGS

1 To make the sauce, trim off the upper leafy part of the lemongrass stalk and the tough end of the bulb. Remove the outer layer of the stalk. Finely slice the stalk and place in a small bowl with the sugar and red pepper flakes. Add the boiling water and stir until the sugar is dissolved, about 2 minutes. Stir in the vinegar. Pour the sauce into a dipping bowl and set on a serving platter.

2 To make the meatballs, combine the cilantro, green onions, garlic, lemon zest, ⅛ teaspoon black pepper, nutmeg, egg, and fish sauce in a food processor. Pulse 4 or 5 times until puréed. Add the pork and pulse 2 or 3 times until the mixture is minced. Do not overprocess the mixture, or it will have a gummy texture.

3 Place a generous amount of flour on a dinner plate. Dip your hands in the flour, scoop up a walnut-sized piece of the pork mixture, dust it with flour, and lightly shape into a ball. Repeat to make a total of 16 balls.

4 Preheat the oven to 400°F (200°C). In a nonstick frying pan over medium-low heat, warm the oil. When the oil is hot but not smoking, gently add the meatballs and cook, turning as needed, until uniformly lightly browned, about 4 minutes. Transfer to paper towels to drain. (The meatballs can be refrigerated for up to 24 hours before proceeding.)

5 Place the meatballs on a rimmed baking sheet, cover with aluminum foil, and bake until cooked through, about 20 minutes. Arrange the lettuce leaves in a single layer on the platter. Place a meatball on each lettuce leaf and serve with the sauce for spooning over the meatballs.

Spicy Meatball Soup

For this simple and filling *sopa de albóndigas,* the *albóndigas,* or meatballs, are bound and enriched by shreds of grated potato. Once browned, the meatballs are simmered in a tomato-based soup flavored with parsley and jalapeño.

4 large russet potatoes, about 2 lb (1 kg) total weight

1 lb (500 g) ground (minced) lean pork

1 white onion, one half minced and one half coarsely chopped

½ teaspoon dried oregano, preferably Mexican

Sea salt and freshly ground pepper

2 eggs, lightly beaten

1 lb (500 g) ripe tomatoes, chopped, or 1 can (14½ oz/ 455 g) chopped tomatoes, drained

4 cups (32 fl oz/1 l) chicken stock

2 tablespoons safflower or canola oil

1 tablespoon all-purpose (plain) flour

1 jalapeño chile, partially slit open

1 fresh flat-leaf (Italian) parsley sprig, chopped

¼ cup (¼ oz/7 g) fresh cilantro (fresh coriander) leaves for garnish

MAKES 6 SERVINGS

1   Peel the potatoes and grate them on the medium holes of a grater. Wrap the grated potatoes in a kitchen towel and squeeze out the excess liquid. In a bowl, combine the potatoes, meat, minced onion, oregano, 1 teaspoon salt, and 1 teaspoon pepper, and toss to mix. Add the eggs and mix again. With your hands, roll the meat-and-potato mixture into 1-inch (2.5-cm) balls. Set aside.

2   Put the tomatoes and the chopped onion in a blender. Process until smooth, adding a little of the chicken stock, if needed, to facilitate blending. Set aside.

3   In a large Dutch oven over medium heat, warm the oil. When it is sizzling hot, working in batches, gently drop in the meatballs and fry until lightly brown on all sides, about 10 minutes. Using a slotted spoon, transfer the meatballs to a plate.

4   Return the pot to medium heat, sprinkle the flour into the hot oil remaining in the pot, and cook, stirring, for several minutes. Slowly pour in the tomato-onion mixture, then add the chile and parsley. Cook, stirring occasionally, until the mixture thickens and darkens in color, about 3 minutes. Add the remaining stock and the meatballs and let the soup simmer, uncovered, for 10–15 minutes. Remove the chile and discard. Taste and adjust the seasoning. Ladle into warmed wide bowls, garnish with the cilantro leaves, and serve at once.

Focaccia Burger

Freshly ground, high-quality beef is essential to a good burger, but the right bread is just as critical. Soft, yeasty focaccia is the perfect wrap. If you don't have an Italian bakery nearby, check an Italian delicatessen for focaccia. This recipe yields more aioli than you need; save any left over as an accompaniment for steamed artichokes.

For the aioli

1 large clove garlic

Sea salt

1 egg yolk, at room temperature

½ cup (4 fl oz/125 ml) extra-virgin olive oil

1⅓ lb (655 g) ground (minced) beef chuck

Sea salt and freshly ground pepper

4 squares plain focaccia, 4 inches (20 cm) each, halved horizontally

1 large tomato, cored and thinly sliced

½ red onion, very thinly sliced

1 large handful baby arugula (rocket), or larger arugula with stems removed

MAKES 4 SERVINGS

1 To make the aioli, in a mortar, combine the garlic with a pinch of salt and pound to a paste with a pestle. Set aside. Put the egg yolk in a small bowl, add a few drops of warm water, and whisk to loosen the yolk. Begin whisking in the olive oil slowly—drop by drop at first, then a little faster once it emulsifies. Whisk in the garlic paste. Taste and adjust the seasonings.

2 Season the meat with salt and pepper. Divide into 4 equal portions and shape each into a patty about 4 inches (10 cm) square and ½ inch (12 mm) thick.

3 Preheat the broiler (grill). Place the focaccia squares on a baking sheet in a single layer, slip into the broiler, and toast, turning once, until lightly crisped on both sides.

4 Heat 2 frying pans, preferably nonstick, over medium heat. Put the patties in the pans, not touching, then reduce the heat to medium-low and cook until browned on the bottom, about 3 minutes. Turn and cook to the desired doneness, about 3 minutes longer for medium.

5 Meanwhile, spread the cut side of each focaccia square with the aioli. When the burgers are ready, place them on 4 of the squares. Top with the tomato and red onion slices and the arugula, then with the remaining focaccia. Serve at once.

Florentine-Style Ossobuco

This version of the famous Milanese dish is much easier to make than the traditional version, since it is not served with saffron risotto or garnished with *gremolata* (minced garlic, lemon zest, and parsley). But it is equally delicious.

4 slices veal shank, each 1½–2 inches (4–5 cm) thick, with bone and marrow

Salt and freshly ground pepper

3 tablespoons extra-virgin olive oil

2 yellow onions, finely chopped

2 carrots, peeled and finely chopped

2 celery stalks, finely chopped

1 cup (8 fl oz/250 ml) dry red wine

3 canned plum (Roma) tomatoes, coarsely chopped

MAKES 4 SERVINGS

1 Preheat the oven to 325°F (165°C). Score the outer edge of each veal shank at the meaty side of the shank opposite the bone with 2 shallow cuts about 2 inches (5 cm) apart, so the meat remains flat during cooking. Generously season with salt and pepper. In a frying pan over medium-high heat, warm the olive oil. Add the shanks and cook on the first side until golden brown, about 4 minutes. Turn and cook until browned on the second side, about 4 minutes. Transfer to a plate.

2 Reduce the heat to medium and add the onions, carrots, and celery to the pan. Sauté, adding a few tablespoons of water if the pan dries out, until the vegetables are softened, about 10 minutes. Add the wine, raise the heat to high, and cook until the alcohol evaporates, about 3 minutes. Remove from the heat and stir in the tomatoes.

3 Lightly oil a roasting pan large enough to hold the shanks comfortably. Transfer the shanks to the pan. Spoon the vegetable mixture over the meat, cover with aluminum foil, and cook until the veal is fork-tender, about 1½ hours. Transfer to warmed individual plates. Spoon the pan juices over the top and serve at once.

Veal Stew with Tarragon

For this recipe, the traditional *blanquette de veau*—an old-fashioned preparation of stewed veal in a hearty sauce—has been updated with new techniques and flavors. The result is a lightly creamy sauce with a bright, intriguing taste.

3½ lb (1.75 kg) boneless veal stew meat, trimmed of excess fat and cut into 2-inch (5-cm) pieces

3 cups (24 fl oz/750 ml) chicken stock

1 cup (8 fl oz/250 ml) dry white wine

3–4 tablespoons chopped fresh tarragon

2–3 tablespoons chopped fresh flat-leaf (Italian) parsley

1 large clove garlic

2 shallots, chopped

2 green (spring) onions, white part only, thinly sliced

½ carrot, peeled and diced

½ celery stalk, diced

2 bay leaves

¼ teaspoon grated lemon zest

1 cup (6 oz/185 g) diced canned tomatoes

Large pinch of saffron threads

Salt and freshly ground pepper

¾ cup (6 fl oz/180 ml) heavy (double) cream

2 egg yolks

Juice of 1 lemon

MAKES 4–6 SERVINGS

1 Place the veal in a Dutch oven and add the stock, wine, and water as needed to cover the meat with liquid. Bring to a boil, then immediately reduce the heat to low and skim off the foam that rises to the surface.

2 Add 1 tablespoon of the tarragon and 1 tablespoon of the parsley to the pot, then the garlic, shallots, green onions, carrot, celery, bay leaves, lemon zest, and tomatoes. In a mortar using a pestle, crush the saffron and add half of it to the pot. Season with salt and pepper. Cover and simmer over low heat until the meat is very tender but not falling apart, 2½–3 hours. Using a slotted spoon, transfer the meat to a bowl.

3 Spoon off any fat from the cooking liquid. Set the pot over high heat and boil until the liquid is reduced by half and intensely flavored, about 10 minutes. Remove and discard the bay leaves. Add the remaining saffron and return the meat to the pot. Reduce the heat to medium.

4 In a small bowl, whisk together the cream and egg yolks. Whisk in a ladleful of the hot reduced liquid until well combined, then pour into the pot, stirring until a creamy emulsion forms. Continue to cook over medium heat until the sauce thickens slightly, taking care not to scramble the eggs, 3–4 minutes. The meat should now be warmed through. Stir in the lemon juice. Taste and adjust the seasoning with salt and pepper. Transfer to a serving bowl, sprinkle with the remaining tarragon and parsley, and serve at once.

ITALY
Prosciutto, Salami, Figs, and Melon

The sweetness of ripe melons and figs makes a perfect foil for cured Tuscan meats. Prosciutto and melon are the most traditional pairing. The prosciutto slices should be almost transparent so that their flavor does not overpower the delicate melon. *Meloni*—or *poponi,* as they are sometimes called in Tuscany—are strictly a summer fruit. Figs are undoubtedly the most sensual of all Tuscan fruits, making their short season—late summer, early autumn—all the more precious.

12 fresh figs, halved lengthwise

½ lb (250 g) semi-aged Italian salami such as *salame toscano* (page 280), thinly sliced on a slight diagonal

1 large ripe cantaloupe, halved and seeded

6 oz (185 g) prosciutto, sliced paper-thin

1 loaf coarse country bread, sliced

MAKES 6 SERVINGS

1 Arrange the figs in the center of a large serving platter. Roll each slice of salami into a loose cylinder and place around the figs.

2 Cut each melon half into 6 wedges, then cut the rind from each wedge. Arrange the melon on the platter. Drape with the slices of prosciutto. Serve with the bread alongside.

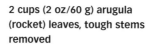

ITALY
Bresaola with Arugula

Usually associated with the far north of Italy, *bresaola,* air-dried cured beef, is a fixture of the Roman Jewish table as a substitute for prosciutto and is popular today for its low fat content. This popular antipasto also makes a fine summer main dish.

2 cups (2 oz/60 g) arugula (rocket) leaves, tough stems removed

Salt and freshly ground pepper

2 teaspoons extra-virgin olive oil, plus extra for serving

16 paper-thin slices *bresaola,* about 4½ oz (140 g) total weight

1½ oz (45g) wedge Parmigiano-Reggiano cheese

4 lemon wedges

MAKES 4 SERVINGS

1 Tear the arugula leaves into a bowl, sprinkle with salt, and drizzle with the 2 teaspoons olive oil. Toss to mix well. Add a grinding of pepper if the arugula is mild; often its own peppery taste is sufficient.

2 Arrange the *bresaola* slices around the edge of a serving platter or individual plates. Place the arugula in the middle. Using a handheld cheese slicer or a vegetable peeler, shave the cheese over the arugula. Sprinkle lightly with salt and freshly ground pepper, and serve at once. Place the olive oil bottle on the table for diners to add to the *bresaola*. Pass the lemon wedges for squeezing over the top.

Italian Salumi

SALAME TOSCANO

The word *salame* derives from the Latin *sal* (salt), salami's traditional preservative. Tuscan salami are made from the lean meat of mature pigs, finely ground and mixed with small cubes of pork lard and peppercorns. A portion of the pig's intestine is used as a casing for the mixture, hence the term *insaccati* (literally "put into a sack") used to refer to sausages and salami in general. The fresh salami are hung in an aging room for about two months to dry and season.

SALAME DI CINGHIALE

Cinghiali, "wild boar," live in the Tuscan woods, where it is not uncommon to come upon a pair of sows and their young walking nose to tail. They are mythical-looking creatures with dark bristly hair and improbably long snouts, which they use to sniff out desirable roots and herbs. *Cinghiale* is also a favorite game meat. It is slowly braised when fresh or made into deeply flavored prosciutti, *salame,* and *salsicce* (sausages).

PROSCIUTTO DOLCE

All prosciutti, whether *dolce* (sweet) or *salato* (salted), are made from the hind thigh of a pig just under a year old. Delicate *prosciutto di Parma* comes from pigs fed, among other things, whey from the process of making Parmigiano-Reggiano cheese. *Prosciutto di San Daniele* is pressed into a violin-like shape, while Parma prosciutti are rounder. Both have dense meat and creamy, white fat, and are considered *dolce* in Florence—*prosciutto toscano* being more salty.

FINOCCHIONA

Finocchiona is an aged *salame* made of minced pork belly and jowl seasoned with wine and fennel. *Infinocchiare* means "to swindle." The word was applied to this sausage in the days when farmers sold *vino sfuso* (unbottled wine) and offered prospective buyers *salame* with fennel seeds, whose aniselike flavor interferes with the ability to taste wine. As a result, an inferior wine tasted better than it really was.

SALAME TOSCANO

PROSCIUTTO TOSCANO

SOPPRESSATA

SALSICCIA DI CINTA SENESE

SALAME DI CINGHIALE

PROSCIUTTO DOLCE

FINOCCHIONA

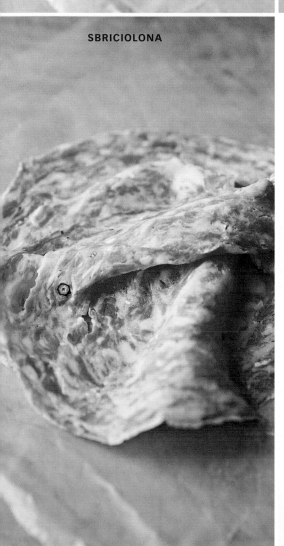

SBRICIOLONA

PROSCIUTTO TOSCANO

While the rest of Italy slightly prefers the more delicate *prosciutto dolce* of the north, salty *prosciutto toscano* is Florence's favorite. The making of *prosciutto toscano* is an age-old art. The fresh hams are refrigerated so that the meat hardens, then they are cleaned, shaped, and salt-cured in aging rooms. Made at private farms in the countryside, it is often boned before curing to facilitate aging and storage.

SOPPRESSATA

Soppressata (or *coppa di testa*) is Tuscany's most humble *insaccato* (see *salame toscano,* left). It is made by boiling the head, tongue, neck, and other leftovers from the pork-curing process for twenty-four hours. The bones are then removed. The meat is cut into chunks and seasoned with salt, pepper, rosemary, garlic, and spices. Then the mixture is transferred into jute sacks, tied by hand, and left to dry for a day. *Soppressata* is eaten fresh, either sliced or cut into cubes.

SALSICCIA DI CINTA SENESE

When fresh and soft, pork sausages are either spread raw on bread or are grilled. When aged, they are sliced like salami. *Salsiccia di cinta senese* is made from the meat of an ancient breed of wild pig. *Cinta senese* pigs are easily recognizable by their black bodies and the broad belt (*cinta*) of bristly white hair that covers their upper backs and front legs. Their meat is dark, well marbled, and flavorful.

SBRICIOLONA

Sbriciolona is essentially a fresher version of *finocchiona.* It is recognizable by its size (it is larger in diameter than *finocchiona)* and even more so by its soft, crumbly texture—hence its name, *sbriciolona,* which means "crumbly." Wild fennel, with tall, feathery leaves and yellow flowers that yield the seeds used as a flavoring, grows throughout the Italian countryside.

Roast Pork with Fennel and Herbs

This simple roast calls for two of Provence's signature ingredients: anise-scented fennel, which grows wild on the region's rolling hills, and *herbes de Provence,* a mixture of lavender flowers, thyme, basil, savory, and fennel seeds that may also contain marjoram, oregano, or rosemary. Pork shoulder, sometimes labeled Boston butt, has a nice amount of fat and is a good choice for this roast.

1 boneless pork shoulder roast, 3½–4 lb (1.75–2 kg), rolled and tied

5 cloves garlic, crushed

3 tablespoons chopped fresh flat-leaf (Italian) parsley

2 tablespoons chopped fresh sage

2 tablespoons chopped fresh rosemary

Salt and freshly ground pepper

12 tablespoons (6 fl oz/180 ml) dry white wine

3 tablespoons extra-virgin olive oil

¼ teaspoon *herbes de Provence* (see above)

¼ teaspoon fennel seeds

1 fennel bulb

1 red bell pepper (capsicum), seeded and thinly sliced lengthwise

3 shallots, finely chopped

½ cup (4 fl oz/125 ml) chicken or veal stock

MAKES 4–6 SERVINGS

1 Preheat the oven to 350°F (180°C). Clip the strings on the roast, unroll it, and lay it, fat side down, on a work surface. In a small bowl, combine the garlic, parsley, sage, rosemary, a large pinch of salt, ¼ teaspoon pepper, 3 tablespoons of the wine, the olive oil, *herbes de Provence,* and fennel seeds. Rub the mixture over the top of the meat, pushing little clumps of it into the crevices. Reroll the meat, tie with kitchen string, and place in a large roasting pan.

2 Roast until an instant-read thermometer inserted into the center of the roll registers 120°F (49°C), about 1½ hours. Meanwhile, cut off the stems and feathery tops from the fennel bulb and discard. Cut the bulb in half lengthwise, remove the core, then cut the bulb crosswise into paper-thin slices. Remove the roast from the oven. Spoon the juices from the pan into a bowl and set aside. Arrange the fennel and bell pepper around the roll. Return to the oven and roast until the bell pepper and fennel are slightly browned in places and an instant-read thermometer inserted into the center of the roll reads 140°F (60°C), about 30 minutes longer.

3 Transfer the meat and vegetables to a platter and cover loosely with aluminum foil. Spoon off any fat from the surface of the juices in the bowl and the pan. Add the shallots to the pan, place over medium-high heat, and cook, stirring, until slightly softened, about 3 minutes. Add the remaining 9 tablespoons wine and the reserved pan juices and cook, stirring, until reduced to 3–4 tablespoons, 5–6 minutes. Add the stock and continue to cook until the liquid is reduced to a flavorful sauce, 3–5 minutes longer.

4 Cut the roast into slices about ¾ inch (2 cm) thick and arrange on individual plates. Pour the sauce over the meat and serve with the vegetables.

Red Roast Pork

Roast pork is a versatile ingredient for which Chinese cooks find many uses: tossed in a stir-fry, diced into fried rice, chopped into noodles or soups, rolled in steamed rice sheets, or minced into filling for dim sum, such as the Roast Pork Buns on page 45. It's also delicious on its own, fanned over steamed rice.

1–2 pork tenderloins, ¾–1 lb (375–500 g) total weight

For the marinade

2 tablespoons light soy sauce

1½ teaspoons dark soy sauce

1½ tablespoons superfine (caster) sugar

1½ teaspoons five-spice powder

¾ teaspoon baking soda (bicarbonate of soda)

1 teaspoon crushed garlic

1½ tablespoons vegetable oil

3–4 drops red food coloring (optional)

MAKES 4–8 SERVINGS

1 Trim the pork tenderloin(s) to remove any sinew, skin, and fat. Cut in half lengthwise, and then cut the halves crosswise into 6-inch (15-cm) pieces.

2 To prepare the marinade, in a wide, flat nonreactive dish, combine the light and dark soy sauces, sugar, five-spice powder, baking soda, garlic, and oil, and mix well. If you want the pork to have its typical red hue, mix in the food coloring. One by one, dunk the pork strips into the marinade, turning to coat evenly, then arrange them in a single layer in the dish. Cover and refrigerate for at least 1½ hours or up to overnight, turning the pork strips occasionally.

3 Position a rack in the second highest level in the oven. Pour 1 cup (8 fl oz/250 ml) water into a drip pan and place it on a rack below. Preheat the oven to 400°F (200°C).

4 Arrange the marinated pork on the upper rack, allowing space between the strips, and roast, about 12 minutes. Turn and roast about 5 minutes longer. The surface should be glazed and slightly charred at the edges, and the meat inside still pink and tender.

5 Remove from the oven and allow the pork to rest before slicing, about 6 minutes. If cooking in advance, let cool completely on the rack, then wrap loosely in waxed paper, and refrigerate for up to 4 days.

Pork Chops with Balsamic Glaze

After only one day in a brine, thick pork chops are seasoned all the way through, not just on the surface. If not overcooked, they will be succulent beyond compare. The sugar helps the chops brown beautifully, and brined meats generally need no additional seasoning. Serve with buttered Brussels sprouts or wilted spinach.

For the brine

7 tablespoons (3½ oz/105 g) kosher or sea salt

¼ cup (2 oz/60 g) firmly packed brown sugar

½ bunch fresh thyme sprigs

4 cloves garlic, halved

1½ teaspoons coarsely cracked pepper

4 center-cut pork loin chops, each 1¼–1½ inches (3–4 cm) thick

1 tablespoon olive oil

2 tablespoons unsalted butter

¼ cup (1½ oz/45 g) minced shallot

2 tablespoons balsamic vinegar

1 cup (8 fl oz/250 ml) light chicken stock, or equal parts canned reduced-sodium chicken broth and water

1 tablespoon minced fresh sage

MAKES 4 SERVINGS

1 To make the brine, in a saucepan over medium heat, combine the salt, brown sugar, thyme sprigs, garlic, pepper, and 8 cups (64 fl oz/2 l) water. Bring just to a simmer, stirring to dissolve the salt and sugar. Remove from the heat, and transfer the brine to a nonreactive container large enough to hold both the pork chops and the brine. Let the brine cool completely, and then refrigerate until cold.

2 Add the pork chops to the cold brine, making sure they are submerged. If necessary, top the pork chops with a plate to weigh them down. Cover and refrigerate for 1 day.

3 Preheat the oven to 200°F (95°C). Remove the chops from the brine and pat dry. Choose a heavy frying pan large enough to hold the chops in a single layer without touching. Heat over medium-high heat. Add the olive oil and swirl to coat the bottom. When the oil is hot, add the chops and reduce the heat to medium. Cook until nicely browned on the bottom, about 10 minutes, adjusting the heat if necessary to avoid scorching. Turn and cook until the chops are no longer pink at the bone, 10–12 minutes longer, spooning off excess fat as it accumulates. Transfer the chops to a heatproof platter and keep warm in the oven.

4 Pour off any fat in the frying pan and place over medium-low heat. Add 1 tablespoon of the butter. When the butter melts, add the shallot and cook, stirring, until softened, about 2 minutes. Add the vinegar, bring to a boil, and boil briefly until reduced by half. Add the stock and sage, raise the heat to high, and boil, scraping up any browned bits on the pan bottom, until reduced to ⅓ cup (3 fl oz/80 ml). Remove from the heat, add the remaining 1 tablespoon butter, and swirl the pan without stirring until the butter melts.

5 Return the pan to low heat. Return the chops to the pan and cook gently, about 1 minute, turning them in the sauce 2 or 3 times. Divide the chops among warmed plates and spoon any remaining sauce over the top. Serve at once.

MEXICO
Grilled Pork Tacos

If you were to order *tacos con cecina* in most parts of Mexico, it would be thinly sliced beef, but in Oaxaca, long, thin strips of chile-marinated pork fill these tacos.

For the chile sauce

5 guajillo chiles, seeded

4 ancho chiles, seeded

Boiling water

6 cloves garlic, unpeeled

¼ cup (2 fl oz/60 ml) white vinegar

½ teaspoon dried oregano, preferably Mexican

10 whole peppercorns, or ¼ teaspoon freshly ground pepper

½-inch (12-mm) piece true cinnamon bark, or ½ teaspoon ground cinnamon

1 whole clove, or 1 pinch of ground cloves

Sea salt

1 pork tenderloin, about 1 lb (500 g), trimmed of excess fat

12 large green (spring) onions, root ends trimmed

12 small Anaheim chiles

2–3 tablespoons safflower or canola oil

4 limes, halved

2 avocados, pitted, peeled, and sliced

Avocado salsa, homemade or purchased

Tomato salsa, homemade or purchased

12 small radishes

12 corn tortillas, homemade or purchased, warmed

MAKES 4–6 SERVINGS

1 To make the chile sauce, heat a heavy frying pan over medium heat. Add the chiles and press with a spatula for a few seconds. Turn and press for a few seconds until the chiles are slightly colored and begin to give off their aroma. Transfer to a bowl, add boiling water to cover, and let stand until soft, about 20 minutes. Add the garlic cloves to the pan and toast, turning, until softened and browned, about 10 minutes. Let cool, then peel and place in a blender. Drain the chiles, reserving the soaking water. Tear into small pieces and add to the blender with the vinegar and oregano. If using whole spices, pulverize in a spice grinder. Add the spices and 1 teaspoon salt to the blender and pulse to form a thick sauce, adding a few drops of the reserved soaking water if needed.

2 Lay the pork tenderloin horizontally in front of you. Starting at one end, using a sharp knife, slice the pork crosswise without cutting all the way through. Turn the tenderloin over and, again not cutting all the way through, make a parallel cut about ¼ inch (6 mm) from the first. Turn the pork back over to the original side and repeat, making another parallel cut. Continue turning the meat and making parallel cuts until the entire tenderloin is stretched out like an accordian. Rub the chile sauce on both sides, fold the meat back into its original shape, and spread with any remaining sauce. Wrap in plastic wrap and refrigerate for at least 2 hours or up to 12 hours.

3 Prepare a charcoal or gas grill for direct grilling over high heat. Lay a double thickness of heavy-duty aluminum foil on the hottest coals. Rub the green onions and chiles with the oil and place on the foil, with the white part of the onions over the coals. Grill, turning frequently, until browned, about 10 minutes. Place in a shallow bowl and toss with a squirt of lime juice.

4 Cut the meat across the folds into long slices and lay on the grill rack. Brush with oil and grill, turning once, until browned, 2–3 minutes per side. Place the green onions, chiles, limes, avocados, salsas, and radishes in separate bowls. Serve each guest a portion of meat and 2 or 3 tortillas.

Pork Braised in Riesling

Tart and aromatic quince makes its appearance in autumn and pairs well with apples. Here, the two form a compote to accompany pork slow-cooked in Riesling.

2 lb (1 kg) boneless pork shoulder roast, trimmed of excess fat and cut into 2-inch (5-cm) pieces

Sea salt and freshly ground pepper

½ cup (4 fl oz/125 ml) olive oil

2 medium yellow onions, diced

6 cloves garlic

1 cinnamon stick

4 fresh thyme sprigs

4 fresh flat-leaf (Italian) parsley sprigs

1 bay leaf

3 cups (24 fl oz/750 ml) Riesling

2 carrots, peeled and diced

½ cup (4 fl oz/125 ml) Calvados

2 teaspoons Champagne vinegar or apple cider vinegar, or to taste

For the compote

3 quinces

3 tart red apples

4 tablespoons (2 oz/60 g) unsalted butter

1 large yellow onion, diced

1 cup (8 fl oz/250 ml) Riesling

¼ cup (3 oz/90 g) honey

1 tablespoon Dijon mustard

Grated zest of 1 lemon

MAKES 4–6 SERVINGS

1 Place the pork pieces in a nonreactive bowl and season on all sides with salt and pepper. Cover and refrigerate overnight.

2 In a Dutch oven over medium-high heat, warm the olive oil. Add the pork and sear on all sides until deep brown, about 8 minutes. Transfer to a plate. Reduce the heat to medium. Add the onions and sauté until lightly browned, 8–10 minutes. Add the garlic, cinnamon, thyme, parsley, and bay leaf and sauté until the garlic is fragrant, about 2 minutes. Pour in the Riesling and deglaze the pan, scraping up any browned bits on the pan bottom. Return the pork to the pan and add enough water so that the liquid comes to the top of the pork. Season with salt and pepper, reduce the heat to low, cover, and simmer until the meat is tender, about 1½ hours. Add the carrots and Calvados and simmer, covered, until the carrots are tender, about 30 minutes longer. Stir in the vinegar and season with salt and pepper.

3 To make the compote, peel and core the quinces and apples, then cut into 1-inch (2.5-cm) chunks. In a saucepan over medium heat, melt the butter. Add the onion and sauté until translucent, 10–12 minutes. Add the quinces, apples, Riesling, and honey, reduce the heat to low, and cook until the fruit is soft, 30–35 minutes. Stir in the mustard and the lemon zest and season with salt.

4 Divide the pan juices and pork among individual plates. Serve at once with the compote.

Pork Stew with Picada

The earthy cuisine of the Pyrenees has as one of its high points *civet de senglar,* a dish of wild boar in red wine. This version of that recipe works well for pork. The *picada* is reminiscent of Mexican mole. To skin the hazelnuts (filberts), toast them in a hot pan until the skins loosen, then rub them off with a dry kitchen towel.

2 lb (1 kg) boneless leg of pork or pork shoulder butt, cut into 2-inch (5-cm) cubes

1 large yellow onion, thinly sliced

2 carrots, peeled and chopped

1 leek, white and pale green parts, chopped

2 tomatoes, chopped

6 cloves garlic, peeled and crushed

½ lemon

8 whole black peppercorns

1 fresh thyme sprig

2 bay leaves

1 bottle (24 fl oz/750 ml) red wine

1 tablespoon unsalted butter

¼ cup (2 fl oz/60 ml) olive oil

3 cups (24 fl oz/750 ml) beef stock, or as needed

Salt

For the picada

1 small slice coarse country bread

1 tablespoon olive oil

6 blanched almonds

4 hazelnuts (filberts), skinned (see above)

4 walnuts

1 tablespoon pine nuts

1 oz (30 g) bittersweet chocolate

Handful of fresh flat-leaf (Italian) parsley leaves

MAKES 4 SERVINGS

1 In a large nonreactive bowl, combine the pork, onion, carrots, leek, tomatoes, garlic, lemon, peppercorns, thyme, and bay leaves. Add the wine, cover, and marinate in the refrigerator, stirring occasionally, for at least 24 hours or up to 2 days.

2 Drain the pork, reserving the marinade. Pat the pork dry. In a Dutch oven over medium heat, melt the butter with the olive oil. Working in batches, add the pork and cook, turning as needed, until lightly browned on all sides, about 8 minutes. Using a slotted spoon, transfer the pork to a plate. Strain the reserved marinade through a colander into a bowl. Set aside the liquid and discard the lemon from the vegetables. Raise the heat under the pot to medium-high, add the strained vegetables, and sauté until the onion is softened and almost all the liquid has evaporated, about 5 minutes. Remove from the heat.

3 In a small saucepan over high heat, bring the strained liquid to a boil and cook until reduced by half, about 15 minutes.

4 Add the pork and the reduced marinade to the pot with the vegetables and pour in enough of the stock to cover the meat (reserving at least ½ cup/4 fl oz/125 ml). Place over low heat and simmer, uncovered, until the pork is fork-tender, about 1 hour. Remove from the heat and, using a slotted spoon, transfer the pork to a bowl. Discard the bay leaves, thyme sprig, and peppercorns. Pass the sauce through a fine-mesh sieve or process briefly in a food processor. Return the sauce and pork to the pot, season with salt, stir well, cover, and simmer gently, adding a little more stock if needed, until the sauce is thick, 10–15 minutes.

5 To make the *picada,* cut the crust from the bread. In a small frying pan over medium-high heat, fry the bread in the olive oil until crisp, about 2 minutes. In a mortar, grind together the bread, nuts, chocolate, and parsley with a pestle until a crumbly paste forms. Stir the *picada* into the sauce and simmer gently, being careful not to let it burn, about 5–10 minutes. Transfer the stew to a warmed platter and serve at once.

FRANCE
Country Pâté with Herbs

Pâtés date back to medieval times, when they were more strictly defined as a seasoned meat, fish, or poultry mixture in a pastry lining, usually served hot. Today the term is used for what is technically a terrine: the pâté of the past minus its pastry, baked in the loaf-shaped dish also called a terrine. In France, the dish is lined with thin, lacy caul fat from a pig's belly, uncured or salt-cured bacon, or *poitrine* (pork belly). If using smoked bacon, blanch it for 2 minutes.

1 large bunch spinach, about ¾ lb (375 g), stems removed

3 tablespoons unsalted butter

1 large yellow onion, chopped

2 cloves garlic, chopped

Salt and freshly ground pepper

11–12 slices lean bacon, about ⅔ lb (315 g) total weight, preferably unsmoked (see above)

1 lb (500 g) chicken livers

1 lb (500 g) boneless pork shoulder, cut into 1½-inch (4-cm) cubes

2 eggs

2 tablespoons heavy (double) cream

¼ cup (2 fl oz/60 ml) Cognac

1–2 teaspoons dried thyme

1 tablespoon chopped fresh tarragon

3 tablespoons fresh flat-leaf (Italian) parsley, chopped

3 tablespoons chopped fresh basil

1 teaspoon chopped fresh rosemary

Pinch of *quatre épices* or allspice

3 tablespoons all-purpose (plain) flour

2–3 bay leaves

Butter (Boston) lettuce leaves

Cornichons

Pickled onions

MAKES 6–8 SERVINGS

1 Preheat the oven to 350°F (180°C). Bring a large pan of water to a boil. Add the spinach and cook until tender, about 3 minutes. Drain, squeeze dry, then chop coarsely.

2 In a frying pan over medium-high heat, melt the butter. Add the onion and garlic, season with salt and pepper, and sauté until the onion is light brown, 6–8 minutes. Let cool.

3 Chop 3 of the bacon slices into small pieces. Trim the livers of discolored areas and connective tissue. In a food processor, combine the chopped bacon, livers, pork, and onion mixture and process to a coarse purée. Transfer to a large bowl. Add the spinach, eggs, cream, Cognac, thyme, tarragon, parsley, basil, rosemary, *quatre épices*, flour, ½ teaspoon salt, and ¼ teaspoon pepper, and stir to combine.

4 Line a 9-by-5-by-3-inch (23-by-13-by-7.5-cm) loaf pan, preferably nonstick, with the remaining bacon, draping the ends over the sides. Press the meat mixture into the pan and arrange the bay leaves down the center. Fold the bacon slices over the top. Cover tightly with aluminum foil.

5 Place the loaf pan in a baking pan and pour in hot water to reach three-fourths up the sides of the loaf pan. Bake until a thermometer inserted into the loaf reads 145°F (63°C), about 2 hours. The sides will have pulled away from the pan and the pâté should be surrounded by melted fat.

6 Remove the loaf pan from the water bath and place on a rimmed baking sheet; do not remove the foil. Place a weighted board on top of the pâté and wrap a towel around the outside of the loaf pan. Let cool to room temperature.

7 Remove the weight and refrigerate the pâté for at least 8 hours. (It will keep, covered and refrigerated, for about 3 days.) To remove from the pan, insert a knife along the edges to loosen the pâté. Gently warm the bottom of the pan in warm water for a few seconds, then invert a plate on top of the pan and invert the plate and pan together. Lift off the pan. Cut the pâté into slices ¾–1 inch (2–2.5 cm) thick and arrange on plates lined with the lettuce leaves. Accompany with the cornichons and pickled onions.

The vocation of *charcutier* dates to the Middle Ages, when anyone who worked with meat had to devise ways to cure and preserve it for long periods. Thus was born such commonplace Parisian *charcuterie* items as *saucisson* and *jambon fumé.*

French Charcuterie

In every Paris neighborhood, on almost every street, you'll find a *charcuterie,* a take-out shop that carries hams, pâtés, and sausages of every description. Some shops specialize in the products of a particular region of France, such as the Auvergne, the Alsace, or the Périgord; others are famed for what they make on the premises, which might include a dozen different varieties of *boudin* or a particularly fine selection of pâtés.

Most *charcuteries* boast a mountain of inventory, but nearly all of them carry the classics, including andouille (tripe sausage; *andouillette* is the smaller version), *boudin blanc* (white sausage of chicken, veal, or pork, sometimes flavored with truffle), *boudin noir* (dark sausage made from pork blood), *crépinette* (a sausagelike patty often wrapped in caul fat), *jambon cru* (salt-cured ham), *jambon fumé* (smoked ham), and *saucisson sec* (sausage, usually air-dried, sliced and eaten cold). In addition, *charcuteries* almost always carry a selection of pâtés, chopped or ground and seasoned mixtures of meat, poultry, or seafood, and terrines, pâtés named for the ceramic containers in which they are made. Along these same lines, you'll find *rillettes,* rich spreads of shredded pork, duck, goose, or, more rarely, chicken or turkey, and galantines, stuffed, boned poultry or meat usually covered with aspic.

In addition to the wealth of cured and cooked meats, most *charcuteries* sell oven-ready trays of snails stuffed with garlicky green butter, various types of quiche, an array of salads, and assorted other ready-to-eat foods. Many shops also offer a take-out hot meal at midday and sometimes early evening, a holdover from the days when Parisian living quarters frequently lacked a stove.

With hundreds of *charcuteries*—old, new, rustic, fancy—from which to choose, selecting only a few to highlight is difficult, but here are four of the best: Charcuterie Charles is known for its many *boudin blanc* varieties, variously flavored with truffles, hazelnuts, pistachios, or prunes. Charcuterie Coesnon is another well-respected maker of *boudin,* as well as of exquisite terrines, salt-cured hams, dried sausages, and *andouillettes.* Schmid is the *charcuterie* to visit for Alsatian specialties, particularly all types of sausages. Finally, the elegant Maison Pou stocks an incredible selection of wines, cheeses, mushrooms, and truffles, along with plenty of handsome pâtés to tempt you.

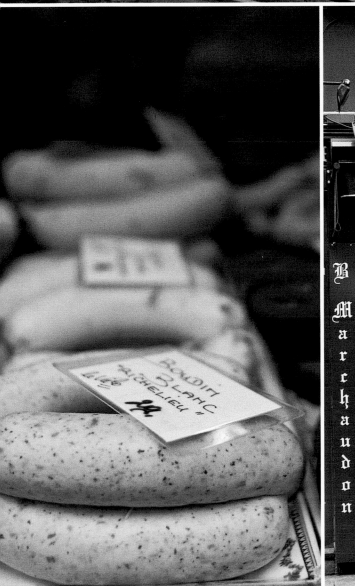

MEXICO
Slow-Cooked Lamb

Once steamed in buried underground pots, the chile-marinated meat known as *birria*—usually mutton or kid—is still long-cooked until it turns into a tender stew with plenty of flavorful broth.

8 ancho chiles, seeded

6 guajillo chiles, seeded

Boiling water

5 cloves garlic, unpeeled

1 cup (8 fl oz/250 ml) white vinegar

2-inch (5-cm) piece true cinnamon bark, ground, or 1 teaspoon ground cinnamon

½-inch (12-mm) piece fresh ginger, peeled and grated

2 teaspoons dried oregano, preferably Mexican

½ teaspoon ground cumin

Salt and freshly ground pepper

4–5 lb (2–2.5 kg) bone-in lamb shoulder, trimmed of excess fat

1 can (14½ oz/455 g) chopped tomatoes

½ cup dry sherry (optional)

For the garnish

Shredded cabbage

Finely chopped white onion

Lime wedges

MAKES 10 SERVINGS

1 Place the chiles into a heavy frying pan over medium heat and press with a spatula for a few seconds. Turn and press for a few seconds until the chiles are slightly colored and begin to give off their aroma. Transfer to a bowl, add boiling water to cover, and let stand until soft, about 20 minutes. Add the garlic cloves to the pan and toast, turning, until softened and blackened, about 10 minutes. Let cool, then peel and place in a blender. Drain the chiles and add to the blender with the vinegar. Process until very smooth. Add the cinnamon, ginger, 1 teaspoon of the oregano, the cumin, 1 teaspoon salt, and ½ teaspoon pepper. Blend to a smooth paste, adding a little water if needed. Taste and adjust the salt.

2 Place the meat in a bowl and coat evenly with the paste. Cover and refrigerate for at least 5 hours or, preferably, overnight.

3 Preheat the oven to 350°F (180°C). Place a rack in the bottom of a large roasting pan with a tight-fitting lid. Pour in enough water to reach just to the top of the rack, then place the meat on the rack. Top with any paste left in the bowl. Cover the pan tightly with aluminum foil and then the lid. Bake for 3 hours.

4 Remove from the oven and raise the oven temperature to 375°F (190°C). Tear the meat into large pieces and spread them on a baking sheet, removing any fat or gristle and the bones and reserving the broth in the pan. Brown the meat in the oven, turning at least once, about 15 minutes.

5 Skim the fat off the reserved broth and transfer 1 cup (8 fl oz/250 ml) to a blender and the rest to a saucepan. To the blender, add the tomatoes and the remaining 1 teaspoon oregano and purée until smooth. Add the purée to the saucepan. Add the sherry, if using, and bring to a gentle simmer. Season with salt, if necessary. Simmer gently, uncovered, about 15 minutes.

6 To serve, spoon the meat into individual bowls and ladle in the broth. Pass the cabbage, onion, and lime wedges in small bowls at the table.

Roast Leg of Lamb with Artichokes

1 bone-in leg of lamb, about
4½ lb (2.25 kg)

3 tablespoons fresh rosemary
leaves, plus sprigs for garnish

8 cloves garlic, slivered

Salt and freshly ground pepper

½ teaspoon dried thyme

3 tablespoons extra-virgin
olive oil

1 head garlic, cloves separated,
unpeeled

1 tablespoon white wine
vinegar, or juice of ½ lemon

3 large or 4 medium artichokes,
about 2 lb (1 kg) total weight

2 cups (16 fl oz/500 ml) dry red
wine

1 cup (8 fl oz/250 ml) beef
or veal stock

MAKES 4–6 SERVINGS

1 Preheat the oven to 375°F (190°C). Make small incisions 2–3 inches (5–7.5 cm) apart all over the lamb. Insert a few rosemary leaves and a sliver of garlic into each incision. In a bowl, combine 1 teaspoon salt, ¼ teaspoon pepper, the thyme, and the olive oil and rub the mixture all over the lamb. Place the lamb fat side up in a roasting pan just large enough to accommodate the lamb and eventually the artichokes. Scatter the whole garlic cloves around the lamb and roast, about 30 minutes.

2 Meanwhile, fill a large bowl with water and stir in the vinegar. Working with 1 artichoke at a time, cut off the stem flush with the bottom, then peel the stem and add it to the vinegar water. Snap off the tough outer leaves until you reach the pale inner leaves. Cut the top one-third off the artichoke, removing the pointed tips of the leaves. Quarter the artichoke lengthwise and cut out the choke. Add the quarters to the vinegar water.

3 Bring a large pot of salted water to a boil. Drain the artichokes, add them to the boiling water, and cook, about 3 minutes. Drain and set aside.

4 Remove the roasting pan from the oven, turn the lamb, and roast, about 15 minutes longer. Turn it again and roast until a thermometer inserted into the thickest part of the lamb (but not touching bone) registers 130°F (54°C) for rare to medium-rare, about 35 minutes longer. About 20 minutes before the lamb is done, add the artichokes to the pan and roast until tender when pierced with a fork. Transfer the lamb, garlic, and artichokes to a serving platter and cover loosely with aluminum foil.

5 Skim off any fat from the pan juices. Place the pan over medium-high heat, add the wine, and bring to a boil, scraping up any browned bits from the pan bottom. Continue to cook, stirring, until the liquid is reduced by half, about 10 minutes. Add the stock and cook until reduced to a slightly thickened sauce, about 5 minutes. Taste and adjust the seasoning.

6 Carve the lamb into thin slices and arrange on a platter. Surround with the artichokes and garlic cloves and moisten the meat with the sauce. Garnish with rosemary sprigs and serve at once.

Grilled Lamb Chops with Shell Beans

Fresh shell beans, served with flavorful lamb, have a creamy, tender quality and are coveted during their short season in late summer.

For the beans

1 tablespoon olive oil

½ small yellow onion, minced

2 cloves garlic, 1 minced and 1 left whole

2 cups (10 oz/315 g) fresh shelled beans, such as cranberry (borlotti), flageolet, runner, or cannellini, or ⅔ cup (4½ oz/ 140 g) dried beans, soaked overnight and drained

4 cups (32 fl oz/1 l) chicken stock, vegetable stock, or water

4 tablespoons (2 oz/60 g) unsalted butter, at room temperature

1 tablespoon red wine vinegar

Sea salt and freshly ground pepper

For the lamb

2 frenched racks of lamb, 8 ribs and 1½–2 lb (750 g–1 kg) each

¼ cup (2 fl oz/60 ml) olive oil, plus extra for brushing

2 tablespoons unsalted butter

¼ cup (1 oz/30 g) dried bread crumbs

1 tablespoon chopped fresh flat-leaf (Italian) parsley

1 teaspoon chopped fresh marjoram

1 teaspoon chopped fresh thyme

MAKES 4 SERVINGS

1 To make the beans, in a large saucepan over medium heat, warm the olive oil. Add the onion and minced garlic, cover, and cook, stirring occasionally, until the onion is tender, about 7 minutes. Add the beans and the stock. Bring to a simmer and cook until the beans are tender, 15–20 minutes for fresh beans, 45–90 minutes for dried beans, depending on the variety. If using dried beans, add hot water as needed to keep the beans covered. In a mortar, crush the garlic clove into a paste with a pestle. Transfer to a small bowl, add the butter, vinegar, ½ teaspoon salt, and ¼ teaspoon pepper, and blend with a fork. Add to the beans. Taste and adjust the seasoning.

2 Preheat the oven to 450°F (230°C). In a large ovenproof pan over medium-high heat, warm the ¼ cup (2 fl oz/60 ml) olive oil. Lay the racks meat side down in the pan and sear to a rich brown, 4–5 minutes. Transfer the pan to the oven and roast, about 7 minutes. Turn the lamb and roast, 5–7 minutes for medium-rare, 8–10 minutes for medium. Remove from the oven, tent with aluminum foil, and let rest, about 15 minutes.

3 While the lamb rests, in a frying pan over high heat, melt the butter. Add the bread crumbs and sauté until lightly toasted, 3–5 minutes. Transfer to a bowl. Stir in the parsley, marjoram, and thyme, and season with salt and pepper. If necessary, reheat the beans over medium heat, stirring occasionally.

4 Brush the lamb with olive oil and sprinkle with the bread crumb mixture, pressing it into the meat. Cut each rack into chops. Divide the beans among individual plates and top with 2 chops each. Serve at once.

Lamb Kebabs with Yogurt Sauce

Tender cuts of lamb are ideally suited to those who prefer quick-grilled or roasted meats. Roast lamb is often served with mint sauce or red currant jelly. This upscale version of a kebab is served with yogurt sauce and a salad with mint.

For the lamb

1 large yellow onion

Juice of 1 large lemon

2 tablespoons extra-virgin olive oil, plus extra for brushing

Freshly ground pepper

2 lb (1 kg) boneless, lean lamb from loin or leg, cut into 1-inch (2.5-cm) cubes

For the yogurt sauce

1½ cups (12 oz/375 g) Greek yogurt or other plain whole-milk yogurt

½ English (hothouse) cucumber, peeled and coarsely shredded

Sea salt and freshly ground pepper

For the salad

6 green (spring) onions, white parts only, thinly sliced

¼ cup (⅓ oz/10 g) fresh mint leaves, coarsely shredded

2 hearts of romaine (cos) lettuce, coarsely shredded

4 large or 8 small pita breads, homemade or purchased

MAKES 4 SERVINGS

1 To prepare the lamb, coarsely grate the onion into a fine-mesh sieve set over a large bowl. Press on the onion with the back of a wooden spoon to extract as much juice as possible. Discard the grated onion. Add the lemon juice and olive oil to the onion juice and season with pepper. Add the lamb cubes, turn to coat, cover with plastic wrap, and refrigerate for at least 2 hours or up to 8 hours.

2 To make the yogurt sauce, put the yogurt in a serving bowl. If using Greek yogurt, whisk in ½ cup (4 fl oz/125 ml) cold water to form a creamy, thick sauce. Add the cucumber, season with salt and pepper, and stir to combine. Cover and refrigerate.

3 Prepare a charcoal or gas grill for direct grilling over medium-high heat. If using wooden skewers, soak them in water to cover, about 30 minutes.

4 To make the salad, in a bowl, combine the green onions, mint, and romaine. Set aside.

5 Remove the lamb cubes from the marinade. Thread the cubes onto the skewers. Season with salt and brush with olive oil. Place the skewers on the grill rack directly over the heat source and grill, turning frequently, until deep brown, 4–6 minutes for medium-rare. Remove the cubes from the skewers and add to the salad.

6 Set the pita breads on the grill rack and grill, turning once, until warm, 2–3 minutes. Split open each pita bread and fill with the salad and lamb. Spoon on some of the sauce. Serve at once.

MOROCCO
Lamb Tagine

4 tablespoons (2 fl oz/60 ml) olive oil

2 yellow onions, finely chopped

3 carrots, peeled and chopped

3 lb (1.5 kg) cubed lamb for stewing

½ cup (2½ oz/75 g) all-purpose (plain) flour

Salt and freshly ground pepper

3 cloves garlic, minced

1 teaspoon ground cumin

¼ teaspoon saffron threads

1 tablespoon peeled and minced fresh ginger

2½ cups (20 fl oz/625 ml) beef stock

1 cup (8 oz/250 g) canned crushed tomatoes

1 cup (6 oz/185 g) chopped dried dates

Grated zest and juice of 1 orange

2 tablespoons finely chopped fresh flat-leaf (Italian) parsley for garnish

MAKES 6 SERVINGS

1 Preheat the oven to 350°F (180°C). In a Dutch oven over medium heat, warm 1 tablespoon of the olive oil. Add the onions and sauté until softened, about 5 minutes. Add the carrots and cook until slightly softened, about 3 minutes longer. Transfer to a bowl and set aside.

2 Pat the lamb dry. Place the flour in a large bowl or plastic bag and season with salt and pepper. Add the lamb in batches and stir or shake to coat thoroughly.

3 Add the remaining 3 tablespoons oil to the pot and heat over medium-high heat. Working in batches to avoid crowding, add the lamb and brown on all sides, 4–5 minutes. Transfer to a bowl and set aside.

4 Return the onion mixture and browned lamb, along with any accumulated juices, to the pot. Add the garlic, cumin, saffron, and ginger and stir to coat the meat and vegetables. Add the stock and bring to boil, scraping up the browned bits on the pan bottom. Add the tomatoes, dates, and orange zest and juice and bring to a boil.

5 Cover and bake in the oven until the meat is tender, 1½–2 hours. If the sauce seems thin, transfer the meat and vegetables to a bowl and boil the sauce on the stove top until thickened. Return the meat and vegetables to the pot. Taste and adjust the seasoning. Transfer the stew to a serving bowl and garnish with the parsley. Serve at once.

DAIRY AND EGGS

By the Dozen

DAIRY AND EGGS AROUND THE WORLD

Though relatively few of us now begin the morning by collecting freshly laid eggs or milking cows, these staples of the farm play vital roles in our day-to-day cooking. Eggs and the many dairy products derived from the milk of cows, goats, and sheep provide valuable nutrients, and their transformational properties allow us to create countless rich entrées, creamy sauces, and delicate desserts.

Milk, cheese, and eggs, in varying forms, are essentials in nearly every kitchen. Fundamental on their own but also endlessly versatile, dairy products can be paired with everything from fresh herbs and vegetables to wild mushrooms, exotic spices, chocolate, coffee, or fruit. From milk comes a variety of creams, a world of cheeses, and rich custards to be either baked, burnt, or frozen. Milk from goats, cows, sheep, buffalo, and camels was central to the early nomadic diets of central and southern Asia, the Middle East, and Africa, and in many countries, herd animals were valued not for their meat but for the nutritious milk they provided on a regular basis. To this day, dairy products are a crucial source of protein for many families, particularly in vegetarian cultures.

The 101 pleats of a tall, white toque, the classic chef's hat, are said to represent the many ways a master chef can cook an egg. French cuisine unquestionably enshrines egg cookery as a serious art. Dessert cooks, in particular, depend on eggs as a basic ingredient in batters and doughs, and as the foundation of smooth custards, airy mousses, high-rising soufflés, and delicate meringues. In addition to chicken eggs, chefs turn to larger, richer duck eggs and goose eggs or to diminutive, speckled quail eggs. Eggs and dairy often appear together as well, the melting smoothness of cheese or cream perfectly complementing the tenderness of eggs. French omelets, soufflés, and quiches, Italian frittatas, and Spanish tortillas are all takes on this classic pairing.

		CHEVRES (con't)			EDAM		HUNTSMAN	
	14.80	~CHABICHOU			EMMENTHALER		IDIAZABAL smoked	
	2.80	~CHAVRIE	3.72		EPOISSES		ISTARA	11.00
VALO	11.30	~CHEDDAR (DOMESTIC)			ESROM		JACKS	
LY	13.00	~CHEVRE d'OR			EXPLORATEUR	11.30	~BLOCK	still 2.75
ERI		~CHEVRE de BELLAY 10.75			FARMERS	4.35	~DIANA	
AIN	7.00	~CORNILLY			FETA		~DRY	7.50
Noire	5.50	~CROTTIN			~BULGARIAN (sheep) 4.90		~EXTRA DRY	9.00
Poitou	7.50	~CHAVIGNOL	4.80		~FRENCH (sheep) 6.20		~GARLIC	
	1.00	~REDWOOD HILL	5.80		~GREEK (sheep) 6.90		~GOAT	9.00
	9.50	~DRUNKEN GOAT (MURCIA)			~ISRAELI (sheep) 5.50		~HOTPEPPER	4.50
	10.00	~GARROTXA (SPAIN)					~HARBENFRO	
		~GOUDA			FOL EPI	11.00	~SONOMA	5.50
		~HUMBOLDT FOG	16.00		FONTINAS		~TELEME not label	6.50
5 varies		~IL CAPRINO/truffle 9.50			~VAL D'OSTA	11.50	JARLSBERG	5.25
CABOT	5.10	~JACK	8.00		~FONTAL	8.00	JARLSBERG-LIGHT	5.05
DIAMOND 6.75		~LAURA CHENEL ASSTD			~DANISH	5.50	~KASHKAVAL (BULGARIA) 6.70	
ANADIAN 6.75		~LE CHEVROT	8.75				KASSERI ~domestic cow	
N BLOCK 4.75		~LE GARIOTIN					KEFALOGRAVIERA	7.00
MERYS or 14.00		~LE LINGOT	6.50		FOURNOLS	7.50	KEFALOTYRI	7.00
ENGLISH		~LE KODIN	4.50		FROMAGE d'AFFINOIS 8.00		KUMINOST	
DWOOD HILL 10.25		~MAITRE SEGUIN	9				LANCASHIRE	12.00
ERBOT	8.00	~PAVE SAVAGE			GAMMELOST (SORRY)		LAPPI	
NSIN (white) 6.50		~PELLIOUTE/BRIE 12.80			GJETOST		L'EDEL de CLERON	12.50
aged 1 yr 7.35		~PICANDOU			GOUDAS		LEICESTER	
MILD 2		~POLIGNY St.Pierre 9.80			~ARINA (goat) 10.00		LEYDEN	5.30
ARIETIES		~QUESO MATERERO 12.75			~AGED (goat) when Avail.		LIMBURGER	4.50
VAILABLE		~REDWOOD HILL ASSTD			~PARRANO (half aged) 8.00		LIVAKOT	11.00
		~SELLES sur CHER 6.20			~PRIMA DONNA			
PELBY'S 12.00		~STE MAURE			~RUBED		MACHEGO	10-12.00
		~TOMME de GRAND MERE			SUBENHARA/NETTLE		~BABY	8.50
		~VALEN CAY	9.00		~YOUNG (red wax) 5.00		~AGED (raw milk) 12.80	
		OTHER VARIETIES often avail					~MONTALBAN	
GOATS		CHIMAY	8.00		GRUYERE CAVE AGE 9.00		~ROSEMARY	12.80
ALE		COMTE	10.00		SWISS ~ RESERVE 7.50		MANOURI	7.00
		COTSWOLD	10.00		FRENCH ~BEAUFORT 14.00		MAROILLES	12.00
DOMESTIC)		COULOMIERS	8.00		COMTE		MASCARPONE	10.50
ERON	12.00	CREAM CHEESE	4				MIMOLETTE	12.00
de QUERCY		CREME FRAICHE	4		GUBBEEN	13.00	MIZITHRA	
PAILLE		CROTTIN POIVRE	10.00		~HAVARTI	4.80	MONTASIO	8.00
OU	2.80				~CARAWAY	4.80	MORBIER raw/past 6.50 8.00	
BERT (Poitou) 7.50		DOUBLE GLOUCESTER			~DILL	4.50		
BERRY		DOUX de MONTAGNE			~EXTR RICH	4.80		
(SPANISH)		DURRUS			~TILSIT (STRONG) 5.50			

Prices Su

TRY Keene's Cheddar $14 lb
ENGLISH FARMHOUSE

COBB HILL FROM VERMONT
A FULL-BODIED FARMSTEAD RAW MILK CHEESE

rp & sly Farmstead Bleu de C
raw milk blue, firm

DAIRY

Raw milk can be boiled down to paste, such as the *khoa* of northern India, or separated with rennet, vinegar, or lemon juice to form curds. Pressing the curds creates fresh cheeses such as *paneer* and *queso fresco,* familiar staples in India and Mexico respectively. Inoculating the curds and aging them under highly localized conditions create the many famed cheeses we've come to enjoy, from Italy's grainy Parmigiano-Reggiano to England's blue-veined Stilton, France's creamy chèvres, and Spain's golden *manchego.* When melted, cheese helps bind other ingredients, creates luxuriously smooth textures, and provides filling richness. Fresh soft cheeses such as ricotta and cream cheese are also the basis of global variations on fluffy cheesecakes.

In the Middle East, where yogurt was first fermented thousands of years ago, countless dishes incorporate the soured milk's tartness and smooth texture. Soured milk products such as buttermilk and yogurt also appear in marinades for their ability to tenderize meat. Southern fried chicken and tandoori are two favorite examples. Straining yogurt thickens its texture and concentrates its flavor. Flavored with *za'atar,* a mixture of dried thyme, oregano, sesame seeds, cumin, and salt, yogurt serves as a refreshing accompaniment to *lavash* bread and slices of cucumber in Arabic cuisines.

When eaten with bread, jam, or fruit, a slice of cheese can become a meal. The celebrated cheese course that traditionally completes dinner in France showcases the country's many famous offerings. In the Middle East, a typical day begins with a breakfast of warm bread, pungent goat cheese, salty olives, and *labnah,* a creamy mixture of thickened yogurt and olive oil. Those with a sweet tooth will choose a softer cheese served with spoonfuls of sweet jam, or yogurt swirled with honey and walnuts. Macaroni and cheese and grilled cheese sandwiches are comfort foods popular with children and adults alike in the United States.

Fresh cream is the base of many desserts. Whipped to airy lightness or gently cooked in a custard, it retains its silken texture. Fermented and thickened cream, such as English clabbered cream, French crème fraîche, and Russian *tvorogm,* add distinctive flavor and richness to dishes, whether spooned as a topping or stirred into sauces.

EGGS

In North America, eggs reign at breakfasts and brunches, but in many other countries they appear more regularly at the lunch and dinner table. Italy's frittata, France's quiche, China's lobster Cantonese, and Japan's savory steamed custards reveal the binding power of eggs while highlighting their smooth richness. In India, hard-boiled eggs star in endless versions of spicy egg curry, their colors and flavors changing with the region and with each family's own recipe. Red-dyed whole eggs, symbolizing fertility and new life, appear at parties in China to celebrate birth and also at Easter meals in Greece.

Hard-boiled eggs are the perfect food to eat on the go. Glass jars of pickled eggs and wire baskets filled with hard-boiled eggs are familiar sights in American delis and French bistros. Asian street vendors tend pots of eggs simmering in a sweet-smoky tea and soy infusion. Cracked slightly while still in the their shell, these tea-marbled eggs are dyed with beautiful patterns by the dark, flavorful liquid.

Chinese cooks like to use eggs that have been preserved in salt brine or in a mixture of clay, ash, and rice straw, which changes their texture and color. Delicate ribbons of egg whites help thicken a whole class of soups served at formal banquets, such as hot-and-sour soup and egg drop soup. In Japan, the test for a new sushi restaurant includes ordering a sweet, rolled omelet called *tamago* to judge the chef's care and talent in presenting his food.

As one of the most complete and easily digestible sources of protein, eggs appear in simple, nourishing soups in many cultures. Stirred into hot broth with garlic, bread, and grated Parmesan cheese, egg yolks thicken *acquacotta,* an Italian soup that is a mainstay in rural communities. For Japanese children, *tamago-gohan* is the epitome of comfort: hot rice topped with egg and *shoyu.* Some versions call for whipping the rice with the egg to a light, foamy texture.

Egg and cress sandwiches are a mainstay of Britain's afternoon tea and appear on the menus of nearly all delicatessens in England. Easy-to-eat deviled eggs are often the first dish to disappear at picnics and barbecues in the United States.

Huevos Rancheros

Colorful, flavorful, and substantial—after all, it originated as a bolstering mid-morning meal for Mexican ranch hands—*huevos rancheros* has become a popular brunch food well beyond Mexico's borders. Variations abound, but this version sticks closely to the basics of the dish: a lightly fried and salsa-dipped corn tortilla topped with refried beans, diced avocado, and a pair of fried eggs.

4 large, thick corn tortillas, preferably stale

1½ cups (12 fl oz/375 ml) roasted tomato salsa or other tomato salsa, homemade or purchased

¼ cup (2 fl oz/60 ml) canola oil, or as needed

8 eggs

Sea salt and freshly ground pepper

1 cup (8 oz/250 g) canned refried pinto beans, warmed

⅔ cup (5 fl oz/160 ml) *crema,* sour cream, or crème fraîche

⅓ cup (1½ oz/45 g) crumbled *queso añejo* or grated dry Monterey jack cheese

1 tablespoon coarsely chopped fresh cilantro (fresh coriander)

1 small avocado, halved, pitted, peeled, and cut into ½-inch (12-mm) cubes (optional)

MAKES 4 SERVINGS

1 Preheat the oven to 200°F (95°C). If the tortillas are fresh, spread them out on a work surface and let them dry out for 5 minutes. Meanwhile, in a wide saucepan over low heat, warm the salsa. In a large nonstick frying pan over medium-high heat, warm the ¼ cup (2 fl oz/60 ml) oil. One at a time, fry the tortillas, turning once, until softened, about 5 seconds per side. Using tongs, transfer to paper towels to drain, then keep warm in the oven.

2 Reduce the heat under the frying pan to medium-low and wait for the oil to cool down. Break 4 of the eggs into the pan and fry them slowly until the whites are set and the yolks have begun to thicken but are not hard (cover the frying pan if you like firm yolks), about 3 minutes. Season with salt and pepper. Transfer the eggs to a roasting pan and keep warm in the oven. Add oil to the frying pan if necessary, and fry the remaining 4 eggs.

3 Remove the tortillas from the oven. Using tongs, dip each tortilla quickly in the warm salsa and place on warmed individual plates. Spread ¼ cup (2 oz/60 g) of the refried beans evenly on each tortilla and top with 2 of the fried eggs. Spoon some of the salsa over the edges of each tortilla and the whites of the eggs, leaving the yolks uncovered. Spoon a little *crema* over the salsa, then sprinkle with the cheese and cilantro. Garnish with the diced avocado, if using, and serve at once.

UNITED KINGDOM
Smoked Fish Omelet

This after-theater supper was created in 1929 for Arnold Bennett. He was living in the Savoy Hotel, doing research for a novel, and reportedly requested the same haddock omelet each night. This recipe is simpler than the Savoy's current luxurious version.

½ lb (250 g) smoked haddock or smoked cod fillet, cut in half

1 fresh flat-leaf (Italian) parsley sprig

3 whole peppercorns

1 bay leaf

2 cups (16 fl oz/500 ml) milk

1 cup (4 oz/125 g) coarsely grated Gruyère cheese

Freshly ground pepper

2 tablespoons unsalted butter

4 eggs, lightly beaten with a pinch of fine sea salt

4 tablespoons (2 fl oz/60 ml) heavy (double) cream

Coarsely snipped chives, for garnish

MAKES 2 SERVINGS

1 Preheat the broiler (grill). Place the fish in a nonreactive saucepan over medium heat. Add the parsley, peppercorns, bay leaf, and milk. Cook until bubbles appear at the edge of the pan. Reduce the heat and simmer until the fish flakes when a knife is inserted into the thickest part, 3–5 minutes. Transfer the fish to a plate to cool; discard the milk mixture.

2 Remove the skin from the fish. Break the flesh into rough flakes, discarding any bones, and place it in a small bowl. Stir in the cheese and season with pepper.

3 Set two 7-inch (18-cm) ovenproof omelet pans over medium-high heat. Melt 1 tablespoon butter in each. Tilt the pans to distribute the butter evenly. Pour half of the egg mixture into each pan. Repeatedly draw a wooden spoon through the egg in each pan until the bottom is set but the top is still liquid, about 1 minute. Top each omelet with half of the fish. Pour 2 tablespoons cream over the top of each. Place in the broiler and cook until the omelets are bubbling and flecked with brown, about 6 minutes. Remove from the broiler, garnish with the chives, and serve at once.

SPAIN
Tortilla Española

½ cup (4 fl oz/125 ml) plus 2–3 tablespoons olive oil

2 lb (1 kg) potatoes, peeled and sliced ¼ inch (6 mm) thick

Salt and freshly ground pepper

2 yellow onions, thinly sliced

6 eggs, lightly beaten

MAKES 6 SERVINGS

1 In a large frying pan over low heat, warm the ½ cup (4 fl oz/125 ml) oil. Add half of the potato slices and cook, turning occasionally, until tender but not browned, 15–20 minutes. Transfer to a plate and season with salt and pepper. Repeat with the remaining potato slices. Leave the oil in the pan.

2 In another frying pan over medium heat, warm the 2–3 tablespoons oil. Add the onions and cook until soft and golden, about 15 minutes. Remove from the heat.

3 In a large bowl, whisk the eggs together. Stir in the onions and potatoes, and season with salt and pepper. Warm the oil remaining in the large pan over low heat. Pour in the egg mixture and cook until the bottom is golden, 8–10 minutes. Invert the tortilla onto a plate, then slide it back into the pan. Cook until the second side is set, about 4 minutes, then transfer to a serving plate. Serve at room temperature.

Artichoke and Leek Frittata

Frittatas are easier to make than omelets and are just as good at room temperature as they are straight from the pan. Leftover frittata, sliced and layered in a baguette with a little mayonnaise, makes a wonderful sandwich.

Juice of 1 lemon

8 baby artichokes, about 2 oz (60 g) each

Sea salt and freshly ground pepper

2 tablespoons unsalted butter

2 or 3 leeks

6 eggs

¼ cup (1 oz/30 g) grated Parmesan cheese

2 tablespoons minced fresh flat-leaf (Italian) parsley

MAKES 4 SERVINGS

1 Fill a bowl with water and stir in the lemon juice. Working with 1 artichoke at a time, snap off the outer leaves until until you reach the tender, pale green heart. Cut about ¼ inch (6 mm) off the top of the heart to remove the pointed leaf tips. Peel the stem and trim the base to remove any dark green parts. Add the trimmed hearts to the lemon water.

2 Bring a pot of salted water to a boil. Drain the artichokes, add to the boiling water, and cook until tender when pierced with a knife, 5–7 minutes. Drain and transfer to a bowl of ice water to cool. Drain again. Cut the artichokes in half lengthwise, then cut lengthwise into slices ¼ inch (6 mm) thick. Pat the slices dry.

3 Trim off the root end and dark green tops of the leeks. Remove any tough outer leaves. Cut each leek in half lengthwise, then thinly slice the white and pale green parts; rinse and drain thoroughly. In a 10-inch (25-cm) ovenproof nonstick frying pan over medium-low heat, melt the butter. Add the leeks and cook, stirring occasionally, until soft, 10–12 minutes. Stir in the artichokes, season with salt and pepper, and cook, about 2 minutes.

4 In a bowl, whisk together the eggs, Parmesan, and parsley just until blended. Add the egg mixture to the pan and stir to distribute the vegetables evenly. Reduce the heat to low and cook slowly, uncovered, until the eggs are almost completely set but still a little moist in the center, 15–20 minutes.

5 While the eggs are cooking, preheat the broiler (grill) and position a rack about 8 inches (20 cm) from the heat source. Broil (grill) the frittata until the top is lightly colored and the center is firm to the touch. Remove from the broiler and, using a spatula, loosen the edges of the frittata. Slide it carefully onto a serving platter. Serve warm.

Stilton and Leek Tart

Stilton cheese became famous in 1740 when Frances Paulet supplied Cooper Thornhill, owner of Bell Inn at Stilton, with her large rounds of nutty-tasting, blue-veined cow's milk cheese. The inn was a day's journey by coach from London, and soon Thornhill was sending coach-loads of the cheese to the capital. Stilton, still made in Nottinghamshire, Leicestershire, and Derbyshire, remains a favorite. Here, it combines with leeks and cream to form a rich and flavorful tart.

For the pastry

1½ cups (7½ oz/235 g) all-purpose (plain) flour

Pinch of fine sea salt

½ cup (4 oz/125 g) cold unsalted butter, diced

3–4 tablespoons cold water

For the filling

5 small leeks

3 tablespoons sunflower oil

3 oz (90 g) Stilton or other strong blue cheese

1 whole egg, plus 1 egg yolk

½ cup (4 fl oz/125 ml) heavy (double) cream

Fine sea salt and freshly ground pepper

MAKES 6 SERVINGS

1 To make the pastry, in a bowl, stir together the flour and salt. Add the butter and, using a pastry blender or 2 knives, cut it into the dry ingredients until the mixture forms coarse crumbs. Alternatively, place the flour and salt in a food processor, add the butter, and pulse 4 or 5 times, then transfer to a bowl. Using a fork, stir in enough of the cold water to form a rough dough. Turn out onto a lightly floured work surface and lightly knead just until smooth, about 30 seconds. Shape the dough into a disk ¾ inch (2 cm) thick, wrap in plastic wrap, and refrigerate for at least 30 minutes or up to overnight.

2 On a lightly floured work surface, roll out the dough into an evenly thick 10-inch (25-cm) round. Carefully transfer the dough to a 9-inch (23-cm) tart pan with a removable bottom, and press it into the bottom and up the sides. Trim the edges even with the rim. Prick the dough with a fork in several places, line with parchment (baking) paper, and fill with dried beans or pie weights. Refrigerate for 30 minutes.

3 Preheat the oven to 400°F (200°C). Bake the tart shell until the pastry looks dry but is not colored, about 15 minutes. Carefully remove the paper and beans. Set the shell aside. Reduce the oven temperature to 350°F (180°C).

4 Meanwhile, to make the filling, trim off the root end and dark green tops of the leeks. Remove any tough outer leaves. Cut each leek in half lengthwise, then thinly slice the white and pale green parts; rinse and drain thoroughly. In a frying pan over medium heat, warm the sunflower oil. Add the leeks and cook, stirring occasionally, until wilted, about 4 minutes. Transfer to a small bowl.

5 Place the cheese, whole egg, and egg yolk in a food processor and purée until smooth. Transfer to a bowl and stir in the cream and then the leeks. Season with a pinch each of salt and pepper. Pour into the tart shell. Bake until the filling is golden brown and just set, about 25 minutes. Transfer the tart to a serving plate and serve warm or at room temperature.

British Cheeses

STILTON

Traditionally eaten at the end of a meal, and in great demand over Christmas, Stilton has an intense, savory taste, a creamy texture, and blue veins that result from the cheese being pierced with needles to allow air in. Every Stilton dairy follows its own recipe. Colston Bassett is made in the traditional way in Nottinghamshire by ladling, rather than pouring, the cow's milk curds into a mold, giving it a particularly creamy texture.

WIGMORE

Wigmore cheese is the understated creation of Anne Wigmore, an analytical cheese maker based in Berkshire, who set about creating new styles of cheese in the mid-1980s. (Her other creations include Waterloo and Spenwood.) Wigmore is made from unpasteurized sheep's milk. To develop delicate flavor nuances, the curds are washed with water to dilute their acidic whey, then are left to ripen for up to six weeks, when the cheese acquires a bloomy rind.

DORSTONE

This lemony, soft, ash-coated goat cheese is made by Charlie Westhead at Neal's Yard Creamery in Dorstone. With its delicate, fresh taste and crumbly, velvety texture, Dorstone is typical of the cheeses Britons like to eat during summer. Matured for only ten days, it has a subtle acidity and flavor that need no further accompaniment than crusty bread or crisp radishes. It is perfect for impromptu picnics.

BERKSWELL

Offering a single cheese at the end of a meal with oat cakes and perhaps quince cheese has become fashionable. One of the best varieties for this is Berkswell, with its floral taste and fudgy texture. It was created by the Fletcher family, who use the unpasteurized milk of their East Friesland sheep for their reinterpretation of Caerphilly, a lightly pressed and brine-soaked cow's milk cheese. Berkswell is matured in basket-weave molds, which leave their imprint.

STILTON

BEENLEIGH BLUE

STINKING BISHOP

MRS. KIRKHAM'S LANCASHIRE

WIGMORE

DORSTONE

BERKSWELL

CHEDDAR

BEENLEIGH BLUE

One of the first new British blue cheeses to arrive on the restaurant scene in the 1980s, Beenleigh Blue is made from the milk of Dorset cross Friesland sheep by Ticklemore Cheese in Devon. Its sweet, nutty taste captivated British cheese eaters, who serve it with a flowery dessert wine or crumble it into a watercress, pear, and walnut salad. Ticklemore later created a rich cow's milk blue called Devon Blue and an intense-tasting goat's milk blue called Harbourne Blue.

STINKING BISHOP

Some of the milk for Charles Martell's pungent semisoft Gloucestershire cheese comes from his small herd of rare-breed Gloucester cows. The rind is washed with perry (pear cider), made from a rare local pear varietal called Stinking Bishop. The cheese has a pale orange rind and a creamy center. The idea of saving an endangered cattle breed and a rare pear by making a tasty cheese makes Stinking Bishop especially appealing.

MRS. KIRKHAM'S LANCASHIRE

Lancashire cheese was rarely found outside England until 1995, when London cheese seller Randolph Hodgson secretly entered Mrs. Kirkham's Lancashire in the British Cheese Awards. It won Supreme Champion and became fashionable overnight. Like her mother and grandmother, Mrs. Kirkham meticulously mixes the cow's milk curds over three days, then molds and presses them to make a golden, hard cheese wrapped in cheesecloth (muslin).

CHEDDAR

Cheddar is a cornerstone of British cheese making, the method having originated near the Cheddar gorge in Somerset and spread around the county. By the seventeenth century, farmers were pooling their cow's milk to make vast truckles of cheese that could be matured for a couple of years. The best modern cloth-bound Cheddars vary, from the buttery Lincolnshire Poacher to the crumbly Montgomery's Cheddar.

Sweet Cheese Tartlets

Cheese tarts are enjoyed all over the Mediterranean, but are especially popular in Greece and Portugal. This particular recipe, traditionally found in the tavernas on the sun-splashed island of Santorini, produces small, delicate tartlets.

For the pastry

2 cups (8 oz/250 g) sifted all-purpose (plain) flour

¼ teaspoon salt

1 teaspoon baking powder

2 tablespoons sugar

3 tablespoons unsalted butter, at room temperature

4 tablespoons (2 oz/60 g) vegetable shortening

1 egg, lightly beaten

For the filling

1 lb (500 g) fresh soft cheese such as ricotta, mizithra, or farmer, or equal parts ricotta and cream cheese

1 cup (8 oz/250 g) sugar

2 tablespoons all-purpose (plain) flour

2 egg yolks

1 teaspoon ground cinnamon, plus extra for garnish (optional)

Grated orange or lemon zest (optional)

MAKES 12 TARTLETS

1 To make the pastry, in a bowl, stir together the flour, salt, baking powder, and sugar. Add the butter and shortening and, using a pastry blender or 2 knives, cut it into the dry ingredients until the mixture resembles coarse meal. Add the egg and 1 tablespoon water and stir with a fork until a soft dough forms, adding a little more water if needed. Gather the dough together and knead until smooth, about 5 minutes. Wrap in plastic wrap and refrigerate.

2 To make the filling, in a bowl, combine the cheese, sugar, flour, egg yolks, 1 teaspoon cinnamon, and orange zest, if using. Stir to mix thoroughly.

3 Preheat the oven to 350°F (180°C). Divide the dough into 12 equal balls. On a lightly floured work surface, roll out each ball into a 4-inch (10-cm) round. Carefully transfer each round to a 2½-inch (6-cm) tartlet tin, and gently press it into the tin, fluting the edges. Place the pastry-lined tins on a large baking sheet. Alternatively, butter a large baking sheet, form the 4-inch (10-cm) rounds into free-form tart shells, pinch the edges to make a fluted rim, and arrange on the baking sheet. Carefully spoon the cheese filling into the tart shells, gently smoothing the tops with a rubber spatula. Bake until the tops are a pale golden brown, 20–25 minutes.

4 Transfer to wire racks and let cool. Sprinkle with cinnamon, if using, and serve at room temperature.

Goat Cheese and Mint Tart

Two ingredients make this Ibiza *flaó,* a sweet cheese tart, something special: the aniseeds in the pastry dough and the mint in the filling. The freshness of the mint cuts the richness of the tart. The recipe calls for *mató,* a goat's milk cheese sold when it's no more than a few days old, but whole-milk ricotta is a suitable substitute.

For the dough

1¾ cups (9 oz/280 g) all-purpose (plain) flour

1 teaspoon aniseeds

¼ cup (2 fl oz/60 ml) anise liqueur such as *anis seco*, Pernod, or pastis

¼ cup (2 fl oz/60 ml) canola or mild vegetable oil

Unsalted butter for greasing

For the filling

1 lb (500 g) *mató* (see above) or whole-milk ricotta cheese

4 eggs, beaten

1 cup (8 oz/250 g) granulated sugar

Grated zest of 1 lemon

4 fresh mint leaves

Confectioners' (icing) sugar for dusting (optional)

MAKES 6 SERVINGS

1 To make the dough, sift the flour into a bowl. Make a well in the center and add the aniseeds, liqueur, and oil. Using your fingers, lightly mix the ingredients until they resemble coarse bread crumbs. Add 3 tablespoons water and continue to mix until a smooth, elastic dough forms, adding a little more water if needed.

2 Butter a 9-inch (23-cm) tart pan with a removable bottom. On a lightly floured work surface, roll the dough into an 11-inch (28-cm) round about ¼ inch (6 mm) thick. Carefully transfer the round to the prepared pan, and gently press it into the bottom and up the sides. Trim the edges even with the rim. Set aside.

3 Preheat the oven to 350°F (180°C). To make the filling, in a bowl, lightly mash the cheese with a fork. Add the eggs, granulated sugar, and lemon zest. Tear the mint leaves into very small pieces and add to the bowl. Mix well and pour into the pastry shell. Bake until the top is pale gold, about 30 minutes. Transfer to a wire rack and let cool completely.

4 To serve, transfer the tart to a serving plate and dust the top with confectioners' sugar, if using.

Pecorino Romano with Pears and Figs

Aged cheeses with fresh fruit and interesting condiments, such as artisanal honeys and fruit preserves, are popular desserts in Italy's best restaurants. In winter, *pecorino romano* might be matched with pears and a jam made from dried figs, while in summer, it might sit alongside fresh figs so ripe they're bursting their seams.

For the fig jam

2 tablespoons hazelnuts (filberts) or almonds

¼ lb (125 g) moist dried figs (about 5 figs), stems trimmed and each fig cut into 4–5 pieces

2 tablespoons brandy

2 tablespoons sugar, or to taste

Grated zest and juice of ½ lemon

6-oz (185-g) wedge *pecorino romano* cheese, aged at least 5 months

2 ripe pears such as Bosc or Anjou

MAKES 4 SERVINGS

1 To make the jam, preheat the oven to 300°F (150°C). Spread the nuts in a single layer on a small baking pan and toast, shaking the pan once or twice, until the nuts darken and give off a pronounced aroma, 10–15 minutes. Transfer to a plate to cool. (There is no need to remove the skins.)

2 In a small saucepan over high heat, combine the figs and ½ cup (4 fl oz/125 ml) water and bring to a boil. Remove from the heat and let stand, about 5 minutes. Put the nuts in a food processor and pulse twice. Add the figs and their liquid, the brandy, the 2 tablespoons sugar, and the lemon zest and juice. Pulse until the figs are coarsely chopped. Taste the jam and adjust the sugar.

3 Using a sharp knife, split the cheese into 4 chunks, then divide them among individual plates. Halve the pears lengthwise and remove the cores. Slice each half lengthwise, keeping the slices together, then fan them out on the plates. Divide the jam among the plates and serve at once.

Fromage Blanc with Apricot Coulis

For the coulis

4 small to medium apricots, about 1 lb (500 g) total weight

1 apple, peeled, cored, diced

2 tablespoons raspberry jam

1½ tablespoons Cognac

1–2 tablespoons sugar

Handful of raspberries

Fresh lemon juice, as needed

1 cup (8 fl oz/250 ml) heavy (double) cream

1–2 tablespoons sugar

¾ lb (375 g) *fromage blanc*

Fresh mint sprigs and raspberries for garnish

MAKES 4 SERVINGS

1 To make the coulis, pit and quarter the apricots. In a heavy nonreactive saucepan over medium-high heat, combine the apricots, apple, jam, Cognac, 1½ tablespoons water, and 1 tablespoon of the sugar. Bring to a boil, reduce the heat to low, and simmer, uncovered, until the fruit is just tender, about 10 minutes, adding water if needed to prevent scorching. Transfer to a food processor. Add the raspberries and purée until a chunky sauce forms. Taste and adjust the seasoning with sugar and lemon juice. Refrigerate until well chilled, at least 2 hours or up to 2 days.

2 In a bowl, using an electric mixer on medium-high speed, whip the cream until light and fluffy. Add the sugar and continue whipping until soft peaks form.

3 Spoon the *fromage blanc* into individual serving bowls. Spoon the coulis over the cheese. Top each serving with whipped cream, mint sprigs, and raspberries.

Chenna and Paneer

Cheese is expensive in India, so families often make their own. *Chenna* is a curd cheese; *paneer* is *chenna* that has been pressed firm. Fried *paneer*—delicious served atop a salad—or a bit of *chenna* with bread and Indian pickle makes a great lunch.

8 cups (2 qt/2 l) milk

3–4 tablespoons fresh lemon juice

All-purpose (plain) flour for dusting

Vegetable oil for frying

MAKES 1¼ CUPS
(10 OZ/315 G) CHENNA,
OR 2 CUPS (10 OZ/315 G)
PANEER CUBES

1 To make the *chenna*, line a sieve with a double layer of cheesecloth (muslin) and place over a large bowl. In a deep nonreactive pot over medium-high heat, bring the milk to a boil, then reduce to a low simmer. Add 3 tablespoons of the lemon juice and stir slowly while the curd forms, leaving behind the thin, yellowish whey, about 1 minute. Add more juice if the cheese does not form completely. Pour the cheese and whey into the sieve and let drain thoroughly.

2 To make the *paneer*, loosely wrap the *chenna* in the cheesecloth, set it in a baking dish, and weigh it down with a water-filled pot until firm, about 1 hour. Unwrap and cut it into ½-inch (12-mm) cubes, then dust with flour. In a large frying pan over medium-high heat, warm enough oil to cover the bottom of the pan. When the oil is hot, add the cubes and fry until light golden, about 2 minutes.

3 Serve the cheese at room temperature or chilled. It can be refrigerated, tightly wrapped in plastic, for up to 5 days.

Making Brie

TYPES OF BRIE

An enormous amount of Brie is mass-produced throughout France each year. True Brie comes from the province where it originated, now known as the *département* of Seine-et-Marne. It is made from unpasteurized milk and has a velvety, white rind streaked with orange mold. Brie de Meaux, with its characteristic soft center, is the most common variety. Connoisseurs prefer the harder-to-find Brie de Melun, with its firmer texture. Look for Brie *fermier*, cheese made from the milk of a single farm.

AGING

Brie gains its nutty flavor and melting texture during aging. Brie de Melun is dried for four weeks, then aged for at least six weeks, while Brie de Meaux is dried for one week and aged for at least four. Brie is one of the only French cheeses often aged in a different region from where it is produced. Many Brie makers ship their products to *affineurs*, who age the cheeses in special cool rooms.

To develop its full character, Brie must be aged on straw mats. In the early salting and drying stages, the mats allow excess water to drain from the rounds, leaving behind the butterfat that is key to the cheese's signature richness. In the later aging stages, the straw leaves striped marks on the rind, adding a hint of grass and earth to the finished product. If a Brie does not have these telltale stripes, it was probably produced in a modern factory, instead of the old-fashioned way on a farm. Both types of Brie are often aged for another two or three weeks at a shop before being sold. Brie is said to be *bien fait*, or perfect for eating, at around ten weeks.

Large wheels of soft, buttery Brie are found at almost every Parisian *fromagerie.* Brie de Meaux, made around the city of the same name, is known as the King of Cheeses and the Cheese of Kings. The kitchen at the court of Louis XIV is said to have had a standing order for fifty wheels a week.

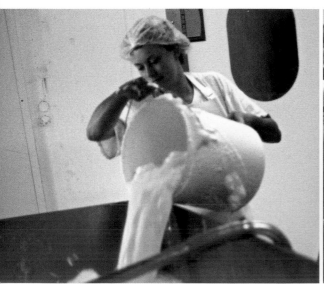

MAKING BRIE DE MELUN

CURDLING THE MILK Milk, still warm from the cow, is poured into a large metal tank, lactic enzymes are added, and part of the cream is removed. The milk is transferred to smaller cisterns, rennet is added, and the milk is left to curdle for eighteen hours.

FORMING THE CHEESES The curds are ladled into large, perforated, round molds to a height of 7 inches (18 cm). The molds are set on straw mats and left to drain for five hours. The curds are then transferred to molds about 10½ inches (27 cm) in diameter—the size of a finished Brie de Melun—salted, and left to drain for one day, sinking to 2 inches (5 cm).

DRYING AND AGING The cheeses are left to dry in a cool room for four weeks, during which time they fall to their final height of 1¼ inches (3 cm). They are then shifted to another cool room, where they age for a minimum of six weeks, during which the interior becomes more buttery and stripes of mold form on the rind. Even at its ripest, Brie de Melun retains a firm texture.

ITALY
Ricotta Torte

The most common ricotta is made from cow's milk, and ricotta made from water buffalo's milk and goat's milk can also be found. But rich, creamy *ricotta romana*, made from sheep's milk, is particularly prized. It is a popular filling for such sweets as *sfogliatelle* (filled flaky pastry) and *cannoli,* and for tarts such as this one.

For the filling

3 cups (1½ lb/750 g) whole-milk ricotta cheese, preferably fresh

¾ cup (6 oz/185 g) granulated sugar

1 teaspoon Strega or Sambuca liqueur or light rum

1½ oz (45 g) bittersweet chocolate, shaved with a knife

For the pastry

¾ cup (6 oz/185 g) unsalted butter, at room temperature, cut into ¾-inch (2-cm) pieces

1¾ cups (7 oz/220 g) confectioners' (icing) sugar, sifted

2 tablespoons honey

⅛ teaspoon vanilla extract

Grated zest of 1 lemon

Pinch of salt

3 egg yolks, plus 1 yolk for brushing, lightly beaten

3 cups (12 oz/375 g) cake (soft-wheat) flour, sifted

1 teaspoon baking powder

MAKES 8 SERVINGS

1 If using fresh ricotta, place it in a sieve lined with cheesecloth (muslin) and set over a bowl. Cover and let drain in the refrigerator until dry, up to 24 hours.

2 To make the pastry, in a bowl, combine the butter, confectioners' sugar, honey, vanilla, lemon zest, and salt. Using your fingers, work the ingredients together just until mixed. Using a wooden spoon, work in the 3 egg yolks. In a small bowl, whisk together the flour and baking powder, then gradually stir the mixture into the butter until the dough comes together. Pat into a rough mass. Cover the bowl with plastic wrap and refrigerate for at least 2 hours or up to 24 hours.

3 Work the dough briefly to form a smooth mass, then divide into 2 pieces, one slightly larger than the other. Form each into a disk and refrigerate the smaller disk. On a lightly floured work surface, roll the larger disk into a 12½-inch (31.5-cm) round about ¼ inch (6 mm) thick. (If the dough becomes too soft, chill it until firm.) Carefully transfer the round to an 11-inch (28-cm) pie pan, and gently press it into the bottom and up the sides. Run a knife around the inside edge of the pan bottom, freeing the dough on the sides. Gather the loose dough, form into a ball, then roll back and forth against the floured surface to create a rope 35 inches (88 cm) long (the circumference of the pan). Lay it around the inside edge of the pan. Using the tines of a fork, prick the bottom crust in several places. Cover and refrigerate.

4 Preheat the oven to 375°F (190°C). To make the filling, put the ricotta in a bowl and beat with a wooden spoon to soften. Beat in the granulated sugar and let rest, about 5 minutes. Stir in the liqueur and chocolate then spread the filling into the pan. Divide the remaining disk of dough into 10 balls. Roll each into a rope 11 inches (28 cm) long. Lay 5 ropes across the filling and the remaining 5 perpendicular to them, to create a lattice pattern. Trim any excess dough. Brush the dough with the remaining yolk.

5 Bake until the crust is a deep golden brown and the filling is set, 40–45 minutes. Transfer to a wire rack to cool. Serve at room temperature.

New York Cheesecake

New Yorkers weren't the first to create cakes based on soft, fresh cheese—various European forms had been around for centuries. But New York cheesecake, a very specific cake, owes its evolution to the invention of cream cheese by the Empire Cheese Company in the late 1800s. Introduced to the new cheese, Jewish bakers created the silken-textured cake that remains a staple in the city's diners.

For the crust

5 tablespoons (2½ oz/75 g) unsalted butter, melted

1¼ cups (3¾ oz/112 g) graham cracker crumbs

2 tablespoons sugar

For the filling

2½ lb (1.25 kg) cream cheese, at room temperature

2 cups (1 lb/500 g) sugar

⅓ cup (2 oz/60 g) all-purpose (plain) flour

2 whole eggs, plus 1 egg yolk

1 cup (8 fl oz/250 ml) heavy (double) cream

1 teaspoon vanilla extract

MAKES 8–10 SERVINGS

1 To make the crust, preheat the oven to 325°F (165°C). Generously butter the bottom and sides of a 9-inch (23-cm) springform pan. In a bowl, stir together the melted butter, graham cracker crumbs, and sugar until the crumbs are evenly moistened. Transfer to the prepared pan and press firmly and evenly into the bottom and about 1½ inches (4 cm) up the sides. Bake until the crust dries out slightly, about 10 minutes. Transfer to a wire rack and let cool completely.

2 To make the filling, place the cream cheese in a large bowl. Using an electric mixer on high speed, beat until smooth, about 5 minutes. In a bowl, mix together the sugar and flour. Add to the cream cheese and beat until well blended. One at a time, add the eggs and egg yolk, beating after each addition and scraping down the sides of the bowl. Add the cream and vanilla and beat until combined. Pour the mixture into the crust.

3 Bake until the cheesecake is set and the center jiggles slightly, 80–90 minutes. Transfer to a rack and let cool in the pan. Cover with plastic wrap and refrigerate for at least 4 hours or up to overnight.

4 Remove the cheesecake from the pan. To cut it, run a thin-bladed knife under hot water and wipe dry before each cut. Serve chilled.

Cherry Cheese Blintzes

The basis for these blintzes is mild and tangy farmer cheese. The white, fresh cheese is a form of cottage cheese from which most of the liquid has been removed. It is sold in a fairly solid loaf. Any sweet or canned tart cherry would be appropriate for this dish. If you use fresh cherries, make sure they are very ripe or poach them for 5 minutes in sweetened water.

For the blintzes

4 eggs

1 cup (8 fl oz/250 ml) milk

1 cup (5 oz/155 g) all-purpose (plain) flour

⅛ teaspoon fine sea salt

2 tablespoons unsalted butter, melted, plus extra for cooking

For the filling

½ lb (250 g) cream cheese, at room temperature

½ lb (250 g) farmer cheese (see above)

¼ cup (2 oz/60 g) sugar

1 egg

1 teaspoon fresh lemon juice

½ teaspoon vanilla extract

¼ teaspoon ground cinnamon

1 cup (6 oz/185 g) jarred cherries, drained and halved, or pitted fresh sweet cherries (see above)

4–5 tablespoons unsalted butter

Fruit jelly or preserves such as apricot

MAKES 22 BLINTZES

1 To make the blintzes, in a blender, combine the eggs, milk, flour, salt, and 2 tablespoons melted butter. Blend for 10 seconds, then scrape down the sides and blend for 20 seconds longer. Place a 6-inch (15-cm) crepe pan or a small nonstick frying pan over medium heat and brush with melted butter. Ladle in 2 tablespoons of the batter and swirl the pan to coat the bottom. Cook until the bottom of the blintz is golden and the top is just set, about 45 seconds. Transfer the blintz to a plate, browned side down; do not cook the other side. Repeat with the remaining batter, brushing the pan with butter between each blintz.

2 To make the filling, in a large bowl, whisk the cream cheese, farmer cheese, sugar, egg, lemon juice, vanilla, and cinnamon with a fork until smooth. Stir in the cherries.

3 Line a platter with parchment (baking) paper. Place 2 heaping tablespoons of filling in the center of a blintz. Fold 2 opposite edges toward the center so they meet over the filling. Pat gently to flatten. Fold in the remaining edges so they overlap slightly in the center. Place, seam side down, on the platter. (The assembled blintzes can be covered and refrigerated for up to 8 hours. Bring to room temperature before cooking.)

4 To cook the blintzes, preheat the oven to 200°F (95°C). Place a large frying pan over medium-low heat and add 1 tablespoon of the butter. When the butter foams, add 4 or 5 blintzes, seam side down; do not crowd the pan. Cook until golden, about 5 minutes. Turn and cook until golden, about 3 minutes. Transfer to a platter, loosely cover with aluminum foil, and keep warm in the oven. Arrange 2 or 3 blintzes on each plate, top each with a dollop of jelly, and serve at once.

ITALY
Coffee Gelato

The most basic gelato flavor in Italy is not vanilla but *crema,* made with deep orange egg yolks and milk rather than cream. This quintessential flavor can be lightly scented with coffee or vanilla beans, lemon or orange zest, or even a splash of *vin santo.* Gelato is soft and malleable, more suited for a spatula than a metal scoop. Serve this version with a bracing cup of espresso. Or, serve the gelato with the espresso poured over it, an Italian treat called *affogato al caffè* (drowned ice cream).

4 cups (32 fl oz/1 l) milk

1 cup (8 oz/250 g) sugar

15 dark-roasted coffee beans

Pinch of salt

6 egg yolks, lightly beaten

MAKES 8 SERVINGS

1 Have ready a large bowl partially filled with ice cubes and water. In a heavy saucepan over medium heat, combine the milk, ½ cup (4 oz/125 g) of the sugar, the coffee beans, and the salt. Cook until small bubbles start to appear around the edge of the pan, about 5 minutes.

2 Meanwhile, in a bowl, whisk together the egg yolks and the remaining ½ cup (4 oz/125 g) sugar until very thick and pale yellow. Whisking constantly, slowly add about ½ cup (4 fl oz/125 ml) of the warm milk mixture to the egg mixture. Pour the egg mixture into the remaining milk mixture in the saucepan and cook over medium heat, stirring constantly with a wooden spoon, until it is thick enough to coat the back of the spoon and leaves a clear trail when a finger is drawn through it, 5–7 minutes. Do not let the mixture boil. Place the saucepan in the bowl of ice water to stop the cooking. Stir occasionally to facilitate cooling.

3 When the custard reaches room temperature, cover with plastic wrap, pressing it directly onto the surface to prevent a skin from forming. Refrigerate until well chilled, at least 2 hours or up to 12 hours.

4 Strain the custard through a medium-mesh sieve into a bowl. Discard the coffee beans. Transfer the mixture to an ice-cream maker and freeze according to the manufacturer's instructions. Unless your ice-cream maker has a built-in freezing compartment, transfer the gelato to a freezer-safe container. Cover and freeze the gelato until firm, at least 3 hours or up to 3 days, before serving.

Gelato

SORBETTO DI LIMONE

Light, tart, and refreshing, this is the flavor for the days when the weather is so swelteringly hot that the cobblestones seem to sizzle and a gelato break is the only way to survive the unrelenting heat. *Limone* is also the flavor of choice on rare formal occasions when *sorbetto* is served to cleanse the palate between courses. It is delicious paired with a more substantial gelato such as *gelato di cioccolato*.

SORBETTO DI FRAGOLA

Italians wouldn't dream of eating North America's anemically pastel-colored strawberry ice cream if they could have a bright pinkish red *sorbetto di fragola* (strawberry sorbet) instead. In Italy fruits are usually—though not always—fashioned into *sorbetti* rather than gelati. *Fragola* tends to be a *gelateria* standard and is always found in late spring when the fruits are at their prime.

GELATO DI NOCCIOLA

Nocciola, or hazelnut (filbert), is one of Italy's favorite nuts. The nuts of the Hazel tree, they are often toasted and are more commonly used in ice creams and baked desserts than eaten out of hand. Hazelnuts define *gelato di nocciola,* but they also lend their character to other gelato flavors, such as *gelato di gianduia,* which takes its name from the popular chocolate and hazelnut cream-filled candies called *gianduiotti.*

GELATO DI STRACCIATELLA

As beloved in Italy as it is throughout North America and elsewhere, *gelato di stracciatella* (chocolate chip) purportedly got its name from the Roman egg-drop chicken soup of the same name. The bits of chocolate, which tend to look more like tiny shavings than actual chips, are said to resemble the egg threads in the soup.

SORBETTO DI LIMONE

GELATO DI CIOCCOLATO

GELATO DI CREMA

GELATO DI PISTACCHIO

SORBETTO DI FRAGOLA

GELATO DI NOCCIOLA

GELATO DI STRACCIATELLA

GELATO DI FIOR DI LATTE

GELATO DI CIOCCOLATO

The *gusto* (flavor) chocolate fans inevitably head for first, *cioccolato* is generally of the deep, dark variety—*fondente,* as it is called in Italy. Some *gelaterie* scatter tiny flecks of dark chocolate over the tub of freshly made *gelato al cioccolato.* A popular chocolate flavor is *bacio* (kisses). It is named after—and made with—Baci Perugini, a brand of foil-wrapped chocolate and hazelnut bonbons, each containing a slip of paper with a romantic quote or bit of poetry.

GELATO DI CREMA

This basic gelato is an eggy surprise to those expecting vanilla. The intense flavor, however, is exactly what aficionados want when they order what is essentially egg-custard ice cream. Artisan-made *crema* has a delicate creaminess that attests to the high quality of the eggs used. Since the flavor of *gelato di crema* relies so heavily on eggs, it is at its very best when its primary ingredient is farm fresh and organic.

GELATO DI PISTACCHIO

Pistachios tend to be associated more with the cuisines of the Middle East than with Italy, where they are also cultivated. Sicily makes frequent culinary uses of *pistacchi,* and they are occasional ingredients in savory fillings or stuffings in other parts of Italy. In Florence, the pale green nuts are found still in their shells on the counter of a bar during the *aperitivo* hour or shelled and incorporated into a delicate, lively colored gelato.

GELATO DI FIOR DI LATTE

Fior di latte (flower of milk), which is also the name used for fresh cow's milk mozzarella, might more aptly be called plain gelato. It is a delicate gelato made without any flavorings other than milk and sugar and is sometimes used as the base for other gelati. The color is a pale milky white rather than the eggy yellow of *gelato di crema.* *Fior di latte* is the first ice cream mothers give to their *bambini.*

Catalan Burnt Cream

Crema catalana is traditionally made for the feast of Saint Joseph on March 16, but it is also an everyday delicacy enjoyed throughout the region. You'd be hard-pressed to find a Barcelona restaurant menu that doesn't feature it. Traditionally, a spiral iron is heated until extremely hot, then used to create the brittle sugar crust. A kitchen torch or broiler can be substituted with excellent results.

8 egg yolks

¾ cup (6 oz/185 g) sugar

4½ tablespoons (1 oz/30 g) cornstarch (cornflour)

4 cups (32 fl oz/1 l) milk

Grated zest of ½ lemon

3-inch (7.5-cm) piece cinnamon stick

MAKES 6 SERVINGS

1 In a small bowl, whisk together the egg yolks and ½ cup (4 oz/125 g) of the sugar until pale and creamy, about 6 minutes. In a large bowl, dissolve the cornstarch in ¼ cup (2 fl oz/60 ml) of the milk.

2 In a heavy saucepan over low heat, combine the remaining 3¾ cups (30 fl oz/940 ml) milk, the lemon zest, and the cinnamon stick and heat until small bubbles start to appear around the edge of the pan, about 10 minutes.

3 Whisk the egg yolk mixture into the cornstarch mixture until well blended. Add a little of the hot milk, whisking constantly to prevent the yolks from curdling. Continuing to whisk, add the remaining milk little by little. Strain the mixture through a fine-mesh sieve into the saucepan used for heating the milk. Heat slowly over very low heat, stirring constantly, until the mixture thickens into a custard, about 15 minutes. Do not boil or it will curdle.

4 Pour the custard into six 1-cup (8-fl oz/250-ml) shallow custard dishes or into a 2-qt (2-l) shallow gratin dish and let cool to room temperature. Cover with plastic wrap and refrigerate until well chilled, at least 2 hours or up to 12 hours.

5 Make the sugar crust no more than 30 minutes before serving, or the topping will be soggy instead of crisp. Dust the surface of the cold custard evenly with the remaining ¼ cup (2 oz/60 g) sugar. Using a kitchen torch, and holding it 2–3 inches (5–7.5 cm) from the surface, caramelize the sugar by constantly moving the flame over the top until it bubbles. Alternatively, preheat the broiler (grill). Place the ramekins or gratin dish on a baking sheet and place under the broiler 3 inches (7.5 cm) from the heat source. Broil (grill) until the top is caramelized, about 2 minutes. The burnt sugar should form a thin sheet of golden brown caramel. Serve at once.

Flan

Flan is a dish whose popularity cuts across all borders. The wobbly milk-and-egg custard with a crown of caramel is one of the most memorable finishes to a meal. It is normally prepared in individual metal pots known as *flaneras,* specially made for the purpose, but individual-sized ramekins or small custard cups may be substituted.

3 tablespoons sugar, plus 1 cup (8 oz/250 g)

2½ cups (20 fl oz/625 ml) milk

1 vanilla bean, split lengthwise, or a few drops of vanilla extract

2 whole eggs, plus 6 egg yolks

MAKES 6 SERVINGS

1 In a small saucepan, combine the 3 tablespoons sugar and 2 tablespoons water. Bring to a boil over medium heat and boil, without stirring, until the mixture becomes a golden brown syrup, about 4 minutes. Pour an equal amount of the caramel syrup into each of six ½-cup (4-fl oz/ 125-ml) ramekins or custard cups, tipping and rotating the molds until the sides are coated about halfway up.

2 Pour the milk into a saucepan, add the vanilla bean, place over low heat, and heat until small bubbles start to appear around the edge of the pan, about 7 minutes. Do not allow the milk to boil.

3 Preheat the oven to 300°F (150°C). In a bowl, whisk together the eggs, egg yolks, and 1 cup (8 oz/250 g) sugar until a pale, creamy mousse forms. Add a little of the hot milk, whisking constantly to prevent the yolks from curdling. Continuing to whisk, add the remaining milk little by little. Strain the custard through a fine-mesh sieve into the prepared molds, dividing it evenly.

4 Place the filled molds in a large baking dish and add boiling water to reach halfway up the sides of the molds.

5 Bake the custards until they are set but the centers still jiggle slightly, 50–60 minutes. Touch the surface of the custard lightly with the point of a knife; it should come away cleanly when the custard is set. Remove the baking dish from the oven, and lift the molds out of the water. Let cool to room temperature, then cover and refrigerate until well chilled, at least 2 hours or up to 6 hours. To serve, run a sharp, thin knife blade around the inside of each mold, and turn out the custards onto individual plates.

ITALY
Zuppa Inglese

The name of this popular Italian dessert means "English soup," referring, supposedly, to its resemblance to British trifle. One of the ingredients, *alchermes,* a bright red, herb-and-spice-flavored liqueur, derives its name from the Arabic *qirmiz,* which is also the source of the English word *crimson.* The composition of *zuppa inglese* may vary, the only constants being cake, custard, and alcohol, preferably some of it red.

For the custard

2 cups (16 fl oz/500 ml) milk

1 large lemon zest strip

1 whole egg, plus 3 egg yolks

⅓ cup (3 oz/90 g) granulated sugar

¼ cup (1½ oz/45 g) all-purpose (plain) flour

1 teaspoon Sambuca

1 sponge cake, homemade or purchased

¼ cup (2 fl oz/60 ml) rum, or more to taste

¼ cup (2 fl oz/60 ml) *alchermes* (see above) or framboise

½ cup (4 fl oz/125 ml) heavy (double) cream

2 teaspoons confectioners' (icing) sugar

About 2 teaspoons grated bittersweet chocolate

MAKES 4 SERVINGS

1 To make the custard, in a saucepan over medium heat, combine the milk and lemon zest and heat until small bubbles start to appear around the edge of the pan. Do not allow the milk to boil. Remove from the heat and let cool slightly, then remove and discard the lemon zest.

2 Meanwhile, in a bowl, whisk together the whole egg, egg yolks, and granulated sugar until well blended. Whisk in the flour, 1 tablespoon at a time, and then continue whisking the mixture until it is thick and pale yellow, about 5 minutes. Stirring constantly, slowly pour the hot milk into the egg mixture. Pour the contents of the bowl into the saucepan, place over low heat, and heat gently, stirring constantly, until the mixture is thick enough to coat the back of a spoon, about 7 minutes. Strain the custard through a fine-mesh sieve into a bowl. Stir in the Sambuca. Let cool to room temperature, stirring from time to time to prevent a skin from forming.

3 Using a serrated knife, cut the sponge cake into slices about 2 by 3 inches (5 by 7.5 cm) and ¼ inch (6 mm) thick. Line the bottom of four 1-cup (8-fl oz/250-ml) bowls, preferably clear glass, with some of the cake slices. Sprinkle the cake with some of the rum. Spread one-fourth of the custard (about ½ cup/4 fl oz/125 ml) over the cake. Top with another layer of cake and sprinkle with 2 tablespoons of the *alchermes.* Spread one-third of the remaining custard over the top. Repeat to make 2 more layers of cake, liqueur, and custard, and then end with a cake layer. Cover and refrigerate for several hours, or preferably overnight, before serving.

4 In a bowl, whisk together the cream and confectioners' sugar until medium-stiff peaks form. Spoon the cream on top of each bowl and sprinkle with the chocolate.

Buttermilk Panna Cotta

A soft and quivery *panna cotta* (literally, cooked cream) with the subtle tang of buttermilk makes a lovely partner for mixed summer fruits. In northern Italy, where the dish orginates, it would be made entirely with heavy cream. Adding buttermilk lightens the dessert and contributes its intriguingly tart taste.

For the panna cotta

Canola oil for coating

1½ teaspoons unflavored gelatin

2 cups (16 fl oz/500 ml) heavy (double) cream

7 tablespoons (3½ oz/105 g) granulated sugar

1 cup (8 fl oz/250 ml) buttermilk

⅛ teaspoon almond extract

For the compote

4 cups (1¼–1½ lb/625–750 g) mixed summer fruits such as pitted and sliced plums, nectarines, peeled peaches, figs, and whole berries

2 tablespoons superfine (caster) sugar, or to taste

2½ teaspoons fresh lemon juice, or to taste

2 teaspoons anise liqueur such as Sambuca, or to taste

MAKES 6 SERVINGS

1 To make the *panna cotta*, moisten a paper towel with the oil and very lightly oil six ¾-cup (6-fl oz/180-ml) ramekins or custard cups.

2 Put 2 tablespoons water in a small, heatproof ramekin. Sprinkle the gelatin evenly over the water and let stand to soften, about 10 minutes. Set the ramekin in a small saucepan, and add water to the pan to come halfway up the side of the ramekin. Place the pan over medium heat and bring the water just to a simmer to dissolve the gelatin. Set the saucepan aside with the ramekin in it.

3 In another small saucepan over medium heat, combine the cream and granulated sugar and bring to a simmer, stirring constantly. Remove from the heat, then whisk in the gelatin. Let cool for 1 minute, then whisk in the buttermilk and the almond extract. Divide the mixture evenly among the prepared molds. Cover and refrigerate until firm, for at least 4 hours or up to overnight.

4 To make the compote, in a large bowl, combine the fruits, superfine sugar, lemon juice, and liqueur. Stir gently to distribute evenly, cover, and refrigerate, stirring occasionally, 4–8 hours.

5 To unmold each *panna cotta*, place the ramekin in a bowl of hot water for about 10 seconds. Then invert a dessert plate on top of the ramekin and invert the ramekin and plate together. Shake the mold gently to loosen the *panna cotta*; it should slip out easily. Surround each portion with the fruit compote, dividing it evenly. Serve at once.

FRUIT, NUTS, AND CHOCOLATE

From the Orchard

In the common language of food, sweetness punctuates our days. There's midmorning *meriendas* with hot chocolate and banana *turrons* in the Philippines and afternoon tea with currant scones to refresh many a Briton. Comforting tapioca pudding, cheerful chocolate chip cookies, rustic fruit tarts, and spectacular layered cakes—there's a sweet for every mood.

Fortunately for us, desserts and snacks have little to do with sustenance and everything to do with the pure enjoyment of some of our favorite ingredients. Though fresh fruit, crunchy nuts, and luscious chocolate can each stand on their own, when gently folded together—whether in cakes, tarts, cookies, ice creams, or custards—they reach new heights of flavor and texture. Fruits harvested from farms and orchards welcome the changing seasons in their fullest glory: the first strawberries of spring, lush peaches on summer's hottest days, crisp apples and pears in autumn, and festive oranges that enliven winter holidays. Cookies and tarts filled with raspberry jam and decanters of whole cherries or peaches covered in brandy reveal delicious ways cooks extend the

sweet flavors of seasonal fruit. The rich, buttery harvest from indigenous nut trees also defines favored treats, both sweet and savory, in every region—from pine nuts in Spain to pecans in the American South to pistachios in the Middle East. Cacao tree pods, from which chocolate is derived, were so valuable in ancient Mayan culture that, for a time, they served as currency throughout Mesoamerica. Today, chocolate can star alone in a dense torte or melt into a complex medley with fruit, nuts, and aromatic flavorings. Classic pairings include simple yet elegant chocolate-covered strawberries, hazelnut and chocolate in Italian *gianduja*, cherry and chocolate in German Schwarzwälder Kirschtorte, and chocolate with coffee in countless mocha desserts.

FRUIT

Families across Europe and North America celebrate the arrival of warm weather with berry-picking expeditions. First luscious strawberries, then dusky blueberries, and finally plump blackberries and fragile, jewel-like raspberries fill pails and baskets to overflowing. Wild berries, such as northern Europe's wild wood strawberry, or *frais de bois,* and the tiny blueberries of New England and Newfoundland, are highly sought for their intensely concentrated flavors. Sprinkled whole over ice cream or lightly sugared and then sandwiched between layers of shortcake, berries are among the easiest fruits to enjoy.

The stone fruit family encompasses cherries, apricots, plums, and peaches, all tender-fleshed fruits that find their way into jams, fresh tart fillings, and summer cobblers. Closely related to almonds, these fruits complement the nut's flavor well, whether nestled in a frangipane tart filling or soaked with almond liqueur. The firmer texture of *pomme* fruits such as apples and pears allows them to hold up to longer cooking. The many versions of apple pies and tarts enjoyed around the world, from caramelized *tarte tatin* to crumble-topped pies, attest to the fruit's appeal. Wrapped in pastry or stuffed with walnuts and raisins, apples can even be baked whole. Pears simply poached in wine make a dramatic autumn dessert.

Oranges, lemons, limes, tangerines, and grapefruits are perhaps the most versatile of fruits. The tart juices add depth to dishes while the zest flavors batters, glazes, and sauces. Special citrus varieties appear in local fare, such as the Seville oranges of Spain that make excellent marmalade or the tiny *kalamansi* limes of the Philippines that are squeezed into drinks. Most oranges and lemons reach their peak in winter, offering a welcome brightness during the colder months.

Under the tropical sun, fruits such as mangoes, papayas, guavas, bananas, and coconuts ripen to intense fragrances and luscious textures. Mango season is eagerly anticipated in India, where nearly a thousand varieties come to market. The Alphonso and the Kesar, considered the king and queen of mangoes for their silky-smooth flesh and perfumed aromas, are now available in the West. The textures of most tropical fruits are best highlighted in simple desserts with minimal cooking, such as custards, mousses, or crepes.

Dried fruits also have an important place in cakes and breads. The currants that sweeten English scones, the rum-soaked raisins and candied orange peel of Dresden's Christmas stollen, and the sugary

dates and apricots enjoyed throughout the Middle East hint of a time when dried fruit was a symbol of luxury. No longer rare and precious, they remain popular for their concentrated flavors, chewy textures, and ability to absorb flavorful liqueurs and fruit juices.

NUTS

In the American South, pecans are highlighted in pies and candies, including New Orleans' famed pralines. In the Middle East, delicate pastries feature pistachios, almonds, and walnuts flavored with a syrup of cinnamon, honey, and rose water. In Italy, hazelnuts (filberts), or *noccioli,* appear in nearly every possible sweet, from creamy gelato to crisp *torrone* nougat. Indian desserts such as *kheer* and *payamsam,* rice puddings served at ceremonies, call for thinly sliced cashews or almonds. Popular versions of *barfi,* a widely enjoyed Indian confection, also include generous sprinklings of nuts.

The smooth texture, pale color, and mild flavor of almonds make them especially versatile. They can be ground into marzipan, a paste that appears in many traditional dessert recipes, or soaked and pressed to create almond milk. Cooks around the world also grind other nuts, such as chestnuts and hazelnuts, into flours or pastes. In China, finely crushed black sesame seeds flavor a sweet soup that ends formal banquets and fill round, sweet-rice dumplings served during the Mid-Autumn Festival.

CHOCOLATE

Ancient Mayans and Aztecs whipped chocolate into a luxurious beverage for court and temple ceremonies. In Europe, chocolate was also enjoyed first as a thick, frothy drink, but it wasn't long before dessert chefs and candy makers realized chocolate's potential to add deep, rich flavors to cakes, cookies, and confections.

Inherently bitter, the cacao of chocolate pods is mixed with sugar and milk in varying amounts to create a range of products from dark, intense bittersweet through semisweet to creamy milk chocolate. Working with chocolate requires special skill, so chocolate makers all over have established their own shops to showcase their luxurious treats. Purists enjoy chocolate truffles finished simply with a light dusting of cocoa. The more adventurous seek out creative confections flavored with liqueurs, nuts, fresh or dried fruits, and unusual seasonings such as pink peppercorns, lavender, and star anise. Mexican-style chocolate—with a hint of chile and almonds—recalls the same ancient recipe first enjoyed by Mayan and Aztec rulers.

Raspberry Tart

Made with *pasta frolla* (short-crust pastry), this tart is as beautiful as it is delicious, whether topped with uniform raspberries or a mix of any fresh berries in season.

For the crust

¾ cup (6 oz/185 g) unsalted butter, at room temperature

1 egg, lightly beaten

⅓ cup (3 oz/90 g) granulated sugar

2 cups (8 oz/250 g) cake (soft-wheat) flour

For the custard

3 cups (24 fl oz/750 ml) milk

8 egg yolks

¾ cup (6 oz/185 g) granulated sugar

¼ cup (1 oz/30 g) cornstarch (cornflour)

2 cups (8 oz/250 g) raspberries or other fresh berries, such as blackberries, hulled strawberries, or blueberries

Confectioners' (icing) sugar for dusting

MAKES 6–8 SERVINGS

1 To make the crust, in a large bowl, using a wooden spoon, combine the butter, egg, and granulated sugar. Add the flour and mix until a homogenous dough forms. Form into a ball, cover with plastic wrap, and refrigerate for at least 2 hours or up to 8 hours.

2 Preheat the oven to 400°F (200°C). Butter a 9½-inch (24-cm) tart pan with a removable bottom. On a lightly floured work surface, roll out the dough into a 10-inch (25-cm) round ¹⁄₁₆–⅛ inch (2–3 mm) thick. Remove the tart pan bottom, lay the dough round over it, and trim off the overhanging dough. Place the dough-lined bottom back into the pan. Gather up the dough scraps and roll into a rope long enough to encircle the pan. Lay the rope along the inside edge of the pan and press it into the bottom and up the sides to a height of ¾ inch (2 cm). If desired, use a knife to create a zigzag along the top edge.

3 Line the tart shell with parchment (baking) paper, fill with dried beans or pie weights, and bake until the crust is pale and dry, about 30 minutes. Remove the beans and paper. Continue baking until golden, about 5 minutes longer. Transfer to a wire rack to cool. Carefully transfer the crust from the pan to a serving plate.

4 To make the custard, in a heavy saucepan over medium heat, warm the milk until small bubbles start to appear around the edge of the pan, about 5 minutes. In a bowl, whisk together the egg yolks, granulated sugar, and cornstarch until pale and creamy. Whisking constantly, slowly add about ½ cup (4 fl oz/125 ml) of the warm milk to the egg mixture. Return the mixture to the remaining milk in the saucepan and cook, whisking constantly, until it thickens and begins to bubble around the edge of the pan, 5–8 minutes. Remove from the heat and stir, about 1 minute longer. Strain though a medium-mesh sieve into a bowl. Let cool slightly, stirring occasionally, then pour into the tart crust, using a spatula to distribute it evenly.

5 When the custard has cooled completely, arrange the berries on top in a single layer. Dust lightly with confectioners' sugar and serve.

Meringue with Blackberries

Dewy blackberries and fresh whipped cream make the perfect dessert for a warm September day. Rather than a pastry crust, here they are layered onto a shell of crisp and chewy meringue that's been flavored with toasted hazelnuts.

For the meringue

⅓ cup (2 oz/60 g) hazelnuts (filberts)

3 egg whites, at room temperature

¾ cup (5 oz/155 g) superfine (caster) sugar

½ teaspoon white wine vinegar

Pinch of fine sea salt

1 teaspoon cornstarch (cornflour)

For the topping

1 cup (8 fl oz/250 ml) heavy (double) cream

3 tablespoons kirsch (optional)

3 cups (12 oz/375 g) blackberries

Superfine (caster) sugar for dusting

Fresh mint leaves for garnish

MAKES 6 SERVINGS

1 To make the meringue, preheat the oven to 350°F (180°C). Spread the hazelnuts on a baking pan and toast until the skins start to darken and loosen, about 15 minutes. Transfer to a kitchen towel and rub vigorously to remove the loose skins. Place the hazelnuts in a food processor and pulse 3 or 4 times until they form very fine crumbs. Set aside.

2 Draw an 8-inch (20-cm) circle on a piece of parchment (baking) paper and place on a baking sheet. Put the egg whites in a large, clean bowl. Using an electric mixer on medium speed, beat until the whites begin to thicken. Raise the speed to medium-high and beat just until soft peaks form. Slowly add the superfine sugar and continue to beat until medium-firm peaks form. Sprinkle in the vinegar, salt, and cornstarch and fold in with a metal spoon. Fold in the ground hazelnuts until incorporated. Spoon the mixture inside the circle on the prepared sheet. Using the metal spoon, neatly shape and flatten into a disk. Place in the oven, reduce the temperature to 300°F (150°C), and bake, about 1 hour. Turn off the heat and leave the meringue in the oven until cold, about 3 hours. The outside will be crisp, and the inside will be soft and chewy. Transfer to a serving plate.

3 To make the topping, in a large bowl, combine the cream and the kirsch, if using. Using a whisk or the electric mixer, whip until soft peaks form. Spoon over the meringue and scatter the blackberries on top. Dust with superfine sugar, sprinkle with mint leaves, and serve at once.

Summer Berry Pudding

The scent of this warm berry pudding is so enticing that it takes discipline to resist turning it out before it has set. The key to a successful pudding is to use a good-quality white bread from a local bakery. The bread should have sufficient body to absorb the juice of the cooked fruits and hold its shape, despite being cut into thin slices. If fresh currants are unavailable, do not substitute dried. Instead, replace them with blackberries or blueberries and adjust the sugar to taste.

2 cups (8 oz/250 g) red currants, stems removed

2 cups (8 oz/250 g) black currants, stems removed

4 cups (1 lb/500 g) strawberries, hulled and halved

1½ cups (12 oz/375 g) sugar

3 tablespoons raspberry or strawberry eau-de-vie (optional)

2 cups (8 oz/250 g) raspberries, plus extra for garnish

8–10 slices good-quality, firm white bread, about ¼ inch (6 mm) thick, crusts removed

Fresh mint leaves for garnish (optional)

1 cup (8 fl oz/250 ml) heavy (double) cream for serving

MAKES 6 SERVINGS

1 In a nonreactive saucepan, combine the currants, strawberries, and sugar. Add the eau-de-vie, if using, or 3 tablespoons water. Cover, place over low heat, and cook, stirring occasionally, until the sugar is dissolved and the fruit releases its juice, about 5 minutes. Stir in the 2 cups (8 oz/250 g) raspberries and cook, covered, until the raspberries just begin to release their juice, about 2 minutes. Let cool. (The fruit will continue to release juice as it cools.)

2 Lightly oil a 3-cup (24-fl oz/250-ml) pudding basin or ceramic or glass bowl with a 6-inch (15-cm) rim and a 3-inch (7-cm) base. Cut out a circle of bread that will fit in the bottom of the basin, and place in the basin. Cut out another circle that will fit inside the top, and set aside. Cut the remaining bread slices into wedges and use them to line the sides of the basin, making sure that there are no gaps between the pieces and that they extend above the rim.

3 Spoon the fruit into the bread-lined basin, packing it gently and stopping ½ inch (12 mm) below the rim of the basin. Reserve any extra fruit and juice in a covered container in the refrigerator until ready to serve. Fold the tops of the bread over the fruit filling and cover with the reserved circle of bread, pressing down gently. Set a saucer on top and weight with a heavy can. Place the basin in a dish to catch any juices and refrigerate for at least 8 hours or up to 2 days.

4 Remove the weight and saucer. Run a sharp knife along the inside of the basin, being careful not to cut into the pudding. Invert a plate on top of the basin, invert the plate and basin together, shake the basin sharply, and carefully lift off the basin. Pour any reserved juices over the pudding and garnish with the reserved fruit or fresh raspberries and the mint leaves, if desired. Pass the cream at the table.

Cherry Clafoutis

Clafoutis, a custardlike pudding thick with locally grown tart cherries, originated in Limousin, in the center of France. The dish has been taken up all over the country, and not only are different varieties of cherries used, but other fruits as well. The cherries are typically left unpitted—if you stick to tradition, warn your guests.

1 cup (8 fl oz/250 ml) milk

¼ cup (2 fl oz/60 ml) heavy (double) cream

⅔ cup (3½ oz/105 g) all-purpose (plain) flour, sifted

3 eggs

¼ cup (2 oz/60 g) granulated sugar

1 tablespoon vanilla extract

¼ teaspoon salt

4 cups (1 lb/500 g) stemmed sweet or tart cherries, pitted if desired

1 tablespoon confectioners' (icing) sugar

MAKES 6–8 SERVINGS

1 Preheat the oven to 350°F (180°C). Generously butter a 9- to 10-inch (23- to 25-cm) round baking dish. In a bowl, combine the milk, cream, flour, eggs, granulated sugar, vanilla, and salt. Using an electric mixer set on medium speed, beat until frothy, about 5 minutes.

2 Pour enough of the batter into the baking dish to cover the bottom with a layer about ¼ inch (6 mm) deep. Put the dish in the oven and bake, about 2 minutes, then remove it. Cover the batter with a single layer of the cherries. Pour the remaining batter over the cherries. Return to the oven and bake until puffed and browned and a knife inserted into the center comes out clean, 30–35 minutes. Dust the top with confectioners' sugar. Serve warm.

Sour Cherry Tart

Visciole are small, sour cherries that grow near Rome. Most *visciole,* like their even sourer relative, *amarene,* go straight into the jam pot, and it is the fate of most jams to end up spread in a thick tart crust. If you are short on time, use any good-quality commercial preserves—about 1 cup (10 oz/315 g)—containing pieces of fruit.

For the cherry jam

1 lb (500 g) sour cherries, pitted

½ cup (4 oz/125 g) granulated sugar

Pinch of ground cinnamon

For the pastry dough

1 whole egg, plus 2 egg yolks

¾ cup (6 oz/185 g) granulated sugar

Pinch of salt

½ cup (4 oz/125 g) plus 2 tablespoons unsalted butter, at room temperature, cut into 6 pieces

3 cups (12 oz/375 g) cake (soft-wheat) flour

For the pastry cream

1 cup (8 fl oz/250 ml) milk

1 large lemon zest strip

1 vanilla bean, split lengthwise

3 egg yolks

¼ cup (2 oz/60 g) granulated sugar

2 tablespoons cornstarch (cornflour)

Confectioners' (icing) sugar for dusting

MAKES 6–8 SERVINGS

1 To make the jam, in a heavy nonreactive pan over medium heat, bring the cherries, sugar, and cinnamon to a simmer, stirring to dissolve the sugar. Cook, stirring frequently, until the cherries are soft and the mixture begins to thicken, about 15 minutes. Set aside to cool and thicken.

2 To make the dough, in a bowl, whisk together the egg and yolks, sugar, and salt. Whisk in the butter a piece at a time. Work in the flour gradually until a smooth dough forms. Divide into 2 pieces, one slightly larger than the other. Form each into a disk, wrap separately in plastic wrap, and refrigerate for at least 2 hours or up to 24 hours.

3 To make the cream, in a saucepan over medium heat, warm the milk, lemon zest, and vanilla bean until bubbles begin to appear around the edge of the pan. Remove from the heat; remove and discard the zest and the vanilla bean. In a bowl, whisk together the yolks, sugar, and cornstarch until thick and pale, about 5 minutes. Whisking constantly, slowly pour the hot milk into the egg mixture. Pour the mixture into the saucepan, place over low heat, and cook, stirring constantly, until thick enough to coat a spoon, 5–10 minutes. Let cool. Cover with plastic wrap, pressing it directly onto the surface to prevent a skin from forming, and refrigerate for at least 30 minutes or up to 24 hours.

4 Preheat the oven to 350°F (180°C). Butter an 11-inch (28-cm) tart pan, dust with flour, and tap out the excess. Place the large dough disk in the pan, and pat evenly into the bottom and about 1 inch (2.5 cm) up the sides. Spread with the pastry cream. Using a spoon, dot the surface with the jam, then, gently spread it to cover.

5 On a lightly floured work surface, roll out the remaining dough disk into an 11-inch (28-cm) round. Cut the round into 10 strips ¾ inch (2 cm) wide. Lay 5 strips across the filling and the remaining 5 perpendicular to them, to create a lattice pattern. Trim any excess. Fold the exposed edge of the dough down onto the filling.

6 Bake until golden brown, 40–45 minutes. Transfer to a rack and let cool completely. Dust with confectioners' sugar and serve.

Mangoes Flambéed with Tequila

To slice a mango with the least mess, cut it in half just off center to avoid the pit. Using the tip of a knife, score the flesh into thin slices without cutting through the peel, then press against the skin side of the peel and cut away the flesh.

½ cup (2 oz/60 g) shredded unsweetened coconut

6 ripe mangoes, about 3 lb (1.5 kg) total weight

3 tablespoons dark brown sugar

3 tablespoons unsalted butter, cut into small pieces

Finely shredded zest of 1 lime

Finely shredded zest of ½ orange

1 tablespoon fresh lime juice

1 tablespoon fresh orange juice

¼ cup (2 fl oz/60 ml) *tequila blanco*

1 qt (1 l) coconut or French vanilla ice cream

MAKES 6 SERVINGS

1 Preheat the oven to 350°F (180°C). Spread the coconut on a baking pan and toast, stirring frequently, until golden brown, 7–10 minutes. Set aside.

2 Raise the oven temperature to 400°F (200°C). Lightly butter a shallow 9-by-13-inch (23-by-33-cm) baking dish. Peel and slice the mangoes (see above). Arrange the slices, slightly overlapping them, in the baking dish. Sprinkle with the brown sugar and dot with the butter. Scatter the lime and orange zest over the top, then drizzle with the lime and orange juices.

3 Bake, uncovered, until the mango slices begin to brown, about 20 minutes. Though best served immediately, the mangoes can be kept warm for about 30 minutes. When ready to serve, sprinkle the tequila over the mangoes and carefully ignite with a long match. Shake the pan until the flames die out. Divide the mangoes among individual plates. Add a scoop of ice cream to each and garnish with the toasted coconut.

Mango Pudding

This pudding, an inspired borrowing from the kitchens of South Asia, has been absorbed into the dim sum repertoire in Hong Kong and Guangdong. For the coconut cream, skim the top layer from an unshaken can of coconut milk.

½ cup (3 oz/90 g) small pearl tapioca, rinsed and drained

⅓ cup (3 oz/90 g) superfine (caster) sugar

1 can (14 oz/440 g) sliced mango

½ cup (4 fl oz/125 ml) coconut cream (see above)

MAKES 4–6 SERVINGS

1 Place the tapioca in a saucepan with ½ cup (4 fl oz/ 125 ml) water and the sugar. Place a colander over a bowl and drain the mango. Measure out 1 cup (8 fl oz/250 ml) of the liquid and add it to the saucepan. Discard the rest; set aside the mango. Bring the tapioca to a boil, reduce the heat to medium-low, and simmer, stirring frequently, until almost all of the tapioca pearls are translucent, about 20 minutes.

2 Add the coconut cream and simmer until the pudding is thick and no white pearls remain, about 6 minutes.

3 Purée the mango in a blender and stir it into the pudding. Divide evenly among individual bowls, cover, and refrigerate until firm. Serve chilled.

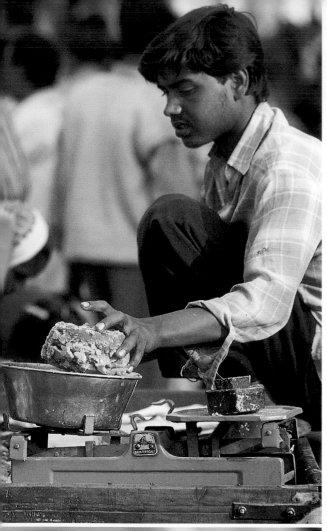

Banana-Coconut Pancakes

Kelapura (*kela* means "banana" and *pura*, "bread" or "pancake") are served all over southern India, where banana and coconut palms abound. The pancakes are made with rice flour and fermented palm sap, which acts as a natural leavening agent. If rice flour is unavailable, substitute cream of rice cereal and let the batter rest for fifteen minutes before cooking the pancakes. Any number of flavorings can be added, from mango or persimmon to toasted cashews or pine nuts.

½ cup (2½ oz/75 g) all-purpose (plain) flour

½ cup (2½ oz/75 g) rice flour or cream of rice cereal (see above)

1¼ cups (10 fl oz/310 ml) coconut milk

½ cup (4 fl oz/125 ml) milk

⅓ cup (2½ oz/75 g) jaggery or brown sugar

½ teaspoon baking powder

1 banana, peeled and mashed

8 green cardamom pods

Vegetable oil or butter for frying

MAKES 8 SERVINGS

1 In a bowl, combine the all-purpose flour, rice flour, coconut milk, milk, sugar, and baking powder. Beat with a whisk or electric mixer until a smooth batter forms. Gently fold in the banana.

2 Pry open the cardamom pods and remove the seeds. Place in a mortar and grind to a powder with a pestle. (Alternatively, enclose the seeds in plastic wrap and crush them with a mallet.) Add the ground cardamom to the batter and mix well.

3 Preheat the oven to 200°F (95°C). Pour oil to a depth of ¼ inch (6 mm) into a nonstick frying pan, and heat over high heat. When the oil is hot, add a heaping tablespoonful of batter to the pan to form each pancake. Cook until the undersides are brown and the edges begin to crisp, about 2 minutes. Turn and cook until nicely browned on the second side, about 1 minute longer. Transfer to a platter and keep warm in the oven while you cook the remaining pancakes, adding more oil if needed. (The pancakes can be set aside, covered, until ready to serve. To reheat, loosely wrap the pancakes in aluminum foil and warm in a preheated 375°F (190°C) oven for about 8 minutes.)

Bananas and Tapioca in Coconut Milk

The soup is a variation on the popular Vietnamese afternoon snack of bananas stewed in coconut milk. Here, the duo is simmered together with rich pearl tapioca.

6 bananas, peeled and cut crosswise into thirds

Salt

¾ cup (4 oz/125 g) pearl tapioca

⅔ cup (5 oz/155 g) sugar

1 tablespoon cornstarch (cornflour) dissolved in 3 tablespoons water

1 can (13½ fl oz/420 ml) coconut milk

MAKES 6 SERVINGS

1   Place the bananas in a large bowl and add water to cover and ½ teaspoon salt. Set aside.

2   In a saucepan over high heat, bring 6 cups (48 fl oz/1.5 l) water to a boil. Add the tapioca, reduce the heat to low, and simmer until the pearls are clear, about 10 minutes. Add the sugar and 1½ teaspoons salt and stir to dissolve. Add the cornstarch mixture and stir until the liquid is lightly thickened, 2–3 minutes. Drain the bananas and add to the saucepan along with the coconut milk. Raise the heat to medium and cook until the bananas are tender but still firm, about 5 minutes. Divide the bananas and liquid among individual bowls. Serve hot or warm.

Caramelized Bananas

⅓ cup (1¼ oz/35 g) unsweetened flaked or shredded dried coconut

2 tablespoons unsalted butter

½ cup (3½ oz/105 g) firmly packed light brown sugar

2 tablespoons dark rum or water

Pinch of salt

4 bananas, peeled

Vanilla or coconut ice cream

MAKES 4 SERVINGS

1   Preheat the oven to 350°F (180°C). Spread the coconut on a rimmed baking sheet and toast, stirring occasionally, until golden, about 3 minutes. Set aside.

2   In a frying pan over medium heat, melt the butter. Stir in the brown sugar. Add the rum and salt and stir to combine. Halve the bananas lengthwise and then crosswise. Place them in the pan cut side down. Reduce the heat to medium-low and cook, turning once, until just tender and golden, about 5 minutes total. Divide among individual plates, add a scoop of ice cream, sprinkle with the coconut, and serve.

Fruit Flambé

FLAMING DESSERTS

Flaming desserts were once the crowning glory of haute cuisine and, although now viewed as charmingly retro and a little kitschy, they still add plenty of flash to the historic dining rooms of New Orleans. At Antoine's, the flaming football-shaped Baked Alaska serves two, and, with advance notice, it may be emblazoned with a personal message. The city's oldest restaurant also sets light to classic cherries jubilee and buttery, orange-scented Crêpes Suzette. At Broussard's, the eponymous Crêpes Broussard are rolled around cream cheese and pecans, then ignited with brandy in a strawberry sauce. At Emeril's Delmonico, the Crêpes Suzette get "kicked up a notch" with citrus chocolate ice cream, and the chocolate-hazelnut Baked Alaska is fired in a Frangelico rum sauce.

Still, Brennan's original creation remains the most famous of all the French Creole flambéed desserts. It is now served at countless other restaurants, locally and nationwide, and has inspired such spin-offs as Bananas Foster pie, shortcake, waffles, and ice cream.

CRÊPES FITZGERALD

Former Brennan's chef Paul Blangé originated many of the signature dishes that are still on the menu at the Royal Street landmark today, including Bananas Foster. Blangé named another fiery dessert for a party of six businessmen from Fitzgerald Advertising who lunched at Brennan's every day for years, always at the same table. Crêpes Fitzgerald are filled with sour cream and cream cheese, then flamed with fresh sliced strawberries in maraschino liqueur.

New Orleans' Brennan's Restaurant created Bananas Foster in 1951 for a *Holiday* magazine feature. Little did anyone imagine that it would become their most requested dish. Brennan's now sets fire to thirty-five thousand pounds (seventeen thousand kilograms) of bananas a year.

MAKING BANANAS FOSTER

HEATING THE SAUCE There's always a sense of drama in the dining rooms at Brennan's when a waiter wheels out the cart for tableside preparation of the famed Bananas Foster. He empties small dishes of butter, brown sugar, and ground cinnamon into a flambé pan, then heats it over a low flame, tipping and swirling the pan until the butter melts and the sugar dissolves.

FLAMING THE BANANAS Next he adds a shot of banana liqueur along with quartered bananas. Just as the bananas are starting to brown, he adds dark rum and tips the pan to ignite the alcohol. Sometimes the flames are so spectacular that nearby diners gasp and lean away while the waiter ladles the sauce in high arcs until the flames extinguish.

SERVING THE DESSERT For each diner, the waiter arranges three or four pieces of banana on top of French vanilla ice cream and finishes the dessert with a generous drizzle of the warm sauce. Fragrant cups of French roast coffee finish things off.

Pear Fritters

2¼ cups (11½ oz/355 g) all-purpose (plain) flour

¼ cup (2 oz/60 g) granulated sugar

Pinch of salt

2 eggs, separated, at room temperature

1 tablespoon extra-virgin olive oil

¾ cup (6 fl oz/180 ml) ice water, or as needed

4 firm yet ripe Bosc pears, about 5 oz (155 g) each, peeled, cored, and cut into wedges ½ inch (12 mm) thick

½ cup (4 fl oz/125 ml) *vin santo*, Marsala, or other sweet wine

Corn or safflower oil for deep-frying

Confectioners' (icing) sugar for dusting

MAKES 6 SERVINGS

1 In a large bowl, whisk together 1¾ cups (9 oz/280 g) of the flour, the granulated sugar, and the salt. Make a well in the center, add the egg yolks and olive oil, and beat the wet ingredients lightly with a fork. Gradually incorporate the flour, adding ice water 1 tablespoon at a time, until a thick batter forms. Cover and refrigerate, 2–3 hours.

2 Put the egg whites in a clean bowl. Using an electric mixer on medium speed, beat until the whites form stiff but not dry peaks. Fold into the chilled batter and set aside.

3 Place the remaining ½ cup (2½ oz/75 g) flour on a plate and the *vin santo* in a bowl. Dip each pear wedge in the *vin santo*, dredge lightly in the flour, and set aside.

4 Pour the oil to a depth of 3–4 inches (7.5–10 cm) into a heavy 6- to 8-inch (15- to 20-cm) saucepan, and heat to 350°F (180°C) on a deep-frying thermometer. Working in batches, dip the pear wedges into the batter, then slip them into the hot oil and fry, turning once, until golden brown, about 4 minutes. Transfer to paper towels to drain. After each batch, make sure the oil returns to 350°F. Dust the fritters with confectioners' sugar and serve at once.

Poached Pears in Spiced Red Wine

6 firm yet ripe pears such as Bartlett (Williams'), about 2 lb (1 kg) total weight

1 bottle (24 fl oz/750 ml) dry, fruity red wine such as Beaujolais

½–¾ cup (4–6 oz/125–185 g) sugar, or to taste

1 cinnamon stick

3 tablespoons brandy or Cognac

¼ teaspoon vanilla extract

2–3 tablespoons Port or *crème de cassis*

Fresh lemon juice, as needed

MAKES 6 SERVINGS

1 Cut a thin slice off the bottom of each pear, then carefully core it from the bottom. Leave the stem intact. Peel the pears and place them on their sides in a heavy nonreactive saucepan.

2 Add the wine, ½ cup (4 oz/125 g) of the sugar, the cinnamon stick, and the brandy and bring to a boil. Reduce the heat to low, cover, and simmer gently, about 10 minutes. Turn the pears and simmer, covered, just until tender when pierced with a skewer, 20–25 minutes. Using a slotted spoon, transfer the pears to a bowl.

3 Return the poaching liquid to a boil and cook until reduced to a syrup, 15–20 minutes; watch carefully to avoid scorching. Taste and add the remaining sugar if needed. Heat, stirring to dissolve the sugar, then add the vanilla, Port, and lemon juice. To serve, stand the pears upright and drizzle with the hot syrup. Alternatively, cover and refrigerate both the pears and the syrup, then serve chilled.

Candied Apples

Before red eating apples were introduced to China, quinces, crabapples, and thorn apples—the tart fruit of an indigenous hawthorn tree—were all available. In Kaifeng, the sugared and honeyed fruit was being sold by street vendors one thousand years ago, and a few hundred years before that, in the Tang dynasty, crabapples steeped in honey and cinnabar were eaten as an elixir of life.

Salt

2 tart apples, peeled, cored, and cut into wedges ⅓ inch (9 mm) thick

⅔ cup (3½ oz/100 g) all-purpose (plain) flour

1 egg

⅓ cup (1½ oz/45 g) cornstarch (cornflour)

Oil for deep-frying

⅓ cup (2½ oz/75 g) superfine (caster) sugar

2 teaspoons Asian sesame oil

2 teaspoons lard (optional)

Ice water

MAKES 6–8 SERVINGS

1 Fill a bowl with lightly salted water, add the apple wedges, and let soak, about 10 minutes. Drain, then spread on a kitchen towel to dry.

2 Place ⅓ cup (1¾ oz/50 g) of the flour in a paper bag, add the apple wedges, close the top of the bag, and shake well to coat.

3 In a bowl, beat the egg lightly until well blended. Beat in the remaining ⅓ cup (1¾ oz/50 g) flour, the cornstarch, and ½ cup (4 fl oz/125 ml) water to make a thin batter.

4 Pour oil to a depth of 2 inches (5 cm) into a wok or deep, heavy frying pan, and heat to 350°F (180°C) on a deep-frying thermometer. Dip half of the apple wedges into the batter and slip them into the oil. Fry, stirring and turning the pieces to prevent them from sticking together, until golden, about 1½ minutes. Using a slotted spoon, transfer to paper towels to drain. Repeat with the remaining apple wedges.

5 Pour off the oil from the pan. Add the sugar, sesame oil, and lard, if using, and cook, stirring constantly, until the sugar is golden brown, 3–4 minutes. Carefully add 1½ tablespoons water and allow it to bubble briefly, then add the fried apple wedges and quickly turn them to coat. Using the slotted spoon, transfer the apple wedges to a plate.

6 To serve, place a bowl of ice water on the table along with the candied apple wedges. Each guest selects a piece of hot apple and holds it in the ice water briefly to harden the toffee before eating.

Tarte Tatin

The origin of this tart has been traced to the early twentieth century and to two sisters, Stéphanie and Caroline Tatin, who ran a small hotel in the Loire Valley town of Lamotte-Beuvron. It seems rustic apple tarts were a specialty of the area, with the upside-down version baked by the *demoiselles* Tatin among the best known.

For the puff pastry

1½ cups (7½ oz/235 g) all-purpose (plain) flour

½ teaspoon salt

1 tablespoon white wine vinegar

2 tablespoons unsalted butter, melted, plus ¾ cup (6 oz/185 g) cold unsalted butter

2 lb (1 kg) Golden Delicious apples, peeled, quartered, and cored

Juice of ½ lemon

6 tablespoons (3 oz/90 g) unsalted butter

1 cup (8 oz/250 g) plus 2 tablespoons sugar

Crème chantilly or crème fraîche for serving

MAKES 8 SERVINGS

1 To make the puff pastry, place the flour in a large bowl and make a well in the center. Add the salt, vinegar, melted butter, and ⅓ cup (3 fl oz/90 ml) water to the well and whisk the liquid briefly. Using a fork, work the flour into the liquid. When all of the flour is incorporated and a dough has formed, knead it briefly until smooth but not too firm. Wrap in plastic wrap and refrigerate, 2–3 hours.

2 Remove the dough from the refrigerator, unwrap, and place on a lightly floured work surface. Roll out into a square about 1 inch (2.5 cm) thick. Using a mallet or rolling pin, flatten the chilled butter to about ¾ inch (2 cm) thick, then center it on the dough. Fold the sides over the butter, rewrap, and refrigerate, about 1 hour.

3 Return the dough to the floured work surface and roll out into a rectangle about 10 by 15 inches (25 by 38 cm). Fold into thirds like a business letter, then rotate the dough a quarter turn. Roll out again to a rectangle. Fold again, rewrap, and refrigerate, about 1 hour. Repeat this process 3 or 4 times, rolling out and folding the dough twice each time and refrigerating for 1 hour in between and for at least 30 minutes after the last rolling.

4 In a large bowl, toss the apples with the lemon juice. Set aside. In an ovenproof 12-inch (30-cm) frying pan, preferably nonstick, melt the butter over medium-high heat. Sprinkle the sugar over the butter and cook until it melts and caramelizes, 6–8 minutes. Tilt and swirl the pan, but do not stir. Arrange the apples on the caramel in a tight single layer. Reduce the heat to medium-low and cook, occasionally tipping the pan and spooning the caramel sauce over the apples, until tender and well coated, 30–35 minutes. Remove from the heat.

5 Preheat the oven to 375°F (190°C). On a lightly floured surface, roll out the pastry into a round slightly larger than the frying pan and about ⅛ inch (3 mm) thick. Lay the round over the apples, tucking in the edges. Bake until the crust is puffed and golden brown, 25–30 minutes. Wearing oven mitts, invert a large plate over the pan and invert the plate and pan together, then lift off the pan. Replace any dislodged apple pieces. Serve warm, accompanying each slice with a dollop of crème chantilly.

Peach Sorbet

Peaches are a favorite summer fruit in Tuscany, where they are often sliced into a pitcher of chilled white wine and left to soak for a couple of hours before serving for dessert. The appeal of *sorbetto* is that it is little more than the fruit itself—the fresher and riper the fruit, the better.

6 peaches, about 3 lb (1.5 kg) total weight

1⅓ cups (11 oz/345 g) sugar

Juice of ½ lemon

MAKES 8 SERVINGS

1 Bring a large saucepan of water to a boil. Score a shallow X on the blossom end of each peach. Slip 2 peaches at a time into the water and blanch, about 30 seconds. Using a slotted spoon, remove the peaches from the water and set aside. When they are cool enough to handle, peel away the skins. Cut the peeled peaches from the pits. In a blender or food processor, purée the peaches until smooth. Transfer the purée to a bowl, cover, and refrigerate until well chilled, about 3 hours.

2 In a small saucepan over medium heat, combine 3 cups (24 fl oz/750 ml) water and the sugar and bring to a boil. Reduce the heat to low and simmer until the sugar dissolves, about 4 minutes. Let the sugar syrup cool, then stir it into the chilled purée. Stir in the lemon juice and return the bowl to the refrigerator, about 1 hour.

3 Transfer the mixture to an ice-cream maker and freeze according to the manufacturer's instructions. Unless your ice-cream maker has a built-in freezing compartment, transfer the sorbet to a freezer-safe container. Cover and freeze until firm, at least 3 hours or up to 3 days.

Peach and Frangipane Tart

This luscious tart, filled with peaches nesting in an almond paste cream, can just as successfully be made with nectarines, figs, or plums. Frangipane is a sweet, creamy filling that always includes almonds and sometimes rum. If your tart pan is black rather than silver, reduce the oven temperature to 375°F (190°C).

For the dough

1 cup (5 oz/155 g) all-purpose (plain) flour, plus extra for dusting

1 tablespoon sugar

¼ teaspoon fine sea salt

½ cup (4 oz/125 g) chilled unsalted butter, cut into small pieces

1½ tablespoons ice water

For the filling

4 tablespoons (2 oz/60 g) unsalted butter, at room temperature

4 oz (125 g) almond paste

⅓ cup (2 oz/60 g) all-purpose (plain) flour

1 egg

For the topping

2 or 3 peaches, about 1¼ lb (625 g) total weight, peeled, pitted, and cut into slices ¼–⅓ inch (6–9 mm) thick

1 tablespoon sugar

1 tablespoon unsalted butter, melted

⅓ cup (3 oz/90 g) peach or apricot jam

MAKES 8 SERVINGS

1 To make the dough, in a food processor, combine the 1 cup (5 oz/155 g) flour, sugar, and salt. Pulse 3 or 4 times to blend. Add the butter and pulse until the mixture resembles coarse crumbs. Sprinkle in the ice water and pulse until the dough just starts to clump. Shape into a disk ¾ inch (2 cm) thick, wrap in plastic wrap, and refrigerate, about 1 hour.

2 Remove the dough from the refrigerator and let soften, about 10 minutes. Put it between 2 sheets of parchment (baking) paper each at least 10 inches (25 cm) square. Roll out the dough into an evenly thick 10-inch (25-cm) round, flouring lightly as needed. Transfer the dough to a 9-inch (23-cm) tart pan with removable bottom. Press it into the bottom and up the sides of the pan, then trim any overhang. Cover with aluminum foil and freeze, about 30 minutes.

3 Preheat the oven to 400°F (200°C). Line the tart shell with parchment (baking) paper and fill with dried beans or pie weights. Bake for 20 minutes, then carefully remove the beans and paper. Prick the bottom of the shell with a fork. Continue baking until lightly browned, 10–15 minutes longer. Transfer to a wire rack to cool completely.

4 To make the filling, in a bowl, combine the butter, almond paste, and flour and, using an electric mixer on medium-low speed, beat until smooth. Add the egg and beat at medium until creamy. Spread the filling in the tart shell.

5 To prepare the topping, in a bowl, toss the peaches with the sugar. Arrange over the filling, starting at the edge and placing the slices close together in a ring. Fill the middle of the ring with more slices. Brush the peaches with the melted butter. Set the tart on a baking sheet and bake until the fruit is tender and the filling is puffed and firm, 30–35 minutes. Transfer to a wire rack and let cool, about 15 minutes.

6 Meanwhile, in a small saucepan over low heat, melt the jam. Pass it through a medium-mesh sieve into a bowl. Thin it slightly with water, then brush on the peaches. Serve the tart warm.

Lemon-Lavender Cake

Londoners like nothing better than lingering in a café over coffee or tea and cake, watching the world pass by. While some prefer French confections, others are fond of simple English cakes like this lavender cake with the fresh, floral taste of the English countryside, embellished with an old-fashioned drizzle icing. The best source for pesticide-free lavender is your own garden or a friend's.

8 sprigs pesticide-free fresh lavender flowers (see above), or 1 teaspoon finely chopped, pesticide-free fresh lavender leaves, plus flowers for serving (optional)

1¼ cups (9 oz/280 g) superfine (caster) sugar

1 cup (8 oz/250 g) unsalted butter, at room temperature

Finely grated zest of 2 lemons

Pinch of fine sea salt

4 eggs

½ cup (2 oz/60 g) sifted all-purpose (plain) flour

1½ cups (6 oz/185 g) ground blanched almonds

¼ cup (2 fl oz/60 ml) fresh lemon juice

For the icing

1½ cups (6 oz/185 g) confectioner's (icing) sugar

Juice of ½ large lemon, or as needed

MAKES 8–10 SERVINGS

1 Preheat the oven to 350°F (180°C). Generously butter a 9-by-5-inch (23-by-13-cm) loaf pan.

2 Strip the flowers from the lavender sprigs. Place in a food processor and add the superfine sugar, butter, lemon zest, and salt. Process until pale and fluffy, 2–3 minutes. Transfer to a large bowl. Add the eggs one at a time, alternating with one-fourth of the flour, beating well with a wooden spoon after each addition. Gently stir in the ground almonds and the lemon juice.

3 Spoon the batter into the prepared pan and smooth the top. Bake for 10 minutes. Reduce the oven temperature to 325°F (165°C) and bake until a skewer inserted into the center comes out clean, 50–55 minutes. Let rest in the pan on a wire rack, about 5 minutes, then run a knife around the edge of the pan and turn the cake out onto the rack. Place right side up and let cool.

4 Meanwhile, to make the icing, sift the confectioner's sugar into a bowl. Using a wooden spoon, stir in the lemon juice, a few drops at a time. The icing should be thick but spreadable. If it is too stiff, add a little lemon juice.

5 Using a knife and dipping it in hot water if it becomes too sticky, spread the icing over the cooled cake, making sure that it drips down the sides. Let stand until the icing is set, about 1 hour. Decorate with fresh lavender flowers, if desired. The cake will keep, stored in an airtight container without the flower garnish, for up to 3 days.

Lemon Icebox Pie

Sweetened condensed milk is a common ingredient in desserts from the Deep South. A convenience in the days before refrigeration, it's now used as a matter of taste, as in this wonderfully refreshing and lemony icebox pie. The flavor is intensified by adding grated lemon zest to both the graham cracker crust and the whipped cream topping. Unlike some versions, the pie is baked, but just long enough to cook the yolks while retaining the fresh flavor.

For the crust

1 cup (3 oz/90 g) graham cracker crumbs

½ cup (2 oz/60 g) coarsely ground pecans

2 tablespoons sugar

2 teaspoons grated lemon zest

4 tablespoons (2 oz/60 g) unsalted butter, melted

For the filling

4 egg yolks

1 tablespoon grated lemon zest

1 can (14 fl oz/440 ml) sweetened condensed milk

½ cup (4 fl oz/125 ml) fresh lemon juice, strained

For the topping

1 cup (8 fl oz/250 ml) heavy (double) cream

1 tablespoon sugar, or more to taste

½ teaspoon grated lemon zest

MAKES 6–8 SERVINGS

1 To make the crust, preheat the oven to 300°F (150°C). In a bowl, stir together the graham cracker crumbs, pecans, sugar, and lemon zest. Stir in the melted butter until the crumbs are evenly moistened.

2 Transfer the crumb mixture to an 8- or 9-inch (20- or 23-cm) pie dish and press it firmly and evenly into the bottom and up the sides. Bake until set, about 10 minutes. Transfer to a wire rack and let cool completely. Raise the oven temperature to 325°F (165°C).

3 To make the filling, in a bowl, using an electric mixer, beat together the egg yolks and the lemon zest until very light and frothy, about 2 minutes. Add the condensed milk and beat until smooth. Stir in the lemon juice. Set aside until slightly thickened, about 15 minutes.

4 Pour the filling into the cooled crust. Bake until softly set, about 15 minutes. Transfer to a wire rack and let cool. Cover and refrigerate for at least 4 hours or up to 2 days.

5 To make the topping, in a bowl, using an electric mixer on medium speed, beat the cream until very frothy. Sprinkle with the sugar and lemon zest and beat until soft peaks form. Spread the whipped cream evenly over the chilled pie and serve at once.

Profiteroles with Chocolate Sauce

For the ice cream

2 cups (16 fl oz/500 ml) heavy (double) cream

1 cup (8 fl oz/250 ml) half-and-half (half cream)

1 cup (8 oz/250 g) sugar

1 tablespoon vanilla extract

Pinch of salt

For the profiteroles

½ cup (4 oz/125 g) unsalted butter

1 tablespoon sugar

Pinch of salt

1 cup (5 oz/155 g) all-purpose (plain) flour

4 eggs

For the chocolate sauce

8 oz (250 g) bittersweet chocolate, finely chopped

¾ cup (6 fl oz/180 ml) heavy (double) cream

2 tablespoons unsalted butter

½ teaspoon vanilla extract

MAKES 6 SERVINGS

1 To make the ice cream, in a large bowl, whisk together the cream, half-and-half, sugar, vanilla, and salt. Cover and refrigerate until cold, at least 2 hours or up to overnight. Pour into an ice-cream maker and freeze according to the manufacturer's instructions. Transfer to a freezer-safe container, cover, and freeze until firm, at least 3 hours or up to 3 days.

2 To make the profiteroles, preheat the oven to 425°F (220°C). In a large, heavy saucepan, combine the butter, sugar, salt, and 1 cup (8 fl oz/250 ml) water. Bring to a rolling boil. Remove from the heat and add the flour all at once, stirring constantly until incorporated. Place over medium heat and stir until the batter forms a ball. Transfer to a mixing bowl.

3 Using a wooden spoon or an electric mixer on medium-low speed, beat the batter to help it cool, 3–4 minutes. In a small bowl, whisk 1 egg. When the batter has cooled, add the egg and beat until incorporated. Add the remaining eggs one at a time, whisking each one first and beating after each addition. After each egg is added, the batter will separate and appear shiny, but will return to a smooth paste with vigorous beating. Let rest, about 10 minutes.

4 Line a baking sheet with parchment (baking) paper. Spoon the batter into a large pastry (piping) bag fitted with a ⅜-inch (1-cm) plain tip. For each profiterole, pipe about 1 heaping teaspoon of batter onto the sheet, forming a mound about 1 inch (2.5 cm) in diameter and spacing them at least 2 inches (5 cm) apart. Bake for 10 minutes. Reduce the oven temperature to 350°F (180°C) and continue to bake until the pastries have risen and are golden and firm, about 25 minutes longer. Let cool.

5 To make the chocolate sauce, put the chocolate in a bowl. In a small, heavy saucepan over medium-low heat, warm the cream until small bubbles form around the edge of the pan. Remove from the heat, add the butter, and stir until melted. Slowly whisk the cream into the chocolate until combined, then stir in the vanilla.

6 Using a serrated knife, carefully cut the profiteroles almost in half. Place the split pastries on individual plates. Set a small scoop of ice cream inside each, drizzle with the warm chocolate sauce, and serve at once.

Note: The pastries can be wrapped and frozen for up to 1 month. Before using, preheat the oven to 350°F (180°C), place on a baking sheet, and bake until crisp, 10–11 minutes.

Chocolate arrived at the French court in 1615, when Louis XIII took a Spanish bride. But several decades would pass before France could claim its first French-born royal chocoholic: Louis XIV reportedly drank hot chocolate three times a week at Versailles.

French Chocolate Shops

Some of the most elegant retail establishments in Paris are *chocolateries* (chocolate shops). Throughout the day, you will see the young and the old, the wealthy and the working class—every one of them a seasoned client—leaving the shops with lovely little bundles concealing cocoa-dusted truffles, creamy *palets*, and fruit-filled *barquettes*.

Chocolate arrived in France with Jewish confectioners who were fleeing the Inquisition on the Iberian Peninsula. They set up processing operations in the region of Bayonne, but the new product was given a cold shoulder at first. Chocolate's place as a prized French commodity was assured only after two kings, Louis XIII and Louis XIV, married Spanish infantas, who served chocolate at court.

Today, France produces some of the world's finest chocolate, both for fashioning into exquisite bonbons and for transforming into elaborate desserts, and a beribboned box of chocolates is considered the perfect gift. All the *grandes épiceries*—Hédiard, Fauchon, Le Bon Marché—and some *pâtisseries* carry chocolates, but many Parisians prefer to go to a shop devoted exclusively to such pleasures, finding the visit a sweet treat in itself.

Jean-Paul Hévin's chocolate shops, with their spare yet irresistible displays, resemble modern jewelry boutiques. Debauve & Gallais has been operating in the same location since 1800, when it was opened by a pharmacist and his nephew, who dispensed both medicines and chocolate. At À l'Étoile d'Or, each chocolate has its own story and its own flavor. La Maison du Chocolat is a sea of choices, every one of them elegant and refined, many of them incorporating Asian spices, fresh fruits, or herbal infusions.

POUDRE DE CACAO

CHOCOLAT NOIR AUX NOISETTES

GÂTEAU DE MOUSSE AU CHOCOLAT

TRUFFES AU CHOCOLAT

CHOCOLATE SAMPLER

Poudre de cacao Dense, rich *poudre de cacao* (cocoa powder) is made by finely grinding the compressed nibs of cacao beans after most of the cocoa butter has been removed. French cafés use the sweetened powder to make hot chocolate, while the unsweetened variety is used for coating truffles and decorating cakes. Although the most decadent Parisian hot chocolates are made from melted chocolate shards, they usually include a touch of cocoa powder to balance the flavor and texture.

Chocolat noir aux noisettes *Chocolat noir*, or dark chocolate, contains at least 55 percent cacao, along with cocoa butter and sugar. A higher percentage of cacao means a more bittersweet chocolate. The addition of roasted nuts and dried fruits is popular, especially at Christmas. Known as *mendiants*, these come in large slabs (broken into pieces and sold by weight), in bars, or in palm-sized disks. The *noisette* (hazelnut/filbert) is the most popular nut and is usually used whole.

Gâteau de mousse au chocolat Rather than bake at home, most Parisians stop by a *pâtisserie* or *chocolaterie* when they are in the mood for cake. The chocolate mousse cake is a classic—layers of mousse and cake moistened with sugar syrup and topped with a perfectly smooth chocolate *glaçage* (icing). Other versions contain coffee or caramel mousse, chopped hazelnuts (filberts), crunchy nougat layers, or chocolate shavings. For a simpler cake, seek out a *gâteau au chocolat*, an egg-rich, flourless chocolate cake with a moist center and no icing.

Truffes au chocolat Chocolate truffles, so-called because they resemble the natural fungi of the same name, are delicate balls of creamy chocolate. The traditional recipe is simple: ganache (dark chocolate mixed with cream) is formed into a ball, thinly coated in chocolate, and rolled in cocoa powder. Some *chocolatiers* offer more exotic versions, such as truffles rolled in toasted coconut or flavored with rum and raisins.

Devil's Food Cupcakes

The cupcake—that icon of American childhood birthday parties—has become the dessert darling of urbanites, who line up at high-end pastry shops for the beautifully decorated treats. This version is chocolate with a buttercream frosting.

½ cup (1½ oz/45 g) Dutch-process cocoa powder

¾ cup (6 oz/185 g) firmly packed light brown sugar

2 teaspoons instant espresso

1 cup (8 fl oz/250 ml) boiling water

½ cup (4 fl oz/125 ml) buttermilk

2 teaspoons vanilla extract

½ cup (4 oz/125 g) unsalted butter, at room temperature

¾ cup (6 oz/185 g) granulated sugar

2 eggs, at room temperature

1¼ cups (6½ oz/200 g) all-purpose (plain) flour

1½ teaspoons baking soda (bicarbonate of soda)

½ teaspoon salt

For the buttercream

1 cup (8 oz/250 g) unsalted butter, at room temperature

2 egg yolks

1 tablespoon vanilla extract

¼ teaspoon salt

2 cups (8 oz/250 g) confectioners' (icing) sugar

MAKES 12 CUPCAKES

1 Preheat the oven to 350°F (180°C). Line 12 standard muffin cups with paper liners or lightly butter the muffin cups and the top of the muffin pan.

2 In a bowl, combine the cocoa powder, brown sugar, and espresso powder. Add the boiling water, stir until smooth, and let cool to room temperature. Stir in the buttermilk and vanilla. Set aside.

3 In a large bowl, using an electric mixer on high speed, beat together the butter and granulated sugar until fluffy and almost white, 3–4 minutes. Add the eggs, one at a time, beating well and scraping down the bowl after each addition. In a separate bowl, stir together the flour, baking soda, and salt. Fold one-third of the chocolate mixture into the beaten butter. Add one-third of the flour mixture, stirring gently to combine. Continue folding in the chocolate mixture and adding the flour until all the mixtures are combined into a smooth batter.

4 Divide the batter evenly among the muffin cups. Bake until a toothpick inserted into the center of a cupcake comes out clean, 15–18 minutes. Let cool to room temperature in the pan on a wire rack.

5 To make the buttercream, in a bowl, using an electric mixer on high speed, beat the butter until fluffy, 3–4 minutes. Add the egg yolks and beat until fluffy. Beat in the vanilla, salt, and confectioners' sugar. Remove the cupcakes from the pan and spread the buttercream evenly over the top of each cupcake.

Flourless Chocolate Cake

This dense chocolate cake, served with crème anglaise, is a fine showcase for rich Italian chocolate, whose purity was the subject of a debate that split the European Union in 2003, with France and Italy fighting to defend their superior products.

For the crème anglaise

1 cup (8 fl oz/250 ml) milk

1 vanilla bean, split lengthwise, or ⅛ teaspoon vanilla extract

3 egg yolks

⅓ cup (3 oz/90 g) sugar

For the cakes

1 cup (8 fl oz/250 ml) heavy (double) cream

7 oz (220 g) bittersweet chocolate, preferably 70 percent cacao, cut into small pieces

2 egg yolks

2 tablespoons sugar

2 tablespoons all-purpose (plain) flour, sifted

Unsweetened cocoa powder for dusting

MAKES 4 SERVINGS

1 To make the crème anglaise, in a heavy saucepan over medium heat, combine the milk and the vanilla bean, if using (if using extract, add it later), and heat until small bubbles begin to appear around the edge of the pan. Remove from the heat and let cool slightly. In a bowl, whisk together the egg yolks and sugar until thick and pale yellow, about 5 minutes. Whisking constantly, slowly pour the hot milk into the egg mixture. Pour the egg mixture into the saucepan, place over low heat, and heat gently, stirring constantly, until it is thick enough to coat the back of a spoon, 5–10 minutes. Do not let the mixture boil. Remove from the heat and remove and discard the vanilla bean, if used. Strain through a fine-mesh sieve into a bowl. Stir in the vanilla extract, if using. Let cool to room temperature, stirring occasionally to prevent a skin from forming.

2 Preheat the oven to 425°F (220°C). Generously butter four ¾-cup (6-fl oz/180-ml) molds or ramekins, dust with flour, and tap out the excess.

3 To make the cakes, combine the cream and chocolate in a double boiler over simmering water, and heat, stirring occasionally, until melted and smooth. Remove from the heat. In a bowl, using a whisk or an electric mixer on medium speed, beat together the egg yolks and sugar until thick and pale yellow, about 5 minutes. Whisking constantly, pour in the chocolate mixture in a thin stream. Gently whisk in the flour. Divide the chocolate mixture among the prepared molds and arrange them on a baking sheet. Bake until the top of each cake is firm to the touch, about 10 minutes. The center will still be liquid. Transfer the molds to a wire rack and let cool, about 5 minutes.

4 To serve, invert a dessert plate over each warm cake and invert the plate and mold together, then lift off the mold. If the cakes stick, ease them out with the tip of a knife. Spoon some of the cooled crème anglaise in a pool alongside each cake. Using a sifter, dust each cake with a little cocoa powder. Pass the remaining crème anglaise at the table.

MEXICO
Spicy Hot Chocolate

In Mexico, chocolate tablets are put into a clay pot with hot milk. A carved wooden *molinillo* is rapidly twirled to create a thick layer of foam, then the chocolate is poured into bowls or cups. The tablets can be found in well-stocked markets.

4 cups (32 fl oz/1 l) milk or water

2 chocolate tablets, about ¼ lb (125 g) total weight, broken into small pieces

1 vanilla bean (optional)

MAKES 4 SERVINGS

1 In a saucepan over low heat, warm 1 cup (8 fl oz/ 250 ml) of the milk. Add the chocolate tablets and stir with a wooden spoon until melted. Add the remaining 3 cups (24 fl oz/ 750 ml) milk and the vanilla bean, if using, and let simmer for several minutes.

2 Remove the pan from the heat. Lift out the vanilla bean and save for another use. Using a whisk, beat the chocolate milk vigorously until a thick layer of foam covers the surface. Pour into cups, distributing the foam evenly. Serve at once.

ITALY
Bittersweet Hot Chocolate

Florentine hot chocolate is so decadently dense that one could easily believe it was nothing but the finest melted dark chocolate. Arrowroot, a thickener similar to cornstarch (cornflour) but with a more neutral flavor, is the secret to its thickness.

For the hot chocolate

¾ cup (2½ oz/75 g) unsweetened cocoa powder

⅓ cup (3 oz/90 g) granulated sugar

3 cups (24 fl oz/750 ml) milk

1½ teaspoons arrowroot (see above)

½ cup (4 fl oz/125 ml) cold water

For the whipped cream

¾ cup (6 fl oz/180 ml) heavy (double) cream, well chilled

1½ teaspoons confectioners' (icing) sugar, sifted

MAKES 6 SERVINGS

1 To make the hot chocolate, in a heavy saucepan, whisk together the cocoa powder and granulated sugar. Place over low heat and vigorously stir in ½ cup (4 fl oz/125 ml) of the milk, a few tablespoons at a time. When the mixture is smooth, stir in the remaining 2½ cups (20 fl oz/625 ml) milk. Bring to a boil over medium heat, stirring constantly. Reduce the heat to low and simmer, stirring often, about 5 minutes. Remove from the heat and let cool, about 5 minutes.

2 Return the hot chocolate to a boil, then reduce the heat to low and simmer, about 5 minutes. Remove from the heat.

3 In a small bowl, dissolve the arrowroot in the cold water. Pour into the hot chocolate. Bring to a boil over medium heat one final time, stirring constantly, then remove from the heat.

4 To make the whipped cream, in a bowl, combine the cream and confectioners' sugar. Using a wire whisk or an electric mixer, beat until the cream is light and fluffy and holds soft peaks, about 4 minutes.

5 Pour the hot chocolate into cups, top with the whipped cream, and serve at once.

FRANCE
Hazelnut Soufflé

No one knows who made the first soufflé, but Antoine Beauvilliers spread the word. In the late eighteenth century, he cooked for French royalty before opening a restaurant in Paris—where, according to legend, every meal included a soufflé.

For the chocolate crème anglaise

1 cup (8 fl oz/250 ml) milk

3 tablespoons sugar

4 oz (125 g) best-quality bittersweet chocolate, coarsely chopped

2 egg yolks

Ice water

½ teaspoon vanilla extract

⅛ teaspoon salt

For the soufflé

1¼ cups (6 oz/185 g) hazelnuts (filberts)

1 tablespoon all-purpose (plain) flour

¼ cup (2 oz/60 g) plus 2 tablespoons sugar

1 whole egg, plus 2 egg yolks

⅓ cup (3 fl oz/80 ml) milk

1 tablespoon brandy or Cognac

3 or 4 drops vanilla extract

6 egg whites

¾ teaspoon cream of tartar

Tiny pinch of salt

MAKES 6 SERVINGS

1 To make the crème anglaise, in a heavy saucepan over medium heat, combine the milk, sugar, and chocolate. Cook, stirring constantly, until the chocolate melts, about 5 minutes. In a bowl, whisk the egg yolks. Whisking constantly, slowly pour the chocolate mixture into the eggs. Pour the egg mixture into the saucepan, place over medium heat, and cook, stirring constantly, until thick enough to coat the back of a spoon, about 5 minutes. Do not let the mixture boil. Strain through a fine-mesh sieve into a bowl. Place in a larger bowl partially filled with ice water and let cool, stirring occasionally, for about 5 minutes. Stir in the vanilla and salt. Cover and refrigerate.

2 To make the soufflé, in a frying pan over medium-high heat, toast the hazelnuts, shaking the pan occasionally, until the skins darken and loosen, 3–5 minutes. Transfer to a towel and rub vigorously to remove the loose skins. In a food processor, process the hazelnuts to a fine powder. Set aside.

3 Preheat the oven to 375°F (190°C). Butter six 1-cup (8-fl oz/250-ml) individual dishes or one 1½-qt (1.5-l) soufflé dish. In a saucepan, whisk together the flour, ¼ cup sugar, whole egg, and egg yolks, then whisk in the milk. Set the pan over medium-low heat and cook, stirring constantly, until the mixture begins to thicken, 4–6 minutes. Do not let it boil. Set aside ¼ cup (1 oz/30 g) of the ground hazelnuts. Stir in the remaining nuts and continue cooking until an opaque custard forms, about 2 minutes. Pour into a large bowl and stir in the brandy and vanilla. Let cool completely.

4 In a small bowl, combine the 2 tablespoons sugar and the reserved hazelnuts. Sprinkle the mixture into the soufflé dish(es), coating the bottom and sides.

5 Put the egg whites in a large, clean bowl. Using an electric mixer on medium speed, beat the whites until foamy. Add the cream of tartar and salt and continue to beat just until firm peaks form. Scoop one-fourth of the egg whites onto the hazelnut mixture. Using a rubber spatula, stir in the whites to lighten the mixture. Scoop the remaining whites on top and fold in just until no white streaks remain. Scoop into the prepared dish(es). Bake until risen and lightly flecked with gold, about 10 minutes for individual soufflés or about 20 minutes for a large soufflé. Serve with the chilled crème anglaise alongside.

Hazelnut Cake

This version of the classic Catalan sponge cake, or *pa de pessic,* features toasted hazelnuts and a spoonful of ground licorice, which gives the cake an aromatic kick. Ground licorice powder can be found in specialty and natural-food stores, or it can be made by grinding dried licorice root in a spice grinder or food processor.

1½ cups (7½ oz/235 g) hazelnuts (filberts)

4 eggs, at room temperature

1 cup (8 oz/250 g) granulated sugar

1 cup (8 oz/250 g) unsalted butter, at room temperature

1 cup (5 oz/155 g) all-purpose (plain) flour

2 teaspoons ground licorice (see above)

Confectioners' (icing) sugar for dusting (optional)

MAKES 6 SERVINGS

1 Preheat the oven to 375°F (190°C). Butter a 10-inch (25-cm) cake pan. Dust with flour and tap out the excess.

2 In a frying pan over medium-high heat, toast the hazelnuts, shaking the pan occasionally, until the skins begin to darken and loosen, 3–5 minutes. Transfer to a kitchen towel and rub vigorously to remove the loose skins. Put half of the hazelnuts into a food processor and process to a fine powder. Wrap the remaining hazelnuts in the towel and gently break into pieces with a mallet.

3 In a bowl, whisk together the eggs and granulated sugar until the mixture becomes a pale, creamy mousse and has tripled in volume, about 5 minutes. Continuing to whisk, add the butter. Then add the flour, ground hazelnuts, hazelnut pieces, and licorice and mix well.

4 Pour the batter into the prepared pan. Bake until a skewer inserted into the center comes out clean, about 50 minutes. Let cool slightly on a wire rack. Run a table knife around the inside edge of the pan to loosen the cake, then invert the cake onto a serving plate. Dust the top with confectioners' sugar, if using. Serve warm or at room temperature.

Pistachio Baklava

Both Greece and Turkey claim this heavenly nut-filled pastry, but it is a favorite sweet throughout the eastern and southern Mediterranean. Spiced ground pistachios and walnuts fill the crisp layers of filo, which are baked and saturated with a honey syrup.

1½ cups (6 oz/185 g) pistachios, plus 3 tablespoons chopped

1 cup (4 oz/125 g) walnuts

3 tablespoons sugar, plus ¾ cup (6 oz/185 g)

1 teaspoon ground cinnamon

¼ teaspoon ground cloves

¼ teaspoon salt

1 lb (500 g) filo pastry sheets, each about 12 by 18 inches (30 by 45 cm), thawed overnight in the refrigerator if frozen

½ cup (4 oz/125 g) unsalted butter, melted

1 cup (12 fl oz/375 ml) honey

MAKES 36 PIECES

1 In a food processor, combine the 1½ cups (6 oz/185 g) pistachios, walnuts, 3 tablespoons sugar, cinnamon, cloves, and salt. Pulse until finely ground. Transfer to a bowl and set aside.

2 Cut the stack of filo sheets in half crosswise to make 2 stacks each about 8 by 12 inches (20 by 30 cm). Stack the sheets between sheets of parchment (baking) paper, and cover with a damp kitchen towel.

3 Brush a 9-by-13-inch (23-by-33-cm) baking pan with melted butter. Place 1 filo sheet in the pan and brush lightly and evenly with butter. Repeat to make 12 layers. Sprinkle with about one-fourth of the nut mixture. Top with 2 more filo sheets, brushing each with butter. Sprinkle on one-third of the remaining nut mixture, then layer with 2 more buttered filo sheets. Repeat once more, using half of the remaining nut mixture and 2 more buttered filo sheets. Top with the remaining nut mixture, then with 12 buttered filo sheets. Brush the top sheet generously with butter and refrigerate, about 15 minutes.

4 Preheat the oven to 350°F (180°C). Using a serrated knife, cut the baklava into 18 rectangles (3 across the short side and 6 across the long side). Then cut diagonally across the rectangles to form triangles. Bake until golden brown, 50–60 minutes. Transfer to a wire rack and let cool slightly.

5 In a small, heavy saucepan over medium heat, combine the ¾ cup (6 oz/185 g) sugar and ½ cup (4 fl oz/125 ml) water and stir to dissolve the sugar. Bring to a boil and cook, without stirring, until the mixture reaches 220°F (104°C) on a candy thermometer, about 5 minutes. Remove from the heat and stir in the honey. Pour the syrup over the warm baklava (being careful not to splatter). Sprinkle with the 3 tablespoons chopped pistachios. Cover loosely with waxed paper and let stand at room temperature for at least 8 hours or up to overnight.

6 Run a sharp knife along the cuts, then remove the baklava from the pan. Store in an airtight container at room temperature, with waxed paper between the layers, for up to 1 week.

Pistachio Cake

Sicily is known for its flavorful pistachios, particularly those from around Bronte, on the eastern side of the island. Cooks use them to make gelato, biscotti, and this orange-scented cake. Accompany with a scoop of *gelato di crema* (page 323).

2 cups (8 oz/250 g) pistachios, shelled

1¼ cups (10 oz/315 g) granulated sugar

1 cup (5 oz/155 g) all-purpose (plain) flour

½ teaspoon grated orange zest

6 egg whites, at room temperature

⅛ teaspoon salt

1 teaspoon vanilla extract

6 tablespoons (3 oz/90 g) unsalted butter, melted and cooled

Confectioners' (icing) sugar for dusting (optional)

MAKES 6–8 SERVINGS

1 Preheat the oven to 325°F (165°C). Spread the pistachios on a rimmed baking sheet and toast, shaking the pan every few minutes, until fragrant and lightly toasted, 5–8 minutes. Transfer to a plate to cool.

2 Raise the oven temperature to 350°F (180°C). Butter a 9-inch (23-cm) springform pan. Line the bottom with parchment (baking) paper cut to fit. Butter the paper. In a food processor, coarsely chop half of the toasted nuts, then remove and set aside. Add the remaining toasted nuts and ½ cup (4 oz/125 g) of the granulated sugar to the food processor and process until the nuts are finely chopped. Add the flour and orange zest and pulse to blend.

3 Put the egg whites in a large, clean bowl and add the salt. Using an electric mixer on medium speed, beat the whites until foamy. Raise the speed to high and gradually add the remaining ¾ cup (6 oz/190 g) granulated sugar and the vanilla, beating until soft peaks form. Sprinkle the flour mixture on the whites and fold in gently. Fold in the butter and reserved chopped nuts. Pour the batter into the pan.

4 Bake until a toothpick inserted into the center comes out clean, about 40 minutes. Transfer to a wire rack and let cool, about 10 minutes. Run a knife around the inside edge of the pan, release the pan sides, and slide the cake onto the rack. Let cool completely.

5 Place the cake on a serving plate. Dust the top with the confectioners' sugar, if desired, and serve.

Almond-Pine Nut Cookies

The first day of November is All Saints' Day in Catholic countries, and Spain celebrates with special foods, including these little, round almond cookies. Similar to macaroons, *panellets* are made with sweetened ground almonds bound together in dough. This is the original version, encrusted with pine nuts. Nowadays, the dough may be flavored with myriad ingredients, from whiskey to candied chestnuts, and might be coated with coconut, chocolate, marzipan, or a variety of nuts.

1 small russet potato, about ¼ lb (125 g), peeled

1 lb (500 g) blanched almonds

Grated zest of ½ lemon, finely minced

2 cups (1 lb/500 g) sugar

1 egg white

½ cup (2½ oz/75 g) pine nuts

MAKES ABOUT 20 COOKIES

1 Bring a small saucepan of water to a boil. Add the potato and cook until tender when pierced with a knife, about 10 minutes. Drain and transfer to a small bowl. Mash with a fork and let cool slightly. In a food processor, process the almonds until finely ground. Add the ground almonds and lemon zest to the potato and mix thoroughly.

2 In a small, heavy saucepan, combine the sugar and 1 cup (8 fl oz/250 ml) water and stir to dissolve the sugar. Bring to a boil, stirring with a wooden spoon until the mixture thickens to a syrup. Continue cooking, without stirring, until the syrup reaches 250°F (120°C) on a candy thermometer. Remove from the heat.

3 Pour the syrup in a thin stream onto the almond mixture and mix well with the spoon. (The dough is too hot to handle.) Let cool for at least 15 minutes. Form the dough into a ball, wrap in plastic wrap, and refrigerate overnight.

4 Preheat the oven to 475°F (245°C). Butter a baking sheet. In a small bowl, lightly beat the egg white. Using your hands, shape the dough into walnut-sized balls. Roll in the egg white and then in the pine nuts, embedding the nuts slightly into the surface. Arrange about 2 inches (5 cm) apart on the prepared sheet.

5 Bake until the cookies are golden brown, 15–20 minutes. Let cool on the pan on a wire rack. Store in an airtight container for up to 1 week.

Spanish Pastry Shops

There is more to the *pastisseries*—literally, "cake shops"—of Catalonia than their name alone implies. Of course, cakes and cookies are their main stock in trade, but many of them also have specialties that set them apart from their competition. Some *pastisseries* have branched out into sweet or savory *coques* (flatbreads), which are usually the territory of the *forns* (bread ovens). Others are known for their croissants, chocolate bonbons, *crema catalana* (burnt custard), or their expertise with sweets from elsewhere, such as panettone or plum cake. Some shops are more like confectioneries, others mainly bakeries. The *pastisseria* is in essence simply a dispensary of good things to eat that are mainstays on the Catalan table but that require too much time or skill (or both) for most people to make at home.

Given the decline of interest in churchgoing in contemporary Spain, it's surprising how much influence Catholicism still has over daily lives. For example, nearly every pastry and cookie has its moment in the religious year, from the *tortell de Reis* made for the feast of Epiphany and the *coca de Sant Joan* for the Feast of Saint John to the *turróns* and *neules* for Christmas. This calendar is strictly adhered to; it's useless to look for *mona de Pasqua* (chocolate Easter cake) in November, for example, or *panellets* (nut cookies) in April.

By and large, Catalan baking, like the food in general, is not characterized by subtlety or great refinement. Its strength resides in the skill with which even simple things can be made delicious. The basis of the repertoire is a rich brioche dough, and the difference between one specialty and another is mainly in the variety of fillings and toppings. It has been further elevated by the influence of nearby France, and almost all *pastissers* now use butter, instead of the more traditional lard, for making cakes. (Vegetarians take note, however: *llardons*, or fried bits of pork, are a common feature of the *coca de Sant Joan* and *coca de Sant Jaume*.)

When in Barcelona, it is well worth taking a tour of some of the city's grand *pastisseries*. Five of the best in town are Escribà, Foix, Brunells, Baixas, and Sacha. They are not only sumptuously decorated but also enormously popular, and it's not uncommon to see lines snaking out the front door onto the street. If your purchase is a gift, say so (*"es per regalar"*) and it will be packed up in a box with ribbons and bows at no extra charge.

In the towns and cities of Catalonia, the *pastisseria* is an institution. Every moment of the day provides an opportunity to visit—from morning croissants and midday slices of *coca* to afternoon *berenars* and elaborate desserts fit for essentially any celebration.

BORREGUETS
SANT ANTONI
2'00 € 60/st

PANELLETS
assortits

BRUNELL

Bourbon Pecan Tart

Broad, leafy pecan trees grew wild along the Louisiana bayous for centuries before they were cultivated commercially, and the trees are still prized by homeowners for the cool shade they provide in summer and the bountiful harvests they produce in autumn. Gooey and sticky sweet, pecan pie is the quintessential southern dessert. Here, it is transformed into a buttery tart that uses less sugar than the original but preserves the crisp top layer of nuts. A shot of bourbon is added for good measure.

For the pastry

1½ cups (7½ oz/235 g) all-purpose (plain) flour

½ teaspoon fine sea salt

½ cup (4 oz/125 g) chilled unsalted butter

3 tablespoons ice water

For the filling

2 eggs

½ cup (4 oz/125 g) sugar

¼ teaspoon fine sea salt

¼ teaspoon ground cinnamon

⅔ cup (7½ oz/235 g) molasses

2 tablespoons unsalted butter, melted

2 tablespoons good-quality bourbon

1¼ cups (7 oz/220 g) pecan halves

MAKES 8 SERVINGS

1 To make the pastry, in a food processor, combine the flour and salt and pulse briefly to blend. Cut the butter into 8 pieces and distribute evenly over the flour. Pulse 10 times, or until the mixture resembles coarse meal. Sprinkle the ice water over the surface and pulse 7 more times. The dough will appear loose but should hold together when pressed between your fingers. Shape the dough into a disk ¾ inch (2 cm) thick, wrap in plastic wrap, and refrigerate, for at least 30 minutes or up to overnight.

2 Preheat the oven to 350°F (180°C). On a lightly floured work surface, roll out the dough into a 12-inch (30-cm) round about ⅛ inch (3 mm) thick. Wrap the round loosely around the pin, then carefully unroll it over the top of a 9-inch (23-cm) tart pan with a removable bottom, allowing the excess to drape over the sides. Press the pastry gently into the bottom and sides of the pan, then roll the pin across the top of the pan, trimming off any excess dough.

3 To make the filling, in a bowl, using an electric mixer on medium speed, beat together the eggs, sugar, salt, and cinnamon until smooth. Add the molasses, butter, and bourbon and beat until thoroughly combined. Stir in the pecans. Pour the filling into the shell.

4 Bake until a knife inserted in the center comes out clean, 45–50 minutes. Transfer to a wire rack, let cool, about 10 minutes, then remove the pan sides and let cool completely. Slide the tart off the pan bottom onto a serving plate.

Pecan Cheesecake

As an alternative to the familiar Mexican flan and rice pudding, many *restaurantes* and *fondas* include cheesecake among their desserts. This version is embellished with a topping of native pecans and *cajeta,* a thick goat's milk caramel syrup. *Cajeta* is available in jars in Hispanic markets, but homemade has a much better flavor.

For the cajeta

4 cups (32 fl oz/1 l) goat's milk

1 cup (8 oz/250 g) sugar

½ cup (4 fl oz/125 ml) cow's milk

¼ teaspoon baking soda (bicarbonate of soda)

1 tablespoon vanilla extract, rum, or brandy

½ cup (2 oz/60 g) pecans, toasted and finely chopped, plus chopped pecans for garnish

Pinch of sea salt

For the crust

1½ cups (4½ oz/140 g) finely crushed vanilla wafers

4 tablespoons (2 oz/60 g) unsalted butter, melted

For the filling

1½ lb (750 g) cream cheese, at room temperature

¾ cup (6 oz/185 g) sugar

1 teaspoon vanilla extract

3 eggs

For the topping

2 cups (16 fl oz/500 ml) sour cream

¼ cup (2 oz/60 g) sugar

2 teaspoons vanilla extract

25–30 pecan halves

MAKES 12 SERVINGS

1 To make the *cajeta,* in a large, heavy saucepan over medium heat, bring the goat's milk to a simmer. Add the sugar and stir to dissolve. In a small bowl, stir together the cow's milk and baking soda. Stirring constantly, ladle in a small amount of the hot goat's milk. Remove the pan from the heat and whisk the soda mixture into the goat's milk. Return the pan to the stove and simmer, stirring frequently with a wooden spoon, until the *cajeta* begins to thicken, about 30 minutes. As it darkens, reduce the heat to low and stir constantly until the *cajeta* becomes a dark caramel color and coats the back of the spoon, about 20 minutes longer. Pour into a bowl and let cool, then stir in the vanilla. Pour half of the *cajeta* into another bowl, stir in the ½ cup (2 oz/ 60 g) chopped nuts and salt, and set aside. Refrigerate the remaining half.

2 To make the crust, in a bowl, stir together the crushed vanilla wafers and butter until the wafer crumbs are evenly moist. Transfer to a 9-inch (23-cm) springform pan and press firmly and evenly into the bottom and about 1 inch (2.5 cm) up the sides. Refrigerate for 30 minutes.

3 Preheat the oven to 350°F (180°C). To make the filling, in a bowl, using an electric mixer, beat the cream cheese until smooth. Add the sugar and vanilla and beat until blended. One at a time, add the eggs, beating until smooth.

4 Drizzle the *cajeta* evenly over the chilled crust, then pour in the filling. Bake until firm, 50–60 minutes. Immediately place in the refrigerator on a kitchen towel. Chill for 15 minutes. Raise the oven temperature to 450°F (230°C).

5 To make the topping, in a bowl, stir together the sour cream, sugar, and vanilla. Pour over the top of the cheesecake and bake for 10 minutes. Transfer to a wire rack to cool.

6 Place a circle of pecan halves around the outer edge of the cheesecake. Cover and refrigerate for at least 24 hours or up to 3 days. To serve, release and remove the sides of the pan. Heat the remaining *cajeta* just until warm. Place slices of the cheesecake on individual plates, drizzle with *cajeta,* and garnish with the remaining chopped nuts.

Glossary

ACHIOTE PASTE This seasoning paste made from the hard, brick red seeds of the annatto, a tropical tree, contributes a mild, flowery flavor and a deep yellow-orange color to foods. It is a typical ingredient in the Yucatán peninsula in Mexico.

AGRODOLCE An Italian sweet and sour sauce with origins in the ancient Roman kitchen, when honey, grape must, or sweet wine provided the sweet, and vinegar or *garum* (a popular fish sauce of the time) the sour. In traditional Roman cooking, wild boar or beef tongue may be cooked in *agrodolce,* as are occasionally red mullet and salt cod.

AJOWAN *Ajowan* seeds (also known as *ajwain*) come from the thymol plant, a close relative of caraway and cumin. Native to southern India, the plant also thrives in Egypt, Iran, Afghanistan, and Pakistan. The seeds resemble large celery seeds. They have a sharp taste and, when crushed, smell strongly of thyme. Ajowan has been used for centuries in India to flavor vegetable dishes, breads, pickles, and *pappadums.* It helps control digestive problems, so it is often added to starchy dishes and those containing legumes. If ajowan is unavailable, thyme imparts a similar flavor.

AMCHOOR POWDER Made from unripe mangoes that have been peeled, dried, and ground to a pale gray-beige powder, *amchoor* powder, also known as mango powder, has a strong aroma and sour tang. It is used as a souring agent, mainly in vegetarian cooking, and to tenderize meat. If unavailable, lemon juice may be substituted.

ASAFETIDA Popular in Indian vegetarian cooking, where certain religious dictates prohibit the use of garlic and onion, asafetida is dried gum resin from the root of the ferula plant, a type of giant fennel grown mainly in Iran, Afghanistan, and Kashmir. It has a strong, fetid smell in its uncooked form. Sulfur compounds give the spice its odor, which is miraculously transformed during cooking into a sweet garlicky-onion aroma. Though asafetida is available in both lump and powder form, there is little difference in quality, and it's more convenient to buy it already ground. Store it in an airtight jar to prevent the smell from lingering or permeating other foods. Asafetida can be replaced with minced garlic.

BLACK VINEGAR One of three main types of Chinese vinegar distilled from fermented rice, black (also labeled brown) vinegar is a dark-colored, subtly flavored vinegar used as a flavoring and condiment.

Balsamic vinegar is a suitable substitution; adjust the amount to taste.

BOUQUET GARNI This French term refers to a bundle of aromatic herbs used to flavor stocks and sauces as they cook and then easily discarded. The typical bouquet garni contains parsley, thyme, and bay leaves, and may also include the outer leaves of a leek or a small celery stalk.

TO MAKE A BOUQUET GARNI, place an 8-inch (20-cm) square of cheesecloth (muslin) on a work surface and in the center set ½ celery stalk, including leaves, cut into 2-inch (5-cm) lengths; 2 or 3 fresh flat-leaf (Italian) parsley sprigs; 2 or 3 fresh thyme sprigs; 1 bay leaf; and 8–10 peppercorns. Fold 4 green outer leek leaves, each about 4 inches (10 cm) long, in half and add to the other ingredients. Bring up the corners of the cheesecloth and tie securely with kitchen string.

CANDLENUTS Resembling small, waxy hazelnuts (filberts), these oil-rich nuts—known in Malaysia and Indonesia as *buah keras*—are used primarily as a thickening agent in spice pastes. Blanched almonds may be substituted.

CASSIA LEAVES The leaves of the cassia tree, also known as Indian bay leaves, have a slightly clovelike aroma and flavor and are available dried from Indian grocers. Despite their nickname, they are not related to European bay leaves (*Laurus nobilis*). If cassia leaves are unavailable, the same quantity of European bay leaves may be used, although they will give a somewhat different taste.

CÈPE MUSHROOM The firm texture, rich flavor, and sweet fragrance of cèpes make them highly sought after throughout Europe. These wild mushrooms have light brown caps topping thick stems. The cèpe mushroom, also known as the porcini mushroom, is most commonly available dried outside of Europe.

CHILES Chiles, whether dried or fresh, have distinctive flavors and degrees of heat, so they cannot be used interchangeably. Look for fresh chiles with smooth, shiny skins and no breaks or cracks. Dried chiles should be relatively supple and without discolored patches of skin.

FRESH CHILES
Anaheim: Familiar long green, mild to moderately spicy chile found in most markets. Similar to New Mexican variety of chile.

Güero: A pale yellow to light green chile. Several varieties may be used, including the Fresno, yellow banana, and Hungarian wax, which vary in degree of heat. Most are rather sweet with a pungent punch.

Habanero: Renowned as the hottest of all chiles, this 2-inch (5-cm) lantern-shaped variety from Yucatán combines its intense heat with flavors recalling tomatoes and tropical fruits. Available in unripe green and ripened yellow, orange, and red forms.

Jalapeño: The most popular and widely available fresh variety, this tapered chile, 2–3 inches (5–7.5 cm) in length, has thick flesh and varies in degree of hotness. It is found in green and sweeter ripened red forms. Available pickled (*en escabeche*) as well.

Poblano: Named for the state of Puebla, this broad-shouldered, tapered, moderately hot chile is 5 inches (13 cm) long and a polished deep green.

Serrano: Slender chile measuring 1–2 inches (2.5–5 cm) long and very hot, with a brightly acidic flavor. Available in both green and ripened red forms.

TO ROAST FRESH CHILES, use long-handled tongs to hold them over a gas-stove burner until their skins are evenly blistered and charred, about 5 minutes; or roast directly over a very hot charcoal or gas grill. Alternatively, roast under a preheated broiler (grill), turning occasionally, until evenly blackened and blistered, 6–8 minutes. Transfer to a paper or bag and let cool for 5 minutes before peeling.

TO PEEL AND SEED ROASTED CHILES, use your fingertips to peel away the blackened and blistered skins. If any areas resist, use a knife or rinse under running cold water. Don't worry if charred bits remain. Slit the chiles open and use your fingertips or a small knife to remove the seeds and white veins.

DRIED CHILES
Ancho: Dried form of the poblano, about 4½ inches (11.5 cm) long, with wide shoulders, wrinkled, dark reddish brown skin. Its mild, bittersweet flavor is reminiscent of chocolate and it has a slightly prunelike aroma.

Árbol: Smooth-skinned, bright reddish orange chile about 3 inches (7.5 cm) long, narrow in shape, and fiery hot.

Cascabel: "Rattle" chile, describing the sound made by its seeds when the medium-hot globe-shaped chile is shaken. It is about 1½ inches (4 cm) long, with brownish red, smooth skin.

Chipotle: The smoke-dried form of the ripened jalapeño, rich in flavor and very hot. Sold in its dried form, it is typically a leathery tan, although some varieties are a deep burgundy. It is available packed in a vinegar-tomato sauce (chipotle chiles in adobo) and lightly pickled *(en escabeche)*.

Guajillo: Moderately hot, this burgundy chile is about 5 inches (13 cm) long, tapered, and with rather brittle, smooth skin and a sharp, uncomplicated flavor.

Morita: A smoke-dried chile about 1 inch (2.5 cm) long, resembling the chipotle except for its almost bluish red color.

Mulato: Looks like the ancho but has dark, almost black skin and a distinctive full, sweet flavor.

Pasilla: Skinny, wrinkled, raisin-black chile, about 6 inches (15 cm) long, with a sharp, fairly hot flavor.

TO SEED DRY CHILES, clean them with a damp cloth, then slit them lengthwise and use a small knife to remove the seeds.

TO TOAST DRIED CHILES, clean them with a damp cloth, then heat a heavy frying pan or griddle over medium heat. Add the whole or seeded chiles, press down firmly for a few seconds with a spatula, turn the chiles, and press down for just a few seconds more. The chiles should change color only slightly and start to give off their aroma.

CAUTION The oils naturally present in chiles can cause a painful burning sensation. When handling chiles, be very careful not to touch your eyes or other sensitive areas. After handling them, wash your hands thoroughly with warm, soapy water. If you have particularly sensitive skin, wear plastic gloves when working with chiles.

CINNAMON BARK, TRUE *Canela,* the type of cinnamon favored by Mexican cooks for savory and sweet dishes, is true cinnamon, the flaky, aromatic bark of a laurel tree native to Sri Lanka. Cinnamon sticks and ground cinnamon are the more aggressive-flavored forms of cinnamon derived from cassia, the bark of another Southeast Asian variety of laurel. If substituting cinnamon sticks or ground cinnamon for true cinnamon bark, reduce the amount used.

COCONUT CREAM, MILK, AND THIN MILK Quality unsweetened canned coconut milk, with an excellent ratio of cream to milk, is a welcome shortcut to making your own. If a recipe calls for coconut cream and/or thin coconut milk, do not shake the can before opening. After you open the can, first scrape off the thick mass on top, which is the coconut cream. The next layer is an opaque white liquid, which is the coconut milk, and finally there is a clear liquid, which is thin coconut milk.

TO MAKE COCONUT MILK OR COCONUT CREAM FROM A WHOLE COCONUT, first pierce one or two of the dots on the "three-dot-face," using an ice pick or screwdriver, and pour out the juice. Then, using a hammer, make several whacks around the equator, first cracking it and then breaking it into pieces. Using a small knife, pry the meat from the shell, then peel off the thin brown skin. Cut the meat into 1-inch (2.5-cm) pieces and pulverize it in a food processor. One coconut will yield about 3½ cups (1 lb/500 g) pulverized coconut. For coconut cream, put the coconut in a bowl and add 1½ cups (12 fl oz/375 ml) hot water. Let steep for 10 minutes, then pour through a fine-mesh sieve into a bowl, pressing against the coconut to extract as much liquid as possible. Place the squeezed coconut in another bowl. This first pressing, about 1 cup (8 fl oz/250 ml), is coconut cream. For coconut milk, add 3 cups (24 fl oz/750 ml) hot water to the same coconut, let steep for 15 minutes, and repeat the straining process. This step yields about 2½ cups (20 fl oz/625 ml) coconut milk. Repeat the process a third time for thin coconut milk. Refrigerate the milk and cream and use within 3 days.

CREMA Although *crema* translates simply as "cream," in Mexico it usually refers to a rich, slightly soured variety, which is found in well-stocked grocery stores. A suitable substitution is crème fraîche, which is similar in consistency, or you can thin sour cream slightly with whole milk.

TO MAKE CREMA, in a small nonaluminum bowl, stir together 1 cup (8 fl oz/250 ml) heavy (double) cream (do not use an ultrapasteurized product) and 1 tablespoon buttermilk. Cover with plastic wrap, poke a few holes in the plastic, and leave at warm room temperature (about 85°F/30°C) until well thickened, 8–24 hours. Stir, cover with fresh plastic wrap, and refrigerate until firm and chilled, about 6 hours. *Makes about 1 cup (8 fl oz/250 ml).*

CRÈME ANGLAISE Made of egg yolks, sugar, hot milk, and vanilla, crème anglaise is a sweet, thin custard used as a sauce for desserts.

CRÈME CHANTILLY This simple French dessert sauce consists of cream beaten until lightly thickened, then sweetened and flavored.

CRÈME FRAÎCHE A tangy fresh cream, crème fraîche is used as a topping for fruit and other sweets and as an enrichment for sauces or soups because it does not separate when boiled. It is widely available in supermarkets.

TO MAKE CRÈME FRAÎCHE, combine 1 cup (8 fl oz/250 ml) heavy (double) cream—do not use ultrapasteurized—and 1 tablespoon buttermilk in a saucepan over medium-low heat. Heat to lukewarm; do not allow to simmer. Remove from the heat, cover, and let stand at warm room temperature until as thick and flavorful as you like, at least 8 hours or up to 48 hours. Refrigerate before using. *Makes about 1 cup (8 fl oz/250 ml).*

CURRY LEAVES These small leaves of a tropical shrub are used whole, either fresh or dried, to add aromatic flavor to simmered dishes. They are also sometimes pounded to a powder to season egg dishes and marinades. Bay leaves may be substituted, although their perfume differs.

CURRY POWDER Used mainly in the dishes of southern India, curry powder is a mixture of spices, not a single spice. The Western-style curry powder that is stocked on supermarket shelves bears little similarity to the carefully blended, personalized mixtures of Indian cooks. Ingredients and their proportions vary among dishes, regions, and cooks, but a typical blend includes coriander seeds, brown mustard seeds, fenugreek seeds, cumin seeds, black peppercorns, cloves, red chiles, roasted chickpeas (garbanzo beans), and turmeric.

EPAZOTE Related to spinach, chard, and beets, epazote is one of the most important herbs used by cooks in central and southern Mexico, where it grows profusely. Due to its intense flavor, it should

be added at the end of the cooking process and used sparingly. Epazote is also used to reduce the gastric distress some people experience after eating beans. Though difficult to find fresh outside of Mexico, epazote is easy to grow from seed. It is sold in dry form, packaged in little cellophane sacks, which is inferior to the fresh herb.

FENNI One seldom hears of *fenni* outside the Indian state of Goa because the Goans love the liquor so much that none is left for export. There are two varieties of *fenni:* coconut and cashew. Centuries ago, the Konkan people of Goa tapped and fermented coconut. Cashew *fenni* is relatively new. Purists sip *fenni* straight, like cognac, but it is more commonly served with lime soda over ice. The cashew liquor is also the secret ingredient in many Goan marinades for seafood.

GALANGAL Similar in appearance to ginger, to which it is related, this gnarled rhizome adds a mustardlike, slightly medicinal flavor to simmered dishes. Known in Thailand as *kha,* in Indonesia and Malaysia as *laos,* and sometimes also referred to in English as Siamese ginger, galangal is available fresh and frozen whole and as dried slices. If only the dried form can be found, use half the quantity you would for fresh. If dried galangal will be pounded or blended, reconstitute it first by soaking in warm water for 30 minutes until pliable. For some soups and curries, the unsoaked pieces can be added directly to the simmering liquid.

GARAM MASALA Garam masala is the typical spice blend of northern India (indeed, *garam masala* simply means "spice blend"). The blend, sold commercially or made at home, features coriander, cumin, black pepper, cardamom, cloves, cinnamon, nutmeg, and mace. It is typically incorporated into dishes at the beginning of cooking, but is sometimes sprinkled over a dish just before serving.

HOISIN SAUCE A thick, sweet, reddish brown sauce made from soybeans, sugar, garlic, Chinese five-spice powder or star anise, and a hint of chile, hoisin sauce can be thick and creamy or thin enough to pour. Used throughout China, hoisin sauce is rubbed on meat and poultry before roasting to lend a sweet flavor and red color. As a condiment, it should be used with caution, as its strong flavor can easily overpower most foods. Hoisin sauce is available in large cans, but smaller jars are more practical and are usually of better quality. Look for it in Asian markets or major grocery stores.

HOT BEAN SAUCE Also known as chile bean paste, hot bean sauce is a thick, salty paste of mashed chiles, fermented yellow beans, seasonings, and oil. The intense flavors in this sauce are appreciated in many Chinese stir-fries and braised dishes.

JAGGERY Jaggery, or dehydrated sugarcane juice, is a by-product of sugar refining. Golden brown and with a flavor resembling maple syrup, it is used in savory dishes to bring out the flavors of other ingredients. Brown sugar, palm sugar, maple syrup, or maple sugar may be substituted, although they do not accurately replicate jaggery.

KAFFIR LIME LEAVES The kaffir lime contributes its rich, citrusy flavor to curry pastes and other savory and sweet dishes through its dried, fresh, or frozen leaves and its gnarled rind. Its juice, however, is not used. Pesticide-free lemon or lime leaves may be substituted.

KARI LEAVES These small, shiny, highly aromatic leaves come from the *kari* tree, native to southern India and Sri Lanka. Although sometimes called curry leaves, and often used in curries, they bear no relation to curry powder and are not interchangeable with it. Nor do they taste of curry. Rather, both their flavor and aroma are citrusy, as befits a member of the citrus family. Fresh and dried *kari* leaves are used extensively in savory dishes throughout southern India and are a characteristic flavor of the region. *Kari* leaves are available in Indian grocery stores. Fresh leaves have the best flavor, but dried are usually more easily found and may be substituted. Use double the quantity of dried leaves as for fresh. If the leaves are unavailable, substitute a mixture of 2 teaspoons minced parsley and 1 teaspoon finely grated lemon zest for every 20 *kari* leaves.

KHEER *Kheer* is the primary dessert of India. Home cooks generally prepare a simple rice-and-milk

version; more elaborate renditions—with nuts, fruits, flower essences, and spice embellishments—are served in restaurants and at wedding feasts.

LARD Rendered pork fat, or lard, lends a rich taste to recipes. When cooking, do not use the processed white commercial variety, which lacks authentic flavor. Instead, look for a butcher shop that renders its own. Or render it yourself, using pork fat from a reputable butcher. Ask the butcher to grind it for you, or chop it finely at home in a food processor before rendering.

TO RENDER FAT INTO LARD, preheat the oven to 300°F (150°C). Spread 1–2 lb (500 g–1 kg) ground (minced) or chopped pork fat in a large roasting pan. Roast until most of the fat has melted, leaving behind light golden scraps of connective tissue, 30–45 minutes. If the lard itself begins to color, reduce the temperature. Remove from the oven and let cool slightly, then pour through a sieve into sealable containers. It will keep in the refrigerator for several months or in the freezer for up to a year.

LARDONS/LLARDONS The French term *lardons* (or, in Catalonia, Spain, *llardons*) refers to small strips or squares of fat cut from the belly of a pig. They are often sautéed and added to salads and other dishes, including stews, fried potatoes, and omelets. In the United States, slab bacon (with the rind removed), which comes from the side of the pig, is a good substitute. Salt pork, which comes from the belly of the pig, or pancetta, an Italian cured, unsmoked bacon, can also be used.

LEVAIN A natural sourdough starter that begins with a *chef,* a mixture of flour and water (or other liquid), which is left to ferment for a few days. Then flour is added to the soured dough, and it becomes a *levain,* or "leavening."

MACE Mace is the bright, lacy membrane that covers the nutmeg seed. When ground, it becomes an orange-yellow spice with a flavor that is a deeper and more pungent version of nutmeg. Ground mace loses its flavor quickly, so purchase it in small amounts and store it in the refrigerator.

MANGO POWDER *see amchoor powder*

MEXICAN CHOCOLATE Mexican chocolate, a mixture of cacao beans, almonds, sugar, and often cinnamon and vanilla, is formed into disks, or tablets, usually weighing 3 ounces (90 g). It has a grainier texture than typical cooking chocolate and is not suitable for baking or candy.

MOREL MUSHROOM The morel is distinguished by a long, oval cap sporting a network of deep crevices and an aroma that is intense and musky. Grit and dirt are easily trapped in the honeycombed caps. Therefore, unlike most other mushrooms, morels need to be soaked briefly in cold water to which a little white vinegar has been added. Drain and dry with a clean kitchen towel before cooking.

PILONCILLO This unrefined sugar commonly comes in hard cones that are grated or chopped before use. The most common ones weigh ¾ ounce (20 g); the larger ones weigh about 9 ounces (280 g). In southern Mexico, the unrefined sugar is often made into thin, round cakes or into bricks. The darker the sugar, the more pronounced the molasses flavor. Well wrapped piloncillo will keep indefinitely. Dark brown sugar may be substituted.

PIMENTÓN Spanish paprika, which is finely ground from dried *nyora* peppers, can be sweet, bittersweet, or spicy hot. Look for *pimentón* in small tins in Spanish or specialty markets, or use sweet paprika in its place.

PORCINI MUSHROOM *see cèpe mushroom*

QUATRE ÉPICES "Four spices" in French, *quatre épices* is a classic spice blend whose mild, sweet, earthy flavor is used to season meats, terrines, pâtés, stocks, and sauces. Plain allspice can be substituted.

TO MAKE QUATRE ÉPICES, in a mortar using a pestle, crush about 1½ teaspoons whole allspice berries and 1½ teaspoons whole cloves and transfer to a small bowl. Grate 1 whole nutmeg and add to the bowl along with 1 teaspoon ground cinnamon. Stir to combine, transfer to a jar, cover tightly, and store in a cool, dark place. *Makes about 3 teaspoons.*

QUESO AÑEJO When *queso fresco* is aged, it becomes *queso añejo,* a tangy, dry cheese, more authentically called *queso cotijo,* which is grated as a garnish for tacos, enchiladas, and other everyday dishes. Feta cheese is a suitable substitute.

QUESO FRESCO Fresh cheeses, or *quesos frescos,* are soft, tangy, lightly salted cow's milk cheeses that are crumbled or sliced for adding to numerous Mexican dishes. They are labeled *queso fresco* or *queso ranchero.*

SAFFRON THREADS The world's most costly spice by weight, saffron comes from the perennial *Crocus sativus.* The crocus blossoms are hand-harvested, then the three stigmas from each flower are delicately removed, also by hand, and dried. Only when dried do they develop their unique aroma and flavor. Saffron is also valued for its brilliant orange-yellow color, which is characteristic of Spanish paellas and many Indian pilafs. Saffron is used sparingly not only because of its cost, but because increasing the quantity doesn't increase the aroma or flavor imparted. It is best to buy saffron threads, the whole dried stigmas. Powdered saffron loses its flavor more rapidly and is subject to adulteration with less costly ingredients, such as turmeric. Before saffron threads are added to a dish, they are typically either toasted in a dry pan over low heat or lightly crushed and then steeped in a warm liquid such as wine, stock, milk, or water.

SALAM LEAVES *Salam* is the Malaysian term for aromatic laurel leaves similar to bay, used either dried or fresh to flavor simmered and stir-fried dishes. Although bay leaves are the usual substitute, some cooks prefer curry leaves.

SAMBAR POWDER This hot spice mixture is used widely in the dishes of southern India. The ingredients and their proportions vary from one cook to another, but the essentials include red and black pepper, turmeric, fenugreek, coriander seeds, cumin seeds, and various types of legume.

SAW-LEAF HERB Known as saw-leaf herb because of its slender serrated leaves, this fragrant herb recalls coriander (cilantro). Called *ngo gai* by the Vietnamese, the fresh leaves are typically added to soups at the table.

SEMOLINA FLOUR This somewhat coarse flour is milled from durum wheat, a variety particularly high in protein. The flour is almost always used in the manufacture of dried pastas. It is also used in some pizza doughs and breads.

TAMARIND The fruits of the tamarind tree, native to India, bear seedpods containing dark brown seeds surrounded by an acidic pulp that is pressed into a liquid for use in soups, salads, curries, meats, and fish dishes throughout India and Southeast Asia. Tamarind is available commercially in block form and as a concentrate. The block form consists of a sticky mass of compressed seeds and pulp. The required amount is taken from the block and soaked

in hot water to extract the flavor; the resulting liquid is known as tamarind water. The more convenient concentrated form is available in jars. Tamarind water is easy to make from the block form.

TO MAKE TAMARIND WATER, cut up ½ pound (250 g) of the pulp into small pieces, place in a bowl, and add 2 cups (16 fl oz/500 ml) boiling water. Mash the pulp to separate the fibers and seeds, then let stand for 15 minutes, stirring two or three times. Pour the liquid through a fine-mesh sieve placed over a bowl, pushing against the pulp with the back of a spoon and scraping the underside of the sieve to dislodge the clinging purée. Transfer to a jar and refrigerate for up to 4 days or freeze for up to 1 month. *Makes about 1½ cups (12 fl oz/375 ml).*

USLEE GHEE *Ghee* literally means "fat." There are two types: *usli ghee* (clarified butter) and *vanaspati ghee* (vegetable shortening). A recipe that calls simply for ghee is understood to mean usli ghee. Indian clarified butter differs from the European equivalent in having been simmered until all the moisture is removed from the milk solids and the fat is amber colored. This gives *usli ghee* its unique nutty taste. Clarification also increases butter's storage life, an important consideration in the many Indian homes without refrigeration. *Usli ghee* may be made from cow's milk or, more commonly in India, from buffalo's milk, which has a higher fat content and gives a cleaner tasting, better colored result.

TO MAKE USLI GHEE, heat ½ lb (250 g) butter in a pan over medium-low heat, uncovered, until it melts. Raise the heat to medium and simmer the butter, stirring often, until the clear fat separates from the milk solids, about 15 minutes. During this process a layer of foam will rise to the top of the butter and the butter will crackle as its milk solids lose moisture. When the milk solids lose all the moisture, the fat as well as the milk residue will turn amber colored. Remove the pan from the heat and let the residue settle on the bottom. Pour the clear fat, which is the *usli ghee,* into a jar, ensuring that no residue is included. Alternatively, strain through two layers of cheesecloth (muslin). Discard the residue. *Usli ghee* may be refrigerated, covered, for up to 6 months or frozen for up to 12 months. Thaw before using. *Makes about ¾ cup (6 fl oz/180 ml).*

Index

Published by Gold Street Press,
a division of Weldon Owen Inc.
415 Jackson Street, San Francisco, CA 94111
www.goldstreetpress.com

WILLIAMS-SONOMA, INC.

Founder & Vice-Chairman Chuck Williams

A TASTE OF THE WORLD

Conceived and produced by Weldon Owen Inc.
415 Jackson Street, San Francisco, CA 94111
Tel: 415-291-0100 Fax: 415-291-8841

In Collaboration with Williams-Sonoma, Inc.
3250 Van Ness Avenue, San Francisco, CA 94109

A Weldon Owen Production
Copyright © 2008 Weldon Owen Inc.
and Williams-Sonoma, Inc.

First printed in 2008
10 9 8 7 6 5 4 3 2 1

ISBN-13: 978-1-934533-11-6
ISBN-10: 1-934533-11-4

Printed in China by SNP-Leefung

A NOTE ON WEIGHTS AND MEASURES

All recipes include customary U.S. and metric
measurements. Metric conversions are based on
a standard developed for these books and have
been rounded off. Actual weights may vary.

WELDON OWEN INC.

Executive Chairman, Weldon Owen Group
  John Owen
CEO and President Terry Newell
Senior VP, International Sales Stuart Laurence
VP, Sales and New Business Development
  Amy Kaneko
Director of Finance Mark Perrigo

VP and Publisher Hannah Rahill
Executive Editor Kim Laidlaw
Managing Editor Karen Templer
Editorial Assistant Julia Nelson

VP and Creative Director Gaye Allen
Senior Art Director Emma Boys
Designer Lauren Charles

Production Director Chris Hemesath
Production Manager Michelle Duggan
Color Manager Teri Bell

AUTHORS

Melanie Barnard, Brigit Binns, Georgeanne
Brennan, Cathy Burgett, Carolynn Carreño, Kerri
Conan, Lori De Mori, Abigail Johnson Dodge,
Maureen Fant, Charity Ferriera, Janet Fletcher,
Joyce Goldstein, Beth Hensperger, Diane
Holuigue, Dana Jacobi, Joyce Jue, Sybil Kapoor,
Elinor Klivans, Michael McLaughlin, Ray Overton,
Lou Seibert Pappas, Jacki Passmore, Paul
Richardson, Julie Sahni, Michele Scicolone,
Constance Snow, Marlena Spieler, Marilyn
Tausend, Thy Tran, Diane Rossen Worthington

ACKNOWLEDGEMENTS

Weldon Owen wishes to thank the following
people for their generous support in producing
this book: Judith Dunham, Lesli Neilson, Nanette
Cardon, Meghan Hildebrand, and Stephanie Tang.